The Rise of Gospel Blues

The Rise of Gospel Blues

The Music of
Thomas Andrew Dorsey
in the Urban Church

MICHAEL W. HARRIS

OXFORD UNIVERSITY PRESS
New York   Oxford

Oxford University Press

Oxford   New York   Toronto
Delhi   Bombay   Calcutta   Madras   Karachi
Kuala Lumpur   Singapore   Hong Kong   Tokyo
Nairobi   Dar es Salaam   Cape Town
Melbourne   Auckland   Madrid

and associated companies in
Berlin   Ibadan

Copyright © 1992 by Michael W. Harris

First published in 1992 by Oxford University Press, Inc.,
200 Madison Avenue, New York, New York 10016

First issued as an Oxford University Press paperback, 1994

Oxford is a registered trademark of Oxford University Press

Library of Congress Cataloging-in-Publication Data
Harris, Michael W. The Rise of Gospel Blues: The Music of
Thomas Andrew Dorsey in the Urban Church / Michael W. Harris.
p. cm.   Includes bibliographical references and index.
ISBN 0-19-506376-7
ISBN 0-19-509057-8 (pbk.)
1. Gospel music—History and criticism.
2. Dorsey, Thomas Andrew.   I. Title.
ML3187.H37   1992   782.25—dc20
91-8987

2 4 6 8 10 9 7 5 3 1

Printed in the United States of America

Mr. and Mrs. Thomas Andrew Dorsey have graciously provided the author access to and permission to use documents and photographs from the Thomas Andrew Dorsey Papers.

To Ernest and Magnolia Kirk

my foster parents

Acknowledgments

I benefited from the aid and advice of numerous persons during the research and writing of the manuscript. First among these was Mr. Dorsey, who gave unselfishly of his time and memories during many hours of interviewing. The story he told has implications far beyond the scope of his biography. He made the point again and again that he considered his biography secondary to the need to have the history of the gospel movement written. His wife, Kathryn, and daughter, Doris, opened the Dorsey home to me as one of the family.

I owe the same thanks to the other interviewees—family, friends, associates, and admirers of Mr. Dorsey. They freely gave me the background and corroborative information that I needed to gain perspective on the gospel blues movement. Wherever I found them, from Villa Rica, Georgia, to Memphis, Tennessee, to New York, to Chicago's South Side, they welcomed me and my electronic gear with unreserved hospitality. I have lumped them together here only because of the need to conserve space. Each deserved more time and study than I could give with only Dorsey on my agenda.

I benefited as considerably from several institutions. Dr. Donald F. Joyce, curator of the Vivian G. Harsh Collection of Afro-American History and Literature at the Carter G. Woodson Regional Library of the Chicago Public Library, was of significant help in making available the Illinois Writers Project papers and related primary materials on black Chicago. I am as deeply grateful for the access granted to me by the Georgia State Archives and Atlanta Historical Society to rare turn-of-the-century sources.

My research and traveling expenses were supported in large part by generous grants from the Southern Fellowships Fund, the Fund for Theological Education, and the Warren and the Wesley Weyman Funds at Harvard University. A Smithsonian Institution Research Fellowship and a Rocke-

ACKNOWLEDGMENTS

feller Humanities Fellowship allowed me to devote the 1979–80 and 1985–86 academic years, respectively, to full-time work on this project.

A number of persons read the dissertation, the manuscript, or both and offered timely advice. I have special thanks for Marcus Thompson, Elizabeth Nordbeck, Pamela Plender, and Janet Piez; each read various parts of the dissertation and helped with editing and proofreading chores. Each of the members of my dissertation committee contributed in a unique way to my understanding and approach to this research. Professor Louise Vosgerchian, with her inimitable pragmatic approach to music analysis, will always stand out in my mind for her admonition that no matter how profound I find any of my discoveries, I must always ask myself, "So what?" Professor Preston Williams, himself raised in the old-line religious tradition, gave timely advice on maintaining a balance in the presentation of all viewpoints. Though he specializes in liturgical music that precedes gospel blues by a millennium, Professor David Hughes, a medievalist, brought depth, breadth, and, not in the least, encouragement through his considerable insight into music and religion. I owe the greatest amount of gratitude to Professor William R. Hutchison, the chairman of my committee. He was a wellspring of advice in working out the conceptual framework of this study. For whatever I am as a scholar, I owe to his patience, understanding, and firm guidance.

At the University of Tennessee, Knoxville, R. Baxter Miller, Diane Morrow, and Rosalind Hackett read and offered major suggestions for several of the revised chapters. Denise Dipuccio patiently edited the early drafts, often coaxing many insights out of the most obdurate of my prose. Research assistants Ellen MacRae and Donna Payne painstakingly typed and edited the transcripts. Chancellor Jack Reese awarded me a timely research grant to conduct much of the Georgia State Archives investigation.

In its final stages, the manuscript benefited from the critical readings of several seminars at Temple University and at Wesleyan University. Also at Wesleyan, Denise Jefferson helped with editing and research, and Robert Lancefield edited and typeset the music examples. William Holshauser became the most dependable undergraduate research assistant one could desire, checking footnotes, editing text, and proofing the music examples.

Members of my family—especially Josephine, Charie, Irwin, Dominiquie, and Clara—gave unselfishly and untiringly of whatever they could to encourage me to "stick with it."

I have reserved the most heartfelt thanks to those who helped shape this study. One of the foremost of these was Arnold Rampersad, who carefully read drafts and corrected many would-be errors as this project evolved from the dissertation into the present book. Gertrude (B.) Palmer read the final draft with both an African Americanist's and copyeditor's eyes; I have her to thank for finding and fixing the inconsistencies and unevenness of seven years of rewrites and additions.

ACKNOWLEDGMENTS

I will be forever grateful to Oxford's Sheldon Meyer for his support in publishing the Dorsey story. His assistants, Stephanie Sakson-Ford, a most patient and thorough copyeditor, and Karen Wolney, a consummate negotiator, have my deepest appreciation. Scott Lenz's editorial assistance is so skillful and thoughtful that I think of it as an art. For the aid her painstaking compilation of the index will provide each reader, Linda Solow Blotner has my special thanks.

For all the help, explicit and implicit, one acknowledges in completing a major project, the responsibility for its failure as opposed to success ultimately falls back on that person. To the extent that I should recognize the wisdom in this statement, I claim all errors in the book. To the extent that I know that I must pay tribute to whom it is due, I disclaim any notion that I could have completed this study without each person's contribution.

Middletown, Conn.   M. W. H.
May 1991

Author's Note to Paperback Edition

On Saturday, 23 January, 1993, Thomas Andrew Dorsey died at his home in Chicago at the age of 93. The causes of his death were related to his long-term suffering from Alzheimer's disease.

Iowa City, Iowa
January, 1994

Contents

List of
Music Examples

LIST OF MUSIC EXAMPLES

Introduction

In the early to middle 1930s, the first notes of gospel blues—a blend of sacred texts and blues tunes—were heard in Protestant black churches in the midwest and northeast cities of the United States. To one group of African Americans who populated these churches, this music was crude: it harked back to the primitive "cornfield ditties" of enslavement.[1] It seemed to confirm blacks' inability to advance by not assimilating the music and liturgical practices of mainline, white Protestantism. To another group, usually composed of recently settled southern migrants, this music rekindled a spirit of worship that had been dampened by the European classical anthems and unimproved hymns sung in these churches.

The large-scale urban in-migrations of the 1920s and 1930s brought these two groups together. Ignoring the storefront religion to which they should have been attracted, southern migrants trooped into the citadels of progressive American black Protestantism. They were lured by offers of housing assistance, employment, and general social support for the adjustment to the North.[2] These churches, moreover, appealed to the sense of upward mobility of former southern peasants, whose move north represented as much a rethinking of their southern—and more likely indigenous African American—religious practices as it did an escape from the tyranny and economic conditions of the South.[3] These new urbanites seemed ready to lay aside the hand-clapping, foot-tapping, and shouting that had characterized their worship for the security and status of an old-line church affiliation.

In the two or three years preceding the first appearance of gospel blues, tension mounted between these groups. New settlers seemed continually less willing to deny themselves their former style of worship and adopt that of the urban elites. By the end of the 1920s, moreover, newcomers to the cities outnumbered their original black populations. The growing presence of migrants slowly eroded the norms of mainline assimilationist worship. Ministers, seeking larger congregations, mixed folk and non-folk preaching styles in order to hold the "allegiance of the shouters and non-shouters."[4] More and more emotionalism crept in, undermining the staid decorousness of the services.

The only part of worship that seemed impervious to the onslaught of migrants' seemingly alien practices was the music. In the years immediately prior to the emergence of gospel blues, choirs were basking in their ever-growing acclaim for performing the staples of the western European classical tradition. At churches in Chicago, for example, one could hear movements from Rossini's *Stabat Mater* or Mendelssohn's *Elijah* during Sunday morning worship.[5]

By the early 1930s, the scene in old-line black urban churches had become that of a perplexing potpourri of white mainline Protestant and southern Afro-American religious rituals. Neither group seemed able to claim an entire worship to its liking. Traditionalists could revel in the pulpitry of the preacher and the shouts of the congregation only to have their spirits muted by Mozart's *Ave Verum*. Progressives quickly felt the afterglow of excerpts from a Schubert mass extinguished by the moaning and chanting of the congregation in response to the minister's down-home preaching.

Thus the advent of gospel blues as a sacred song style represented the arrival of old-line churches at an uncomfortable consensus for a new mode of religious expression. Its appearance altered the dominant musical praxis of the day—the only part of mainline black Protestant worship that was seemingly immutable to the influence of migrant African Americans. But those who lamented the disestablishment of old-line liturgical practices composed a distinct minority. Judging by the swiftness with which gospel blues spread through the churches, first in Chicago like "wildfire," then to St. Louis, Detroit, Cincinnati, Philadelphia, and on, it represented the sentiments of a majority of black Protestant Americans.[6]

Despite the extensive impact of gospel blues on black religion and on black culture in general, it has received little extended scholarly attention. To some extent this is to be expected, since gospel blues has social, religious, cultural, and even economic roots and thus seems to require a corresponding range of methods in order to analyze it. Thus one can find partial discussions of gospel blues in a wide range of works representing a variety of subject areas. E. Franklin Frazier, a sociologist, wrote about it in his study, *The Negro Church in America*. St. Clair Drake and Horace Cayton, anthropologist and sociologist respectively, noted its impact on religion as part of their comprehensive study of the Chicago black community between World Wars I and II. In the major cultural history of Afro-America, *Black Culture and Black Consciousness,* Lawrence Levine treated gospel blues as the capstone of the development of black sacred song.[7]

With the exception of Levine's study, no other has examined the intellectual forces behind this music or, more important, the intellectual milieu out of which it evolved. At the root of this lack of attention lies the problem of sources: few of them are written. The intricacies of the thought underlying the evolution of gospel blues, moreover, make the discussion of both the music and its history all the more difficult to investigate even were there a well-laid trail of written sources. This study of Thomas Andrew Dorsey, based in large part on oral sources, is an attempt to overcome these problems.

Thomas Andrew Dorsey, the acknowledged "father," if not leader, of the early gospel song movement, provides a biographical, and thus micro, perspective from which to unravel this story. A brief look at Dorsey's activities during the introductory years of gospel blues shows that he was its central figure. He was the first to publish a gospel piece, *If You See My Savior* (1928). An examination of the more than 400 gospel songs that he published (not necessarily composed) indicates that he is still today the most prolific composer/publisher in the movement. His best-known work, *Take My Hand, Precious Lord,* has become a staple of the Protestant hymnody of both black and white Americans. He was one of the founders of the first gospel chorus to be organized in Chicago's mainline churches in 1931 and probably in the United States. In August 1933, he and two associates chartered the National Convention of Gospel Choirs and Choruses, the largest association of gospel singing groups in the United States.[8] He still serves as its national president. From the late 1930s until the middle 1950s, this organization sent out agents to metropolitan areas to organize choruses. These in turn became the predecessors of the gospel choral groups found in most black churches today.

To focus on Dorsey as a leader of the gospel blues movement surely illuminates certain elements of the evolution of that song style. But to do so excessively overshadows aspects of his life that lead to a deep understanding of the social milieu out of which gospel blues evolved. This is even truer in Dorsey's case since he personifies—almost uniquely so—the thought and social forces that forged the culture in which this music was shaped.

For example, throughout his life Dorsey was buffeted between the assimilationist and indigenous value systems that divided the two groups discussed above and that exemplify the historic duality, or, as Du Bois put it, "twoness" of Afro-American life.[9] As a child, at Mt. Prospect Baptist Church in Villa Rica, Georgia, he heard two contrasting styles of church music: one, improvised spirituals similar to slave sacred songs, and the other, shaped-note hymnody that was composed by his uncle but that was actually a song style belonging to traditional southern white folk religion.[10] In becoming familiar with both types of song, young Dorsey unknowingly embraced one of the major polarities in black religious ritual.

When he began his piano career, he encountered the same dichotomy. He was introduced to blues piano playing in the theaters and brothels of Atlanta's red-light district. When he tried to take formal lessons, however, he realized that his improvisational playing style would have to yield to note reading. Not only was the contrast musical, it was environmental. A black person could rarely obtain classical piano training in any part of town except the residential area around Morehouse College and Atlanta University where Atlanta's black aristocracy lived. From the quiet, tree-lined streets of this neighborhood to the strange music he found himself making there, Dorsey encountered a radically alien culture. Within a few months, he quit piano lessons and returned to selling popcorn at the Eighty-One Theater. There he caught the pianists between shows and got them to teach him the newest tunes and riffs.

The dichotomization of African American culture manifested itself in Dorsey's life in ways other than in music. If one considers the black urban-northern migrations not only as broad expressions of dissatisfaction with the social and economic conditions of the South but to some extent as a search for cultural reorientation, then each step of the migrant's trek to the North was one consciously made in repudiation of former non-assimilationist ways. In this sense Dorsey is once again archetypal: he participated in the two major Afro-American migrations before World War II. In 1908, at the age of ten, he moved with his family to Atlanta along with thousands of other peasants from the rural to urban South. Then in 1916, the year of the largest wave of migrants from the South, Dorsey moved to Chicago—clearly in an effort to find something new. In both instances self-advancement was his aim. This he achieved, but not without experiencing the scorn and derision shown to migrants because of their supposed backward ways. Thus was the sense of progressiveness—at the expense of black social and cultural ways—deeply infused in him.

At the heart of this study of gospel blues is the premise that ideas—as opposed to events or other more concrete data of history—are the generative structures of culture. By extension, blues is thought as opposed to mere music. The rise of gospel blues will thus be treated here not as the appearance of a form or style of music but as the emergence of a concept—a "feelin'" as Dorsey would say. Without doubt there is a music to examine here in its own right, although the usual customary classifications of blues by number of bars and by the repetition of texts and chordal progressions does not apply readily to the musics in this study. More accurately, this study assumes that ideas and music share a continuum and that the former occupies the left-most position while the latter picks up somewhere toward the right of it. Making a judgment as to where, or if, the thinking leaves off and the musical expression comes into its own has determined the organization of this study.

The connection between ideas and culture is hardly something new and profound. It seems, however, to have been overlooked in the study of African American life in the United States mostly because of the unconventional—that is, non-literary—sources available for writing black intellectual history.

Perhaps surprisingly, it is this very lack of written sources that has generated the research design of this study. For example, one would think that Dorsey's 116-page typescript autobiography, heretofore unknown, ought to function as the major primary source. For the most part it does. But this work, having been completed around 1960, includes numerous errors and some distorted interpretations of events. In order to resolve these problems, I conducted over 30 hours of interviews with Dorsey over an 18-month period, using the autobiography as a guide literally to cross-examine him. But then, in order to supplement and corroborate information from these interviews, I found it necessary to locate and interview his living relatives and associates, as well as agents for the Convention, members of his early choruses, and various choir directors in Chicago, St. Louis, Detroit, Cincinnati, New York, Atlanta, Memphis, and other cities. Supplementing the oral accounts is a considerable mass of information that I have found in metropolitan black newspapers (e.g., the *Chicago Defender, Pittsburgh Courier,* and *St. Louis Argus*), as well as manuscripts from the WPA Illinois Writers Project files of the Vivian G. Harsh Collection of the Chicago Public Library, church programs and histories, and other miscellaneous printed memorabilia in the possession of the Dorsey family. In general, this method has produced a sort of triangular network of corroboration that contains internal checks at each point: 1) the Dorsey autobiography and interviews verifying one another; 2) the supplementary interviewees providing checks against one another's narratives and each against Dorsey's; and 3) the printed sources providing descriptive cross-references to events and to persons, in turn verifying the other two points in the source matrix.

Even Dorsey's written gospel blues cannot be relied on as a conventional documentary source. None of his 400-plus published songs contains the ornamentation that is added during performance. This lack of notated embellishments actually reveals a fundamental performance practice: the printed gospel song contains text and music which the singer is free to interpolate at the time of utterance. In other words, when a gospel singer looks at a Dorsey song, she has before her a set of textual and musical notes from which she can improvise a sermon in music. Thus Dorsey's written songs inform this study less than do the improvisations which accompany those works such as the placement of textual interjections (for example, "My Lord," "Thank you, Jesus," and "Praise Him") and the configurations of embellishments—each of which varies from performance to performance.

Judging by these research methods, this study would seem to fall into the category of oral history. Again, however, the sources belie the assumptions one would be inclined to make about them. To the extent that histories based on unwritten sources are generally not considered to be the histories of ideas, the classification of this study of gospel blues as oral history would be misleading. The black American experience argues this point better than I: from the anti-literacy laws of slavery to the innate spontaneity of Afro-

American art forms, one can find reasons for the paucity of literary sources when researching black intellectual history. Obviously African Americans have thought as much as any people; they merely have used different modes to express and record ideas—especially those having to do with such overarching cultural concepts as duality. Black thought thus can be mined from many veins of culture and often may be found nestled among a variety of forms of peculiarly black expression.

My point is not to dissociate this study of gospel blues from oral history so much as it is to disclaim the license sometimes taken by oral historians to compromise the standards of careful scholarship. Although the major sources for this study are oral, they have not displaced any of the available documentary evidence that I have been able to find. I have taken, moreover, two steps to convert the oral sources as much as possible into written ones: 1) the interviews have been transcribed. I consider these 2000-plus pages of transcriptions to be a set of documents akin to the slave narratives. As such, they will be cited in the text as if they were letters, journals, books, or other types of written primary sources. After publication of this study, these transcripts will be placed in the Center for Black Music Research at Chicago's Columbia College for scholars to examine. 2) The transcripts have been typed into a computer to form a database that generates concordances for items such as names, locales, events, dates, and, in limited cases, ideas. This process serves to integrate non-notated and notated source bases and helps to verify them against one another.

I have used speech and written sources without regard for their expression of ideas. In doing so, I have rejected the urge to employ the journalistic practice of editing speech into prose. While unedited speech tends to read often as muddled ideas, there is much to argue for the untidiness of spoken thought. For example, the pause or the utterance of several "ah's" as one works through an idea can be read as important nuances; to delete them simply for the purpose of crafting a more pithy statement is to tamper with the subtext of *how* one puts her thoughts into words. Thus the interview excerpts appear verbatim, with the exception that they have been relieved of excessive and/or repetitive verbiage, and, of course, they have been punctuated. I have also merged commentary from several interviews when the topic was the same, the goal being to collate disparate conversational bits into single statements. There is no indication of this process in the text except for citations which include all sources for each quotation. The juxtaposition of speech and written sources is most evident in the form of the text. I have placed all but the most brief comments into indented, blocked paragraphs. The idea has been to give the reader a sense of the dialogue that I have between myself as author and various other sources from which I draw—especially Dorsey, whose both spoken and written thoughts have prompted this study.

At this point it should be clear that whatever is biographical in this study serves a purpose beyond that of the customary life story of an individual. This study above all probes an incident in the history of a concept that is lodged firmly in the African American mind: duality, the sense of double consciousness. The emergence of gospel blues into the black old-line church setting of the 1930s is the incident; it provides some more detail of the duality. In the broadest sense, therefore, this biographical portrait of the rise of gospel blues comprises part of the history of a sociocultural phenomenon that has occupied a unique place in the lives of black Americans and that has been exemplified by aspects of the life, mind, and music of one Thomas Andrew Dorsey.

The Rise of Gospel Blues

1

Religion and Blackness
in Rural Georgia:
1899–1908

Daniel Alexander Payne, the sixth bishop of the African Methodist Episcopal (AME) Church, was so disturbed by the presence and behavior of "Praying and Singing Bands" that he devoted over four pages of his *Recollections* to criticizing these groups as the "strange delusion that many ignorant but well-meaning people labor under":

> About this time I attended a "bush meeting," where I went to please the pastor whose circuit I was visiting. After the sermon they formed a ring, and with coats off[,] sung, clapped their hands and stamped their feet in a most ridiculous and heathenish way. I requested the pastor to go and stop their dancing. At his request they stopped their dancing and clapping of hands, but remained singing and rocking their bodies to and fro. This they did for about fifteen minutes. I then went, and taking their leader by the arm[,] requested him to desist and to sit down and sing in a rational manner. . . . To the most thoughtful and intelligent I usually succeeded in making the "Band" disgusting; but by the ignorant masses, as in the case mentioned, it was regarded as the essence of religion.[1]

In many ways, this account describes the general cultural ferment of post-Emancipation black America. There were blacks who, in clinging to Afro-American folkways, expressed their allegiance to the self-contained culture of their slave ancestors. Among these people the ring shout, so bothersome to Payne, thrived along with the spirituals, hand clapping, and foot stomping that gave it life. There were other blacks who found indigenous black culture an impediment to the assimilation of Afro-Americans into the mainstream culture. Singing was one way they could demonstrate that they deserved a place in the white culture to which they were still denied access.

More can be gleaned, however, from this incident than its representation of the cultural factionalism among late nineteenth-century black Americans.

After all, the tension between ethnicity and the melting pot has figured in the histories of numerous American ethnic groups. What is unique about Afro-American history and of significance to a deep understanding of the shaping of post-Emancipation black American culture is that this clash occurred in a church setting and that it was provoked by a church leader in reaction to an established church ritual.

The place of black churches as battlegrounds for rival cultural forces was virtually foretold by the manner in which many of them were founded during the first years of the post-Emancipation period. Numerous black churches came into existence with the aid of the northern-based, white missionary organizations that had entered the postwar South with the stated purpose of uplifting former slaves. Generally, these groups sought to provide education and ministerial training for those freedpersons and their children who possessed leadership potential, devotion to religion, and what these white emissaries would regard as a modicum of intelligence. These newly trained agents would build a following—usually a congregation—that would absorb what were, in fact, white cultural values. These small flocks would in turn spawn more ministerial trainees. Within a decade after the Civil War, northern white church organizations had founded scores of missions, elementary schools, colleges, and theological seminaries.[2]

One of the more active of these groups was the American Baptist Home Mission Society. By 1868 it was supporting thirty missionaries who ran schools for the training of "Christian leaders"; and by the 1880s it had established a number of institutions that were forerunners of many of today's prestigious black colleges. Its stated purposes were:

> . . . the appointment of general missionaries to win men to Christ and to gather them into churches; to impart education to all in order that they might read and understand the Scriptures; and to instruct ministers through classes organized at central points. . . . The dominant theory of the Society in this work, from the outset, has been that emphasis must be laid upon the training of competent, consecrated Christian leaders for the uplift of the race; and that Christian culture and character are fundamental thereto.[3]

In addition to the Baptists, the Congregationalists also played an important role in the postwar South through the American Missionary Association. Whereas the American Baptist Home Missionary Society was most noted for establishing churches and training ministers, the American Missionary Association concentrated on setting up Christian educational institutions for freedpersons. It followed the Union army into the South, declaring that "in accordance with the great Christian aim, it seeks to reach the people where they are, and to lift them, by charitable and educational means, as well as by preaching of the Gospel, to the high plain [sic] of Christian civilization."[4]

By the late 1870s, these organizations—along with the Freedmen's Aid

Society of the Methodist Episcopal Church, the Committee on Missions to Freedmen of the Presbyterian Church in the U.S.A., the Quakers, and the United Presbyterians—were conducting most of the educational and church work among former slaves. Competing with one another, they virtually overbuilt schools, especially colleges and universities. There were more "universities" for black Americans by 1895 than universities of any kind in both Britain and France. This institutional designation was actually misleading in that only 22 of the 54 schools that referred to themselves as universities offered college-level courses, and barely 750 students were enrolled in them.[5]

Not all of Bishop Payne's incident with the "bush meeting" people can be explained by the deculturation of former slaves through the Bibles and primers of northern white missionaries. Clearly, some blacks cooperated with white missionary societies and acted as funnels for the inpouring of non-black values into black society. But Payne was bishop of the African Methodist Episcopal Church, the first independent denomination to be formed by black Americans. The answer to the question of why it, too, would promote the divesting of Afro-American cultural traits from its members adds another perspective from which to view the shaping of post-Emancipation black culture.

The forces underlying the origins and growth of the AME Church would seem to foster the evolution of non-African-American cultural values. From its inception, the AME Church justified its existence by citing a need for a separate worship experience for blacks who attended white churches. The explicit reason for this need stemmed from the second-class membership that blacks experienced in white churches. An equally compelling but more subtly stated reason was rooted in blacks' desire for praying, preaching, and other rituals of worship to conform more to a style they preferred. For seven months prior to walking out of St. George's Methodist Episcopal Church in November 1787, blacks had been holding organized prayer meetings and were in the process of searching out a "place of worship for the colored people." This group later formed Bethel Church. By then, a considerable number of small, unattached congregations had separated themselves from the white parent congregations that had discriminated against them. "Taking into consideration their grievances," they came together "to secure the privileges" of independent worship and, in 1816, organized the African Methodist Episcopal Church, the first black denomination in the United States.[6]

Richard Allen, the pastor of the Bethel congregation and first bishop of the AME denomination, and his fellow AMEs found joy in more than their achievement of non-segregated worship. In Methodism they found a natural resonance with the worship style they had cultivated. Indeed, this compatibility had a long history among black Americans. Slaves were known to have responded favorably to the Methodist circuit rider's whosoever-will-may-come message with "tears streaming down their faces." They rejected the Quakers' introspection and the Church of England's catechism for the catharsis of the conversion experience. Wrote a former slave, John Thompson:

> My mistress and her family were all Episcopalians. The nearest church was five miles from our plantation and there was no Methodist church nearer than ten miles. So we went to the Episcopal church, but always came home as we went, for the preaching was above our comprehension, so that we could understand but little that was said. But soon the Methodist religion was brought among us, and preached in a manner so plain that the way faring [sic] man, though a fool, could not err therein.
>
> This new doctrine produced great consternation among the slaveholders. It was something which they could not understand. It brought glad tidings to the poor bondman; it bound up the broken-hearted; it opened the prison doors to them that were bound, and let the captive go free.
>
> As soon as it got among the slaves, it spread from plantation to plantation, until it reached ours, where there were but few who did not experience religion.[7]

The free blacks of Philadelphia, searching for a denominational home, echoed Thompson's sentiments. They flirted with the Church of England but were persuaded by Richard Allen to join the Methodist connection:

> . . . I was confident that there was no religious sect or denomination [that] would suit the capacity of the colored people as well as the Methodist; . . . [because] the plain and simple gospel suits best for any people; . . . [because] the unlearned can understand, and the learned are sure to understand; and . . . [because] the Methodist is so successful in the awakening and conversion of the colored people, [with its] plain doctrine and having a good discipline. . . . We are beholden to the Methodists, under God, for the light of the Gospel we enjoy; for all other denominations preached so high-flown that we were not able to comprehend their doctrine. Sure am I that reading sermons will never prove so beneficial to the colored people as spiritual or extempore preaching. I am well convinced that the Methodist has proved beneficial to thousands and ten times thousands.[8]

This early preference among unaffiliated blacks for a denominational alliance that met their expectations for praying and preaching seems incongruous with the later zealousness of Bishop Payne in quashing the bush meetings. Given the reasons for which the AMEs first organized, Bishop Payne's crusade to abolish the old ways would have found as little precedence among the founders as it did among the later followers whom he scolded for their quaint practices.

From their beginning the AMEs seemed almost preoccupied with proving that they deserved their independence. Much of this predilection can be traced to the struggle of pre-AME blacks with their white mother churches over matters ranging from ownership of church property to the appointment of ministers for administering sacraments. While white Methodists welcomed the exodus of blacks from their congregations, they were reluctant to let blacks govern themselves. Ostensibly their reticence stemmed from a desire to observe Methodist Episcopal rules. But to Richard Allen, and evidently to many of his co-organizers, church rules were a subterfuge for paternalism. The record is inconclusive as to which motive dominated. Nevertheless, with whites so willing to scrutinize their every move, blacks lost few opportunities to show that they not only could oversee their affairs but could do so as effectively as whites.

Richard Allen took every chance he could to bring to whites' attention the good citizenship and moral character of his parishioners. One of the earliest examples of his vigilance can be found in his *A Narrative on the Proceedings of the Colored People During the Awful Calamity in Philadelphia in the Year 1793; and a Refutation of Some of the Censures Thrown Upon Them in Some Publications*. Here Allen recounts the activities of black Philadelphians during an outbreak of yellow fever. Again and again he tells of the heroic conduct of blacks who, often at risk to their lives, nursed and then buried whites when other whites would not. "Many of the white people, who ought to be patterns for us to follow after," he chided, "have acted in a manner that would make humanity shudder."[9]

Allen continued his campaign by urging the newly formed AME body to adopt rules of discipline for the Methodist Episcopal Church in order to "exhibit to the Christian world the rules of government and articles of faith by which [AMEs would be] influenced and governed." Of the few extant records of the denomination, a "Journal of Proceedings of Bethel Church" for the years 1822–31 indicates that the AMEs were rigorous in overseeing the conduct of individual members. Bethelites set up disciplinary councils modeled after those in white Methodist churches. These councils heard testimony, deliberated, and set punishment for infractions ranging from indebtedness to sexual immorality. Other examples of AME assimilation of white church standards can be found in Allen's publication of a hymn book in 1818. The collection of 314 compositions closely followed that of the official Methodist Episcopal hymnal. So intent was Allen on re-creating the decorous worship of the white Methodist churches that he expunged all of the folksier, camp-meeting songs that had appeared in an earlier version of his hymnal. The older one had been used by blacks after they had left St. George's but before they united as AMEs.[10]

What Allen and the early AMEs began, Payne pursued almost with a vengeance. He boasted in his *History* of the AMEs that the church as an "independent hierarchy" helped blacks to "feel and recognize our individuality and our heaven-created manhood." Like the earlier church fathers, however, he had more faith in the idea than in the realization of black individuality. Indigenous religious song manifested a certain type of blackness that he found especially backward. With an arrogance bloated with righteousness, he campaigned ceaselessly for a "higher" standard of music. His enthusiasm for ridding the church of black music bordered on the fanatical to many. For one congregation that refused to allow him to pastor in 1850, his stance on black music constituted but one symptom of his chronic and overbearing elitism:

> The stewards told me at the official board meeting that the people . . . had no fault to find with my character, but that I had too fine a carpet on my floor, and was too proud; that if one of the members should ask me to take tea with them, I would not; and lastly, that I would not let them sing their "spiritual songs."

Payne defended himself by countering that the songs were no more than "'Corn-field Ditties'" and should be put aside with the other older practices he found distasteful. Ultimately these confrontations did little more than embolden Payne: he became the major force behind bringing European classical instrumental music and choirs into the AME church.[11]

As its refusal indicates, the congregation deeply opposed Payne's crusade. Far from being just an expression of cultural chauvinism, this resistance reflected how deeply rooted in the AME Christianity of Payne's time were the worship traditions of enslavement. To those whose ring dancing he despised, Payne was not elevating them to an enlightened Christianity; he was asking them to forsake their religion. Thus when the pastor said, "Sinners won't get converted unless there is a ring," Payne replied, "You might sing till you fell down dead, and you would fail to convert a sinner." The two continued to talk past each other, with Payne issuing the call: "The time is at hand when the ministry of the A.M.E. Church must drive out this heathenish mode of worship or drive out all the intelligence, refinement, and practical Christians who may be in her bosom."[12]

The AME Church was not alone in this ambivalence toward black folk culture. As the oldest black denomination, it offers the longest record of this struggle. After Emancipation, however, the problem confronted other major black denominations. Carter G. Woodson, the black historian who has written the only comprehensive history of organized black religion to date, devoted a chapter to discussing the mind-sets of "conservatives" and "progressives." The concern was not simply singing and dancing: it was, as in the case of the early AMEs, a matter of blacks taking control of their religious organizations. Conservatives resisted independent denominations; progressives founded them.[13]

Clearly, there were three minds—the white missionary, the assimilationist, and the traditionalist—that set out under the banner of Christianity to shape the culture of post-Emancipation black America. That two of these wanted to recast that culture in the mold of white mainline culture and the third wanted to remain more insulated is little more than arithmetically significant. Of greater importance is that two of these minds—though of the same race—disagreed about the appropriate cultural expression of that race. Indeed, it is the division between these two black minds that provides the starting point from which to examine the dualities that were present in the late nineteenth-century African America into which Thomas Andrew Dorsey was born.

Perhaps no other issue provides clearer evidence of the struggle between these two minds than that of the organization of the black family during this period. To grasp the complexity of this division, one can turn to the work of W. E. B. Du Bois, the leading black sociologist of that time and, though he had an abiding respect for indigenous black culture, a prominent advocate of assimilation at least for its social and economic benefits. Using data he collected, he wrote an essay, "The Development of a People," in which he describes three typical households in a small Georgia town during the last decades of the nineteenth century. At the lower end of the social structure he finds "a little one-room box with a family of eight." The mother and father are not married. He works irregularly, and what little income she derives from being a laundress, she "squanders." Du Bois implies that this family structure perpetuates itself: "the nameless child of the eldest daughter makes the last member of the family."[14]

Du Bois could have been describing Silvey Plant, Dorsey's maternal grandmother. She was a single parent. Not all of her eight living children (she had eleven) were fathered by the man whose surname, Plant, she gave them. Indeed, neither Dorsey nor Silvey's other surviving grandchild, Carrie Lee Hindsman Phillips, remembers seeing his or her grandfather: "You know back in them days," explains Ms. Phillips, "how people, some of them came up; [how] old folks back in those days did." Silvey Plant's children have been described as mulattos and others as having features more characteristic of black African ancestry. Dorsey implies that the man whom he assumed to be his grandfather was at most an intermittent presence at Grandmother Plant's home: "He lived somewhere . . . in the neighboring towns. I didn't know much about him." As if not to leave one detail of Du Bois's stereotype unmet, a small child belonging to Jennie, one of Silvey's unmarried daughters, lived in the home. Carrie Lee, however, was not nameless.[15]

Du Bois considered a family across the street from the family of eight slightly above this "dumb misery": "a better house—a mother and father, two sons and a girl." Not only is this family a more traditional nuclear family, but, Du Bois adds: "They are hard-working people. . . . They read and write a little and . . . they are seldom idle." He faults them, however, because they are "unskilled, without foresight, always in debt and living from hand to mouth."[16]

Dorsey's paternal grandparents conform to Du Bois's second model, though not as closely as Silvey's family fits the first one. Andrew and Lucy Dorsey were married in 1863. Eight of their twelve children survived childhood. Andrew and Lucy were unlettered but made sure that each of their children was schooled. Unlike most blacks in agriculture in Georgia during the late nineteenth century, Andrew rented a farm—a testament to the initiative and industry that characterized Du Bois's second family type. Du Bois would have found one significant indicator of the tentativeness of the Dorseys' improved status, however: two of Lucy's and Andrew's grandchildren lived with their unmarried mother, Rebecca, in the Dorseys' "better" house.[17]

Although Du Bois could trace the conditions of these families to the degradation of slavery, he nonetheless cringed at their presence. At this particularly early stage of his profession, Du Bois apparently had inflated hopes for social science. He worried that blacks would fall behind "the virile races" of the world because women from families like these had a higher birthrate than "the better class" of black women:

> It is not sufficient to have the increase of the race come from the one-room cabins of the plantations and the hovels of the alleys, while the better class homes and better educated girls neglect the duties of motherhood. It is not only insufficient, it is fatal to rapid progress; since each generation will start far behind the generation that preceded it.

As one who held up the German *Kaffeeklatsch* to educated black young women as the ideal economical entertainment, Du Bois could conceive of almost no circumstances in which the Silvey Plants and the Dorseys could of themselves rise to such levels of enlightenment. They could improve their lives and guarantee better lives for their children, however, by looking just up the street to the home of the black "ideal-maker."[18]

In comparison with the homes of most whites or blacks in this town, the house of this local leader "is among the best." To be sure, ". . . a Dutch housekeeper would find undiscovered corners, and a fastidious person might object to the general scheme of decoration," but these shortcomings were but traces of a degenerate past long since discarded for the ways of a higher civilization. This man had either a vocation such as butchering or carpentry or a profession such as teaching or preaching. Thus it was through education and thriftiness that he achieved his status. As a result of interacting with and mimicking this man, the Plants and Dorseys could get their "ideals . . . thoughts . . . and notions of life." Du Bois believed that family disorganization and the poverty, crime, and ignorance that were related to it were symptoms of one problem: a clash between "two different standards of culture." Through his training and frugality, the leader became exposed enough to both cultures to assume the role of "priest" in bringing to his own people the benefits of the one culture he had been trained to consider superior.[19]

Lucy and Andrew Dorsey did follow the lead of the "ideal-maker." One of the Dorseys' sons, Thomas Madison, became a preacher and, after marrying Etta Plant Spencer, Silvey's second eldest daughter, settled in a small Georgia community, Villa Rica, to become a member of Du Bois's model priesthood. To understand the matrix of values in which the Dorseys' son, Thomas Andrew, was nurtured, one must examine Thomas and Etta Dorsey's journeys from their respective farm and alley hovels.

If anything made the assimilationists a formidable force—one a young Thomas Madison could hardly avoid—it was their unanimity on education as the key to an enlightened black America. Payne was convinced of the classroom's effectiveness early in his professional life: he began it as a teacher. From then on he labored ceaselessly to establish educational institutions for blacks, including Wilberforce University in Ohio, the first AME seat of learning. He knew that an "intelligent ministry" was the church's best means of ridding itself of old practices. Du Bois was just as driven and, therefore, exemplary. From his years at Fisk University, an American Missionary Association institution, Du Bois was a living witness to the "essential humanity" that one gained through knowledge. Of course, the missionary associations had already demonstrated their faith in education by establishing hundreds of schools throughout the South.[20]

Thomas Madison Dorsey entered the assimilationists' educational program at a critical point in its evolution in Georgia. In 1893, "progressive" (or separatist) black Baptists had seceded from the Baptist Northern Convention's Georgia association in order to form a black-administered Baptist association in Georgia. This assertion of black rule was less than successful since all of the black Baptist schools and colleges in Georgia were administered by the Baptist Northern Convention through the American Baptist Home Mission Society. The Georgia movement occurred as just one of a rash of black independence struggles tearing at the Northern Baptist Convention's schools throughout the South. Black Baptists were split over the issue of white paternalistic rule after some Georgia black Baptists had severed their ties with the state organization. Dorsey graduated from Atlanta Baptist College a year after this schism. This was a time when the fundamental assimilationist values of the institution were under attack by the very people—such as Dorsey—who were to be educated in it. Black faculty members at the school, already willing partners in Christian acculturation, were forced to draw the line separating them from their brothers more distinctly. Perhaps, then, Dorsey studied at some point under the Atlanta Baptist College black professor who wrote in 1896 that without white education "progress would have been impossible" for the "degraded" freed slaves. As a counterforce to the thinking of this sort by a black professor at his white-run school, there was the independence movement emerged among the state's black Baptists, an event that Dorsey must have witnessed. He may have listened to the more radical rhetoric of Bishop Henry M. Turner of the AME Church, who preached about a "black God" and advocated black emigration to Africa. Or, three months before his graduation, Dorsey could have read about or even have known some of the Atlanta blacks who departed for Africa as part of Benjamin Gaston's colonization plan.[21]

As the denomination containing the largest number of blacks, the Baptist Church gave "special attention to the religious education of the colored preachers." It thus had a special interest in a young man such as Thomas Madison Dorsey. He came from one of those homes that produced highly trainable black men. His brother, Joshua, became a druggist and drugstore owner in Chicago; another, James E., worked variously as a barber, excavator, grocer, and pastor in Atlanta. In 1867, the American Baptist Home Mission Society established the Augusta Institute in Augusta, Georgia, as one of its major educational institutions in the state. In 1879 it altered the focus of this institution considerably by moving it to Atlanta. There it became Atlanta Baptist College, with its charge, as the name implies, to train "competent, consecrated Christian leaders for the uplift of the race." At some point between 1879 and 1894, when the school's name and principal instructional charge were once again changed, Thomas M. Dorsey entered.[22]

But the Reverend Thomas M. Dorsey who left Atlanta Baptist College in 1894 did not become one of the "Christian leaders" that the Society thought it had graduated. Instead, he became an itinerant preacher. This abrupt change of course reflected a deep ambivalence toward assuming his duties in the acculturative church over which the Society had trained him to preside— the temple in which the white missionaries would have him administer the last rites to black folk culture and in which Payne would find neither cornfield music nor stomping. Considering the turmoil surrounding the values upon which the school was founded and the virulent resurgence of black nationalism that was swirling about him as he pursued his studies, Thomas Madison had good reason to question his role in the Society's program. In the absence of any other information, this seems a plausible explanation for his decision not to take a settled pastorate. Except for one brief appointment, he never pastored, according to his son:

> He was known by his preaching. He was kind of an itinerant preacher. He didn't want to pastor. He didn't, I don't think he wanted a church. He was known all over.

Sometime between graduation and October 1895, when he married Etta Plant Spencer, Dorsey's wanderings brought him to Villa Rica, Georgia.[23]

The fact that Etta, given her family environment, married a rising—if resistant—member of the black leadership such as Thomas Madison Dorsey attests both to the inaccuracies of Du Bois's models and to Etta's extraordinary drive to achieve. The prevailing thought among sociologists and historians has been that single-parent families resulted from a failure to emulate the white social norms to which blacks who considered themselves upwardly mobile then aspired, and that unmarried mothers were numerous where impoverishment and illiteracy were rampant and where the black church was ineffective as an "agency of social control."[24] That Silvey Plant's case can be placed so confidently in one of these categories—particularly given the lack of information on her—is doubtful. If her male children, Charles and Phillip, are indicators of her social standing, then those categories may well apply: "Charlie" was a bootlegger and "Phil" was a hobo and itinerant musician. Yet if one considers, instead, Silvey Plant's three daughters, her unmarried status does not fit the stereotypes so easily. Mollie was a respected domestic worker in Villa Rica. Jenny married Corrie Hindsman, one of Villa Rica's first black schoolteachers and a member of one of its more prestigious black families. And Etta was widely admired in the community for her active participation in the church and for her education.[25]

Such a glowing reputation for Etta indicates that, like Silvey, she had achieved through persistence and luck far beyond expectations for one of her family origins. Etta was born in 1870, just as the missionary societies were beginning to establish church schools for freed slaves. Certain descriptions of her—"very religious," "church worker," "well read"—indicate that Etta had a formal, though probably rudimentary, education and a distinctly fervent attachment to religion, quite possibly through a mission institution. Also distinctive—indeed quite unusual at that time for a black person of whatever socioeconomic level—was the traveling occasioned by her marriage to Charlie Spencer, a railroad workman. She was able to accompany him during his work, visiting with some regularity Atlanta, New York, Washington, and other cities along the east coast. During these visits she undertook enough private music study in piano and voice to gain a reading knowledge of music and at least a minimal performing ability. Unfortunately, her husband's untimely death precluded any sustained musical development: Spencer, in a tragedy Etta witnessed, was crushed under the wheels of a train he was about to board.[26]

The most convincing evidence of her drive and shrewdness can be found in the land records of Carroll County, Georgia. In November 1894 she paid $580 for two parcels, one being a two-acre lot in Villa Rica and the other approximately fifty acres of farmland outside the city. The fact that Etta purchased this land as "Mrs. Etta Spencer" may illuminate the circumstances of this transaction. It is improbable that a married woman would have bought land without her husband's name appearing on the deed. The widowed Mrs. Etta Spencer was most probably the purchaser. If so, her ability to pay almost $600 in cash might have been related to Charlie Spencer's tragedy, perhaps through an insurance settlement.

Whatever the reason, Etta—in the eyes of Payne, Du Bois, and the missionaries—made a wise choice with her money. Over half of the farmers—white and black—in Georgia at this time were tenants, and their numbers were increasing. Even so, "the soil, abused but still rich," was the most available form of savings for blacks who would escape economic slavery. Etta's purchase of land capped a striving for social and economic standing that began with her marriage to a railroad worker, whose steady and relatively well-paying employment boosted them into the black laboring class.[27]

To the wandering preacher who had come to Villa Rica no earlier than June of 1895 to conduct a series of revival meetings, the recent widow embodied virtually all of the values he had been trained not only to live by but to teach: she was moral, literate, and thrifty. Thomas evidently lost little time in letting her know that he found her attractive. Etta, however, at first unimpressed, found him too fat and generally "undesirable" physically. Her initial aversion notwithstanding, the two were married by the Reverend Jerymiah Hindsman on October 15, 1895.[28]

After their wedding, all that remained for Thomas and Etta to do to become the "ideal-maker" couple of Villa Rica was to move into a house and for Thomas to take a pastorate. But for at least the first four years of their marriage, Thomas and Etta wandered through Georgia, Alabama, Tennessee, and Florida. On the surface it would seem that they shared this impulse to live so peripatetically: she had been awakened to the world beyond Villa Rica by traveling with Charlie Spencer; he found the life—and perhaps the notoriety—of the traveling preacher/revivalist more appealing than a settled ministry. Etta, moreover, was a major attribute to his work in that she could provide music when he needed it.[29]

But their unexpected change of direction might not have been as willful as it appears—particularly if one takes into consideration some of the major financial trends and the black church situation in Villa Rica in the last years of the 1800s. For all the wisdom that Etta's decision to buy land indicates, the economics of agriculture during these years would suggest that she should have made another investment. She purchased the property in 1894, one year after a major financial panic developed in the United States; this was followed by a depression that lasted until the end of the decade. She had enough money to purchase the land but not enough to begin farming. She would have found borrowing an impossibility considering her race and gender and the financial conditions in Georgia at the time. Indeed, Villa Rica, like most small towns in Georgia, had no bank when Etta bought the land and needed financing. Circumstances were also as bleak for Thomas to begin his ministry in Villa Rica: none of Villa Rica's four black churches had an opening for a pastor. With neither Etta nor Thomas able to generate income, they were prevented from putting the capstone of their "ideal-maker" role into place: they could not afford to build a house, especially one that Du Bois would coo about as "among the best" in town.[30]

There were advantages, however, to Etta and Thomas's apparent aimlessness: she could indulge her desire to travel; he could continue in quest of the next pulpit and its attendant notoriety. Even Du Bois, who could describe in such glowing terms what Etta and Thomas would attain with her land and his profession, understood their condition in the context of the economic history of blacks from the time of Emancipation: "Then the struggle began and lasts to our day—the struggle of the black man to earn a living, maintain a home, and lay aside savings for the future." Ironically, by 1909, the year Du Bois wrote these words, Etta and Thomas had lost the struggle. Beginning sometime between November 1898 and the following January when Etta must have realized that she was pregnant with her first child, Thomas Andrew Dorsey, she and Thomas Madison attempted to bring their wandering lifestyle to an end and to transform the mere trappings of black leadership into the influence and financial security it should have brought them. In short, they tried to make a home.[31]

The first years of Thomas Andrew Dorsey's childhood were trying ones for his parents. Although Etta gave birth to him in Villa Rica on July 1, 1899, she and Thomas decided once more against settling there. Etta mortgaged part of her farm property on May 16, 1900, and apparently used the money to move her family to Atlanta. One month later they were enumerated in the 1900 Census as living in a rented house at 161 Harris Street in Atlanta along with two of Thomas's brothers and one of his sisters. Not surprisingly, Thomas was listed as being unemployed. From Atlanta they went to Forsyth, Georgia (approximately sixty miles southeast of Atlanta), where, according to Etta, Thomas pastored a church. If his "defaulter" status in the 1901 Carroll County Tax Digest is an indication, Thomas's earnings from this position were barely at subsistence level. They lived there for two years during which Etta had another son, Samuel, who died in infancy.[32]

Their return to Villa Rica from Forsyth sometime in 1903 marked the point at which they must have realized that Thomas's professional training could not provide an income to support the family. Etta's land afforded an opportunity for Thomas to farm for income and still to be a guest preacher when possible. Perhaps their need to buy the supplies and equipment to start planting indicates why land records show that in April 1903 Etta borrowed against her city lots. This was a common means of financing farm ventures in Georgia between the early 1890s and 1930. In order to obtain short-term credit for planting crops and financing other farm-related expenses, farmers mortgaged their land. But during this same period, prices for Georgia's major crop, cotton, were severely depressed. For Thomas to support a family, he needed to farm more land by either buying it or entering into a sharecropping arrangement. He and Etta were hardly in a position to invest in land; indeed, by April the following year Etta had to sell part of the town property. Thus Thomas was forced into sharecropping, one of the most pernicious systems of agricultural financing ever to exist.

In return for placing a lien against the year's crop, a merchant would advance a sharecropper food, clothing, seed, fertilizer, and any other goods needed to raise a cash crop. Because these were such high-risk loans, the interest rate ranged from 25 to 75 percent. Between the high cost of the lien and the low price for cotton, most farmers were driven increasingly into sharecropping and land tenancy. Etta and Thomas were no exception. County tax digests for the years 1903 through 1908 show that the Dorseys owned livestock and farm equipment. Until 1907 the aggregate value of their land, household goods, animals, and implements increased more than seven-fold to $310. Yet this amount evidently did not provide them with financial stability, since it did not amount to their indebtedness. Thus Thomas Madison Dorsey, like most African Americans who were one generation removed from slavery, found that economically, at least, he was no more "free" than his forebears. Even as one of the educated, professional black elite, Thomas and others like him could subsist no better than many of the most unschooled and unskilled of his people.[33]

Thomas Andrew Dorsey's recollections of his childhood are riddled with mentions of the dual status of his father. In the opening paragraph of his autobiography, for example, he alludes both to Thomas's profession and to the peasant work he resorted to in order to provide for the family:

> I was born in Villa Rica, Georgia, a little town about 30 miles west of Atlanta on the Southern R.R. that goes to Birmingham, Alabama. My parents were poor. My father, Rev. Thomas M. Dorsey, was a share-cropper and a hard working man. He farmed and he pastored two small country churches; also taught in a rural school (the three winter months Negro children could attend school). . . . Although we were poverty stricken, my father succeeded in acquiring an education. He was a graduate of Atlanta Baptist College, now called Morehouse College.[34]

In Dorsey's eyes, his father, victimized by the sharecropping system, could barely provide enough for the family's needs: "He worked for Jim Taylor, a nice old white man, who rode about over the fields in a cart with four tires instead of wheels." Taylor could be "nice" about paying his tenants because "at harvest time [he'd] rob you for most of [what you earned]." Since highly productive agricultural techniques were unknown then, "the land would not yield anything but peas and sweet potatoes," and these were mostly for family consumption. Cotton was the only marketable crop he recalls his father planting, and this was equal yearly to "just about one wagon load."[35]

Dorsey recalls that his father, the minister, had to work so hard with his crops that preaching became almost a "sideline" for him. He was able to preach only during the three months that remained after he had planted and harvested. But despite the rigors of tenant farming and its limitations on Thomas's career, Dorsey nonetheless recalls that his father was "known all over" as a good preacher.[36]

His father's divided identity constituted one of the primary influences that shaped young Dorsey's perception of the world about him. As a young boy he became directly involved in his father's two roles and developed distinct attitudes toward them. For example, as a young farmer, Dorsey suffered feelings of distaste for the occupation and of failure that were similar to those he sensed in his father:

> My father would take me to work with him in the field. He would let me plow. And I being so small, the old mule (Chuck) would not mind me when I would tell him to gee or haw, but he would take me and the plow out across the field where he could eat the green grass.

> When every plant came up you had to start hoeing it and taking care of it to keep the grass from eating it up. So it was a whole full-time job, farming. You never got a chance to rest. When the grass got in this field here, you got it out of this field. Over in the other field or whatever you had over there, [grass] would [then] be in there.[37]

On the other hand, Dorsey enjoyed some of the happiest times of his childhood as a vicarious recipient of his preacher-father's prestige and reputation:

> My dad and I were good pals. He'd take me and I'd like that traveling around. We'd travel around and get good food everywhere you went. . . . Nothing but good food in the country in those days. You'd get to meet different people. Me being the pastor's son, well naturally, they'd make over me.

Dorsey enjoyed another benefit of his father's pastoral duties: he attended the elementary schools his father ran as an auxiliary occupation for approximately three months each year. Children could attend these schools only for the three to four months during which they were not engaged in crop work. As early as age three, Dorsey remembers accompanying his father to school.[38]

Thus Dorsey recognized early the disparity in status between his father's two occupations. He naturally found himself more attracted to the one with which he had the more pleasant associations. In a revealing statement, Dorsey speaks of how he imitated Thomas in his capacity as a preacher:

> I had a church under our front porch. The porch was high and under there was my church. . . . They bought me some kind of little cane; my father had a cane too. And I['d] go down under the house and hang my cane up and then I'd start talking to what would be my audience as if they were there. . . . Yeah, I['d] go in and I'd hang my cane up just like he'd go in and hang his cane up.

The "good food" and being "made over" were not the only attractions of the ministry. Dorsey also sensed the respect and authority his father commanded when in the pulpit—an authority clearly absent from his role as a tenant on Jim Taylor's farm. Dorsey probably realized, since Thomas's cane appeared only in the pulpit (he had no known ailment that would require its use), that his father used it for the dramatic assertion of his image as a minister.[39] Such demeanor was missing, of course, from the daily tasks of plowing fields, slopping hogs, and the like. In any event, the effective "transformation" of his father in the context of his religious vocation made a profound impression on young Dorsey. Quite possibly, the style as well as the fact of his father's ministry was one of the major factors in the formation of Dorsey's religious values. The passion for fame, a flair for the dramatic, and a yearning for devoutness—all to become traits of Dorsey's character—were there for the young Dorsey to observe and absorb as he moved between the world of the Reverend Mr. Dorsey and that of Thomas, the sharecropper.

Dorsey's childhood memories of Villa Rica focus largely on his family's socioeconomic status; consequently, Thomas, the father and provider, is the central figure. He seems to have had no knowledge of Etta's landownership and how it aided the family. Thus he tends to obscure Etta's role in his upbringing. In the chapter of his memoirs concerned with Villa Rica, Dorsey mentions eleven incidents directly involving his parents: of these, seven refer to his father, three to both Etta and Thomas, and only one to Etta alone (her previous marriage). Etta's involvement and influence in the shaping of young Dorseys' character, therefore, can be gathered only from secondary accounts and by inference. Even so, Etta's role appears no less important than her husband's; and in some instances it may have even been more significant.

In Dorsey's most complete description of a mother's role, an essay entitled simply "Mother," maternal and religious nurturing are one. In essence, "Mother in her office holds the key of the soul, and she it is who stamps the coin of character and makes the being, who would be a savage but for her gentle cares, a Christian man." Whether Etta herself is the subject here or only Dorsey's sense of motherhood in general, Dorsey underscores the strong maternal influence in the acquisition of religious beliefs. Assisted by her husband, Etta was the central figure in providing Dorsey's early religious training. Both father and mother "would read every passage in the Bible in a year; you couldn't eat until the Bible was read." They discussed it often, "and I had to sit there at the table and listen; . . . I drank it in too."[40]

At an even deeper level, however, Etta seems to have been the source of Dorsey's basic religious sensibilities. In contrast to Thomas, who represented the dramatic display of religious authority, Etta deeply impressed her son with her simple day-to-day piety. For example, Dorsey comments on Etta's provision of food and hospitality to the many hobos and tramps who came to their house because of its proximity to the railroad tracks. Similarly, he remembers her constancy on the night he and his father lost their way during a thunderstorm: "[Etta stood] out in the rain frantically calling" them "at the top of her voice" until they arrived home, guided mostly, one would presume, by the sound of her voice. Perhaps this sense of her devotion was behind Dorsey's admiration in his essay on a mother's "gentle cares." She had "stamped" on him her strength and constancy as spiritual values.[41]

To Dorsey, his father's and mother's involvement with religion constituted differing professions of faith: Thomas's represented the priestly calling or vocation; Etta's, the simple avowal of beliefs. This variance between the religious outlooks of the two principal figures of his childhood likely made his earliest conception of religion dichotomous. The melodramatics of a cane-wielding pulpiteer and the quiet piety of a gentle believer were vivid images, respectively, of the use—perhaps even exploitation—and the practice of faith. He imitated the former and "drank in" the latter—able, as children seem to be, to accept the presence of such antithetical models without perceiving their inherent inconsistency. The idea of religion as paradoxical, as an entity comprising two competing inclinations, nevertheless had been implanted. In his early years, Dorsey encountered no set of circumstances that demanded that one tendency suppress the other. Later in life, however, the question of which was to dominate would lie at the root of the several religious crises he would face.

The one parental influence on young Dorsey for which his mother was solely responsible was that of music. Etta seems to have created an ambience in their home, the musical aspect of which was totally her doing. Her singing and constant humming, the family "sings" that she led, as well as hymn or spiritual singing with relatives and neighbors—these together constituted the earliest musical stimuli leading Dorsey toward his life's work. Etta's musical influence was not simply nurturative in a general way; her playing of the organ was the specific catalyst for his actual development as a musician, enough so that Dorsey feels that "it sprang my musical career."[42]

The organ was no common piece of furniture in the homes of rural southern blacks, but some made sacrifices—perhaps unwisely—in order to own one. Booker T. Washington deplored the presence of one in the home of a backwoods Tennessee family where there was only one fork for four persons. An Atlanta University study of average turn-of-the-century Georgia black families shows the purchase of a $75 organ by a farm household of twelve persons with a combined yearly income of only $819.35. Even though their income was just as low, Thomas and Etta had reason to risk more deprivation by buying an organ: Thomas wanted it for Etta to play when he was pastoring the church in Forsyth. The fact that a parsonage was one of the perquisites of this job may have further prompted Thomas to buy the instrument; certainly an official church residence provided a more suitable setting for an organ than did those Washington and the Atlanta study describe. Furthermore, Thomas must have considered the portable organ, played by his talented wife, an asset to his ministry.[43]

Dorsey must have been fascinated by the organ, since he maintains that it "sprang" his musical development. He set out at once to learn to play it, but because of his size, "couldn't pump it." In spite of this difficulty, he continued his attempts to make the organ sound. Etta seems to have been the source of this determination; by the time Dorsey wanted to play, Etta had gained a wide reputation for playing the organ. Dorsey almost bragged when he spoke of this: "Oh yeah, she played for the church. She played for many of the churches around [in] the country." From Etta's church performances, young Dorsey could see that the organ had rewards other than its pleasing sound. In a revealing statement about his mother's musical activities, Dorsey claims to remember more of her performances away from home: "You do that [i.e., remember] when you go out, for you pay less attention to the home setting." The organ itself, then, only partly "sprang" his career: etched on his mind, as much as the music was on his ears, was the significance of playing that instrument before an audience and the transformation of Etta thereby into a person who commanded admiration and respect.[44]

To Dorsey, Etta's playing of the organ in church became the analogue of Thomas's dramatic preaching. When Dorsey attempted to play the organ, therefore, he was as imitative of his mother as he had been of his father when pretending to preach under the porch. This mimicking suggests that he desired the esteem and favorable regard he perceived as his parents' reward for engaging in these activities. In the world of young Dorsey, music and religion coalesced strongly about the notion that they were assured means to acceptance and approval. His feelings of attraction, at this age, toward preaching and music were thus predicated on his understanding of their social benefits. The same tendency would underlie his later decisions to commit himself in varying degrees to music and religion.

Dorsey remembers only two other individuals, both musicians, whose influence during his childhood may be considered formative. One was Etta's brother, Phil Plant, a musician who sang, played the guitar, and wandered about—mostly as a hobo on freight trains. As a kind of bard in rural Georgia, Phil probably performed what has come to be known as country blues. Thus he may have been important as the earliest performer of secular music to whom Dorsey was exposed consistently.

One of the most distinctive elements of country blues playing around the turn of the century was a guitar style known as "picking." It differed from the strumming or other chordal styles most often associated with guitarists in that the performer played the melody line and attempted to imitate the voice—particularly vocal embellishments—with the instrument itself. Dorsey, of course, was "too small to think anything much of [Phil's] music." But the music to which he was regularly exposed—Etta's singing and playing and religious music in general—was certainly distinct enough stylistically for Dorsey to be able to hear the difference between it and country blues "picking." In any event, Dorsey typically seems to have taken less notice of the quality of Phil's music than of the popularity of it:

I was too small to think anything much of his music, but he could play it all right; I can remember him playing. He could really play it. . . . He must have been popular, for he was always gone. He . . . was king 'round up in there.[45]

The other person—possibly next in importance to Etta—who influenced young Dorsey's musical growth was Corrie M. Hindsman, Etta's brother-in-law. As one of the more prominent members of Villa Rica's black community at that time, Corrie served for many years as the "respected and thorough school-master" of the local one-room school. Although almost no information exists to shed light on his educational background, it is certain, nevertheless, that he must have had some formal education which included piano and composition as indicated by a collection of hymns he wrote and published, *Inspirational Songs*. In Villa Rica, he conducted his teaching and musical activities at Mt. Prospect Baptist Church, founded in 1887 by his father, J. M. Hindsman, and six others.[46] The Dorseys worshipped here when Thomas was not on the road preaching.

Hindsman may have hoped to use as many opportunities as possible beyond the classroom to teach music, or his training may have made him critical of the style and narrow repertoire of the typical worship music found in a rural black church. Whatever the reason, he instituted "shaped note singing" at Mt. Prospect. Stylistically, this music departed radically from the improvised spirituals that dominated black rural congregational singing in turn-of-the-century churches such as Mt. Prospect. Dorsey recalls that at that time, "the people mostly patted their feet and sang what they could sing," that "most of the spirituals were spontaneous, [i.e.] the people sang from their very hearts," and that the spirituals were "about all our folks had to sing that came out of their creation." Hindsman offered a fundamentally different style, one in which the harmonic texture was homophonic as opposed to the call-and-response "polyphonic homophony" of spirituals. This contrast seems to be the basis of Dorsey's impression:

> The shaped note singer didn't want no accompaniment; they wanted to blend their harmony. They wanted nothing but pure harmony. The shape of the note gave you the tune and the pitch. And I mean every man and every woman knew their place [i.e., part: soprano, alto, tenor, or bass]. It was beautiful singing. You wouldn't hear any better singing now than those folks did in those days.[47]

Although Dorsey makes no mention of it, the difference between the reading of the words of the shaped note songs and the rote singing of the spirituals must have accounted for some of the impact of shaped note music on the congregation and on Dorsey himself. Thus Hindsman's tutoring was no small achievement: it brought unschooled persons to a level of musical literacy needed to perform music as unfamiliar to them as that found in his collection. For example, song No. 22, *Sailing on the Ocean*, has a refrain that has antiphonal singing between the bass and upper voices. Song No. 40, *The Lord's My Shepherd,* contains not only antiphonal part singing but considerable chromaticism as well. Ironically, however, for all the music he knew and taught, Hindsman never gave his young nephew any formal training.[48]

Other than the slave spirituals, the white Protestant hymns, and shaped note music, Dorsey describes a type of "moaning" as the only other style of religious song he recalls. As a source of his musical development, "moaning" is significant for three reasons. First, Dorsey associates it with no particular individual. The personalities of Etta, Corrie Hindsman, and Phil Plant were inextricably bound up with Dorsey's perception of the music they played, so much so that no description of the *music*—at least from Dorsey—exists. The "moaning" itself, not a personality, struck Dorsey:

> That moan . . . is just about known only to the black folk. Now I've heard them sing like this when I was a boy in churches, and that kind of singing would stir the churches up more so than one of those fast hymns or one of those hymns they sang out of the book [shaped note].

The emotional effect of "moaning" is the second reason this music figured so significantly in Dorsey's development. Dorsey was no stranger to the emotion common to black worship in general—especially since he traveled to many churches with his father. But the indefinable, mysterious quality of pathos in "moaning" as Dorsey saw it affect others was apparently responsible for the distinct impression he remembers it having on him:

> They'd get more shouts out of the moans than they did sometime out of the words, for the people, they didn't, everybody couldn't read back there, see? But it kind of brings the people up, puts them on their feet, starts them to thinking. After a while it hits the heart and they start to holler, hollering "hallelujah" or something like that. I don't know what it is, but there's something to it that nobody knows what it is; I don't know.[49]

Finally, "moaning" had no prescribed or limited context; its use was widespread. As Dorsey describes and performs it, "moaning" may be considered a set of performance practices, usually embellishments, that were applied to any of the genres of religious song that blacks then sang. In Example 1-1, for instance, Dorsey "moans out" *Amazing Grace.* Though he keeps the original melody prominent, Dorsey is able to recast the mood of the song through his use of ornaments. This ability to express oneself through the melody without singing the text made "moaning" adaptable to widely varying circumstances. "Moaning" was prompted by "something from within" and not tied to an arbitrary set of musical or ecclesiastical situations: "I've heard my mother and other folk get together, get around and get to talking and then start moaning." At church the congregation would sing a spiritual or hymn, "then they [would] moan it out."[50]

Ex. 1-1

Amazing Grace ("moaning style")

In sum, because "moaning" was derived from no single musician, was deeply associated with emotional expression and release, and was pervasive in practice, it would become the dominant musical source for Dorsey's gospel blues. And yet as a child he could barely have fathomed the emotional depths it could penetrate. But if not profoundly swayed by it, he was at least sensitive to "moaning" as a medium for the expression of feeling; and such expression was distinctively the intent of the music he would compose later in life. This is not to say that his tendency to focus on the glamorous rewards of music was altered by what he thought of "moaning." Instead, he finally began to understand that music could not only impress people but move them as well.

Dorsey's father never succeeded in gaining a steady, official position in Villa Rica commensurate with his educational background and training. At the age of 36, some fourteen years after his emergence as one of the select few graduates of a black theological seminary, Thomas found his goals and his desired life-style taking him beyond Villa Rica. Two more children, Lloyd and Lovie, had been born, swelling the size of the family to five; but Thomas had gained no comparable increase in his earnings from sharecropping. Etta, at the same time, seemed to "grow tired of the country life."[51] These conditions prompted the Dorseys—around 1908—to move to Atlanta. In doing so they joined a steadily growing stream of migrants from rural to urban Georgia who, for reasons almost as plentiful as their numbers, looked to the city for what the country was unable to provide.

By 1907, when Dorsey began his eighth year, the matrix of dualities that accounts most for the formation of his social, cultural, religious, and music values was in place. He had sweated and toiled as a dirt farmer as much as he had been pampered and flattered as the son of one of rural Georgia's black petty elite. He had sat among the congregations that thrilled to the pompous pulpitry of his father and among the family in quiet rapture at the pious Bible reading of his mother. He had seen neighbors enthralled by the plaintive twang of his uncle's blues guitar and church members lulled into meditative calm by the muted reeds of his mother's organ. And while he marveled at the pathos of the moaning spirituals, he was intrigued by the vocal demands of the shaped note songs.

The Paynes, Du Boises, and white missionaries who prescribed the world in which the children and grandchildren of slaves should become civilized would have been discouraged at finding these dualities representing the old and the new so much a part of young Dorsey's life. Their design had not allowed for blackness to thrive so well in the very culture they had conceived of to replace it. The question must be asked, even though it probably cannot be answered: was the world that the Du Boises, Paynes, and white missionaries envisioned one in which succeeding generations of ex-slaves could realistically expect to live? If the answer is yes, how does one explain the absence of most of that world for Etta and Thomas? How does one explain, more importantly, the pervasiveness of indigenous African American culture in the offspring of this ideal couple whose achievement alone stood for a repudiation of the native African American ethos? Neither of these questions fazed young Dorsey. In his world, blackness and whiteness could not have been conceived as much more than abstractions. But as Dorsey grew out of his boyhood in a black America that was evolving as quickly out of its own infancy, blackness and whiteness would emerge as realities with which both he and black society would grapple repeatedly over time.

2

Music, Literacy,
and Society in Atlanta:
1910–1916

In Atlanta, Thomas and Etta were forced to alter radically their pattern of living from what it had been in Villa Rica in order to overcome the economic hardships they faced. For the first time since being married, Etta had to do work in addition to that of a homemaker:

> She worked, taking in washing and ironing. [She would] go and wash a big batch of clothes and maybe get a dollar for it. That's about all a woman got to do down there in the south at that time.

Thomas apparently never taught school in Atlanta, nor did he engage in any occupation—other than occasional guest preaching—that required his training as a minister. Although he was listed in the *Atlantic City Directory* for the years 1913–14 as "Reverend," the possibility that he actually pastored is remote: no church was mentioned with his name although it was the practice of the *Directory* to designate a church with a pastor's listing. He was listed as a "laborer" or a "porter" for 1909 and 1912–15. Most of the information available about him supports this designation. According to Dorsey:

> He was a gardener [and would] go around and work the folks' gardens. Work the white folks' of course; we didn't have any. This business of gardening, he expanded it. He'd work certain days for Mrs. Bernard and another day somewhere else and another day somewhere else. He worked for those rich people out there toward the park, Grant Park.

The *Annual Catalogue of Morehouse College*, which lists the professions of alumni, shows that Thomas worked more in occupations other than pastoring. From 1916 through 1920 he reported working as a "florist" instead of "minister," as he had previously been listed.[1]

Dorsey's adjustment to urban living was as difficult for him as it was for his parents. The celebration of his first Christmas in Atlanta was threatened, he recalls, by Etta's poor health and Thomas's lack of employment. Only when Thomas's brother and sister-in-law, James and Sarah, bought presents and food for the family was a "sad" Christmas averted. The cow, Lilly, that had been a pet as well as a dairy food source had to be sold so that Thomas and Etta could buy other essentials. Dorsey recalls:

> I will never forget the butcher's name, Ed Campbell. He paid me twenty-five cents to drive Lilly to the slaughter house. There I saw her killed. I never got over that. . . ."

Even referring to his new house called for an adjustment:

> I know [our house] was 84 Delta Place. [It] had a number. That's what we didn't have in the country. And I had to accustom myself to remember where I lived.[2]

These were unimportant issues compared with the psychological adjustment Dorsey had to make to the most serious consequence of his family's move to the city: the loss of prominence they had enjoyed in Villa Rica. Thomas and Etta represented archetypal black Atlantan immigrants, having to live in the squalor of the side streets of the West Side and, like nearly "a third of the state's black labor force," having to work in domestic and personal services for whites.[3] At least in Villa Rica, Thomas had counterbalanced his sharecropping role with his quasi-professional status as a minister and educator. Etta had also offset her private unacknowledged domestic chores with her more public reputation as a "church worker" and organist. As a child in Villa Rica, Dorsey identified strongly with his parents' prestige—particularly his father's. In Atlanta, however, Thomas was not a preacher or a teacher; nor did Etta play the organ "at all" after moving to Atlanta. The pleasant times Dorsey had experienced traveling to churches with his father and listening to his mother's organ playing in Villa Rica were seldom, if ever, recaptured in Atlanta.[4]

The shock of moving to Atlanta and its attendant loss of status were in no way more apparent to Dorsey than when he attended the Carrie Steele Orphanage School. In Villa Rica, Dorsey's connection to his parents' prestige was based in part on his status as the son of a preacher, who was also the local schoolteacher. He was able to attend school at an earlier age than most children because his father ran it. It was in this environment that he felt privileged because he was the preacher's son. On the contrary, when he started at Carrie Steele he was demoted. Evidently, he was unprepared for the third grade to which he had progressed prematurely in Villa Rica.[5]

These initial problems of adjusting to the school had a direct effect on Dorsey's social development. He became sensitive about his appearance and thought of himself as a "'homely looking' piece of humanity." The darkness of his skin and the Africanness of his facial features were not aspects of his appearance Dorsey would have felt encouraged to take pride in at this time in Atlanta. At the cosmetic counters in black drugstores, he must have seen the skin whiteners and read the advertisements for them that said, "There is no need for anyone to endure a dark, swarthy complexion. . . ." He surely must have thumbed through the *Atlanta Independent,* the major black news-paper, and wondered whether "Her-Tru-Line" really "takes out the curls and kinks" of which he was now so aware.[6]

Dorsey grew to have even less regard for himself as he experienced the way in which differences in complexion and other physical attributes of blackness formed the basis of class distinctions among black Atlantans. He learned painfully that this virtual caste system locked one into its ranks not only by economic status but by looks as well:

> I was always barefooted, while many of the children of the "high tone class" wore shoes. Some of the children were able to wear shoes all the year around. I was looked upon as one of the common class.

As self-serving justification for maintaining his low self-esteem, Dorsey could look to the instances in which he was socially ostracized:

> During that time when we were about the age of ten, the boys and girls would have their birthday parties. They didn't invite me, even though they knew me very well. I guess I was not good enough, they thought, to mingle with their friends. I used to stand outside and look through the windows yearning for some of that youthful pleasure.[7]

Dorsey's problems with the radical recasting of his parents' roles and with his self-image became most evident in his disenchantment with formal education. As a child, Dorsey had often accompanied his father to the school-house but not always as a student. He was educated, at least initially, somewhat on his own terms: he learned when he wanted to and was strongly motivated by the pleasure of accompanying his father. Indeed, when he finally attended school regularly, he did so as a second-grade student: "I never was in first grade . . . even in the country." In Atlanta, however, "They had a system there when you go from one town to the other, you start back where they want you to start." Adding to the profound setback he faced in being demoted in the Atlanta school system, Dorsey also found it to be the scene of the most direct social rejection—in reaction to his looks—he had experienced:

> None of the girls at school would give any attention to me. While they would rave over the other boys, who were more handsome than I, I would go away and sit in a quiet place in the school yard and eat my lunch, which consisted of the following: white bacon, corn bread and a cup of syrup.[8]

Dorsey's feelings of alienation seem all the more appropriate when con-sidering the facilities of the Carrie Steele Orphanage School. Founded in

1889, by Carrie Steele Logan and her husband as a home for abandoned black children, the school was annexed by the Atlanta school system in 1909. Arriving in Atlanta in 1908, Dorsey was humiliated and isolated not just by the upper classes of Atlanta's black society but by its virtual outcasts as far as the school system was concerned. Dorsey remembers it as "a one room affair" in which three grades were taught. According to records, at the time it became an Atlanta public school, Carrie Steele had 112 pupils taught in one room in two four-hour shifts by two teachers whose salaries totalled $45 per month. Thus Dorsey's embarrassment at being demoted back to the first grade was aggravated apparently by his being able to observe second and third graders just across the room taking the lessons that should have been his. Added to this was the "affliction of double sessions," the unsanitary conditions, the poor lighting, and the lack of seats—all of which were conditions found in most of Atlanta's black schools. As late as 1921, the playground where Dorsey lunched in loneliness was rated the lowest in the Atlanta system, having scored 17 out of a possible 125 points. The building itself scored even worse: 80 out of 1000, putting it in the classification of structures "no child should be required at any time to attend. . . ."[9]

Dorsey left Carrie Steele after completing the fourth grade and "didn't go back anymore." As a thirteen- to fourteen-year-old fourth grader, Dorsey understandably became impatient with schooling, since the classroom had intensified his identity crisis. The allure of the streets, of making money, and of becoming a young man without the social stigmas he encountered at school proved powerful incentives for Dorsey to leave his school books. With the third highest percentage of illiterates among cities of its size at that time, Atlanta harbored many like Dorsey who became discouraged by the decay and confusion of the school system. One can only surmise whether, given the protective privilege of his father's status in rural Georgia, Dorsey would have made the same decision had his family remained in Villa Rica. That Dorsey was required by the circumstances of black urban subsistence to make this decision, however, mounts a serious challenge to the idealism and formulaic solutions the Paynes, Du Boises, and white missionaries held out to freedpersons and the next several generations of their children.[10]

Dorsey's religious development also suffered considerably during his initial adjustment to Atlanta. With church no longer the focal point of his parents' lives, Dorsey began to feel a waning attraction to it. Thus religion—as an avenue to a special identity—no longer existed. In the face of the challenges to his self-esteem, Dorsey saw the religious sentiments that he fostered in his earlier years, those generated by his parents' church activities, quickly dissipate:

> My religious feelings? I just went [from] church to church, from place to place, hall to hall. I felt religion, but I didn't want to go to church too often. I wasn't very religious at that time.[11]

Thus the effect of the transition from rural to urban living was sudden and deep. By the age of eleven or twelve, after only two years in Atlanta, Dorsey had developed an inferiority complex, had dropped out of school, and had become demonstrably disenchanted with the idea of religion in his life. Such a response to urban relocation may well have been typical among the many black Americans making a similar move at that time. Cities like Atlanta, Washington, D.C., and Birmingham were filled with masses of recent migrants who suffered from a crisis of identity, who were illiterate, and for whom the church was no longer a cohesive force. Dorsey, therefore, was not the only one who had reached a low point in his life; rather, many people with whom he came in contact, including his parents, shared his condition. His escape from an almost total immersion in such suffering was mainly a matter of will:

> These things never discouraged me or quenched my spirit. Being poor, shab-
> bily dressed, homely looking, did not stop me. I had hope, faith, courage,
> aspiration and most of all determination to accomplish something in life. . . .
> I resolved to make a mark for myself.

If this resolve can be considered half the battle in overcoming these conditions, music can be considered the other half. By the age of sixteen, approx-
imately eight years after moving to Atlanta, Dorsey would become one of the most noted blues pianists in the black community. Thus when Dorsey says, "[I] developed my music ability in Atlanta," he did so as much in order to survive the exigencies of a new and strange environment as he did to develop his love for music. The remaining narrative of his boyhood in Atlanta describes this development.[12]

Dorsey's thoughts about music as a career were spurred by his first exposure to show business. As a boy of eleven or twelve, he often "followed a crowd" of his friends to Decatur Street, at that time the "downtown" of Atlanta's black community, to attend the children's matinees at the Eighty-
One or Ninety-One Theater. These theaters served as two of at least five film and vaudeville houses for "colored people" that were scattered throughout the Atlanta black business district by 1914. As one of the more popular forms of entertainment, movies earned as much as $1000 in gross receipts weekly per theater from admission prices of between five and ten cents per person. The live entertainment provided in these theaters consisted of a vaudeville show of the kind just beginning to appear in cities as the counter-
part of the tent, carnival, circus, and minstrel shows that toured throughout the rural south. Dorsey remembers seeing at the Eighty-One "noted show folk" such as "Ma Rainey, Bessie Smith, String Beans, Skunton Bowser, [and] Buzzin' Burton." While attending these performances, he first felt "a desire for music" that later became so strong that he considered himself "aspiring" to become a pianist like those he was hearing.[13]

Dorsey was first able to make music because of the availability of an organ at home and a piano at his relatives' nearby. At the time his father had bought an organ, Dorsey, although intrigued by it, had been unable to play it because he was too small to pump it. Now, as an older boy, he could "pick out" tunes he heard. When he says that the organ "sprang" his music career, he probably means that the organ was the first musical instrument available to him. Although the first, the organ was not the only instrument to which Dorsey had access as a young boy. James E. Dorsey, Thomas Madison's brother, worked in excavation, a lucrative enough trade to allow him and his wife, Sarah, to afford non-essential furnishings including a piano. Indeed, they were "almost the only ones" in the community able to own a piano. Dorsey had access to this instrument almost as much as to the organ in his home.[14]

Dorsey began an active pursuit of music by "hanging around" the Eighty-One Theater as often as he could in order to meet the entertainers and learn what he could by watching the pianists. Later, after he was a regular, he got a job there as a "butch boy" selling soft drinks and popcorn during intermissions. This job allowed him to associate even more with musicians, particularly Ed Butler, the Eighty-One's main pianist. Dorsey would go to the theater early before his duties began so that Butler could show him "how to play that song [that] so and so sings."[15]

Dorsey made yet another effort to become involved in music: he began to associate with pianists who played at dances. Like most teenagers, Dorsey found his major social outlet in the parties and dances held in various houses, clubs, and community social halls. Pianists provided the music for these affairs and they always played blues: "didn't no dance go on without the blues."[16]

In addition to associating with pianists, Dorsey made an intense effort to learn as much music as he could on his own:

> . . . we had an old fashioned organ on which I would practice. If I heard a new song at the theater or a party, I would come home and sit at the organ until I could play it that very night. If it was 10 o'clock when I got home, or 11 o'clock, I'd go home; I'd play it, pick it out, practice it at night before going to bed.

Thus by "age 12," Dorsey boasts that he "had learned to play the piano very well" and that within "sixteen months" thereafter he "was considered an accomplished pianist."[17]

Dorsey's claim that he had learned to play the piano "very well" by twelve, after what had been at most a year of experience, sounds unbelievable until one understands the manner in which he acquired this skill. He was first trained by rote, that is, "nothing was written." The pianists from whom he learned showed him how to play. When he heard a piece, he would go home and "pick it out": "I didn't have any trouble learning anything; I could play anything I heard." The pianists whom Dorsey watched and imitated, moreover, played for the most part in situations requiring improvisational techniques. For example, James Hennenway and Lark Lee, two dance pianists from whom Dorsey first learned, composed blues over a standard harmonic progression that they varied rhythmically and melodically according to the mood or the tempo of a dance. As part of his job at the Eighty-One Theater, Ed Butler cued pictures with his piano music. According to Dorsey, Ed Butler "made up" this music in order to accompany the action in the film.[18] While blues idioms and harmonic structures can be learned quickly, a mastery of them is a complicated process, probably requiring years of experience. Thus, when Dorsey speaks of the unusually narrow span of time it took him to develop into a pianist, one should assume that he is speaking of the time necessary for him to learn enough of the melodic, harmonic, and rhythmic rudiments of a playing style from musicians like Lee, Hennenway, and Butler for him to be hired for parties and dances. He was, moreover, prone to measure his success with playing by the jobs that he was hired for rather than his actual keyboard ability.

The clearest evidence of the improvisational orientation of Dorsey's playing lies in the music he remembers playing and in his descriptions of the situations in which he performed. At parties, Dorsey recalls having to play for as long as two or three hours, during which he was "changing around" or "slow dragging":

> Sometimes you, the fella, who has got knowledge enough, can make up as he goes. The little unexpected things get [the people]; it comes with you while you're playing. The slow drag, that's just one of them things you know; it was something you dragged.[19]

Dorsey demonstrated his improvisational techniques while he worked with a rather limited amount of material. Measures 1–4 in Example 2-1, "Dance Blues ('fast')," and 2-2, "Dance Blues ('slow drag')," consist of two variations of a "standard introduction" that Dorsey remembers "the folk would scream about" when he played it.[20] Although each example contains a basic six-pitch sequence, Dorsey plays each with a different rhythm. The result, however, is more than rhythmic variation: it is a shifting of the emphasis on certain pitches in the sequence as well. Such melodic variation, apparently built on the technique of shifting accents, enabled Dorsey to disguise the repetitious use of these few pitches. Furthermore, this technique gave Dorsey the means to use the same material to set contrasting moods. Example 2-1 (mm. 1–4) indicates a use before a fast dance ($\quarternote$ note = c. 152), while measures 1–4 of Example 2-2 show the sequence introducing a slow dance ($\eighthnote$ note = c. 144), and measures 7–8 consist of the same sequence serving as a bridge to a cadential phrase.

Another indication of Dorsey's early use of improvisation can be found in the harmonic progressions in his music. In Example 2-1 (m. 5) and 2-2 (mm. 5–6), the harmonic patterns are identical (IV_7-ii_6-IV) even though they occur

Ex. 2-1

Dance Blues ("fast")

mm. 1-2

mm. 3-4

m. 5

Ex. 2-2

Dance Blues ("slow drag")

Ex. 2-2 (cont.)

mm. 7-8

mm. 9-11

in different dances—a fast and slow one, respectively. In measures 10–11 of Example 2-2, Dorsey plays the same sequence of chords, but this time as a means to reach a cadence. His alteration of the sub-dominant chord (IV) to a diminished chord by raising its root (IV$_4^\circ$) provides a leading tone to the dominant seventh chord (V$_7$) and thereby an authentic cadence to the tonic (IV$_6^\circ$-V$_7$-I). In Example 2-3, Dorsey demonstrates a typical rhythmic embellishment of this cadential sequence—one he may have used according to his "feeling."

Although Dorsey remembers little about the theatre cueing he learned, he can recall that it was no less improvisational than his dance music:

> You play something to go where the picture is going. If it was a solemn picture, you would play solemn music and [so forth]. You could just make up as you went along, if you're a good musician.[21]

If Example 2-4 is representative, picture cueing, though improvisational, required technique different from that of dance music. With the exception of

Ex. 2-3

Cadential Sequence

the introductory material, most of the dance music Dorsey remembers stresses harmonic as opposed to melodic material. Example 2-4, however, has a melody played by the right hand and the supporting harmony almost all in the left hand where, in order to provide rhythm, it is set in a broken eighth-note figure (see mm. 2–5 and 14–15).[22]

Learning the techniques of improvisation accounted for only part of Dorsey's rapid development and recognition as a pianist. The sheer effort it required for him to gain notoriety—working in the theater in order to be around pianists, practicing at night after returning from his job or parties until he learned a piece—indicates motivation beyond the simple desire he might have had to master the piano. From the beginning his early attraction to piano playing was nearly devoid of any consideration of the music itself:

> At that time I didn't understand blues or nothing. And didn't even under-stand other types of music too much. All of the music sounded just about alike to me.

Thus when he first heard Ma Rainey, the famous blues singer whom he would later accompany, he "didn't even know what she was singing. She was howling something out there. I don't know if I liked what she was singing or not." At the root of his phenomenal progress lay Dorsey's need to develop an identity that would bring him respect. He was acutely aware of the social importance of pianists: "a piano player could go anywhere; they'd be glad to welcome [him] and he didn't have to worry about no girlfriends." His de-scriptions of his popularity as a pianist—once he sensed that he had gained it—clearly indicate that the piano was the means to a social end:

> I could play almost anything I heard. The "high-tone class," who had shun-ned me at their parties earlier, were glad to have me attend all of their parties now that I was considered an accomplished pianist, equal and even superior to any in their select circle.

Ex. 2-4

Theatre Cue

mm. 1-5

mm. 6-9

mm. 10-12

mm. 13-16

Dorsey, the pianist, now enjoyed the friendships and mobility that Dorsey, the son of migrants from Villa Rica, the school dropout, the social recluse, never dreamed of:

> By this time I had become very popular with the younger set, or now you would say the teenagers, and I had lucked up on a few good-looking clothes, so was always welcome when I entered any of the affairs that were in progress. In my town there were gangs of boys who would not let fellows from the other parts of town come into their community to visit the girls. I never had any trouble with these fellows, because I could play piano and any piano player could go anywhere in town and not be run out.
>
> I lived in a part of Atlanta called Reynolds Town, but I covered all the communities: Edgewood, Fourth Ward, Darktown, Tanyard Bottom, Westside, Mechanicsville, Pittsburgh, Summerhill, Peoplestown and Decatur. I was a favorite in these communities and young friends would want to go along with me for they felt that they would not be chased out by the local gang. I always carried a crowd that followed me.[23]

Still a novice among pianists and still a boy, Dorsey had little hope of playing professionally, inasmuch as the "old aces had that area." The only way left for him to gain some experience came through offering his services where a pianist was needed but not always available: at "rent" or "chittlin'" parties. Only persons with pianos in the community could have these affairs. As the names suggest, the income from the admission charged—"usually ten or fifteen cents a person"—helped pay the rent and perhaps the note on a piano:

> See, they'd keep agendas there, and mark them down: "party such and such a place, at such and such a time." Well, boys like us, we just drop in at the party and I was the piano player, see. "Come on in and play." A little get together, little functions, a few people give to sell their chittlins or sell their beans. Those who had pianos were kind of scarce at that time. Everybody didn't have a piano. Those that had a piano could do that. And they wanted somebody to come and play it anyhow. You could, a piano player, there, if you could play any at all, they welcome you. "Come on, play my piano."

Dorsey also found that he could play in bordellos "if they let me in":

> Oh, I guess I was twelve, maybe thirteen, or fourteen. I'm getting to the place now I'm a pianist; I can play and I love myself for it. I think I'm good. They had places you know, well, let's put it like this: the fellows come in, they want to spend the money and they want to meet and flirt with the girls. The girls, well, they were after their part too. I don't call them sporting houses exactly and then there were some of those too.[24]

Dorsey grew dissatisfied, however, with being able to play only for "chittlin'" parties and sporting houses. He received little money, if any, for his services:

I'll put it like this: you got all the food you could eat, all the liquor you could drink, and a good looking woman to fan you. Now take these parties. If you left the party with seventy-five cents or a dollar, you had a good night and yet you done played about two or three hours.

Dorsey's reputation suffered among his acquaintances for his association with the bordellos and their clientele. They called him "Barrel House Tom":

I ran with the folk and them down [on] Decatur Street and in the alleys, so I guess some of those places, well, anything could happen. All refuse goes in the barrel. They used barrels for refuse, you know—junk, trash. If you wasn't no good, nobody wanted you, they call you barrel house. I was Barrel House Tom and they didn't want to bother with me.

And since he played alone at the parties and houses, he was now cut off from the professional music community and therefore unable—since he learned by rote—to advance by hearing what those pianists were playing:

You mostly had to go downtown, get in with somebody. Now, that's the [reason] I got in with show business, because they had plenty of music around there and I liked that and that was a place for me to kind of practice and bloom out from.[25]

Although Dorsey had achieved some success, it was apparently of a questionable sort. Undoubtedly, he was an "accomplished" pianist by age fourteen, but his accomplishment meant playing mainly on the rent-party circuit and in Atlanta's red-light district, places most professional pianists avoided. Undoubtedly, too, he had learned to play "very well." But the music idioms he had mastered so quickly became almost as rapidly mere clichés as his isolation from the music community and the limitation of his performance opportunities combined virtually to freeze his repertoire and thus stunt his musical growth. Even the recognition that he might have thought he had achieved was doubtful, for it came not as much from those of the "high-tone class" who had always "shunned" him as it did from those who "ran" in the alleys. Thus Dorsey began the second phase of his evolution as a pianist: He had realized that the origins of his present reputation comprised the most serious threat to his further success. Moreover, he lacked the acknowledged musicianship and performance opportunities that would gain him unequivocal respect as a pianist and as an individual. These limitations brought Dorsey to forsake the seventy-five-cent parties and brothels for the chance to associate with professional pianists.

As Dorsey describes it, the community of black professional pianists in Atlanta was divided into two groups: those with a reading knowledge of music and those without. This division did more than set an arbitrary boundary between those who had taken lessons and those who had not—especially considering that it delineated professionals in both camps. It split the community ideologically between those who were trained in music for which a reading knowledge was fundamental and those who were trained in music that was learned by ear:

> There were different pianists for different places. Dance hall pianists didn't have to read no music if he knew enough songs. In the theater, them guys would come there with music and they put it up there and wanted the pianist to cut it.

Whether accurately or not, Dorsey sensed a certain hierarchy, at the top of which stood those in greater demand—the reading pianists. The two men he speaks of almost reverentially were Ed Butler and Eddie Heywood, pianists at the Eighty-One and Ninety-One Theaters, respectively:

> If anybody had something they wanted, you know, where they had to use music, well, they were the music men and music readers. [They] played for some of the swell functions [around] there. I envied these men for their ability to read and write music.

As he entered the professional community, Dorsey belonged to the non-reading group. But this was by default rather than by ideology; he simply had had no opportunity for formal training. He both "envied" those who read and deprecated his own accomplishments: "I wasn't a good musician. I could play almost anything I heard, but I was a poor reader."[26]

Another division among black professional pianists resulted from the scarcity of quality pianos in their communities. The number of pianists far exceeded the availability of dance halls and theaters to employ them or the accessibility of homes, churches, or other such establishments with instruments on which they could practice or perform. The measure of success among pianists, therefore, depended not only on the ability to play but as well on the ability to claim a locale where one was recognized as the pianist: "There was no union then, but them fellas loved their jobs and wasn't going to let nobody come there and challenge them."[27] If having an organ at home and a piano at a nearby relative's was advantageous when Dorsey began playing, it soon proved inadequate in terms of the performance base he needed as a professional.

In order to gain identification in the wider professional community, Dorsey first of all had to seek formal training: "See, I was trying to make a career out of music and these fellas come and talk this stuff and I had to talk it too." He began lessons with a Mrs. Graves, who was affiliated with Morehouse College and had a music studio in her home:

> She was a good musician as to what type of music she played. She taught all of the musicians, I mean, the upper-crust music performers. I'd have to walk from Reynolds Town, where I lived, to the other side, the West Side. She charged about fifty cents a lesson. I'd have to go out and cut grass or something to get the money. She taught, you know, "do, re, mi, fa sol," and then spaces and lines and everything, how to use your fingers.[28]

The music of Morehouse College and that of the theaters and dances occupied opposite ends of the Atlanta cultural spectrum, along with the people to which each type appealed. The "upper-crust" musician was someone trained in a tradition—probably western European classical—who, because of that training, implicitly rejected the more indigenous Afro-American music. Even though pianists Butler and Heywood read, it was a music with which Dorsey was familiar, and it was the music of the people with whom he lived and for whom he performed. Dorsey suddenly encountered a subtle but significant division between musicians, one that transcended the petty distinctions between readers and non-readers and those with or without access to pianos. It was the wall between the East Side and the West Side, between "the fellas" and the "upper crust," between one form of blackness and another: "See, she [Mrs. Graves] wasn't a jazz musician. She taught around Morehouse. The music most the folk [Lee, Hennenway, etc.] were playing was by ear."[29] Dorsey saw another division between the Graves/ Morehouse/West Side milieu and his own: in the former his training was a reflective—almost cerebral—study of music; in the latter it was the rote— more intuitive—process of "picking up" musical knowledge as he played.

As a pre-adolescent school drop-out, Dorsey had already declared his aversion to the learning process if it was too structured and not—to him— immediately applicable to his purposes. In some respects, then, Dorsey's venture to the West Side to learn music was predestined to fail. He was seeking advancement not only in a profession in which he had been involved at best marginally for over two years but in one for which his present study of music had little or no relevance. That he would be able to succeed at all would be more a testament to his determined independence than to the rules of the classroom and studio:

> I knew about as much as I needed to know: how to play songs and things like that. I started a harmony course at Morehouse, but I wasn't there long. [It] didn't do me no good much, for the kind of music I wanted they didn't have it at the College. [With Mrs. Graves] I took, I think maybe the first grade of music. Well, heck, I felt I knew, that's all I needed to know about music. I'm quick.

Dorsey returned to the theater as his classroom, determined, more than ever, to learn all that Butler and Heywood could teach him:

> I didn't have time to take too much time to go to school. What's the need of me going over there, staying all the year for them to tell me when I could play or how good I was? I just go over somebody's house and practice and play [what] I heard at the show. I heard all the songs; I had a pretty good ear.[30]

Dorsey found that he needed more than the art of reading to play in the theater. A "show" consisted of a movie and live entertainment. Dorsey had become skillful at picture-cueing within a year or so after he started work at the theater (see Example 2-4). But because of his lack of training, playing for the acts—something for which reading ability was a given and for which sight-reading and arranging were important additional skills—had been virtually impossible. Given his aversion to formal training, all he could do was admire Butler and Heywood from a distance:

> Many times I'd see Eddie Heywood and Ed Butler, they'd sit up [at] the piano there with the lights on over the piano and make the arrangement until the next show start. Then they play the show [and afterwards] finish it up. That may be something for somebody they had to have the next day or the next week. They were hired, they were making the arrangements. See most of the shows go[ing] through, when they had something new they can't get the new show together, this guy writes all the music down.

Not to be outdone, and with a tenacity and aggressiveness that were becoming more characteristic of him, Dorsey "sent away and got books, self-teaching books," and taught himself the rudiments of notation.[31]

Dorsey could pride himself on having worked his way through the ranks from "butch boy" to learning the skills of a theater pianist and, finally, to music reader. At best, however, he had gained the privilege to be among the readers, but not their full acceptance. He never became more than someone "hanging around." He jokes about it: "I was a showman before I ever had anywhere to perform, for I learned the business there. I've always hung around the theater." Even if Dorsey enjoyed a higher ranking within the professional community, he still would have been idle, awaiting a nod from the house pianist before he could display his newly acquired skills:

> He had to send you. You didn't go out and take it. You couldn't just go in there, I don't care how good you was. You couldn't go in there and sit down, no one. Not in the theater to cue pictures or even to make an opening before the show, I mean before the curtain goes up.

Any playing Dorsey managed to do with the vaudeville shows was incidental. He recalls, for example, once working on a "mini-bill" with Bessie Smith, the famous blues singer. At that time she was another teenager like Dorsey who would "hang" around the Eighty-One Theater "practicing in the backyard." He also recalls that he "wasn't writing anything"; thus his arranging and composition skills, if he had learned anything from his "self-teaching books," remained untapped.[32]

With the theater serving as little more than a learning experience, Dorsey began to re-evaluate his skills in regard to how they affected his ability to earn a living and reputation:

> I didn't have a professional job and I wasn't called professional. You see a profession, you got to be doing something up there that will at least advertise the profession. [I] could read the music. I could do all of this, but you've got to have a place to do it and you've got to have somebody to hear it.[33]

To solve this problem, Dorsey turned once more to the sites of his earlier successes: house parties and dances.

The social outlets for young people, particularly blacks in Atlanta, were limited, according to Dorsey:

> Saturday night stomps and dance halls, theaters, weddings, that's about all [there was]. Saturday night stomps—[after] everybody go to a theater and see a show, that's about the next music you'd get. Go to folk who had pianos.

Among those who played for stomps and other similar affairs, more than among theater pianists, access to pianos was crucial:

> There were plenty of piano players there, but they had no place to play. [Those] who had pianos, they wouldn't let nobody play 'em. What's the need of having a piano and wouldn't let nobody play it? I guess they must be afraid they'd break the piano or something like that.

Dorsey would realize that his earlier decision to leave the small parties was not as advantageous to his budding career as it had seemed at the time. Nor was his move back to the dance/party circuit all rosy: it was wise for the purpose of establishing his professional credentials but problematic considering the number of pianists with whom he had to compete. Still, the sense of fraternity among the players allowed for infrequent opportunities:

> If you had anyone else [who] could play, you let them play. That's the way I got around. Piano players go around and help the others out, help one another.

This largesse hardly allowed one to become well known or to earn a living: "You let them play, but if you got anything for playing, you put it all in your own pocket."[34] The only way for one to establish oneself unquestionably, therefore, was to compete for and win substantial public attention.

Beginning soon after July 4, 1915, Dorsey and the other wandering pianists could take advantage of a new opportunity to display their talents competitively. This was the first Sunday after the opening of the Odd Fellows Roof Garden and was thus the first chance to begin what would become a Sunday afternoon tradition of informal playing sessions. Since dancing was banned in Atlanta on the Sabbath, and since the theaters were closed as well, young people, who mostly "courted" on Sundays, had almost no place to socialize. In order to help solve this problem, the Odd Fellows organization opened the Roof Garden:

> They didn't have any dancing, but they let the young folk or old folk, whoever wanted to, go up to the Roof Garden. You could meet whoever you wanted over there; they had no food; they just opened it up. [You] could go about three o'clock and stay till eight; they sent them home early. You couldn't dance—no kind of thing like partying on Sunday. They [just] let young folk congregate in there and meet one another.

Because the Roof Garden was built for almost any other social activity but dancing, its piano was not reserved for the use of one of the "old aces." The Roof Garden, therefore, had probably the most well-placed open piano in Atlanta. The large group of aspiring and certainly frustrated pianists such as Dorsey recognized this rare opportunity to promote themselves:

> The piano player who could play could go up there and show [his] skill. They would go up some steps, we would call an orchestral stand now, but they would go up there and if a piano player was good, the folks standing on the floor there would stand up and look at him and give him a big hand.

If a pianist played well, he could expect to be hired for parties:

> Piano players come to show off, see. And get a chance to play before the people. You go there and show what you got, and the folk give parties and things, you get a job.[35]

If the Roof Garden offered Dorsey the visibility he needed, his actual keyboard style gave him the popularity he craved. Something the party-givers heard in Dorsey's playing made him highly appealing for circumstances far less genteel than Sunday afternoon at the Roof Garden. To understand this quality and how Dorsey cultivated it, one need only look at the conditions under which he played frequently. With the exception of the theater and dance hall, neither of which Dorsey played at with any regularity, each of the situations in which Dorsey plied his craft was plagued by the threat of "the law." There was prostitution at the bordellos, rowdiness at the house parties, and, considering that Atlanta was "bone dry," the possibility of police raids at both. Dorsey recalls vividly an escape he had to make by climbing out of a second-story window and gradually inching himself to the ground by using his elbows as a wedge when police invaded "one of the houses there on Decatur Street" and began making arrests. At parties, even if no alcoholic beverages were served, the possibility of arrest was still imminent:

> Down there in Atlanta, it's warm weather most of the time. You had to throw the windows open. You could hear the piano playing a block away almost, and when the folk get in there and they get noisy, the neighbor called the law and the law come in there. Sometimes they didn't bother anybody, see what's going on. But if it was one of those places you know, where they handle bootleg liquor, anytime they'd come, they'd pull around the wagon down there and run them in.[36]

The type of mingling and dancing that occurred in brothels and house parties was distinct from that in dance halls and other places in which Dorsey might have played. The purpose of a bordello was understood before one entered. At house parties—particularly given that they flourished as alternative or perhaps after-hours entertainment—varied forms of dancing and intimate association were the rule. Thus, even before his professional career began, and then well into it, Dorsey understood the need to be scarcely seen and barely heard:

> I'm alone. Nobody there on drums. Drums just got in the picture; I mean nobody that's giving a party wanted the drum. You get those folk excited, you'll never get them back. The folk upstairs don't want to hear that drum and the folk there don't want to hear it when they get to those parties. The piano player got to answer for drum and everything else—unless it was a guitar. But, see you had to play that thing soft and low.[37]

As a result of his having to "change around," "slow drag," "make up as you go" for periods lasting as long as three hours, under conditions where the rhythm and melody could be present only enough for slow, intimate dancing but never too pronounced or loud to break the mood or the law, Dorsey became proficient in—and subsequently famous for—an improvisational style virtually unique among pianists in Atlanta. His popularity stemmed, therefore, from his capacity to adapt an already superior playing ability to situations for which his type of playing was needed. Added to this was Dorsey's shrewdness in being able to survive professionally. The combination made for the kind of success that had so often eluded Dorsey:

> I got the jobs just like I got a music publishing company. I [was] just a little bit more aggressive. But they liked my style. Some of the fellows, you know, bump, beat, you know, they played loud and folk get loud and [others] called the law. But I played soft and easy, you could drag it out and hug the woman at the same time. Let the lights down low and they'd have to give attention to hear the piano.[38]

Dorsey once again found a niche in which he could function successfully. As with his earlier arrival at a similar point, however, the achievement paled in light of his desire for a solid career and respectable reputation. After all, the notoriety that he now enjoyed was gained by mastering the style that thrived among the very group of pianists from whom he had once attempted to dissociate himself. Any pride he might have taken in being popular had to have been tempered by the fact that he was still no more than a good background pianist on Atlanta's underground house-party circuit. Thus Dorsey could boast:

> . . . I ranked No. 1 with the leading and best [local] pianists of the time such as Edgar Webb, Ed Butler, Eddie Heywood, Sr., Lark Lee, Harvey Squiggs, Soap Stick, Arthur Hennenway, Long Boy, Nome Burkes, Charlie Spann, and many others.

But he knew that when he assessed his chances of a career among these pianists plus the "many others," he was no better off than they were. Thus he came to the inevitable conclusion that Atlanta was no longer the place for him to continue his search for professional status:

> Seemed the old town did not have much charm for me anymore. I had a yearning to move up higher. . . . I wanted bigger and better things and I wanted to go where the lights were brighter and you didn't have to run to get the last street car at midnight.[39]

3

Blues—From
"Lowdown" to "Jass":
1921–1923

Dorsey was driven to leave Atlanta by his desire to become a professional musician. But, along with the vast majority of black American urban immigrants, he had other reasons for moving north, the most prominent of which were racism and the hope for a better life. The *Chicago Defender,* one of the leading black newspapers, played a key role in arousing these sentiments through its "pronounced radical utterances, its criticisms of the South, [and] its policy of [advocating] retaliation" against racism. The climax of the paper's campaign was its organization of "The Great Northern Drive" for May 15, 1917, whereby "the poor brethren" of the South in one mass exodus would escape their oppression.[1] Dorsey was encouraged by the *Defender*'s articles in his decision to move north: he speaks of reading in the *Defender* about "the great opportunities . . . for my people in the north." Indeed, beginning with its first commentary on migration in March 1915 and thereafter until 1917, the paper's efforts to rally southern blacks coincided with Dorsey's struggles to make a name for himself.[2]

But black Americans like Dorsey were not about to take steps northward in search of a racial utopia alone; such idealism would hardly feed or house them. Life in the North was thought to be better for a more tangible reason: one had the opportunity to advance economically. Indeed, the possibility of earning substantially more money working in northern industries encouraged a number of southerners who, like Dorsey, were contemplating a move. The factories of the North heavily recruited in the South for black workers, who—when they could find work at all—earned a fraction of what they could in the North. Dorsey recalls reading recruitment notices in the *Chicago Defender* and seeing billboard advertisements "all over" Atlanta. At a time when he barely eked out a living playing piano through the night, Dorsey found these calls to the North alluring.[3]

Dorsey had any or all of these reasons to move north, but one racial incident, coupled with the thought of "making big money," provided the catalyst. As a teenager, Dorsey and his friends loitered around the business district, often "keeping a lot of noise or something like that." During one such time, a white storeowner came out to chase the boys away. As Dorsey remembers it:

> Some of the boys see a white man come like that, naturally [they] ran. But I don't know why, I didn't move fast enough and he kicked me.

This was not the first time that Dorsey had experienced physical abuse from a white person. He vividly remembers being "rocked" by white boys when he had the misfortune of being caught alone or in an outnumbered group of blacks in a white neighborhood. The kick, however, seems to have caused more than physical injury, for he remembers making up his mind then and there: "I'm gonna make all white folks pay me back." Already disillusioned with his piano career, Dorsey became bitter after this incident. He could no longer disregard Atlanta billboards saying "the government needs help" in the naval yards in Philadelphia. Friends of his had gone there a few months earlier and were writing back about the large amounts of money they were earning. Dorsey wrote for a job and was hired immediately. He prepared to travel to Philadelphia, but, curiously, "via Chicago."[4]

Leaving Atlanta for Philadelphia in July 1916, Dorsey apparently traveled via Chicago because a number of his father's relatives, including Joshua Dorsey, the druggist, lived there. He never left Chicago, however, to complete his journey to Philadelphia. He felt more secure in Chicago with family around him because "if hard times came," he would have more support than if he moved to Philadelphia where he "didn't know nobody." He worked odd jobs through the summer and fall and also played at parties similar to those at which he performed in Atlanta. He was, however, unable to adjust to the winter weather in Chicago and returned to Atlanta by the winter of 1916. He would repeat this cycle for the next two years, traveling to Chicago to work in the summer and returning home "before it got too cold." This seasonal traveling between Chicago and Atlanta might have continued for several years had Dorsey not faced a new problem on his eighteenth birthday, July 1, 1917: the draft. He had no desire to enter the armed forces. In Chicago he was satisfied with his work, at that time in the Gary steel mills, and with his sporadic opportunities to play music. Under the mistaken impression that people who worked for the government or the railroad were exempt from the draft, Dorsey attempted to avoid conscription by becoming a "dining car cook" for the "CR&P" railroad company. Although he did have to register on September 7, 1918, he never served in the armed forces because he became one of the early victims of the 1918 flu epidemic and was exempted from his first call. The Armistice of November 1918 was signed shortly thereafter. Once the draft was no longer a threat,

Dorsey returned to Atlanta for the winter. Finally, he settled in Chicago shortly after the race riot of July 27 to August 8, 1919.[5]

Dorsey chose to settle in Chicago at a time when both northern and southern cities had become "concentration points" for rural southern African Americans. Chicago's case was particularly dramatic. Between 1910 and 1920, its black population increased by nearly 150 percent from 44,103 to 109,594. In 1916, when Dorsey first traveled there, the largest increment of this population growth occurred: almost 50 percent. Prior to this large influx, Chicago's black community had been rather insignificant in size and had posed little threat to whites. By the end of World War I, however, this situation had changed, one direct result being the 1919 race riots in which 38 persons were killed, 537 injured, and over 1000 left homeless.[6]

The rapid swelling of the numbers of newly arrived blacks created intraracial problems as well. Blacks living in Chicago prior to the great migration watched their area become overpopulated, with more than 90 percent of the 100,000 blacks in Chicago by 1920 concentrated between Twelfth and Thirty-ninth streets, and Wentworth Avenue and Lake Michigan. "Old settlers" blamed their newly arrived brethren for racial problems: "There was no discrimination in Chicago during my early childhood days, but as the Negroes began coming to Chicago in numbers it seems they brought discrimination with them." The urban culture that had arisen among established blacks contrasted sharply with that of migrants, who were often ridiculed because they "didn't know how to act" and "spoiled things."[7]

Although Dorsey's choice of Chicago might have been ill-advised considering the general social situation there during the second decade of the century, it was advantageous to his musical development, particularly during the years 1916 through 1919, when he first joined the community of musicians in Chicago. Many other musicians, especially those from the Mississippi Delta and New Orleans, had sought haven in Chicago since the early 1900s for reasons similar to Dorsey's. By the second decade, Chicago, along with St. Louis and New Orleans, thrived as a ragtime center chiefly because of the migration of black pianists. The first black-owned establishment for the nickelodeon type of music that Dorsey performed in Atlanta was the Pekin Theater, opened in 1905. Its owner, one of the "gambling lords" of black Chicago, started the theater as a cover for his illicit activities. It became widely known for its "fare of ragtime, cakewalks, and 'coon songs', " which were then the staples of the nascent black vaudeville industry. At the time Dorsey began traveling back and forth to Chicago, the community of black musicians found itself in the throes of one of its most significant stylistic transitions caused by the influx of musicians from the famed New Orleans "tenderloin" district, Storyville. Officially established in 1897 in order to contain vice within a single area, Storyville spawned the precursors, originators, and later some of the most noted practitioners of the conglomeration of styles that first became known as "jass" and later "jazz."[8]

Dorsey arrived in Chicago representing the hopes, fears, and aims of the two groups of new settlers most responsible for fundamentally reshaping the black experience: the migrant worker and the migrant musician. Understanding the commonality and divergency of these two personalities provides a clear perspective from which to analyze Dorsey's first years in Chicago. Both types of migrants idolized the North as a frontier of freedom; it became the spatial synonym for unlimited opportunity. They differed, however, in the manner in which they claimed the urban promise. The laborer accepted it as a means to an end: it gave him the chance to toil and thus the chance to succeed. For the musician the promise itself was the end; that is, the mere act of playing was success. Considering his "yearning to move up higher" and his choice of a northern city as the locus of his ascent, Dorsey became both the archetypal migrant urbanite and musician by working in various service jobs on the railroad while vying for success by seeking opportunities to perform. Thus what could have been the typical migrant experience for Dorsey became one subsumed, instead, by his status as a musician. He found Chicago to be not only the northern, urban haven for the restless, former southern black but the place to play himself "up higher."

He was in good company. Chicago was rivaled only by New York as a center of "commercial exploitation and mass diffusion" of music. Perhaps more than any other, this characteristic lured gifted musicians there in search of "better opportunities."[9] Thus Chicago was not so much a gathering place for the novice or the developing musician—though to be sure all levels of musicianship were represented—as it was a mecca for migrating professionals seeking the greater recognition and monetary benefits that a major metropolis could provide. Scott Joplin, Joseph "King" Oliver, Jelly Roll Morton, Louis "Satchmo" Armstrong, and W. C. Handy were merely the more notable in a long line of musicians, including Thomas A. Dorsey, who had come to Chicago to peddle their music for fame. Thus money and notoriety were clearly the arbiters of success within the community of African American musicians Dorsey joined upon moving to Chicago. To some extent he was well suited to such an environment because of his experience in Atlanta. The aggressiveness Dorsey displayed in order to learn the piano and to find playing jobs, together with the pragmatism with which he approached music in order to play under widely varying circumstances, had been crucial to his success in Atlanta and would become the keys to his survival in the more demanding Chicago community. On the other hand, Dorsey's actual style of playing was basically that of an earlier form of blues ("gutbucket," as he would describe it), closer in sound to the rural blues than the derivative played at that time in Chicago: "jass." "Jass" was the style New Orleans Storyville musicians produced by using blues and ragtime instrumental techniques to imitate the blues vocalist. The resulting "dirty tones" were obtained by employing a wide variety of devices such as soda bottles, plungers, cups, and other materials as mutes. By the time this performance style had reached Chicago and had merged with others, it had developed into a form of blues vastly different from the "lowdown" blues to which Dorsey had been accustomed. As the New Orleans "jass" became popular, the blues Dorsey played was relegated to less and less prominence among musicians and certain audiences.[10]

As a pianist, Dorsey entered the Chicago music community unaware that he represented a style of playing that was for most purposes out of vogue and perhaps even archaic to those who had been living in Chicago. He thus had a rather naïve impression of his success as he began playing in Chicago:

> My first night in Chicago my future began shaping up. I made my way to Thirty-seventh and State Street to a wide-open cabaret known as the Kelley Garden. I went into the wine room where the folk were dancing to piano music played by a young woman of about twenty-two. I asked if she would like to rest some. She replied yes and I took over the ivories. When I finished playing I had made a name for myself.[11]

Located in the backs of bars, wine rooms existed for women who at that time were prohibited from being "up front in the bar." Men could come to the wine rooms where "there was dancing" and "the same liquor" was sold. Because of the wine room's disadvantageous placement, musicians did not compete with one another to play there. The wine room, therefore, was ideal for Dorsey, since, as an unknown pianist, he could not have walked into the bar area of the Kelley Gardens and "taken over the ivories"; the system of protocol in Chicago's music community demanded that Dorsey "sweat" for such an opportunity. Ignorance amounted to bliss in this case: because Dorsey had been unable to play steadily in the dance halls and clubs in Atlanta, the bottom of Chicago's ranking of performance opportunities was more than suitable for him.[12]

Dorsey continued to "frequent the place just to get a chance to play and be known in Chicago." Probably because of the "name" he made in the Kelley Gardens, he was hired to play for rent parties and in establishments peculiar to Chicago—"buffet flats." One observer believes that buffet flats first served Pullman porters who sought an imitation of the "'high-class' night clubs where tuxedoed maître d's . . . [arranged for] sexual liaisons." Dorsey describes these establishments as big business for the proprietors, called "landladies," but not for the musicians. Other than for sex, buffet flats were popular because they served as "after-hours or Sunday" drinking establishments. Like the wine room and the rent party, they provided employment for the lower echelon of pianists in the community.[13]

If Dorsey truly believed that these performance opportunities marked his achievement of real success in Chicago, he must have been ignorant of, or indifferent to, the organization of the music community. He had earned a "name," but not any differently than he had in Atlanta: he played for insignificant affairs in both cities. The distorted perspective from which he viewed his renown can be explained partially by the even greater "name" he had achieved in Atlanta merely because he had performed in Chicago:

> I had been to the North and lived. For one thing it kind of made me stand out around there [Atlanta]. I didn't figure that I knew anymore than they did, but [when] you come down to it, I did know some things that they didn't know for they'd never been there [Chicago]. I had some songs and music they didn't have. That kind of helped me stand up and make them listen to me.[14]

Apparently his illusion of fame in Chicago was fed by his inflated conception of it in Atlanta.

Dorsey's sense of his popularity in Chicago was not altogether false, however. By the summer of 1919, the Eighteenth Amendment had been ratified. The buffet flats and rent parties which had once been insignificant now became the main settings for the illegal alcohol trade "when the town went dry":

> More buffet flats opened. It was nothing strange at all for one of the land-ladies to call me at 2 or 3 a.m., saying, "I have a swell bunch from the north side and they want music." The word[s] "swell bunch" meant they had money. I would get dressed, hop a cab, rush over and sometimes the bunch would stay until daybreak. I would leave with $15 or $20.

The "law" had been enough of a threat in the places where Dorsey played in Atlanta that he was no stranger to these circumstances. Musically, he found himself in demand for the same reasons as in Atlanta:

> I made good playing the Buffet Flats, because I had the kind of touch, beat and volume the landladies wanted. I was a soft smooth player and I sang softly with my playing, so I got more work and was better paid than the loud banging type pianist. . . . I was on the landladies' payroll. His kind of playing late at night would call the law or attract the police and the place might be raided. The best pay the loud banging pianist could get was a few dime tips. I was called the "whispering piano player."[15]

The demand for Dorsey's playing indicated in part a preference for the practicality of his blues for illegal situations. For many patrons of the parties and buffet flats, the style of Dorsey's blues was preferable to the jazz blues then prevalent in Chicago:

> No, jazz is a new name on the scene. I was here when it started and remember there were folk who you couldn't go in and call it, [or] say jazz. [If] you say the name jazz in some folk['s] house, "We don't want that; don't come in here with that stuff, jazz." Well, it's just like everything else: the people had to get used to it.

Whatever the following for jazz, it apparently did not represent a cross-section of the black community. Other than the "swell bunch" types who were clearly the exception rather than the rule in the establishments where Dorsey played, those who frequented the parties—and maybe the buffet flats—were the "lower-class, working people, and the small-time people. People who couldn't go to the more expensive affairs, or rub shoulders with the elite, the high class." Because of migration, the numbers of these "lower-class" persons had increased drastically during the years when jazz was emerging. The blues Dorsey played was familiar to this group, who had come from the South as recently as Dorsey had. Jazz, on the other hand, appealed to a "higher class" and to those musicians who were not inclined to play the party and buffet-flat circuit: "They didn't attend these things. They had their own, you see. They were in a class to themselves."[16]

The disparity between the older blues Dorsey played and the newer jazz was even more evident in the moods each style evoked. According to Dorsey's interpretation, jazz was "pep or hot, blues was slow." Because of the variance between the tempos, different techniques were required to play each style:

> [Jazz], your execution was a little faster. . . . All the piano boys were trying to get those extra keyboard frizzles and nimbling in their fingers to make [their music] sound jassy. That's why I didn't bother much with it. [It] took too much energy. You couldn't last an evening. Too much barnstomping. You bump, beat, be wore out.

Whereas jazz was "peppy," blues was "feeling bad; woman, man, feeling bad; ain't got no whole lot of pep to jump around like the jazz."[17]

Though Dorsey is unable to remember the names of jazz dances, to "jump around" was more appropriate to jazz than to the older blues. Much of the early jazz repertoire was in essence the older blues "brought up to dance tempo" by some of the "arrangers and orchestra leaders." Dorsey is speaking, of course, of the "syncopated orchestras" (and bands) that began forming in Chicago around 1915 and by 1919 or 1920 were popular, such as Dave Peyton's Symphonic Syncopators and the orchestras of Erskine Tate and Wilbur C. Sweatman. The "slow drag" and "shimmy" (also "shimmy-she-wobble") were dances for the blues. If New Orleans is representative, since 1910 the slow drag had become increasingly more popular than the dances for rag and rag-blues music. Dorsey, of course, had been slow-dragging since the beginning of his career around 1912. When he arrived in Chicago, the "shimmy had just come out and got popular" and was "just a more modern name for the slow drag." The slow drag and shimmy were so much in demand, not only because they were quieter dances and thus suited to house parties and buffet flats but because the opportunity for intimacy was so much greater:

> They want to get close. You couldn't do no shimmy alone, by yourself. They danced all night. You look around and nobody be moving. They'd just be shimmying.

Even when player pianos began appearing in the buffet flats and thus threatening the incomes of the pianists, Dorsey, because of his blues style, was unaffected:

> Piano rolls when made at the factory were cut or played by more refined pianists. I played the old gutbucket style where you could shimmy or slow drag. Therefore, piano rolls did not supply competition.[18]

Several aspects of Dorsey's performance of the blues make it rather obvious why his music could fit into the blues milieu so well. Example 3-1, *A Good Man Is Hard to Find,* is one of the pieces that Dorsey would "feature, way in the night, drag easy, and play soft and low [in order] not to disturb the folk underneath." The accompaniment is almost devoid of embellishments, leaving the right hand (which usually plays the embellishments) merely to answer the weak beats (two and four), and the left to play the bass in octaves on the strong beats (one and three). The result is an accompaniment that supplies the steady beat required for dancing but that is performed in a manner that undergirds rather than competes with the voice. Indeed, the rhythm, the actual time values of the notes—as opposed to the underlying pulse or beat—results from the interaction between the declamatory delivery of the text (which Dorsey "just talks out") and the unaccented, unadorned pulses of the accompaniment. With the exception of measures seven (beat four) through twelve (beat three) and seventeen through twenty-four (beat three), the melody consists of but one principle pitch with the minor third above or the fourth below that pitch—and intervening pitches—used as ornamentation.[19]

Given the paucity of melodic material, Dorsey's description of how he "just talks out" the melody becomes significant: the only expression available for the voice is rhythmic. Having to perform under the restraints he did—playing "soft and low, dragging easy"—Dorsey had to resort to indirect accentuation supplied by an extensive use of syncopation. Almost none of the vocal phrases begins or ends on a beat. Dorsey thus creates the maximum rhythmic complexity possible under the circumstances: linear variation of rhythmic values in the voice and cross-accentuation between the voice and the accompaniment.

Dorsey achieved an important contrast to this rhythmic complexity—while still remaining within the constraint of "not disturbing the folk"—by ceasing, except vocally, all rhythmic activity at the two points in the text where such contrast seems necessary in order to highlight the meaning. These are measures ten through eleven and eighteen through twenty-one. In the first instance, the text speaks of deception: " . . . then you find that rascal hangin' 'round there with some other gal." In the second it admonishes, "Love him in the mornin', kiss him late at night," and so on. Dorsey stops the steady beat in the accompaniment, replacing it with a sustained chord. For the syncopation, he substitutes duple eighth notes in the first set

Ex. 3-1

A Good Man is Hard to Find (Dorsey's version)

mm. 1-2

mm. 3-4

Ex. 3-1 (cont.)

mm. 5-6

You— al-ways get that——— oth- er kind.—

mm. 7-8

——— You get a good man,———

mm. 9-10

think he's your pal, then you find that ras-cal hang in' 'round there

Ex. 3-1 (cont.)

mm. 11-12

mm. 13-14

mm. 15-16

Ex. 3-1 (cont.)

mm. 17-18

my ad- vice.— Love him in the morn- in',—

(8vb) - - - - - - - - -⸗ loco

kiss him late at night, give him plen- ty lov- in',—

mm. 19-20

treat him—— right, for a good man—— now- days,—

mm. 21-22

8vb - - - - - - - - - -

Ex. 3-1 (cont.)

of measures (canceling temporarily the pulsation of triplet values) and quarter-eighth-note figures on the beat in the second set of measures. He then complements this rhythmic contrast with an equally compelling melodic contrast that he produces by widening the range of the melody to an octave and varying the kind of melodic movement between diatonic and chromatic sequences and between leaps of thirds and fourths.

In essence, these stylistic qualities appear to be a set of performance parameters applicable to music originally composed in styles vastly different from Dorsey's blues. *A Good Man Is Hard to Find,* for example, was written originally as a popular song. It became well known after Sophie Tucker's featured performances of it on Broadway and elsewhere in New York in 1918. Dorsey may well have first heard of it through Tucker before he "featured" it at the rent parties he played. *There'll Be Some Changes Made* was another popular song to which he recalls "couples would drag around the floor . . . when the night was getting old and the lights down low." From early on in his career, Dorsey, as part of his acquisition of technique, had cultivated the ability to take "popular numbers and drag them out." His playing, therefore, functioned as a means of translating one mode of musical expression into another, the latter being the one with which his listeners—mostly recent migrants—could identify. The resulting synergism, sometimes of the most disparate musics, exposed Dorsey's listeners to forms of musical expression from which they might otherwise have remained isolated.[20]

Beyond these moods, dances, and stylistic qualities, the most profound difference between blues and jazz can be found by examining the ethos in which each flourished. The "feelin' bad" versus "peppy," the slow versus fast dances, and the "bump and bang" versus "low and soft" techniques were not only indices but manifestations of two contrasting ambiences with one purpose in common: they offered release. Dragging to the "lowdown, gut-bucket" songs of lost love was as anomalous to the Lincoln Gardens, the De Luxe and Dreamland Cafes, and the Vendome and Grand Theaters, as two-stepping to the refined musicians' *Black Bottom Stomp* or *Doctor Jazz* was to the nameless "get togethers" in crowded tenement houses:

> . . . Blues were not played or sung in high-class places, or in smart society clubs, but were heard in the black and tan joints, the smoky little places, the hole-in-the-wall joints, broken-down roadhouses, and second-rate vaudeville houses.

One might be persuaded to think that Dorsey believed the difference was mostly one of class. He speaks, however, of something more complex, of something more like the feeling for which one seeks out a particular setting: "Blues is a low down and grievous, grieving tempo; it hits you below the belt." Among the people for whom Dorsey played, the sense of suffering and agony was pervasive; they would gather together almost as if to commiserate:

> . . . Some have asked what is the blues. It would be hard to explain to anyone who has never had a love craving, or had someone they loved dearly to forsake them for another, a wounded heart, a troubled mind, a longing for someone you do not have with you, and many other things I could mention. . . . Blues would sound better late at night when the lights were low, so low you couldn't recognize a person ten feet away, when the smoke was so thick you could put a hand full of it into your pocket. The joint might smell like tired sweat, bootleg booze, Piedmont cigarettes and Hoyttes Cologne. . . . The piano player is bending so low over the eighty-eight keys, you would look for him in time to swallow the whole instrument. He is king of the night and the ivories speak a language that everyone can understand.[21]

As a pianist steeped in the musical idioms of the Atlanta blues tradition, Dorsey, through his "ivories," spoke an old tongue in a new land. Everyone who understood it attested to the benefits of sharing mutual despair through music. Unwittingly, Dorsey was helping to preserve the old ways of migrants, precisely at the time when they were attempting to adjust to the city where such ways were held in disdain. The rent party—the kind at which Dorsey played—thus became the secular counterpart of the church, especially for alienated new settlers. Eventually, Dorsey would be as effective in the church as he was now in the rent party.

To Dorsey's fellow musicians, his style of playing must have been quaint compared with the vaudeville, jazz, and other rag-blues styles that prevailed in Chicago's music community. The first printed music to include the word "blues" in the title was three pieces published between August and September 1912. The most famous of these was W. C. Handy's *Memphis Blues*. Its structure and harmony were those "already used by Negro roustabouts, honky-tonk piano players, wanderers and others of their underprivileged but undaunted class from Missouri to the Gulf. . . ." It was hardly a new music, but merely a folk sound notated and adapted by the trained composer. It differed enough in sound, nonetheless, from the original blues style that musicians familiar with Handy's style would consider Dorsey's that of the "honky tonk" pianists.[22]

If the response in New York was any indication, a pianist like Dorsey could expect from his professional colleagues anything from mild condescension to outright contempt for "gutbucket" playing. James P. Johnson, a dance-hall pianist in Manhattan in 1913, played his *Mule Walk* or *Gut Stomp* for "southerners" because "they were country people and they felt homesick." Another pianist playing at a bar in New York, Willie "the Lion" Smith, recalls:

> Our soft, slow, four-o-clock-in-the-morning music got to those folks from the South. . . . By this time we had learned to play the natural twelve-bar blues that evolved from the spirituals. . . . They wanted us to get-in-the-alley, real lowdown. Those big Charleston, South Carolina, bruisers would grab a girl from the bar and stomp-it-down as the piano player swung into the gut-bucketiest music he could.

Perry Bradford recalls less gentle or uniform responses from about 1918:

> . . . the average folks up there had been taught not to "mess up" with that "phony blues tripe" music. . . . It was confusing to see some of those "Hate Blues" hypocrites, who were preaching and brainwashing before the public how much they detested the blues, yet whenever the same so-called sophisticated intellectuals and top musicians would hear some lowdown blues sung and played at a House-Rent-Party or some hole-in-the-wall speakeasy, they'd let their hair down, act their age, be themselves and go to town by belly-rubbing and shouting, "Play 'em daddy—if it's all nite long."

In the light of such attitudes, Dorsey sensed that he was not well received in all circles of the music community and that he was at the lowest ranking among trained musicians. He must have also realized that the "low people" for whom he played in Chicago were no different from those who frequented Atlanta's "chittlin' stomps" and rent parties.[23]

When Dorsey wanted to improve his position in Atlanta, the solution had been merely a matter of "going downtown" and "getting in" with the theater musicians. The simple division of musicians in Atlanta, however, was replaced by a caste system in Chicago. There, he could not—as he had in Atlanta—take a menial position in some establishment as a way of associating with musicians. Neither could he "hang around" hoping to meet people: "I . . . was too young and not well-known enough to mingle or associate with the old-line music men . . . who were then great musicians of the theater." A more formidable barrier than age or anonymity, however, was the

Musicians Protective Union: "Those old guys would call me 'boy.' I had to soft soap those guys in order to get in." The only work besides house parties that Dorsey could find was to replace pianists who failed to appear for a job. Quite often such substituting was illegal because Dorsey had not been assigned officially by the union:

> Back at that time you could kind of get by from the Union. The Union wouldn't come out to those small places, at least the walking delegate wouldn't bother you.

Dorsey did form a band some time between 1916 and 1919, but he was seldom able to find jobs for it: "We played most of the time for ourselves."[24]

Thus in 1923, the most active point of his career so far, Dorsey could be described as a somewhat prospering pianist, but on the periphery of the professional musicians' community. In addition to the general obsolescence of his style, Dorsey faced two other problems that kept him out of the Union: his technique was substandard compared with that of trained, professional pianists; and, as a result, he was unfamiliar with the literature that union musicians would be expected to know. As he points out,

> There wasn't too many that could really tow the line up to the point where the union wanted to send them out for hire. I couldn't make the point; I buffaloed, bluffed my way through.[25]

Undoubtedly, though, his greatest barrier to success was the size of the Chicago musical community. The opportunities were greater than in Atlanta, but so were the numbers of musicians who sought them. Dorsey realized, as he had in Atlanta, that he must alter his goals if he desired to "make it."

As Dorsey looked over the professional community, he came to the realization that in Chicago, as in Atlanta, musicians were divided on the question of notated music: "You couldn't find five musicians at that time out of a hundred that could write the melody down, but they could read music." Reading skill among black musicians was a relatively new development brought about by the increase in the size of groups of musicians playing together and the attendant problem—particularly for those playing inner parts—of learning the music by rote. The higher-paying opportunities to perform came with the syncopated bands and in the theaters, where improvisation was minimal. It was clear to Dorsey that these reading musicians needed parts and that preparing music was "where the money was." He saw too that he could finally fulfill his dream to be like Butler and Heywood at the Eighty-One Theater. He, therefore, made the decision to build on the smattering of composition and arranging he had learned from Butler and Heywood by enrolling in the "Chicago School of Composition and Arranging." This move proved a wise one, for throughout the remainder of his career, whenever he was unable to play for a living, he had more than ample work as a composer/arranger. Evidently, he learned within a short time. By

October 9, 1920, he had registered his first composition at the United States Copyright Office, *If You Don't Believe I'm Leaving, You Can Count the Days I'm Gone.*[26]

Dorsey's registration of one of his blues compositions is unusual when one considers the way in which blues was regarded among his colleagues at that time. In addition to a degree of condescension and contempt toward it, there was also a certain sense of communal ownership:

> All blues, we didn't put them no where. They wasn't paying nothing much for them anyway. Blues was blues. All the blues belong to you. What're you gonna steal? Nothin' you could do with it if you steal it. . . . Well all blues sounded alike for a while anyway, so we never bothered about the other fellow. If he got somethin' [of yours] out, that's O.K. I'd just let him take me out to dinner or somethin' like that. And if he thought I infringed on him, there never was no money transaction, no.

Indeed, the act of composing blues was something musicians joined in for fun:

> We used to have "who can rhyme music." [We] would say, "I'm gonna play something and you put words to it." [I would] compose right as I go along. Some of those guys could do pretty good.

With this widespread casual attitude toward blues' ownership, Dorsey's copyrighting of *Count the Days* seems unusual, especially since he had performed it with his small band as early as 1918. Considering several events in New York in August 1920, however, Dorsey's move to protect his music was well timed.[27]

Though Dorsey and his friends joined in playing "who-can-rhyme" games, Perry Bradford, a vaudeville pianist and songwriter in New York, encountered hostility from his colleagues at the Colored Vaudeville and Benevolent Association:

> . . . when I would park my bony-self on the piano stool . . . and began drifting into the lowdown, melancholy strains of the levee-camp "jive," someone would yell to detract [*sic*] my attention. . . . anything to keep me from whipping out those distasteful blues.

In spite of this general lack of respect for the blues, Bradford believed there was money to be made from performing blues songs. In June 1918, mostly in an effort to find off-season employment, Bradford and several performers wrote a "put-together-quickie" blues revue. Entitled *Made in Harlem,* it played, often to capacity audiences, first at Harlem's Lincoln Theatre and then at the North Pole Theater. Bradford viewed this development as somewhat of a coup since he had "tried for six years to make these uppish Harlemites blues conscious."[28]

Following *Made in Harlem,* Bradford sought to conquer yet another frontier: the recording industry. In February 1920, after several years of unsuccessful attempts with various companies, Bradford persuaded General Phonograph Company (OKeh Records) to record a "colored girl" named Mamie Smith. Because of a pending lawsuit by the Starr Piano Company against Columbia Phonograph Company and Victor Talking Machine Company for a release of the monopoly they held on a cutting process, the record was not available to the public until the beginning of August. But word of the recording spread far in advance of its release, for blacks were not unaware of its significance: finally, a white company had "stuck their neck out." In the March 13 edition of the *Chicago Defender,* an article announcing OKeh's signing of Smith appeared along with a statement that "we [black Americans and/or the *Chicago Defender*] are here for their service." OKeh responded by placing an advertisement for the record in the July 31 edition, to which the *Defender* appended an article urging blacks to buy the record "as encouragement to the manufacturers for their liberal policy. . . ." Evidently, blacks did not find it disconcerting that Smith recorded her two songs, *That Thing Called Love* and *You Can't Keep a Good Man Down,* in the white popular song style of the day accompanied by white musicians chosen by General Phonograph. During the first month of the record's release, over 10,000 copies were sold. One outlet, the Melody Music Shop in Harlem, sold over 2000 copies within two weeks.[29]

With the record's national success and *Made in Harlem*'s local fame, Bradford sought next to combine their impact: recorded sound—then a novelty—would serve as the medium for bringing to prominence an underrated and misconstrued song form. He had no problem convincing OKeh that a vast market had been tapped and that another recording should be made, this time with a "Negro jazzband" so that Mamie Smith "would be at liberty to strut her stuff." The most popular song of *Made in Harlem* was *Harlem Blues*. Smith's rendition had drawn as many as "ten encores" at performances. Bradford changed the title of the song to *Crazy Blues* because he had "used the same lyrics three times before."[30]

Finding the "Negro jazzband" that would be familiar with the blues idiom was difficult in New York:

> . . . the men who could play blues and jazz . . . were scarce in Harlem at that time. . . . It was a hard nut to crack, to find men that would touch the style of music I wanted to play, because those same musicians had scorned W. C. Handy just because he played blues when he made his first appearance at the Lafayette in 1918.

Bradford had Handy to thank for at least one musician he used in the band. Johnnie Dunn was a cornetist well known for his *Bugle Blues* with Handy's Memphis Blues Band. The other instrumentalists were Ernest Elliot, clarinet, Leroy Parker, violin, and Dope Andrews, trombone—all known for their blues playing. Bradford literally had to scrounge around Harlem cabarets to find what became known as "Mamie Smith's Jazz Hounds." On August 10, 1920, *Crazy Blues* was recorded along with *It's Right Here for You*. A resounding success, this record netted Bradford as composer $53,000 in royalties. Bradford now had even more reason to rejoice than he did after the first recording when he declared that ". . . Mamie could now for a releasing moment rejoin that part of ourselves which we have sacrificed to civilization."[31]

Even though Mamie Smith and her Jazz Hounds' music was not the "lowdown, gutbucket" blues that Dorsey played, their recording sparked a reassessment of blues among black Americans. Smith was, after all, a vaudeville singer, and the instrumentalists accompanying her were jazz or vaudeville musicians. Yet the blues, even when adulterated for public consumption, as was the so-called "classic" blues, was unmistakably the music of black Americans.[32] Suddenly, blues was no longer "wee-hour of the morning" music, a vestige of rural backwardness, or an opiate of the unassimilated. Thousands of black Americans sacrificed a dollar in 1920 to purchase *Crazy Blues*. In a sense, each purchaser was implicitly acknowledging a new understanding of the blues, which had previously been relegated to hole-in-the-wall joints.

When Smith's recording of *Crazy Blues* was released in late summer, Dorsey describes what appears to have been an explosion of interest in the blues among musicians:

. . . blues singers began to pop up here and there and their popularity began to sweep the country. . . . Many recording companies began to record and distribute the records of these singers to the four corners of the USA. . . . This was something new and a thriving business. Everyone was aspiring to become a blues or jazz singer. Songwriters were popping up like popcorn. . . .

It was in this milieu that, in all likelihood, Dorsey decided to register *Count the Days* at the Copyright Office. Henceforth, the idea of communal ownership of the blues was dead.[33]

By October 1920, Dorsey had clearly developed his written compositional skills—as evidenced by his having copyrighted *Count the Days*—and as clearly had achieved a reputation as a blues pianist. The writer-performer was a rare combination even among the vast number of musicians in Chicago. With the blues enjoying a new wave of popularity, Dorsey seemed poised to claim a unique position of regard among Chicago musicians. Ultimately, he would do so. But by late fall of 1920, his schedule of playing parties and buffet flats at night, working at other jobs during the day, and studying music somewhere in between "proved too much" for what he himself describes as "a feeble, gaunt fellow of 128 pounds." As the result of this demanding schedule, and probably also frustration with his career, he suffered the first of two nervous breakdowns. So serious was his condition that his mother had to travel to Chicago to take him back to Atlanta because "he had fallen off so small until he was just skin and bones."[34] As would be his fate more often than not, Dorsey, at the moment opportunity seemed his for the taking, was prevented from grasping it. In this instance, while he was convalescing, his fellow musicians were gathering the first fruits of the infant blues recording industry.

4

Blues—From
"Jass" to "Lowdown":
1924–1928

Until 1921, Dorsey's religious involvement had been passive. During his childhood, the disparity between the religious practices of his mother and father caused him to conceive of religion as a hodge-podge of antithetical images. During his adolescence in Atlanta, the church—no longer the site of his parents' prestige—became for him merely a place to socialize. As he recovered from his nervous breakdown, around the age of 22, he seemed no longer prone to become religious. His mother's all-too-frequent admonition, "serve the Lord, serve the Lord," diminished in importance before his greater urge to return to Chicago and continue his career.[1] Early on in his life, therefore, circumstances seemed to determine that a religious experience— in order to have any meaning—would have to be cathartic.

Not long after his return to Chicago in 1921, Dorsey's Uncle Joshua invited him to attend the last session of the National Baptist Convention that had been meeting in the city from September 7 to 12:

> I said, "Oh, I haven't got time for I got something to do." I was in the . . . blues business, I *wanted* to be. I [wasn't] a member of anybody's church— there, my father's, nobody['s]; didn't want to be a member. But it was [at the] big Eighth Regiment Armory. My Uncle prevailed with me and I decided to go. I went and I sat—quite a distance from the front.[2]

The Convention was hardly the religious setting he had expected. Young women paraded about in "home-laundered white" outfits, while men strutted in their tuxedos, Prince Albert coats, cutaways, and silk hats. To the outsider, the Convention was as much a bazaar as a spiritual convocation:

> One would have thought that there was a convention of the National Booksellers' associations. Iron-throated vendors of the blattering of some puny scribbler in Massachusetts or Louisiana tramped the aisles of the great hall

filching the pockets of the unsuspecting of their money for a few dry and empty pages. Everything was sold on the floor from hair tonic to a man's soul.

Having had to pay a dime admission to this carnival-like worship hour, Dorsey must have regretted having followed his uncle's suggestion, that is, until he heard "Professor" W. M. Nix sing *I Do, Don't You?* Whatever example, admonition, and even illness had been unable to accomplish in the cause of Dorsey's religious development, the fervency and expressive quality of Nix's singing that Sunday morning did:

> My inner-being was thrilled. My soul was a deluge of divine rapture; my emotions were aroused; my heart was inspired to become a great singer and worker in the Kingdom of the Lord—and impress people just as this great singer did that Sunday morning.[3]

Nix's fervor that morning can be traced to more than the desire to convince people of their religious shortcomings. The 1921 Convention presented an opportunity for Nix to promote the first official songbook of the National Baptist Convention, *Gospel Pearls*. Nix's presence on the Music Committee, the group charged with compiling *Gospel Pearls,* obligated him all the more to present his selection as favorably as possible. The National Baptist Convention had been grappling with a way to fulfill the "urgent demand for real inspiring and adaptable music in all . . . Sunday Schools, Churches, Conventions, and other religious gatherings." Three years after *Gospel Pearls,* the Convention published its first hymnal with the same purpose in mind, but more explicitly articulated:

> It must be noted that there seems now to be a tendency to get away from that fervency of spirit and song that characterized the church and altar worship of other days, and which contributes so much to the stability of our religion. With the thought, therefore, of the preservation of the good old soul-stirring hymns of days gone by. . . . "The Baptist Standard Hymnal" has been compiled.[4]

The variety of styles found in *Gospel Pearls* reveals to a certain degree the Convention's strategy for curing the declining "fervency of spirit." The first section, "Worship and Devotion," contains a set of standard religious songs composed of ". . . hymns and tunes that cling so closely to the heart, that try as you may, you can not get away from them." These include songs of Isaac Watts, Charles Wesley, Lowell Mason, Thomas Hastings, and Fanny Crosby and thus represent the Anglo-American hymn and gospel song traditions. The other major styles included in *Gospel Pearls* can be traced back to two song types widely used among black composers of sacred song: tabernacle or gospel songs similar to those made popular by Ira D. Sankey, Philip P. Bliss, and Homer A. Rodeheaver (white songwriters/evangelists associated with the prominent evangelists Dwight L. Moody, D. L. Whittle, and Billy

Sunday, respectively), and "spirituals," or "jubilees," derived from slave music. Songs by Lucie Campbell, W. J. Harvey, Carrie Booker Persons, and C. A. Tindley represent the first group and are all in a section called "Revival." (Campbell, Harvey, and Persons were Baptist songwriters and members of the National Baptist Convention Music Committee.) The second group of songs is located in a section called "Spirituals" and is composed almost entirely of the arrangements of John Wesley Work, Sr., and his brother, Frederick J. Work. John Work taught Latin and history at Fisk University, until around 1900, when he revived the defunct Fisk Jubilee Singers and led them on concert tours throughout the United States until 1916. He is credited with being the first black American to collect extensively and arrange black folk music. In 1901 the Work brothers published *New Jubilee Songs*, followed in 1907 by *Folk Songs of the American Negro*.[5]

Nix's delivery on that Sunday morning was influenced by at least one factor other than the need to "sell" *Gospel Pearls*. As one of the most prominent of the group of singing evangelists in the National Baptist Convention, Nix needed to show that the new song book was "especially adapted for soul-winning." According to the Music Committee, *Gospel Pearls* was to be "a boon to Gospel singers." In order to demonstrate its effectiveness, Nix, already known to be successful at "soul-winning," had to sing the songs convincingly; he had to produce results as he had been known to in the past—to "inspire the believer." Evidently he achieved this goal. Even the secretary departed from a rather bland style of writing the minutes to state that "Professor Nix, the popular evangelist, thrilled the Convention."[6]

The music Nix sang that morning is irretrievable. From Dorsey's recollection of it, however, one may discern at least the elements of Nix's style, as well as insight into what it was that struck Dorsey so forcibly and that led virtually to his conversion. Nix's performance was rooted in improvisation. A superficial comparison of the melody as published (Ex. 4-1) shows that it is no more than the framework for Dorsey (Ex. 4-2). Nix must have thought that generation of the feeling that "thrilled" the Convention was tied to the freedom to alter the music. As a singing evangelist, Nix probably approached his written music much in the same manner as the black preacher approached his sermon: his delivery was not restricted to what was written. In this instance *I Do, Don't You* served as a vehicle for Nix's personal testimony:

> The whole text was good news, good news for him, for he was expressing himself, what he did. Gospel is good news and you sing that; you're singing good news to the people and they were susceptible. The thing that sold the song was the personal pronoun, *I*; Nix made it [the song] popular at the Convention.[7]

In Nix's performance, melodic embellishment seems to have assumed a crucial significance as a means for achieving expression. While a certain

Ex. 4-1

I Do, Don't You? (original)

words and music by E. O. Excell

mm. 1-2

I know a great Sav-ior, I do; don't you? I

mm. 3-4

live by His fav-or, I do; don't you? For

mm. 5-6

grace I im-plore Him, I wor-ship be-fore Him, I

mm. 7-8

love and a-dore Him, I do; don't you?

degree of improvisation is the norm in religious music performed by blacks, Nix's singing evidently contained embellishments of a sort that surprised Dorsey and the Convention:

> These turns and trills, he [Nix] and a few others brought that into church music. Hymn singers, they couldn't put this stuff in it. What he did, I wouldn't call blues, but it had a touch of the blue note there. Now that's the turn and the feeling that really made the gospel singers.[8]

According to Dorsey's demonstration, Nix embellished the melody in two ways. The first was by various ornamentations: "the turns and trills" with "a touch of the blue note." In measure one of Example 4-2, for example, the fourth beat is a double appoggiatura, the first note of which is a lowered third ("F flat"). This note is considered a "blue note" in this context

Ex. 4-2

(Dorsey's version
with melodic and
rhythmic analysis)

I Do, Don't You*

mm. 1-2

I know a great Sav–ior   I do, don't you? And I

mm. 3-4

live   by his fa- vor   I   do,_____ don't you?   I

mm. 5-6

want Him to bless me,   to   own_ and con- fess me, com -

mm. 7-8

plete - ly   pos-sess me   I   do, don't_____ you?

Symbols: + = melodic accent
           ○ = shortened value
           □ = elongated value

* N.B.: In measures 1-4, Dorsey sings words to the first stanza; in measures 5-8,
  words to the fourth.

Ex. 4-3

Melodic Accent Summarization

(comparison between Dorsey's and published versions of
I Do, Don't You)

Dorsey

Original

inasmuch as such notes are derived from the lowered third, fifth, seventh, and even sixth degrees of the major scale.[9]

Nix alters the actual pitches of the melody as his second manner of embellishment. A singer, by altering pitches, can change the shape or contour of the melody and, therefore, can shift the point at which the melody climaxes. In Example 4-3, the melodic accents (points where the direction of the melody changes, up or down) of Dorsey's and of the original version are illustrated. The resulting melodic contours show that the alteration of the pitches occurs at points so different from one another that in Dorsey's version the climactic point comes at the beginning of the last phrase, resulting in the following contour:

In contrast, the original climaxes at the mid-point of the third phrase, resulting in the following contour:

The expressive effect of each version differs, owing not only to the variance of the contours but also to the way in which the climax of each contour is approached. In the original, the two phrases preceding the climactic one ascend, but in a disjointed manner. Dorsey's phrases at the same point follow the original with negligible variation. Had his melodic high point not come later, the structural similarity between the two would have continued to the end, and his version would have peaked at the same pitch level as the original. But Dorsey's climax is a surprise in that he delays it for two phrases. In order to continue following the descending pitch level of the original—if such was Dorsey's purpose—his version descends as suddenly as it rose (this time a minor tenth) and continues similarly, though with greater variance than in the phrases preceding the climax.

In addition to the melodic embellishments of Nix's style, there are also rhythmic ones. Without a metrical marking or any other designation, one cannot ascertain if a difference in tempo exists between Dorsey's performance of *I Do, Don't You* and the tempo used normally in the performances of other evangelistic singers or that intended by the composer. Since childhood, Dorsey had believed that slower songs could convey the content or thought of the text better than faster ones:

> When I was a boy, back there in Villa Rica, they had jubilees, or fast songs. They called them jubilees in that day. They [jubilees] had a tempo, and they used the words of the Lord. A lot of folk didn't like fast [songs]. They would sing them slow songs; [they] had an easier chance to grasp the message.

As Dorsey sees it, tempo is a major element of improvisation. The slower the music, the greater the potential for expression, and the more expression, the more the performer can communicate "the message." Tempo, therefore, seems to be used to expound the meaning of the text. This is the idea that must have guided Nix's choice of tempo that Sunday morning.[10]

The meaning of the message, however, is revealed not by tempo alone, but by tempo in conjunction with the alteration of rhythmic values. Tempo as a variable by itself provides only for the duration of rhythmic values. The meaning—within the tempo Dorsey (or Nix) used—was supplied by an alteration of the rhythmic values at points where certain syllables or words were to be emphasized. Thus through his choice of tempo, Dorsey could add or take away the expressive potential of the music. But the actual expression itself was articulated by altering the rhythmic values in order to emphasize parts of the text.

Only two types of rhythmic alteration are possible: the abbreviation or elongation of values. In Dorsey's performance, there is no consistent use of elongated values for one type of expression or abbreviated ones for another. At a point where he lengthens values, for example, he shortens the same value at a subsequent point that is structurally identical. Measure one, beats four through five (Ex. 4-2), and the same beats in measure three, where the following patterns occur, respectively, illustrate this point: ♫♩ , ♩ ♩. . In this instance, the emphasis is made even greater by the way in which Dorsey contrasts alterations with one another.

The most convincing example of the alteration of a rhythmic sequence in order to make textual emphasis occurs, coincidentally, at the climactic point of the melody in Dorsey's version (m. 6). This measure is the only one in which all the values are altered. Such change was necessary because the high point of the melody (beats five and six) is also the greatest point of elonga- tion of any altered rhythmic value in Dorsey's version: four times greater than the value in the original. The original version was written to stress rhythmically the thrice-repeated rhyme scheme, "bless me," "confess me," "possess me." Possibly for this reason, the three musical phrases descend in pitch level. In this stanza, as well as in the other three, a type of submission is implied by each repetition. Dorsey, and perhaps Nix as the evangelist, evi- dently wanted to mark the beginning of each of the phrases because of the emphasized pronoun "I," thereby establishing a pattern of emphasis from the upbeat, or anacrusis, to the first and second beats of each of the phrases. "Completely," as the only adverb in a series of infinitive phrases, achieves its own prominence in spite of its position on the anacrusis of its phrase, which is twice the focus of Dorsey's emphasis. In stretching this note, Dorsey had to shorten the previous values (in order for the six-beat structure to remain intact), because, contrary to previous occurrences, "completely" was to be *on* the beat and to be held. The resulting emphasis would convey the impor- tance of the extent rather than merely the fact of possession. Whether or not Nix chose to emphasize this idea is inconsequential. What Dorsey's demon- stration shows is that Nix had—quite literally—to recompose music in order to make his delivery effective.

The stylistic elements of Nix's performance of *I Do, Don't You* lie at the foundation of Dorsey's ideas about gospel music. Undergirding this thought is the "moaning" he was exposed to as a child. The similarity between Examples 1-1 and 4-2 indicates that in matters of ornamentation and tem- po, Nix's style, as Dorsey recollects it, was a derivative, if not an immediate descendant, of "moaning."[11] Another component of that thought can be found in the singing styles of the various vocalists with whom Dorsey worked as a blues pianist. Given the despair, grief, and loneliness Dorsey projected through his blues, he had to be aware that Nix's singing conveyed feelings of the same order and that the similar elements of both lowdown blues and the Nix styles provided for an expression of feelings not unrelated to one another.

Considering its individual and collective effects, Nix's performance demonstrated, if only in a modest way, the potential for an indigenous style of black music to function in urban Baptist churches. By doing so, Nix may well have been as significant to members of the National Baptist Convention as Perry Bradford and Mamie Smith had been, in secular music, to black Americans at large. Because of the size of the Convention, its membership reflected the attitudes of a large segment of black Americans, north and south. In a religious census completed five years after this convention, black Baptists comprised 61 percent of the 5.2 million black church members in the United States. Nix was able to sing a white gospel hymn in his style and make it appealing, just as Smith had been able to put blues into the white popular song style she first recorded. Nix helped to bring back into prominence—judging by the reception he received at the Convention—qualities of religious music that many black Baptists (especially in the large northern urban churches) would have rejected as backward and more suitable for religious "holes-in-the-wall" (storefront churches) or other such institutions that harbored the religious practices of the unassimilated. Nix may well have been able to adapt the thought of Bradford in his time of triumph: black Baptists could now for a releasing moment rejoin that part of themselves they had sacrificed for another religion.[12]

Dorsey immersed himself in his newfound inspiration "to become a great singer and worker in the Kingdom of the Lord and [to] impress people just as [Nix] did that Sunday morning." Within a year, he wrote his first sacred song, *If I Don't Get There*. And, as he had learned to do with his blues songs, he registered it at the U.S. Copyright Office on September 11, 1922. It also appeared in a later edition of *Gospel Pearls* as song No. 117. Soon after, he wrote *We Will Meet Him in the Sweet By and By*, which appeared in *The Baptist Standard Hymnal* in one of its early editions (No. 621). These pieces are patterned after the gospel hymns that appear in *Gospel Pearls* and in the *Standard Hymnal*, but they are not the best index of his new religious enthusiasm. A clearer indication of the extent to which Dorsey's religious fervor manifested itself is found in his work as director of music at New Hope Baptist Church on Chicago's South Side.

In several ways, Dorsey's experience at New Hope paralleled his blues experience in Chicago. He describes the congregation's singing of spirituals "like down home"; they also clapped their hands to this music. They sang from a "hymn book" that contained some of C. A. Tindley's music. This hymn book could have been *Gospel Pearls*, since several of Tindley's songs appeared there.

New Hope thus appears to have been the sacred counterpart of the rent party. Its members maintained and nurtured the practices of worship that belonged to their former southern life. On the other hand, New Hope's membership seems to have had a tolerance for the revised derivatives of their "down home" religious music, provided that (as with Nix's performance of white gospel music) the new music contained some of the familiar idioms. Dorsey was adept at this translation, having played popular music in blues style at rent parties. When Dorsey speaks of playing the derivative form at New Hope, his language here is strikingly similar to his description of his role at the parties:

> I had the prerogative to take a church song and put more in it. I could change anything I wanted if I thought it would [be] something that would make it better and more noticeable and more appreciated. When you don't have a voice, with these expressions and embellishments, you can express yourself. These little extras are a part of me; that's the way I did it when I was a boy.

Dorsey probably would have been out of place taking such liberties in some churches. But at New Hope—as at rent parties where he had thought of himself as "king of the night" and of his "ivories" as speaking a language that everyone understood—he found himself in the position to enjoy a strong rapport with the congregation:

> They go along and clap with you now, for you are the master. Whoever is the pianist, is the master. You handle people like you want them. Tell them what you want them to do. I get up there and hold the whole church in the hollow of my hand. If somebody don't shout there, I'll give you $10. Got to know how to work on the people.[13]

Even though his life had changed, Dorsey's playing consisted basically of the same improvisational idioms he had learned when he first started piano playing. At one time they would have been unacceptable for religious purposes. Now with "a touch" of them, he could lead others, as he had been led, to a new life. He was, especially since his illness and the religious urgings of his mother, as close as he had ever been to a resolution of the conflict between his career and his religion. He was playing gospel blues.

But Dorsey's conversion was ephemeral—a fragile respite from the war of powerfully competing psychological forces. As a child he had developed a dichotomous perception of religion from the distinctly different religious lives his parents led. The conversion he was now experiencing would be short-lived because it lacked the element of piety that marked his mother's religion; he was led, instead, by an impulse to gain the authoritative identity through religion that he sensed his father had as a preacher and that he had idolized as a child. Dorsey's goals at the time of the Baptist Convention were to "become a great singer" and to "impress people," not to achieve a new religious consciousness. Both strivings had been too powerful in his childhood, however, for him to ignore either one successfully as an adult. This lack of personal commitment to complement his quest for religious identity affected his work at New Hope. Thus when he sensed the other similarity between New Hope and his old blues haunts—that it too was a "second-rate" establishment—his ardor slackened. He had been at New Hope only "a few months" before he decided to give up the church and accept an offer to join Will Walker's "The Whispering Syncopators" in order to "make some quick and real money."[14] The promise of forty dollars every week, compared with a "donation every three or four weeks," was more than enough to weaken and finally rupture the inspiration Dorsey derived from *I Do, Don't You*.

A "syncopated" ensemble could consist of any assortment of instruments from a group of winds to an orchestra of banjos, mandolins, and pianos. As a music term itself, however, "syncopated" defined the rhythmic treatment given to the widely varied styles—spirituals, rag-blues, jazz, popular, vaudeville—in which syncopated groups played. By the end of World War I, the term "syncopated orchestra" (or band) denoted the basic organizational unit in the professional music community, particularly in New York and Chicago. As in prewar years, groups were distinguished from one another either by their style of music or by the type of occasion for which they performed. A glance at the *Chicago Defender* for the years 1922–23, when Dorsey played with "The Whispering Syncopators," shows that "jazz" was the most frequently used designation, with various forms of the word "syncopated" a close second; apparently no group used "blues" as a designation. Issues of 1922 listed "Mary Stafford's Jazz Orchestra," "Vassa's Super Jazz Band," the "Georgia Minstrels," and the "Synco Septette." In 1923 appeared the "Society Syncopators." Perhaps the ultimate combination used in a descriptive title for the music itself was "Jassaway Jasscopation."[15]

Playing in a "syncopated" group represented a new direction in Dorsey's career. Since "The Whispering Syncopators" played "theater dates, clubs, dances, and went on the road," Dorsey must finally have met the union's playing standard for musicians performing for these occasions. His salary was certainly an indication of this status: $40 per week was commensurate with the pay of professional theater musicians.[16]

Dorsey's playing ability itself did not lead to his new status—especially since "piano players were a dollar a dozen." Instead, the steadily growing blues industry in New York began to attract the best musicians from Chicago. Their departure most likely created openings for a lesser-known circle of performers and composers, among whom was Dorsey. Though not of the caliber of those musicians leaving Chicago for New York, Dorsey had begun to socialize with them between 1921 and 1922:

. . . the "House of Jazz Music Store," on State Street just south of 31st Street . . . was a hangout for jazz musicians and showfolks. I would drop into the store now and then just to have some place to go and be around musicians. There I met W. C. Handy of *St. Louis Blues* fame and the prominent pianists and composers Spencer Williams, Charlie Warfield, Clarence Johnson, who cut piano rolls . . . and Clarence M. Jones, who led the orchestra at the Owl Theater. . . .

"About 1922," Clarence Williams, the owner of the store, "and many of the other musicians and songwriters" moved to New York. They were drawn there by the recording industry and many of its support services, such as music publishing. For example, Lloyd Smith, "a young pianist and songwriter," perhaps as relatively unknown as Dorsey, became the new owner of the House of Jazz. He renamed it the "Original Home of Jazz." Even though most of the established musicians left before Dorsey became acquainted with them, he was able from the brief encounters at the House of Jazz to develop some good contacts, one of whom was Will Walker, leader of the Whispering Syncopaters.[17]

Dorsey probably did not have to alter significantly his southern style of playing blues upon joining Walker's group. Indeed, evidence exists that such blues—at least in its classic style—was becoming more fashionable. Between 1921 and 1922, the recording companies released an average of one blues record per week. And in spite of its announced intention to cover a broad spectrum of musical styles, the newly formed black recording company, Black Swan Records, made successful sales only with its blues recordings (e.g., Ethel Waters's *Down Home Blues* and *Oh Daddy*). Thus Dorsey exploited the growing popularity of the music in which he specialized. Indeed, if the name "The Whispering Syncopators" was an indication of the style of the group, Dorsey benefitted not only from the general popularity of the blues but specifically from the style for which he was already noted. His career from its beginning in the bordellos of Atlanta to the buffet flats of Chicago had thrived on his ability to play soft dance music: whispering syncopation.[18]

Playing around Chicago, the band became popular. Ben R. Harney, a white pianist who was "brashly billed" as the person who created ragtime songs, soon offered "The Whispering Syncopators" the opportunity to tour the West Coast with him. Dorsey was not invited, however, since Harney had no need of another pianist. Dorsey's colleagues accepted, leaving him in Chicago without a job. Apparently, Dorsey played with the Syncopators barely four months: he remembers "about four weeks of rehearsals" and "twelve weeks" of theater and road dates. In spite of the brevity of this job, it lasted long enough and was significant enough to distinguish Dorsey from the general run of pianists in the community.[19] Indeed, at this point in his career, late in 1922, Dorsey began to enjoy some prominence as a blues pianist, though to what extent is unknown. A new development in the blues recording industry, however, may have been even more responsible for his new prominence—not as a performer but as a composer.

Between 1923 and 1926, blues records were being marketed on more than fifteen labels. Most of the recordings in 1923, however, were made by eleven artists, some singing under different names for different companies. With the demand for records mounting daily, the recording companies moved to develop more sources of talent by hiring scouts, particularly to search the areas outside of New York City. In Chicago, J. Mayo "Ink" Williams worked as the primary scout and manager for blues singers. There was a need for widely varied and plentiful sources of new music so that each artist could develop an individual repertoire as much as possible. Williams's job thus was both to recruit performers and to court composers. When he and Dorsey met, as the latter remembers it, they were "hanging around" the "Original Home of Jazz": "He was trying to make it, and I was trying to make it."[20]

Through Williams's efforts, Chicago became increasingly a second center of the recording industry and, subsequently, of the blues songwriting and publishing industry. As early as 1921 and no later than 1926, the four largest companies—Victor, Paramount, Columbia, and OKeh—each had a studio in Chicago in addition to New York. Paramount closed its New York studios and recorded exclusively in Chicago beginning in 1926. Dorsey recalls that this flurry of blues recording in New York and Chicago signaled "the beginning of the blues era":

> Blues singers were dropping in [the "Original Home of Jazz"] to learn new songs; record scouts were in frequently to see what was good for recording. . . . I began to write more prolifically and one blues after another fell from my pen. I met songwriters, blues singers and instrumentalists by the score. I played my songs for them and taught them to the singers.[21]

During 1923, Dorsey composed—or at least registered for copyright—seven songs (not including *If I Don't Get There,* his one sacred song up to that time): *A Heart There Was for You,* February 17; *I Just Want a Daddy I Can Call My Own,* March 7; *That Brown O'Mine,* March 26; *Muddy Water Blues,* May 24; *Don't Shimme No More,* June 28; *Riverside Blues,* July 27; and *Miss Anna Brown Blues,* October 1.

This group of songs was composed in a style vastly different from the blues Dorsey had composed. His abrupt switch illustrates his ability to adapt to a new style that he had reason to think advantageous. More than any other piece in the 1923 collection, *A Heart There Was for You* illustrates this point. Registered February 17, 1923, this song exemplifies the popular sentimental style of the early twenties for which composers such as Jerome Kern and Irving Berlin were noted. It has the four-bar phrase unit, asymmetrical binary form (|| a ||: b b1 :||), 3/4 meter waltz style—none of which was characteristic of blues songs as Dorsey performed them. W. C. Handy had set the compositional model for this style as early as 1914 with, for example, his *St. Louis Blues* and *Yellow Dog Blues.* In establishing it, Handy had deviated radically from the format he used "when common simplicity was believed to make for larger copy sales." The new form was essentially the popular song form with the following alterations: 1) twelve-bar phrase unit; 2) symmetrical binary form, consisting (in order) of an introduction, optionally a "wait until ready," or "vamp," section (usually two or three bars), and two or more verses, all of which comprised the "A" section, and a repeated "chorus" that comprised the "B" section; 3) syncopated rhythmic patterns throughout the piece; 4) altered thirds and sevenths; and 5) melodic embellishments.[22]

But the bland text ("Dearie, I'm so lonely since you went away/... A heart there was for you my dear, before you went away") compared with the "lowdown" gutsiness in Dorsey's other songs and with the harmonic structure that lacked the typically altered blues notes, made it unlikely that any blues singer would have included this or the other 1923 songs in her repertoire. Nevertheless, Dorsey had good reason to believe that these blues would be recorded and would sell. All he had to do was to look back at Monette Moore's recording of his *I Just Want a Daddy [I Can Call My Own]* in January 1923: "The release only sold about five thousand records." With this genuine blues song on record and with it becoming somewhat popular, Dorsey probably thought he could succeed as well with the popular as with the blues style. The market undoubtedly was there. With the popular music industry located in New York, however, a little-known composer from Chicago had almost no possibility of publishing for that market.[23]

The composition of blues after Handy's model—indeed the very act of composing a blues song—imposed an artificial quality on blues performance. For example, composers were aware that performers had no need for written embellishments—nor perhaps even music—since the essence of the song was realized through improvisation. Mamie Smith "moaned" well enough to be catapulted to fame singing quasi-blues music accompanied by musicians themselves unfamiliar with blues. Even in teaching his songs to blues singers, Dorsey usually had to give them only the basic idea:

> [I'd] just get the song out there, hand it to them and say "now you just follow me." I [didn't] teach them the music now. They didn't read the music. Only teach them the tune.[24]

With this understanding between composers and performers, one may conclude that, other than the "tune," the stylistic qualities of the blues songs as they appeared in published form were merely publication conventions. Handy earned his title as "father of the blues" not from his origination of that style itself but from deriving the format for its publication.

The process was, in essence, one of packaging the music of one culture for marketing to a distinctly different culture. As long as Dorsey played for tips instead of fees, performed at rent parties instead of at clubs and theaters, and improvised instead of composed, his blues music was unaffected by the marketplace. But Chicago's commercialism compromised—indeed virtually seduced—aspirants like Dorsey by making the success they craved conditional upon their adoption of marketability, rather than stylistic authenticity, as a goal. Dorsey's 1923 compositions, therefore, present an unmitigated display of opportunism. With his compositional skills, his cunning, and his desire for success, all applied toward achieving prominence in an industry that thrived on opportunism, Dorsey had reason—perhaps compellingly so—to write as he did and thereby to alter fundamentally the identity of his music.

By the end of 1923, his strategy had worked. That year Jack Mills, Inc., in New York published his *I Just Want a Daddy I Can Call My Own* as a "fox-trot," and Monette Moore recorded it. In August 1923, she recorded his *Muddy Water Blues*. Undoubtedly, his greatest achievement of that year was Joe "King" Oliver's recording in October and December of his *Riverside Blues*. With one piece published by a large popular music company, and three recorded by two of the most famous artists of that time, Dorsey had become at last one of the major blues composers in Chicago. In little more than a year, Dorsey had risen from relative obscurity to a position of prominence.[25]

On February 15, 1923, the day Dorsey filed the copyright application for the first of his 1923 series of songs, Columbia Records made its first recordings of a "tall and fat and scared to death" singer, Bessie Smith. During the ten years that had intervened since Smith and Dorsey were teenagers "hanging around the Eighty-One" in Atlanta, their careers had followed markedly similar paths. As Dorsey had in Atlanta and Chicago, Smith developed her artistry before listeners who were deeply sympathetic to her style and delivery. Her audiences varied from patrons of a "lowdown dive" and touring minstrel shows in the South to a cabaret and certain small theaters in Philadelphia and Baltimore. Her first 'break,' comparable perhaps to Dorsey's with "The Whispering Syncopators," came with Charlie Johnson's show during the same year (1922). She sang at the Paradise Gardens in Atlantic City, "one of the hottest spots in town."[26]

Among northern professional musicians, her blues—as Dorsey's had been—was apt to be regarded with amusement by some and with contempt by others. Sam Wooding described Smith's singing at the Nest Club in 1923:

> This is one reason she didn't go over too big with New York musicians. She would sing something like "Baby I love you, love you mo' and mo'." I'd go to the bathroom, come back and catch the rest of the verse, "I hope you never leave me, 'cause I don't wanna see you go." She had dragged out each word so that I hadn't missed a thing.

Fred Hager, artistic manager at OKeh Records and the man lauded by the *Chicago Defender* and Perry Bradford for having "stuck [his] neck out" to give a "colored girl" the opportunity to record, rejected Smith because her voice was "too rough." She had also failed in an audition in 1921 for Black Swan Records. Given Black Swan's significance as the only black-owned record company and its success with Ethel Waters's blues performances, Smith's rejection by them must have been difficult for her to accept.[27]

The stylistic standard for blues had been set by the smooth, refined, and sophisticated voices and artistry of New York's professional female theater singers who also performed in well-known clubs, restaurants, and touring shows. With their proximity to the recording studios, these women dominated the making of blues records, and, thus, their vocal quality became the industry's standard production referent.[28] Smith was thus made all too aware—as Dorsey had been by "jass" in Chicago—that she and New York's recording artists were separated by a wide gap. Though these singers were black, Smith had been served notice that they and their "blues" were of another culture—one of which neither she nor her public was a part.

Were it not for the unexpected increase of record sales and the proliferation of recording companies by 1923, Smith and singers like her might have remained excluded from the recording studios by the dominance of the professional vaudeville standard. The demand, however, forced recording company executives to become more flexible concerning vocal quality and to hunt further afield for new talent. Thus Frank Walker, supervisor of recording at Columbia Records, recalling a memorable performance of Smith's he had heard in Alabama six years earlier, instructed his contact for black musicians, Clarence Williams, to "go down there and find her and bring her back up here." Williams, who had accompanied Smith on her unaccepted test recording for OKeh a few weeks before, knew this time that he must make sure that she was well rehearsed. Probably he hoped not only to teach her songs written and performed by recording artists but also to refine some of her unsophisticated "downhome" blues technique as well.[29]

It was more than a coincidence that on that Thursday in February 1923, both Bessie Smith and Thomas A. Dorsey found themselves ready to attempt a career in the blues industry. She stood before a megaphone in a New York City studio ready to record her new repertoire of vaudeville blues after being "prepared" by a coach. Dorsey stood before a clerk in the Chicago copyright office about to register his first popular song after adopting a new mode of composition. Were the stories of countless other southern musicians as accessible for scrutiny as Smith's and Dorsey's, they would probably reveal the same pattern. The aesthetic that was dominant among professional black musicians in the North differed radically from that of their southern counterparts. For downhome musicians to succeed in the North, they had not only to renounce their previous training and experience but also to persevere in the face of the disdain of northerners. The process was so fundamentally acculturative that it could be compared to attempting to "pass."

The coincidence between Smith's and Dorsey's careers ended with the completion of her recording session the following day. Dorsey continued throughout 1923 successfully espousing—at least through his compositions in Handy's style—the norms that he had assimilated. The northern aesthetic, however, was easier to adopt as a composer than as a performer. No amount of Williams's coaching could erase the effect on Smith's voice of years of hollering; neither could new lyrics mask stylistic traits that had become second nature to her.

To Walker, however, Smith's studio performances of *Downhearted Blues* and *Gulf Coast Blues* must have reminded him of the time he listened to her in Alabama in 1917. Her so-called shortcomings were not hers but those of the industry's—specifically its failure to look beyond Harlem's music halls for a market. But Walker did not make this mistake. Before the release of Smith's February recordings, he had her return to make nine more. And he organized a road tour through the South for her to promote her records. By June, when the tour was to begin, he had engaged and recorded another southern artist, Clara Smith. Bessie was to be billed as "Queen of the Blues" and Clara as "Queen of the Moaners." Walker was about to take something of the same risk with his Smiths as Hager had with Mamie Smith at OKeh a few years before. Perhaps Walker's was the greater risk; although his "Queens" would almost certainly be popular in the South, they could prove ineffective in the North, where they had to use the unfamiliar recording medium of the North's vaudeville, or "classic," blues singers.[30]

Concerns of this nature proved unwarranted, however. The sale of Bessie Smith's February recording amounted to 780,000 copies within months of its June release. Two conclusions are, therefore, unavoidable. First, the northern professional vaudeville singer could no longer determine the stylistic trends of the recording industry. Just a year earlier Alberta Hunter, who jointly wrote *Downhearted Blues* with another singer-pianist, Lovie Austin, had herself made a recording of it that "sold well." Since 1920, Hunter had been one of the more popular "classic blues" artists, having introduced three of Handy's hit songs.[31] In spite of Hunter's notoriety, however, and the success of her recording of her own *Downhearted Blues,* Smith's recording outsold Hunter's by thousands more than expected.

The second unavoidable conclusion indicated by Smith's success is that most black Americans who bought blues records preferred the southern blues tradition. Smith was undoubtedly the "biggest-selling blues artist of the period." In 1927, when production for the entire recording industry exceeded 100 million records sold, "race" records (those marketed exclusively for blacks) accounted for an estimated 5 percent of those sales. Smith, therefore, commanded her lead in a market of 5 million records all told. In 1923, when sales of race records were lower than 1927 figures, Smith may have led with as high as 20 percent of the total race sales with the 780,000 purchases of one of her recordings. Given her popularity throughout the years when the demand for race records was the greatest, statistics showing that she accounted for one-fifth of the market—at a time when her style was the only contrasting one—are believable. For almost six months, anyone who wanted the then unusual sound of southern blues, as evidently thousands did, had only Bessie Smith's record to buy.[32]

Neither Dorsey nor any other professional musician in 1923 could ignore the meaning of Bessie Smith's sudden sweep of the blues market. Even though she had attempted the same sort of transformation that had made for his more modest success in Chicago, Dorsey must have found her ascendency to national fame deeply ironic; she had become successful, after all, by singing precisely the style of blues he had forsaken in his climb to the upper echelons of Chicago's music community. His nostalgia over their times together at the Eighty-One must have been tinged with envy.

Dorsey had little reason, however, to do more than reflect on Smith's sudden fame. Judging by the recordings of his music, he had no indication that Smith's success would eventually affect his own career: "I . . . devoted my time to music and songwriting. . . . I felt that I had hit the jackpot as a young musician and had started on the road to ultimate success." Not only had his *I Just Want a Daddy* been published, but it had been recorded by Monette Moore as well in January 1923. His *Muddy Water Blues* was recorded just seven months later by the same artist. The inner circle of the industry—composers, talent managers, and record producers—would have noted such rapid successes. They were the contacts Dorsey had been cultivating at the "Original Home of Jazz" in order to make more records. His glad-handing bore fruit when his *Riverside Blues* was recorded by Joe "King" Oliver's Creole Jazz Band in December 1923. Because of his band and its personnel, Oliver is still considered to have been "at the top of the jazz world." This reputation began with a series of recordings in late 1923 and especially with the "genius" of a recent and unknown addition to the Creole Jazz Band, Louis Armstrong. The recording was evidently a greater hit than all the others by Oliver, according to the *Chicago Defender* advertisement: "King Oliver is sure there on this one." From this record Dorsey received his first public mention in print. The *Chicago Defender* published an article entitled "Dorsey Busy" in its March 1, 1924, edition, mentioning that Dorsey "made the special arrangement of 'Riverside Blues' for King Oliver's Creole Jazz Band when that organization recorded that number for the Paramount people." The article went on to mention Dorsey's other songs from the 1923 series and closed by noting that Dorsey "has several other real things ready for early release."[33]

If the writer of that article was referring to new compositions Dorsey was about to release, however, they did not appear for almost three and a half years. Dorsey's burst of publicity was the last he and almost every other composer of blues—in the style and manner Handy pioneered—would enjoy. The enthusiastic announcement about Oliver's recording of *Riverside Blues* was but one line of an almost half-page advertisement in the *Chicago Defender* announcing Paramount's "discovery" of Gertrude "Ma" Rainey, "Mother of the Blues." Between the lines of commercial rhetoric, the message was clear. Paramount, like OKeh and soon other companies, was vying for the market over which Columbia records had a virtual monopoly because of Bessie Smith's records:

"Moonshine Blues"—the first record by Madame "Ma" Rainey, the wonder-ful goldneck woman who starred for five years in three theaters in Pensacola, Atlanta, and Jacksonville! If it's Blues you want, here they are. . . . the only blues singer in the world elevated to the height of Madame.[34]

If Dorsey failed to detect a trend when Smith scored a success singing blues as he and she had performed them in Atlanta, he could not possibly ignore Rainey and the significance of this advertisement.

The importation of the southern blues singer not only supplanted the dominance of the vaudeville blues singer but also foreshadowed all but the demise of the vaudeville blues composer. Southern or "downhome" perform-ers relied on songs that usually were unwritten.[35] Their music was inten-tionally amorphous, achieving form only in performance, because composi-tion and performance were but one continuous creative process. The blues industry in the North, on the other hand, had subsisted by dividing this process into two professions. From Handy's first published compositions in 1912 to those such as Dorsey's in 1923, vaudeville blues songs were written compositions. With the rise of the recording industry, the composer became as essential to northern vaudeville blues as did the singer. The success of each was predicated on the cultivation of their roles as distinct from one another: the former became the shaper and purveyor of music as thought and the latter of music as practice.

But by the spring of 1924, blues composition must have been little more than an anachronism, judging by Dorsey's production. Having registered eight songs the previous year (and having composed at least a dozen more, according to his memoirs), Dorsey registered only one other song in 1924, *Carolina Blues*. He did not file his next application until August 1928, after he had composed *When You're in Love*. The format of *Carolina Blues* is as much an indication of the effect of these developments as is the sudden reduction of Dorsey's output. *Carolina Blues* appears only with the melody line and one verse, whereas all of Dorsey's previous songs had included full scores (vocal and piano accompaniment) and contained all of the verses. This new format was called a "lead sheet" and was adopted by the blues industry as the format for registering songs for copyright. All of the eleven blues songs Dorsey copyrighted after 1928 were "lead sheets." This format, appearing as it does in February 1924 in Dorsey's music (followed by a compositional hiatus of several years), pinpoints the time at which Dorsey felt the effects of the new (or, to him, old) style of blues. At this time he switched from composing to arranging blues.[36]

Although he had few if any options besides arranging blues, Dorsey's entry into this aspect of the music business was timely. Recording companies had long been engaged in the questionable practice of copyrighting the songs performed by artists even if the song had been registered by the composer. Their argument was that because of the improvisational quality of her performance, the blues singer actually recorded an arrangement of a composed piece rather than the piece itself. The company was not obligated, therefore, to pay royalties if it owned the copyright of the arrangement. With the emergence of southern singers who seldom sang from music, this practice became more widespread. Dorsey's switch from composing to arranging, then, not only was fortuitous given the blues market but also was dictated by that market.

Arrangers seldom worked alone. In order to make money they had to have access to singers and record companies. Dorsey reached his artists through the Chicago Music Publishing Company, founded and owned by one of the more colorful and notorious personalities of the blues industry, J. Mayo "Ink" Williams. Williams had discovered Ma Rainey and referred her to Paramount Records. With this referral, he became the main talent scout for Paramount, expected especially to provide talent from the South. In an effort to outwit the recording companies, Williams duplicated their copyrighting practices—with the help, perhaps not unwittingly, of Dorsey. To carry out his plan, Williams supplied recording companies, mainly Paramount, not only with artists but with each artist's repertoire—all arranged and copyrighted. Dorsey's job was to make the arrangements, copyright the music, and train each artist.[37] If the Melrose Brothers Music Store in Chicago is a gauge, Dorsey was "busy" and Williams rich. The Melrose Brothers copyrighted over 3000 songs from many artists, including well-known ones such as Jelly Roll Morton, without paying royalties. As Williams's accomplice, Dorsey could hardly avoid being aware of the outright thievery of Williams's operation. In some cases he was a victim; in others the victimizer:

> . . . Williams owes me some money from way back in the '20s and early '30s. . . . A guy'd come in with a song, and he'd sing it. He had nobody to arrange it, put it on paper. So I put it on the paper. And see, and then the company would copyright it, see. Vocalion or Chicago Music Co.—we were all mixed up in the Chicago Music Publishing Co. under Ink Williams. I haven't seen a sheet of music they published yet![38]

Not all of Dorsey's work at the Chicago Music Publishing Company was of such dubious value, however. Because of his background, training, and experience, Dorsey was uniquely qualified to coach southern singers to perform in the recording studio. With the exception of the previous two years, approximately all of Dorsey's playing experience had utilized the improvisational blues style he had learned in Atlanta. He also knew the vaudeville style, having learned it from theater pianists in Atlanta and, most reently, having composed in it. Combining his ability to write and arrange music with his success in the recording field, Dorsey bridged the gap between the southern and northern traditions—particularly since his reputation in both sprang from his mastery of the expressive qualities of each:

I taught most of the singers who sang for Paramount Records [and the Chicago Music Publishing Company]. I was the man that had to hear them. I could make any embellishments that I wanted to in the song. I'd do that and then teach it to the artist that was going to perform. Some of them needed a lot of changes too; some of them come in there was terrible.

Dorsey was most effective in helping the singer to interpret the lyrics. Even the southern composer/performer evidently needed polishing in order to achieve good delivery:

[The songs] had no expression. The writer didn't know what to say at some places for the punch. I would take them, feel the words out and then feel the music out and accent them in a way that it will grasp the public and set them up straighter.[39]

Eventually, Dorsey's ability to bridge the stylistic gap between northern and southern blues brought him opportunities beyond those of an in-house coach. Paramount Records had noticed the rich market in the South for blues even before Bessie Smith's recording and thus had cultivated a large southern mail-order business. Since Ma Rainey had come to Paramount as a famous southern singer, having traveled in shows since 1902, the company assumed that her appeal lay mostly in that region and that a southern tour was the logical promotional scheme. She would need a new pianist, however, since Lovie Austin, who had accompanied her in her recordings, was unable to leave her steady employment at the Monogram Theater. Responsible for finding Rainey's pianist, Williams probably knew that of the many accompanists available, Dorsey was the most suitable because his expressive style was the complement of Rainey's: "She wouldn't have to sing any words; she would moan and the audience would moan with her." As Dorsey recalls it, their first meeting was a success:

She was grand, gracious and easy to talk with. I played some songs for her and then rehearsed her on a couple of the blues tunes that she was to use on the road. She was impressed with my playing and hired me as her accompanist and director of her "Wild Cats Jazz Band" which I was to assemble and organize.

This meeting represented a watershed in Dorsey's career; it marked his return to performance as a profession and to "lowdown, downhome" blues as a performance style.[40]

In 1912, the *Chicago Defender* counted 635 theaters in Chicago plus another 110 at various stages of construction. How many of these were accessible to blacks is unknown, but apparently enough were to make a wide range of entertainment available to the community. The Grand and Monogram theaters appear to have been the houses most available to black artists, judging by the fact that they were the only theaters consistently reviewed (almost every week) in the *Chicago Defender,* beginning May 7, 1910. By 1923, the Grand Theater had more quarter-page advertisements than the other theaters; thus it was perhaps the most widely known house on Chicago's Southside.[41]

It is precisely the Grand's stature among theaters that makes Rainey's appearance there at the opening of her tour a surprise. Rainey was well known to her record fans, but not enough of them were thought to be in Chicago to guarantee her a crowd if she appeared alone at the Grand. Paramount Records knew the importance of that theater and decided to let her appear as an added attraction to the Salem Tutt Whitney vaudeville show:

> I don't think Ma had ever appeared in Chicago. The only singing she did around Chicago here was for the record company. . . . We felt that if we had an opening in Chicago, it would give us a good tryout for the show before we hit the circuit. . . . She had fame, but she went over there [to the Grand] because she wanted to get into a big theater where there was going to be a crowd.[42]

The precaution was unnecessary. Tony Langston, the noted reviewer for the *Defender,* wrote of Rainey as the "featured attraction." She clearly proved that with her "Jazz Wild Cats" she was far superior to any of her predecessors; with her blues, Rainey was the first of the "downhome" southern singers to perform at a first-rate Chicago theater. Even Bessie Smith, with her proven fame, had been reluctant to perform in northern cities. But to Smith's surprise, when she finally performed in Detroit in October 1923, it caused a "near riot." She waited until May 1924 to make a Chicago appearance and then did so at the smaller, lesser-known Avenue Theater; again her success earned her a "standing welcome."[43]

For Dorsey, opening at the Grand Theater was a personal triumph. In the brief span of some thirty months, beginning in early 1922, he had pursued practically every whim of the blues industry in an effort to establish himself. Each pinnacle of success to which at times he almost desperately struggled had become a meaningless plateau at the moment he laid claim to it. The "Whispering Syncopators" disbanded and left him just as he had reached the Union's performance standard and had "sweated" to be appointed to what was surely a coveted opportunity for a pianist. A year's compositional output and artistic contacts became valueless within months as he observed the nationwide success of the very blues he once had considered useless to his professional career. But on that night in April 1924, Dorsey could assume that fame for him was no longer illusory. The band that he directed and for which he composed now sat on the stage at the Grand Theater; he was playing his "gutbucket, lowdown" blues as accompaniment for the woman whose performance personified them—a woman to whom he once had hawked his concessions at the Eighty-One Theater and had thought it a privilege to do so. All of this was taking place before an enraptured audience in perhaps the most prestigious black theater in Chicago. Dorsey understandably remembers this concert as "a most exciting event in my life . . . me, playing and directing a band on the stage for such a great singer as Ma Rainey."[44]

The personal triumphs of Smith, Rainey, and now Dorsey had implications beyond their respective careers. The exact composition of their audiences in northern theaters—either mostly former migrants or northern established blacks—is impossible to ascertain. But descriptions of their performances and the reactions of their northern audiences indicate the popularity of, if not the demonstrated respect for, the southern aesthetic as represented by their performance styles. The emotive power, the group commiseration, and the sense of despair and agony that once suffused the rent party, the second-rate vaudeville theater, and the most tawdry joints now brought responses in the grandest performance halls as Dorsey's description of one of Rainey's performances indicates:

> The room is filled with a haze of smoke, she walks into the spotlight, face decorated with Stein's Reddish Make-up Powder. She's not a young symmetrical streamed-lined type; her face seems to have discarded no less than fifty some years. She stands out high in front with a glorious bust, squeezed tightly in the middle. Her torso, extending in the distance behind, goes on about its business from there on down. She opens her mouth and starts singing:
>
>> "It's storming on the ocean, it's storming on the sea.
>> My man left me this morning, and it's storming down on me."

> When she started singing, the gold in her teeth would sparkle. She was in the spotlight. She possessed her listeners; they swayed, they rocked, they moaned and groaned, as they felt the blues with her. A woman swooned who had lost her man. Men groaned who had given their week's pay to some woman who promised to be nice, but slipped away and couldn't be found at the appointed time. By this time she was just about at the end of her song. She was "in her sins" as she bellowed out. The bass drum rolled like thunders and the stage lights flickered like forked lightening:
>
>> "I see the lightning flashing, I see the waves a dashing
>> I got to spread the news; I feel this boat a crashing
>> I got to spread the news; my man is gone and left me
>> Now I got the stormy sea blues."

> As the song ends, she feels an understanding with her audience. Their applause is a rich reward. She is in her glory. The house is hot. Then she lets go again:
>
>> "Lawdy, Lawdy I hear somebody calling me,
>> If it ain't my regular, it must be my use-to-be.

If I had wings and could fly like Noah's dove,
I'd heist my wings and fly to the man I love."

By this time everybody is excited and enthusiastic. The applause thunders for one more number. Some woman screams out with a shrill cry of agony as the blues recalls sorrow because some man trifled on her and wounded her to the bone. [Ma Rainey] is ready now to take the encore as her closing song. Here she is tired, sweaty, swaying from side to side, fatigued but happy. Then she sings:

"Honey, Honey, Honey, look what you done,
You done made me love you, and now your woman done come.
If anybody ask you who wrote this lonesome song,
Tell 'em you don't know the writer,
but a lonesome woman put it on."[45]

5

Old-Line Religion
and Musicians:
1920–1930

The years between 1924, when Dorsey made his debut with Ma Rainey at the Grand Theater, and 1926, when he suffered his second "trouble," were rewarding ones. Rural, downhome, "moanin'" blues was well on its way to becoming the most popular style of recorded blues, traceable in no small part to the popularity of Ma Rainey and her "Wild Cats Jazz Band," which Dorsey organized and directed for her:

> I went out to find musicians for the band; I found many unemployed or half-interested, but they were reluctant to travel and did not want to leave town. I came across Albert Wynn, a young trombone player, who thought the idea was fine and he was anxious to go out of town. Fuller Henderson, a coronet player, after talking it over with his wife, thought the tour would be fine for him (he was the only married man in the band). Gabriel Washington, a young drummer, said he would go, for he had never been out of town. We went into rehearsal for four straight weeks, five hours a day. After that we were in pretty good shape and knew from memory all of the music for the show.
>
> Everything then was ready for the road, billed as Ma (Gertrude) Rainey and Her Wild Cats Jazz Band, Paramount Record Artist, Mother of Blues Singers.[1]

Full instrumental accompaniment for classic blues singers who performed the older-style blues was an uncommon and complicated arrangement. Regular instrumental accompaniment was a luxury rarely afforded. Few singers were popular enough to pay the substantial additional costs of a traveling band. Only four classic blues singers—and only while each was at the apogee of her career—toured with a band: Mamie Smith, Bessie Smith, Lucille Hegamin, and Ma Rainey. If, however, a less popular singer performed in a theater in which an instrumental ensemble (band, orchestra, or some combination of the two) was resident, she could reasonably—though not always—expect that group to accompany her pianist. But blues played by instrumental groups tended to sound like "jass," as it was then identified. Blues singers, therefore, had to be careful programming numbers that had instrumental accompaniment, since such music differed in style from the more intimate, familiar blues sung to the customary piano accompaniment.[2]

In choosing to have a band, therefore, Ma Rainey faced two potential problems: 1) how would it work in conjunction with the resident ensemble she might find in one of the theaters on her tour, and 2) how would its music alter the blues for which she was known? Her solution to the first problem was to allow her band to perform solo numbers and to have them seated with her on the stage. They were clearly delineated from the house band, therefore, and seen as belonging to her act. She worked around the second problem by making only limited use of the "'progressive,'" trained musicians who worked in jazz, preferring instead "'knockabout,'" less sophisticated performers who were known more for their feeling for the music rather than their technical proficiency.[3] Given these considerations, Dorsey's organization, direction, and management of the "Wild Cats" for Rainey was a formidable undertaking, one of the major factors that made 1924 to 1926 the most rewarding years of his career until then.

But a broader perspective exists from which to view Dorsey's accomplishments with the "Wild Cats." The Chicago music community was organized so that even a musician like Dorsey with expertise in both blues and jazz was unable to play professionally in both styles. Musicians were stereotyped. As a pianist, Dorsey was seen as a downhome performer; jazz was at most his sideline. In addition, he was one of the few composers/arrangers among black musicians. Engaging in these activities made him appear more as one who prepared rather than played performances. As a result, his earnings and chances of exposure had been severely limited by the perception that he was a well-known, but insignificant, downhome blues pianist who coached for a living. Ironically, it was organizing Ma Rainey's band and composing for it that helped Dorsey break away from his image as one at the lower strata of the Chicago music community. Rainey needed musicians with backgrounds similar to Dorsey's, because they could play the blues for which she was known. Dorsey found instrumentalists who were intimately familiar with rural, southern styles but who knew some jazz, too. One was not even a member of the mostly "jass" Musicians' Protective Union, and the others, though evidently accomplished musicians, were unemployed at the time he recruited them. They were musicians who, like himself, functioned outside of the main Chicago music community. They were like Dorsey, too, in that even though they were southern bluesmen playing in a style for which reading was not a prerequisite, they *did* read, inasmuch as Dorsey wrote out much of the band's music.[4] Thus the task of assembling a group of misplaced musicians like himself for the already-famous Ma Rainey unified Dorsey's disparate careers and helped to make him more famous.

Bringing together the appropriate personnel, however, was only part of Dorsey's satisfaction in managing Ma Rainey's band. The most rewarding aspect of his work was the opportunity to compose music of different styles. Ma Rainey's "Wild Cats" functioned in three roles: as downhome musicians accompanying her rural blues songs, as urban blues musicians accompanying her popular and vaudeville repertoire, and as jazz musicians when playing alone. Dorsey had to write and otherwise produce these three sounds using the same instrumentalists. The music Dorsey wrote for the show—from overture to finale—spanned these styles and became a common outlet for the varied stylistic elements in his background in a way that he had been unable to attain previously.

The popularity Rainey gained during her tours may be traced in no small degree to the panorama of musical styles in which she performed with the aid of Dorsey as composer, arranger, and conductor of her band:

> I shall never forget the exciting feeling when the orchestra in the pit struck up her opening theme which I had written especially for the show.
>
> The curtain rose slowly and those soft lights played on the band and we picked up the introduction for her first song. I arranged the music for the band. We looked and felt like a million. Ma was hidden in a big box-like affair built like a Victrola. . . . This stood on the other side of the stage. A girl came out and put a big record on it. The band picked up "Moonshine Blues"; Ma sang a few bars inside the big Victrola, then she opened the door and stepped out into the spotlight with her glittering gown that weighed twenty pounds, wearing a necklace of $5, $10, and $20 gold pieces. The house went wild. It was as if the show had started all over again. Ma had the audience in the palm of her hand. Her diamonds flashed like sparks of fire falling from her fingers. The gold piece necklace lay like golden armor covering her chest. She was deservedly called the lady with the golden throat.
>
> My greatest concern was how the crowd would receive our feature band number. Ma did three songs and made her exit, which was the cue for the band to come on. The house lights dimmed down as the spotlight came on the band and we were in the spotlight. We struck up "Tiger Rag." We featured each man. I stood up and played the piano which was then a great novelty.[5]

Dorsey had one other reason to feel that from 1925 onward his life was more fulfilling. In August 1925, he married Nettie Harper, whom he first met while she was rooming at his uncle's house, where Dorsey also lived. One of the few black druggists in Chicago, Dorsey's Uncle Joshua (his father's brother) usually found himself serving as a physician of sorts as well. Joshua Dorsey hired a professional nurse, Frankie Harper, to assist him and invited her to live with his family in their home since she had to move from Philadelphia in order to take the job. At some point, Frankie Harper's sister Nettie joined her in Chicago and also lived with the Dorseys. Soon after

Nettie and Dorsey met, they began courting. Dorsey wanted to marry right away, but Nettie wanted only to talk about it:

> I had saved a nice sum of money on my tours and I felt it was time to take a wife. I knew a number of girls throughout the country where I had traveled. But this lovely little maid from Georgia who lived at my uncle's home in Chicago won my heart. I had a rival who was giving me a close run for her hand. The truth of the matter was that at some time before I met her she was his girl. I suppose she liked me best. I could play the piano and croon to her in the cool of the evening when the lights were soft and low. I thought I had won her heart and asked her to marry me. She never gave an answer. I wrote and asked her mother for her blessings and her daughter's hand in marriage and neither did her mother answer me. I was then somewhat bewildered and perturbed and did not know what to do next. I knew I loved her, and I was sure she loved me, but would not say so.

After delaying for several months, Nettie finally consented to his proposal. They were married on August 1, 1925, during one of Dorsey's tour breaks. On August 2, they left Chicago to travel with the show.[6]

It was not just being married that changed Dorsey's life so much. Upon hearing that Dorsey had a wife, Ma Rainey hired Nettie as her wardrobe mistress, an occupation in which Nettie had no experience. No benefit of early married life seemed to delight Dorsey more than being able to have Nettie travel with him on Ma Rainey's tours. Rainey's decision might not have been as altruistic as it appeared, for it increased her hold on Dorsey. Musicians were reluctant to travel on tours for fear of being stranded if the show was canceled. Thus the turnover of personnel was high—particularly if the musicians could readily find jobs in Chicago or New York. Also, Ma Rainey's tours were booked on the Theater Owners' Booking Association (TOBA) circuit. Since its inception in 1909, this group of theaters had garnered a reputation for providing some of the worst performance accommodations in the business. Conditions were so harsh that the acronym for the Association's title was taken by some to mean "Tough on Black Artists." For others it meant "tough on black asses."[7] It behooved Rainey in more ways than one, therefore, to keep Dorsey happy—even if to do so entailed hiring an inexperienced wardrobe mistress.

Nettie was inexperienced as well at a matter even more critical to her and Dorsey's domestic happiness:

> Having my wife along with me, I had double responsibility of looking after the music for the show and of taking care of her. I had to go shopping for food and she was a poor cook at the start. She would burn nearly everything. Cooking on a stove heated by wood, when she had been used to gas, it was quite a problem for her and a lot of burned food for me. But it was a joy, just like a big long honeymoon.[8]

Being married, having his wife accompany him while touring, and having the opportunity to develop his blues and jazz styles and his compositional and arranging skills as the musical director for "the mother of the blues," Dorsey for the first time faced few, if any, of the conflicts that had plagued him since he began his professional career. This peaceful and productive period lasted only two years, however. For all the successful integration and application of his talents that he was able to accomplish up to 1926, his failure to arrive at some similar balance regarding his religious sentiments marred the professional satisfaction he had gained in the meantime. The next six years would be ones of religious struggle in the life of Thomas A. Dorsey.

Dorsey's search for a resolution of the religious conflicts that were until then more or less dormant in his life was not explicitly clear to him at the time he embarked upon it. He had just returned from one of Ma Rainey's most successful tours. Several times during the tour, in fact, Dorsey had had to cut the show to all but Rainey's part so that it could run twice and all of those who wanted to hear her could "get in and out" in one evening. Then one night in 1926 while playing at a club on the outskirts of Chicago with just members of the band, Dorsey first noticed a slight "unsteadiness." This problem "stretched out into days, into weeks, into months, into two years," incapacitating him musically. Because he was unable to perform, compose, or arrange, it soon grew into a deep depression:

> I knew not where to turn. It was a sad thing to me; it was hard to bear. Those were desperate years. I wanted comfort for my wife, yet I could only take it from her. My distress made my illness and mental confusion worse. Our money was soon gone. We had no income and no one to look to for help.
>
> I went from doctor to doctor; they could not find anything wrong with me. I spent two weeks in the Cook County Hospital; they could not find anything wrong. Then I went to a private hospital in Gary, Indiana, and they did not do me any good. . . . I . . . was a pitiful sight to look upon—weighing only 117 pounds and looking like a skeleton. . . . [Nettie] took a job in a laundry where she spent her days working for one whole year to support us. When she came home in the evenings, she nursed me. All of her care was to no avail, as I did not seem to improve. The show had gotten another piano player and had left on a tour of the Southwest. I was perplexed, sick, disturbed and a bundle of confusion.

Dorsey's despair was so great that he even thought of attempting suicide:

> I was just standing out there ready maybe to jump in [Lake Michigan], if it wasn't nothing else to do. I didn't feel exactly like that but something had to happen.[9]

Coming from the religious background that he did, however, Dorsey seems almost to have been destined, once finding himself at such a low ebb, to seek solace in the church. Yet when his sister-in-law convinced him to attend church with her one Sunday, he probably did not anticipate the events of that morning:

> It's hard to describe what happened. I thought more seriously about God than I had in many years, though I was a confessed believer and went to church. I shall never forget. The Minister was Bishop H. H. Haley and he spoke gently and quietly to me: "Brother Dorsey, there is no reason for you to be looking so poorly and feeling so badly. The Lord has too much work for you to do to let you die."

Dorsey then describes how Haley pulled a "live serpent" out of his throat. From that moment on he claims to have suffered "no more," to have been "going ever since," and to have pledged: "Lord, I am ready to do your work."[10]

As convincing as the supernatural might have been to Dorsey, tragedy soon tested his commitment to the new life. Within a few weeks, a good friend of his who lived in the apartment below took ill one morning and died suddenly that night. This death was deeply perplexing to Dorsey; his inability to understand it, however, seems to have inspired him to seek an even deeper level of religious devotion:

> I was very much saddened by his death and I couldn't understand! I had been sick for over a year and this young man was sick for just one day and then he died. My mind went back to what the minister told me when my sister-in-law took me to church. His words thundered in my ears again: "Have more faith; the Lord has a great work for you to do; you will not die, you will attract attention of the world and grow strong." So from that day I took on new faith, consecrated myself fully to God and grew stronger and stronger physically, mentally and spiritually.[11]

From this incident came the inspiration for Dorsey to write his first gospel blues, *If You See My Savior, Tell Him That You Saw Me.*

The idea of writing sacred music was logical considering that Dorsey was intent on leading a deeply religious life and that he was an accomplished composer and arranger. But it was also predictable given his ideas about blues. As a performer he noted often that people responded similarly to blues whether heard in the theater or at an intimate gathering. Their responses, moreover, were virtually identical to moments of similar emotional appeal in churches:

> I seen women in the audience jump up, so touched—guess a good man had left them, left them cold or something like that—jump up like you shouting in church. I've seen that right in the theater. Whatever it is that touches them, they jump up and wring and shout just like we would in church. It gets low-down. Now what we call low-down in blues doesn't mean that it's dirty or bad or something like that. It gets down into the individual to set him on fire,

dig him up or dig her up way down there 'til they come out with an expression verbally. If they're in the church, they say, "Amen." If they're in the blues, they say, "Sing it now."

Different types of music, "whatever it is, blues, jazz, or gospel," have a similar effect because each is a "vehicle for your feeling":

> If a woman has lost a man, a man has lost a woman, his feeling reacts to the blues; he feels like expressing it. The same thing acts for a gospel song. Now you're not singing blues; you're singing gospel, good news song, singing about the Creator; but it's the same feeling, a grasping of the heart. If it's in your public, they holler out "Hallelujah" or "Amen" in church. In the theater they holler "sing it again" or "do it again" or something like that.

No doubt Dorsey also had in mind religious phrases that singers would voice while performing the blues, such as that in his account of Ma Rainey singing her *Stormy Sea Blues:* "Lawdy, Lawdy, I hear somebody calling me. . . ." He could have been thinking too of blues singers' free borrowing of religious imagery such as in Rainey's "If I had wings and could fly like Noah's dove. . . ."[12]

Since blues elicits "the same feeling" as church music, the same "grasping of the heart," Dorsey suggests that blues should be evaluated less as a sound than as a "feeling":

> Blues notes are on the piano; been on the piano just like opera and its trills and things. A blues note? There's no such thing as a blue note. Blues don't own no notes. The world of music owns the notes and sounds on the piano. You're talking about the old blue seventh. We gave the blues that seventh. But it can be in anything. It's up to the individual to know how and when to bring it out.

In one sense, then, blues is almost musically neutral: it is a set of harmonic, melodic, and rhythmic configurations associated with a set of emotions and their attendant responses. The manifestation of such "blues," at least among blacks, Dorsey believes, transcends the traditional boundaries between the sacred and the secular—boundaries that have been blurred throughout African American history.[13]

Dorsey further supports his view of the neutrality of blues by asserting that music and religion are inseparable. A culture's music—such as the blues of Afro-America—is inextricably bound to its worship:

> Music is a universal something. It was here when we come here and it was here when other generations came. [There] is not a people or a race or a nation or anything in creation that is human that doesn't have its song. I may not know it. I may not like it. I may not be able to sing it. But everything, everybody, I'm talking about every nation, every human being that came

across the earth had a song and sang in some way to their god. They could sing some way in their power.[14]

Acting under the same human urge, African Americans sang music in order to express certain feelings, both of which—the music and the feelings—came to be called "blues." These were simple, "common songs we sang out of our hearts, our feeling." Blues, Dorsey thus feels, was never just music to black Americans; the emotions it conveyed were connected to religious feelings:

> . . . blues were really born shortly after slaves were free and they were sung the way singers felt inside. They were just let out of slavery or put out, or went out, but they hadn't gotten used to freedom. Their spirituals had a kind of feeling, you know, a depressed feeling. They poured out their souls in their songs. They still had the feeling for a number of years, but not the persecution and all that. But blues is a digging, picking, pricking at the very depth of your mental environment and the feelings of your heart. Blues is more than just *blues*. It's got to be that old low-down moan and the low-down feeling; you got to have feeling.[15]

Because of its history and the more recent efforts of the recording industry, however, blues had become associated more and more with subject matter and experiences that were not only secular in nature but to some extent profane:

> Now people look down with derision, discontent, vulgarity on the blues; after all I don't see anything wrong with the blues unless you use vulgarity in it. But the blues itself, the music itself? It can't hurt. [It] can do more good than it can do harm. But people take it and do harm with it because they use it in unsavory places—not so up to date. I guess too what I am trying to say is places where sometimes fights and killing, things like that come off. But I don't pay any attention to that.[16]

Nevertheless, throughout his career as a blues pianist and composer and then as the pianist for one of the two most popular female blues singers of the time, Dorsey had been an active, if unwitting, promulgator of this narrower, more negative application of popularized blues.

This commercialization nearly obscured the function of the blues as an element of black religion. Indeed, the more popular blues became, the more reason black churches, especially those that emulated white liturgies, had to consider it inappropriate. Dorsey sensed that blues had been recontextualized to the extent that many Afro-Americans thought it was inappropriate as religious song. To Dorsey, however, such denigration of the blues was indefensible, especially when he thought of it as the music of slaves and associated it with the "moaning" he heard in church as a child. Later, as an adult, he witnessed the evoking of the emotions of both of those experiences from the stage. He was struck by the historical continuity of the blues:

"Those on down who wrote about the blues and wrote the blues, I think they made a great contribution." Many blacks, however, disavowed this heritage by seeking a religious ethos that excluded blues and the emotion that accompanied it.[17]

In light of his renewed commitment to "serve the Lord" and his profound moments with blues in both its sacred and secular contexts, Dorsey considered it a valid undertaking to place blues on an equal footing with the type of music then prevalent in black churches—certainly old-line ones:

> Blues is as important to a person feeling bad as "Nearer My God to Thee." I'm not talking about popularity; I'm talking about inside the individual. This moan gets into a person where there is some secret down there that they didn't bring out. See this stuff to come out is in you. When you cry out, that is something down there that should have come out a long time ago. Whether it's blues or gospel, there is a vehicle that comes along maybe to take it away or push it away. A man or woman singing the blues in the church will cry out, "Holy, holy, holy."[18]

In a purely musical sense, blues to Dorsey was a collection of keyboard improvisational techniques, "trills and turns and embellishments." Dorsey began his career playing for dances and parties, in theaters and bordellos, where he had to improvise, or "make up," as he went along. Even after learning to read music, Dorsey's playing skill rested mostly on his ability to "change around" or improvise over a pre-existing harmonic pattern or even over known melodies and popular songs. His advocacy of blues religious music is an admonishment to approach church music in the same manner:

> If you can see where you can do something for a song, you do it. And if a pianist, any kind of accompanist, whoever it is, if they can't enlarge on a song—I don't care if it is a dance or a show or the church—they won't sound like nothing. Give me a song, I stick to the note and play it like it is, you won't pay much attention to it. In fact it won't go anywhere. You got to always have something: a little trick, a little embellishment or something. I don't go and take it just straight; I got to put something in it to get over.[19]

In Dorsey's notation of gospel blues, the music as written served no other function than that of a guide, a point from which to embark upon spontaneous creativity. Dorsey never intended that everything to be performed in gospel blues—as with other blues—should be notated. On the basis of his past experience, he assumed that most of the pianists or vocalists who performed his music would probably be unable to read music. Moreover, once written out, blues ornamentation as Dorsey knew it appeared too complex:

> If you write too many embellishments and they see too many notes, they won't play it. They say it's hard. We always made it simple. You can't put all that stuff up there on that paper. They can't read it.[20]

Even those prospective performers who could read music did not want "all that stuff in there." To write embellishments was to pre-empt both a sacred right and a rite of a blues performance. Blues was a conduit for feeling, but the particular feeling at a given performance and the embellishments and other performance techniques used to express or evoke it were options exercised solely by the performer. Particularly for gospel blues this freedom of choice was important, for in the matter of religion, whether expressed in music or speech, one had to surrender oneself to the inspiration of God:

> Every singer who performs, speaker also, preacher, anybody, you don't stick exactly to your script. You got to have something that comes from inside of you that Providence or something gives to you while you are performing. Well now, we call that, religiously, you call that the voice of God speaking through you. See you got to always be—everybody who performs or does anything, even talk—susceptible, openly susceptible for whatever comes in the heart or the mind or your ear.[21]

Dorsey's idea that one be "susceptible" to non-musical forces at the moment of performance complements his notion that the composition of gospel music comes only in response to some event or experience:

> Something's got to happen. That is the way many of my songs come. I either saw something or I heard something or somebody did something; something happened somewhere, had to happen to get the song: gospel song or blues, anything else. Something got to happen before you get the idea. You can't get up, try to write anything, I don't care how many schools that a man has been to or a woman has been to, how many universities, or what not. You got to have enough in the thing that you are going to deliver to the public to grasp the thought, the heart, the feeling and the sense of the public that you are serving. Even the newspaper man has to see something to give a good report [in] the newspaper.[22]

To Dorsey, the essence of a gospel song, at its start (composition) and finish (performance), is its revelation of personal experience.

The connection between Dorsey's blues and his "gospels" was implicit, given that his rationales for composing and performing both were identical. But the connection was also explicit. Dorsey recognized that, despite his new religious commitment and his forsaking of blues as a career, his gospels were derivatives—directly so—of his earlier blues:

> The only thing about all the music is the words are different, see. You use different words and then you take that blue moan and what they call the low-down feeling tunes and you shape them up and put them up here and make them serve the other purpose, the religious purpose. And then too, the [blues] lilt, tempo, expression, the feeling all go together to make gospel songs what they are and to make blues what they are.[23]

Indeed, Dorsey attributes the appeal of gospel music among black Americans to stylistic traits that he considers uniquely "blues":

> I wouldn't have been as successful in gospel songs if I hadn't known some of these things, trills, turns, movements in blues. It's the trills and turns in it that you can't get into anything else but blues and gospel songs. There are moans that you can't get into anything else but blues and gospel songs. Now you take some of the gospel singers—some of the best ones were good blues singers.[24]

An instance of the blues traits in Dorsey's performance of religious song can be found in Examples 5-1, 5-2, and 5-3, where he plays *Amazing Grace*. Dorsey's choice of this hymn is rather fortuitous, for the history of traditional American religious music is replete with embellished versions of *Amazing Grace*.[25]

Example 5-1 is Dorsey's recollection of *Amazing Grace* as it was most often performed in old-line churches without the improvisation he advocated. "You see, there's nothing in there, no embellishments," he remarked after playing this. Perhaps the most striking features are the rhythm and tempo. According to George P. Jackson, *New Britain,* the source tune for this version of *Amazing Grace,* is in a triple meter. Older black churches' renditions, Dorsey explains, must have been in a compound meter—in this instance, 6/8. The iambic accentuation of the text is compromised, however, in 6/8, because of the duple, almost even accentuation of that meter, that is, nearly equal stress on both feet of the text. On the other hand, the quarter-note, half-note pattern of the original 3/4 melody conforms exactly with that of iambic meter. The absence of syncopation seems also to be a factor in Dorsey's dislike of this version. At a tempo of MM = c. 54 for the dotted quarter, emphasis is on the two pulses of the dotted quarters as opposed to six eighth-note pulses. The intent, in fact, seems to be to establish a slow march cadence. The beat would be less marked if it were syncopated.

Examples 5-2 and 5-3 contrast strongly with Example 5-1 because they are arhythmic. Even though each is notated in a triple meter, melodic ornamentation and arbitrary lengthening and shortening of the rhythmic values render almost nil any of the inherent accent patterns of either the text or the melodic meters. But these patterns are of little concern anyway, since preset textual and rhythmic accentuation is nearly useless when virtually every element of the music is to be determined by the performer at the time of each performance. The same fundamental alteration occurs in the melody. Even without the embellishments, the melodic lines of both examples differ distinctly from the "old way" example (5-1).

Such deep textual and rhythmic changes in this music are not without design. They manifest Dorsey's ideas that music in the church must be approached like music in the blues halls and joints; that the performer must get "low-down," that is, inside the listener and prick the heart; that experiences

Ex. 5-1

Amazing Grace (old way)

from life, especially those that make one "feel bad," are to some extent relived and relieved when music is performed in this manner; that the origin of embellishments, moans, and other improvisations is solely the performer's, who employs them at the moment of utterance as the Spirit, feeling, or audience demands; and that, above all, God and the long and sometimes tragic history of black Americans have decreed that music in the black church—if that church is to remain true to its believers—must be performed by these standards.

Ex. 5-2

Amazing Grace (Dorsey's style—1)

The religious music that Dorsey proposed called for a drastic departure from the music practices of the large Protestant black churches in Chicago. Most of these establishment "old-line" churches descended from the oldest black religious organization in Chicago, the Wood River Association (Baptist), which was founded around 1838 and was comprised of two congregations: Zoar and Mount Zion. These merged in 1853 to become Olivet Baptist Church. Between 1882 and 1920, at least nine groups split from Olivet, each beginning as a prayer band or house meeting group—or both—

Ex. 5-3

Amazing Grace (Dorsey's style—2)

mm. 1-2

mm. 3-4

Ex. 5-3 (cont.)

saved   a   wretch————————like

mm. 5-6

me!

m. 7

led by a deacon, growing in size until its membership was large enough to establish a church. Although not as well documented, Quinn Chapel and Bethel, the two oldest AME churches in Chicago, experienced the same sort of schism. From these "splits" came Berea, Bethesda, Ebenezer, Liberty, Monumental, Pilgrim, Progress, Provident, and Salem Baptist churches. By the middle 1920s, each of these churches numbered no fewer than 500 members each and, as a group, had become the major religious bodies in black Chicago.[26]

The black church has served historically as an institutional means of social control and as an avenue for assimilating non-Afro-American values. The replacement of indigenous music practices (such as congregational singing, hand-clapping, foot-patting, and other demonstrative behavior) by choirs directed by trained musicians was lauded early in the development of the black church as a clear sign of social progress. Bishop Daniel Payne chastised the "opposition," those who were set against the introduction of choirs and musical instruments into AME churches:

> . . . [these persons] cared only for those "corn-field ditties" which could produce the wildest excitement among the thoughtless masses. Such persons are usually so because they are non-progressive, and, being illiterate, are consequently very narrow in views of men and things. A strong religious feeling, coupled with a narrow range of knowledge, often makes one a bigot.

Old-line churches in Chicago continued this long and almost sacred rejection of indigenous traditions by resorting to any means at hand—in this instance choirs and non-traditional music—to continue what they believed to be the cultural advancement of their congregations.[27]

The choir's prominence as a cultural force in Chicago's old-line churches was for the most part established around the turn of the century. If the Chicago Choral Study Club at Olivet Baptist Church is typical of the first choirs formed in Chicago's old-line churches, cultural advancement was unabashedly their goal, for the Study Club "was organized to create a desire for better music among Chicago Negroes and to render musical numbers of the higher type." The Club became noted for its performances of such works as Handel's *Messiah,* Gall's *Holy City,* and the choral music of Samuel Coleridge-Taylor and for numbering among its members "'Old Chicago's prominent musicians.'" Evidently other groups were organized along the same lines as the Chicago Choral Study Club: Glenn Dillard Gunn writing for the *Inter Ocean* newspaper mentioned "similar organizations" which were not as prominent as the Choral Study Club.[28]

With the establishment of choral study clubs in old-line churches, the role of these churches in the history of non-traditional black music in Chicago's black community began to emerge. At first the clubs or choirs allied themselves with these churches for pragmatic reasons. Churches were able to provide the money, the personnel, and the place for the performance of classical music. The first opera to be sung by blacks in Chicago was performed by the Bethel AME Church choir in December 1921. Its director, James Mundy, recalls being able to raise the $1000 for production costs by asking for a special collection. With members of the Chicago Symphony playing the orchestral accompaniment (another historic first for Chicago blacks), the Bethel choir performed Von Flotow's *Martha* to capacity audiences for two successive nights.[29]

The alliance between old-line churches and the clubs or choirs was made secure when old-line ministers noted a direct relationship between the success of their music programs and the sizes of their congregations:

> The larger the church the bigger the choirs and the greater the demand for good music. Consequently, the churches hired the top musicians and they paid them good salaries for training their choirs.[30]

Once it was clear that their reputation hinged on their music, old-line churches and their choirs embarked on a joint mission unprecedented for its impact on black Chicago: they sought and nearly succeeded in altering the presentation and choice of music not only in old-line churches but also in the community at large.

One of the first results of this joint mission was a new prestige for trained musicians as choir directors in old-line churches. Ministers competed fiercely for good choir directors. In 1918, for example, Dr. Lacey K. Williams, pastor of Olivet Baptist Church, traveled to Springfield, Massachusetts, in order to hire Edward H. Boatner. Boatner had studied at the Boston Conservatory, the Longy School of Music, and with the famous black tenor Roland Hayes. In addition to leading the choir in Springfield and founding and directing the first black choral group in Boston, Boatner was a soloist with Boston's Ebenezer Church quartet. Williams lured Boatner to Chicago with the promise of a high salary and full support for whatever he wanted to do with the music program. Later, as an inducement for Boatner to continue at Olivet, Williams created the position of Music Director of the National Baptist Convention, something well within his power as its president. Then in 1926, Boatner was sought out by the newly arrived Reverend J. C. Austin, Sr., at Pilgrim Baptist Church, who needed a replacement for James Mundy, who had just resigned. Austin successfully wooed Boatner from Olivet and his post with the Convention by offering to double his salary. Boatner would later leave Pilgrim in disgust over Austin's successful bargaining for another choir director, Thomas A. Dorsey, whose job would be to organize a gospel chorus to provide music along with the choir. Mundy, who apparently held the music post in more old-line churches (Olivet, Pilgrim, Bethel, Quinn Chapel) than any other director, recalls in each instance moving because the minister offered more money and the freedom to expand the extant music program.[31]

As was inevitable, the rivalry between ministers soon became one between old-line choir directors. At Pilgrim Baptist Church, a twenty-seven-piece orchestra was organized to accompany the choir during worship—evidence of the lengths to which churches went in order to establish their music superiority. Even direct competition between choirs sprang up. The *Chicago Defender* on April 5, 1930, reported that a "choir contest" between the Mundy Singers and the Metropolitan Church choir (conducted by J. Wesley Jones) would occur the following Sunday afternoon. The repertoire chosen by the directors is another indication of how far they would go in order to maintain or improve their reputations. Mrs. Bertha Curry, a choir member at Pilgrim, recalls as follows:

> We did Mendelssohn's *Elijah,* Bach Cantatas, *The Seven Last Words* by [Theodore] Dubois, Haydn's *Creation,* all from cover to cover with instrumentalists. The music was wonderful, wonderful, wonderful.[32]

As accomplished musicians increasingly trained choirs to sing major choral works, the worship service became less and less adequate for a choir to display its ability. The competition for members who might be attracted by classical music was hampered by the inappropriateness of a full rendering of large works during Sunday morning services. During worship, the choir at Pilgrim could sing only one movement ("Inflammatus") of Rossini's *Stabat Mater,* and that in English. At a later concert, the complete work was performed in Latin. In order to satisfy further the choir's need to perform music for music's sake, a concert was scheduled once a month, usually on a Sunday afternoon; it was called the "monthly musicale."[33]

By the early 1920s, the monthly musicale had become an institution within old-line churches. "Reputations were made and lost on your musicales," remembers Augustus Evans, an assistant director at Pilgrim. Such a major role and high visibility for the musicale may be considered convincing evidence of its use as a promulgator of the new cultural tastes that were an integral part of old-line religion. If the musicale at Metropolitan was typical of those at most old-line churches, the popularity of the event shows the degree to which black Chicagoans were amenable to those new tastes:

> All the Chicago musicians, music lovers and friends are anxiously awaiting the great musicale to be given by the celebrated Metropolitan Solo Choir, under the direction of their popular and efficient choirmaster, Prof. J. Wesley Jones, Sunday, Sept. 23, at 7:30 p.m. Miss Nellie M. Dobson, one of Chicago's sweetest sopranos, will sing "La Caparina," by Benedict. Emmit Berger, Chicago's leading baritone, will sing a selection from "Carmen." Carol McCoy will give a select reading. The big choir will sing "O Southland" by Johnson; "Spirit Imm[o]rtal" from "Attilla," [by] Verdi; "Chariot Jubilee," by Dett; "Bridal Chorus" [from] Rose Maiden [by] Cowen; two spirituals, "Gave Way Jordan" and "I Want God's Heaven to be Mine." . . . Dr. Wm. D. Cook will welcome the monster crowd. H. A. Hawkins has ordered a large number of chairs to take care of the overflow patrons.[34]

The Reverend Esther Greer describes first-hand the musicales at Metropolitan during the 1920s:

> Every fourth Sunday, if you didn't get to Metropolitan by five—and of course the musicale didn't start until 7:30—it was all over the city of Chicago and nearby places like Gary, South Bend, and St. Louis, that if you didn't get to Metropolitan by five, wear some comfortable shoes because you were going to stand up. And it grew to the place that we used to try to keep the doors closed until six, but it was always so many people on Grand Boulevard at that particular time that the police department demanded that the doors be opened. Then it became that at five o'clock you came in, rushed in and got yourself a seat, because the musicales were tremendous. During Professor Jones' lifetime we enjoyed I think the greatest glory musically that has been enjoyed by any congregation in the city of Chicago.[35]

Given its role in worship, its partnership with the church's cultural mission, and the effectiveness of its monthly musicale, the choir may be considered one of the most visible cultural forces in old-line churches. So integral was the importance of culture to religion there that music became, in essence, a cultural ministry of those churches. Music in old-line churches was thus more than sound; it was religious ideology.

In several respects, the church's cultural role was exemplary. The Sunday musicale provided blacks an opportunity to hear music many could not have afforded at concerts in downtown Chicago, where they would probably not have been welcome in any case. A generation of trained black musicians was given the chance to display the talent that the Chicago music establishment had shown no inclination to recognize. Numerous black music organizations such as the Apollo Ensemble, the Chicago Music Association, the Nathaniel Dett Club, and the Imperial Opera Company could trace their beginnings to the senior choirs in various old-line churches. As late as 1940, the church was recognized as the "most utilized outlet" for music among black Chicagoans.[36]

Its benefits notwithstanding, however, the cultural mission of old-line churches was built on a weak supposition: black progress was to be undertaken without regard to black cultural heritage. Progress, therefore, was measured in terms of the virtual annihilation of as many vestiges of black worship customs as possible.

In face of the growing prominence of trained choirs, congregational singing became less a part of old-line worship. Congregational singing must have been particularly annoying to those who valued a more sophisticated worship hour, and as a result it suffered the attack of two forces, both of which sought the complete reform if not replacement of music associated with indigenous black worship. The more comprehensive of these in its effect was the effort to adopt white hymn-singing practices. The second force was represented by the "Negro Spiritual" tradition that traces its origins back to the post-Emancipation efforts to re-compose sacred slave songs.

Since their earliest exposure to Protestant Christianity in the United States, Afro-Americans have sung the hymns of white Christians. Numerous accounts tell not only of blacks' apparent predilection for psalmody, Watts hymns, camp-meeting songs, and other genres of white Protestant hymnody, but also of their unique style of delivery when singing this music. Such accounts are of little aid in reconstructing the sound of these performances, thus making comparative analysis impossible. But the actions that accompanied such performances are described sufficiently for one to conclude that even though blacks and whites sang the same songs, the general performance practices of the two races differed greatly.[37]

Since at least 1910, black congregations in Chicago (in most instances the forerunners of old-line churches) had used the standard hymnals of the denominations of which they were affiliates. They performed these hymns in a traditional manner, however, so that even though their music was of white origin, their performance—as had historically been the case—was distinctively their own. Despite the general constraint to be non-demonstrative, hymn-singing in old-line churches could still be described as "joyous" and "spontaneous." Particularly in Baptist churches, former practices such as the lining-out of hymns and singing "Dr. Watts" in long or common meter flourished. These practices were carried out in the "prayer service" or "testimonial service" held prior to Sunday morning worship. These services represented some of the last remaining forms of traditional black worship ritual in old-line churches. During such services, the older style of congregational singing had its most unfettered opportunity for expression. Thus selections like *Amazing Grace, Master, the Tempest Is Raging,* and *I'm so Glad Jesus Lifted Me* were sung in the same style and evidently with the same frequency as blacks had been accustomed to, whether they were recently from the South or old settlers in Chicago.[38]

At Pilgrim Baptist Church under the pastorate of Dr. S. E. J. Watson, the congregation customarily sang five or six hymns during Sunday morning worship. By 1926, when the Reverend J. C. Austin had succeeded Watson, the congregation sang only two hymns and the choir, three anthems. As part of his restructuring of the worship, Austin also discontinued the prayer service, thereby eliminating the only form of traditional black worship music that had actually been institutionalized. Austin probably was aware of the extreme difficulty he would face in his attempt to stop the pre-worship prayer service. It was both popular with the membership and conducted by the Board of Deacons, his employer. Nevertheless, he found a way to remove the testimonial portion of the worship service. He had the deacons conduct their service with the choir in the basement. Formal worship then began with a choir processional to the accompaniment of what was probably considered more ennobling music, *All Hail the Power of Jesus' Name.*[39] Within its first ten years, Pilgrim had ceased virtually all of the practices associated with traditional black worship.

The effort to abolish customary congregational singing was actually part of the struggle to control—if not eliminate altogether—demonstrative behavior:

> In the twenties and thirties, people were becoming more intelligent; preachers were studying and trying to take us from our jumpy side and from our emotional side to be still and hear what's being said. The music was part of that. They didn't stop people from shouting; you give vent to the Spirit. But I mean it grew so that people became more quiet and wanted to hear. This meant that our pastors, they wanted good music. They wanted that that would make you listen.

Ministers seemed reluctant to indulge their congregations' traditional singing because they feared that the response would be uncontrollable. After all, except for the selection of the hymn, the congregation governed all other aspects of its singing. One of the Reverend J. C. Austin's parishioners remembers his words as he spoke to his congregation about his reform of the worship music at Pilgrim: "'We are intelligent folks here and we don't do a lot of hollering and so forth and carrying on.'" Such an explicit rejection of southern performance practices from the pulpit apparently had its effect: "They don't ever sing now like they did."[40]

It is unlikely that any minister, choir director, or anyone else advocating or implementing the new worship standards stated publicly that his goal was to imitate white churches. The imitation, however, was implicit and inevitably occurred. The disparity between black traditional singing and Mozart's *Alleluia*, Peter D. Koch's *Thee, God, We Praise* and other anthems was too great to be ignored—especially when the choir was as important as the preacher in maintaining a church's reputation and increasing the size of its congregation. The ethos of white churches was undoubtedly, therefore, the standard:

> You must remember that our hymns, the standard was set by the white folks ahead of us. The white Baptists, you wanted to be a white Baptist. You followed his hymns. See? The [black] Methodists followed the Methodist hymns, and so we sang the hymns the white folks had. The hymns and anthems, there was not difference. We played them pretty much like we heard them in white churches.

Far from being "joyous" and "spontaneous" as in the earlier singing, the congregational style now was "more straight," with an "emphasis on the harmony" instead of the rhythm. In effect, the delivery was "just like theirs [the whites]."[41]

The mimicry of white music standards might have proceeded unchecked had not choir directors with the support of ministers begun to reconsider their extensive use of non-black worship music. The feeling seemed to be that in their search for high standards of worship, directors had too readily discarded their own music: "We were being hincty [snobbish] toward our own music. It was rejected. We just didn't want to sing our music."[42] In an effort to compensate for this rejection, choir directors turned to traditional black religious music—not, however, in its original form, but arranged and titled the "Negro spiritual." This was the second force to which congregational singing was subjected.

Even in an apparent surge of "race consciousness," old-line directors were unable to lay aside the values that had initially caused them to forsake their traditions. The evolution of the arranged or anglicized Negro spiritual indicates this problem. Since almost immediately after Emancipation, when ex-slaves seemed to want to discard them as unpleasant reminders of their bondage, spirituals were pawns in one of the many battles over black cultural identity. At the heart of the controversy was the question of the proper context for their use among freed persons. One side seemed to want to make the spiritual an art song, to have it appreciated with minimal reference to the experience and feelings out of which it had originated. The other side argued that the spiritual belonged within the context of the traditional black religious experience—especially since emotional performance and equally emotional response were intrinsic to black worship.[43]

Writing from Fisk University in 1915 after several successful tours with the Fisk Jubilee Singers as their director, John Wesley Work was a ready proponent of the former argument:

> In truth, the general adaptability of this music to a high degree of development is its hope of gaining artistic recognition. It deserves to be put into a finished form; it lends itself admirably to such a purpose; and those who would keep it as it was first reduced to writing, in their mistaken zeal would doom it to stagnation and to the contempt of highly musical people.

Work's purpose was to make the spirituals the music of "educated Negroes," by shaping it into a form befitting their advancement. For this reason he encouraged and praised the study of these songs as conducted at black colleges (for example, Hampton, Atlanta University, and Tuskegee Institute) and by individuals such as C. J. Ryder, the former president of the American Missionary Association, Harry T. Burleigh, one of the pioneer composer/arrangers of spirituals, and Antonín Dvořák, the noted Czech composer, who on his sojourn in the United States suggested that "inspiration for truly [American] national music might be derived from the negro melodies. . . . "[44]

Arguing as forcefully for the preservation of the original spiritual, C. W. Hyne noted that the qualities of folk musicianship, namely "quarter-tones, slurrings, and unusual harmonies" are lost and "sacrificed to conventional orthodoxy when the folksongs are reproduced . . . [and when there is] the attempt to 'dress them up' unduly." He criticized the lack of spiritual singing in black churches, "except [for those churches] in the rural sections where the Spiritual clung to life and survived because of the sheer desire to sing on the part of the men and women in the congregation." "Denatured Spirituals," he wrote, "remind one of the attempt of one race to remove the curl from the hair and of the other to put it in."[45]

Both sides agreed on the issue most critical to the spiritual: spirituals should be collected and transcribed. The treatment of the spiritual after its gathering and notation was the issue under debate. The arguments Work and Hyne represented, therefore, were created by and apparently of interest only to transcribers and arrangers. For, having been frozen by notation, the spiritual over which they argued was no longer a dynamic expression of Afro-American thought.[46] It was an artifact whose discoverers offered widely differing opinions as to how to exhibit it. Given the cultural awareness and the musical skill required to perform it, Work's spiritual could be none other than the song of the exalted Negro. With the inherent limitations of western music notation, Hyne's spiritual had been denatured long before he thought of criticizing its lack of slurs and quarter-tones.

Like that of Hyne and Work, the race consciousness of old-line music directors was qualified. They had little, if any, reason to regret the loss of the spiritual in its classic form. After all, they held their positions in old-line churches because of the new religious order there—one in which the spiritual was the symbol of backwardness. Indeed, the very survival of these directors' positions depended on their demonstration of the spiritual's obsolescence; this they accomplished most effectively by leading their choirs through some of the most complex choral works of the western European classical music tradition. In the presence of the choir's anthems, the congregation's hymns, and the minister's discouragement of shouting, the spiritual had become an anachronism in old-line churches. Moreover, choir directors had been no less than the perpetrators of its demise:

They [the directors] didn't know nothing about singing these spirituals then, what are you talking about? They were contiguous with slavery, see? So no one wanted to be identified with slavery. We pooh-poohed them.[47]

Thus the black music that old-line directors sought was some proper, objective allusion to the slave past such as the tasteful Negro spiritual. As early as the 1870s this form of the spiritual had been available in an edited and arranged format. "Jubilee" singers from Fisk, Hampton, and other black schools in the South had sung this spiritual throughout the United States and Europe. In addition to bringing in much-needed funds for their institutions, these black singers were living proof that they represented "the highest average of culture among the colored people." They substantiated the recently expressed belief that "a sense of dignity had come with freedom." Behind the development of this spiritual, however, stood the white teachers who taught in southern black schools. Before Work's 1901 publication, no record exists to indicate that blacks had anything to do with the collection and transcription of their religious music. Indeed, the record is replete with accounts of blacks' resistance—particularly among those who were educated—to singing "slave songs" and with the urging—perhaps even insistence—of whites that blacks not allow their musical heritage to die. For example, John Work recalls that students at Fisk would give only "cold silence" when asked by Adam K. Spence, the white principal there, to sing spirituals. Work credits Spence for being "largely responsible for the salvation of . . . Negro music" at Fisk.[48]

This spiritual certainly should have appeased the old-line directors' demand for black music that would be appropriate for worship in their churches. But their desire was not only that the music meet certain standards of worship but that it meet certain standards of the music profession as well. Virtually none of the transcribers/arrangers of this type of spiritual was a musician trained in composition. They were mostly teachers with music experience. The music they wrote was adequate for its purpose: to demonstrate that the spiritual could be dignified. But it was substandard when compared with the anthems being sung by old-line choirs. Even though these arrangements were readily available (for example, *Gospel Pearls* contained a section set aside for them [Nos. 144–63]), they were seldom, if at all, performed by choirs:

> These old collections of spirituals, the early spirituals, were arranged like hymns. They [the arrangers] never did any long, what you call harmonizations. No, no, nothing like an anthem; they were just hymns. They were simplified.

From both old-line directors and a number of black musicians, the spiritual met with a disdain rooted in a scorn for the pity "white hearers" showed who were "touched and moved with deepest sympathy for the 'poor Negro.'"[49]

Whereas old-line directors had considered the spiritual in its classic form to be crude and its first descendent musically trite, they found the anthem/octavo spiritual a worthy medium through which to restore some aspect of their racial heritage to the liturgy from which it had been so effectively expunged. But another reason for their immediate acceptance of anthem spirituals was their sense of fraternity or commonality of consciousness with the blacks who composed them. The first generation of trained black composers evolved during a period when a resurgence of nationalism was taking place in American music. The movement can be traced to 1895 when Antonín Dvořák scolded American composers for their bias toward western European music—particularly the classical tradition—almost to the exclusion of any interest in indigenous American music. Dvořák's chiding spawned a group of nationalist composers (Indianist, Negrophiles, and Anglo-Americanists) who drew from the traditional music of various American ethnic groups.[50]

Composers of this persuasion sought to integrate folk music into the compositional process. To black composers, many of whom were trained by whites of the older school, this process must have helped resolve the sense of ambivalence encouraged by their practice of an art form alien to their racial culture. Beginning in 1907 with one of Dvořák's students, Harry T. Burleigh, black composers published numerous pieces indicating a wide, if not total, embracing of this compositional philosophy.[51]

Once old-line directors knew of them, anthem spirituals were swiftly included in the repertoires of old-line choirs. At the 1915 Lincoln Jubilee Half-Century Exposition in Chicago, Azalia Hackley, long noted for her encouragement of black professionally trained musicians, opened a booth in order to sell the anthem spirituals of two black composers, Harry T. Burleigh and Nathaniel Dett:

> Burleigh had his own music published and Dett had his published, but there was no market for it, because the community was saturated with a desire for the white man's music. She stuck her neck out. She talked about it and talked about it: "Buy this music; help these men get started." We bought it. I was the first one who fell in line with her. So she sat in the exhibition and sold copies. So that started the choirs to buying octavo music. She broke down the barriers. That's the frontier we crossed there.[52]

Old-line directors who were sufficiently trained also composed anthem spirituals. Edward Boatner, who directed at Pilgrim and Olivet Baptist churches, wrote *Twelve Gates into the City* (1923), and *Trampin'* (1927). With the support of Mrs. A. M. Townsend, chairman of the Music Committee of the National Baptist Convention, he compiled and arranged a complete collection entitled *Spirituals Triumphant Old and New*.[53] Dr. William Henry Smith, who directed at Olivet, was well known for his arrangements of *Walk Together Children* and *Ezekiel Saw the Wheel*.[54]

As it had been practiced in old-line churches from the time of their formation and thus, to a great extent, from the time of the institutionalization of the black church, congregational singing no longer existed by the end of the 1920s. It had been all but obliterated by the imposition of white hymn-singing standards. The hearts that once were quickened by its strains were now subdued by its newly acquired dignity. Perhaps some members of old-line congregations reacted similarly to those about whom Zora Neale Hurston wrote:

> I have noticed that whenever an untampered-with congregation attempts the renovated spirituals, the people grow self-conscious. They sing sheepishly in unison. None of the glorious individualistic flights that make up their own songs. Perhaps they feel on strange ground. Like the unlettered parent before his child just home from college. At any rate they are not very popular.
>
> This is no condemnation of the neo-spirituals. They are a valuable contri-

bution to the music and literature of the world. But let no one imagine that they are the songs of the people, as sung by them.[55]

Old-line ministers and choir directors were oblivious to the fact that their headlong pursuit of proper worship demeanor could precipitate such deep dissatisfaction. They were no doubt often self-righteously complacent that "the people [had] adjusted themselves to formal music." And they were satisfied that through benign coercion "the more [the people] were exposed to [formal music], the more it became a part of them."[56] This was the fatal flaw of the ideology that undergirded music praxis in old-line churches during the 1920s. Surely most members of old-line congregations—regardless of their socioeconomic status or length of settlement in Chicago—wanted evidence of their progress. Such a desire was involved in the very act of joining churches that formed the citadels of black urban culture. To assume that such desire was actually a new zeal to forsake the past was the misjudgment of those most active in establishing the new order in old-line churches. As formal music symbolized their contribution to black cultural advancement, so gospel blues was destined to represent the errancy of their ways.

6

Old-Line Religion
and Urban Migrants:
1920–1930

Among the crowds of eager concertgoers who waited for hours to hear the Sunday musicales stood one Thomas Andrew Dorsey. He idolized old-line choir directors as much as he did the jazz greats of the time, often speaking of them in virtually the same breath:

> I then began to hit the night spots, but was too young and not well known enough to mingle or associate with the old-line music men like Will Dorsey, Charles Elger, Dave Peyton, Tony Jackson, Erskine Tate and others who were then great musicians of the theater. At that time J. Wesley Jones was a great choir director on the West Side of Chicago, presenting programs of Negro Spirituals; and James A. Mundy was directing the choir at old Bethel AME Church at 30th and S. Dearborn Street, while George R. Garner was heading the music at Olivet Baptist Church which at that time was at the corner of 27th and S. Dearborn Street.

These were the directors he held in awe, savoring the chances just to meet them, shake their hands, and say, "I enjoyed your performance."[1]

Apparently Dorsey was not as enamored of the music of these performances as he was of the mere significance of witnessing them. In speaking of Jones, Dorsey noted that he was "good at spirituals, but nobody cared for the anthems."[2] Since these spirituals had been "denatured" and bore little resemblance to the "moaning" spirituals he had heard from childhood or the newer gospel blues he was now advocating for the church, Dorsey likely had little more than a passing appreciation for the spirituals that J. Wesley Jones directed. As for the classical music that Jones programmed, Dorsey's assertion that "nobody" liked it at least has to include himself. Somewhere between his gushy reverence for old-line directors and his lackadaisical attitude toward their music, then, lies the motivation Dorsey possessed to attend their musicales.

The basis of Dorsey's ambivalence toward the musicale is hinted at by the timing of the events he refers to in the above description. When he writes that he "began to hit the nightspots," he is referring to his first years in Chicago: specifically after 1919—as indicated by reference to the Volstead Act (October 1919) and the Chicago race riot of that year—but before 1923, as indicated both by the fact that he was still living at his Uncle's house where he slept "in the back" and by the fact that Metropolitan Church and its musicales were being held in the auditorium of Wendell Phillips High School. That Dorsey began attending these events as a recent migrant is significant in that he was even more prone then—perhaps like other migrants—to have a less than earnest preference for old-line music. In order to understand Dorsey's motivation for attending the musicales, then, one must explore the dynamics of the relationship between migrants and old-line churches.

More likely than not, migrants attended such musicales since many of them were members of old-line churches. It has long been the consensus among investigators that newcomers populated the storefront churches on Chicago's South Side. Supposedly, these churches preserved the old ways, such as the one-man or one-woman style of leadership and emotional demonstrativeness, both of which were thought to be attributes of earlier, more primitive—that is, southern—black religion.[3] These conclusions are accurate insofar as they indicate that migrants were likely to prefer worship similar to that found in their former churches. Statistics show, however, that the actual movement of migrants to storefront churches was not so predictable.

Most recent migrants who sought a church affiliation joined the large old-line congregations that formed the original core group of Baptist and Methodist churches in Chicago. Within this group, Olivet Baptist alone increased its membership by over 11,000 between 1916 and 1921. In 1928, it was the "largest Protestant church in the world," with a membership of just under 15,000. Even the AME churches, which generally did not attract migrants as much as the Baptist ones did, claimed an increase of 5000 during the migration period. Considering that between 1916 and 1926 the average membership of all black churches in the United States changed merely from 116 to 122 persons, and that the first years of this period saw as much as a 150 percent increase in growth in Chicago's new settler population, it is obvious that the equally phenomenal growth in old-line church membership in Chicago was mainly attributable to the increase in the migrant population. These churches continued to swell at an above-average rate well into the 1930s: the average number of members of 56 major black churches in Chicago in 1933 was 1,003.[4] In short, large churches as well as storefronts enjoyed increased memberships attributable to the influx of migrants.

More questionable now, however, are those statistics that show that both storefront and old-line congregations drew from the same group of newcomers. The religious ideology of migrants was apparently not monolithic.

For some, the move north marked the deliberate rejection of their southern culture. In some cases, this included forsaking the church in general. One study showed that "well over one-half" of a group of "lower-class" persons had no church affiliation. Another showed that

> [Although] slightly over half of . . . 100,000 lower-class adults *claim* to be church members, . . . a careful analysis of church records indicates that fewer than a third of the lower-class adults were actually dues-paying members of any church . . . [and that] an even smaller number organized the greater part of their leisure time and their emotional life around the church and religion.

"Lower-class" in both of these studies is a term connotative of recent migrants and those maladjusted to urban living. But these were migrants for whom the move was a continuation of an acculturative process that may be traced to the influence of educated ministers in black southern churches. Many of these ministers were encouraged to adopt white cultural values while being trained in southern black colleges; they, in turn, transmitted these values to members of their congregations.[5]

Almost upon arrival, a southerner such as Dorsey was confronted by merciless reminders that he was the less fortunate, unsophisticated inferior of the northern black, that he came from "filth and uncleanliness," that his ways were crude, and that to be tolerated meant to "keep your mouth shut." In addition, he faced deep resentment that the "price" of his northern presence was increased racial discrimination for all blacks where formerly it had been thought to be nearly absent.[6]

The newspaper that played a major role in instigating the migration, the *Chicago Defender,* was also a major voice in setting standards for migrants' social behavior. In a typical editorial written during the early phase of the migration, the paper admonished old settlers to show concern for this "upheaval of the labor market":

> [Organizations] shall seek to instruct the migrants. As to the dress, habits and methods of living necessary to withstand the rigors of the northern climate. As to the efficiency, regularity and application demanded of workers in the North. . . . Every Race man owes this to himself as well as to the newcomers, for what affects one affect[s] all. . . . It is your burden. Will you take it up?[7]

Any migrant with the slightest disposition toward adopting new, northern ways was almost under a barrage of encouragement to do so. The large migrant presence in old-line churches reflected to some extent these pressures.

Old-line churches functioned, moreover, as more than institutions of worship. As early as World War I, they had established programs to aid new settlers in finding housing and employment. By 1920, the settlement program at Olivet included "a full-time professional staff of sixteen [that] operated a labor bureau, kindergarten, nursery, and welfare department." These churches also sought to provide for migrants' social adjustment. At Pilgrim Baptist Church, the congregation was divided into four "armies," each led by a "general," in order to facilitate contact between old and new members and to provide a network for close contact between the pastor or his staff and every member. The church's most noted pastor, Junius C. Austin, Sr., organized groups of women who served essentially as social workers:

> He would send missionary women out, all in the community, all in the city of Chicago, to find the poor folk who were not getting their due, like food and clothing. And he would beg white organizations to bring clothes here to the church and leave 'em, so they could be given to the poor people every day of the week.

Perhaps one of the most enduring social efforts was the organization of the Home Finders' League by Pilgrim Baptist and several other large churches "to encourage Negroes to buy homes and live in them like they used to down south." In cooperation with the two black-owned banks in Chicago, the Binga State Bank and Douglas National Bank, the League purchased houses and financed them at low rates to "reliable" new settlers.[8]

The storefront congregation was probably less the particular choice of migrants than it was the refuge of the religiously disaffected old settlers and newcomers in general. The large percentage both of non-churched and inactive, church-affiliated, "lower-class" persons who were reported as members of storefronts suggests that those religiously disaffected persons who were migrants more frequently forsook religious organizations altogether rather than created or joined churches that were composed of their own. Indeed, migrants had more reasons than not to dislike the storefront, for it represented not only a return to old social patterns but a return to the church in an authoritarian capacity as an agency of social control. In the North, migrants could engage more in secular life; the church no longer constituted a focal point as it had in the rural communities of the South.[9]

Perhaps the most persuasive evidence in support of viewing religious disaffection rather than migrant religious preferences as the main factor in establishing storefront churches is the fact that groups other than either migrants or those thought to be migrants were establishing religious institutions. Between 1928 and 1938, increases in the size and number of congregations occurred among groups at all social levels. Presbyterian, Disciples of Christ, Seventh-Day Adventist, Roman Catholic, and Lutheran churches, mainly white denominations, grew appreciably in south Chicago, as did the mainly black Holiness and Pentecostal churches. Black congregations of predominantly white denominations were attractive to middle- and upper-class blacks, while Holiness and Pentecostal churches found adherents chiefly among economically deprived groups.[10] Religious disaffection therefore was a motive among widely diverse groups across a range of social strata. It was less pronounced among upper-class groups not necessarily because there was less evidence of their disaffection but because their numbers were minuscule in relation to those of the lower class, and thus their religious mobility was less conspicuous.

Had migrants flocked to the storefront churches, as has been the prevailing notion, their vast numbers alone would have made storefront religion the dominant form of religious expression in the Chicago black community. As it was, only about 10 percent of the "lower-class" adults in Chicago worshipped in storefronts.[11] As with other groups disaffected with old-line religion, migrants weighed the options of forsaking organized religion altogether or building alternative churches against the benefits of an old-line affiliation. They least of all preferred to start new churches.

As the established and major congregations in black Chicago, old-line churches stood at the midpoint of the range of religious expression in the city. Beginning with the first wave of migrants in 1916, these churches served as the religious melting pot of new and old settlers, rural and urban customs, and southern and northern ethoses. Among the reasons given by those dissidents who elected to leave old-line churches was the desire to define more sharply a philosophy of worship. But this vagueness of ethos—the compromise between extremes—was precisely the source of the wide appeal of these churches. Theirs was a consensual religion: in the face of rising numbers of migrants in their congregations, old-line churches found compromise critical to their survival as black Chicago's most populous religious institutions. Because of the social backgrounds of the leadership and the urban locale of these churches, a distinct northern ethos—classical music, non-demonstrativeness, subdued preaching—enjoyed an uncontested prominence. As early as 1920, however, this old-line spirit was threatened by the sheer size of the southern invasion. The "mingling" of old and new may have been tentative and conciliatory at first, but it soon became an element of old-line stability.

From 1920 on, old-line religion was shaped by the mounting sociocultural impact of migrant southerners. Descriptions of the churches show that the shift to an ethos of compromise was at first subtle. In the early 1920s, old-line churches were described as having "not completely discarded the emotionalism of traditional Negro religion," but definitely as moving "toward a more decorous order of worship and a program of broad social concern." By the late 1920s, they were "transition" centers, with a "strange mingling of the old and the new," but where there was still the attempt to do away with "rural practices." This was indicated by few if any "'amens,' shoutings, [or] spirituals [as opposed to hymn singing]." By the late 1930s, these churches would be identified as "mixed-type" or "mass" because their leaders faced the problem of holding the "allegiance of 'shouters' and 'non-shouters.'" This tension was relieved only by having a "variety of organizations and activities" and "by modifying the ritual so as to put the older middle-class people and the lower-class members at ease." One other "concession" in these churches by the middle 1930s would be the "gospel chorus," organized to provide music other than the hymns and anthems of the senior choir.[12]

Each of these shifts coincided with or was followed by a high point in the influx of southerners. The largest increase occurred in a short period of years, 1916 to 1918: Chicago's black population grew by nearly 50 percent. The longest period of uninterrupted migration occurred between 1920 and 1930, as the black population moved from 4 to 7 percent of Chicago's 3.3 million people.[13]

From its beginning, the compromise ethos seems to have been determined by the increase in congregational participation. Here was potentially the most divisive issue for the congregations of old-line churches: where spirited emotion was the hallmark of traditional black worship, minimal congregational response epitomized the northern services. As migrant membership rose, the degree of compromise could be measured by how much noise—shouting, "amens," and moaning—could be heard in worship. The resulting ethos, however, could be characterized as more a truce than a compromise. Until the gospel chorus became widespread, proponents of traditional worship seemed generally satisfied with expressing themselves in response to preaching, while those who advocated old-line customs seemed assured that their standard of worship was upheld by the music of the choir.

Preaching was almost inevitably a touchstone for those of southern orientation. The black preacher had historically been the central figure of black religion; crucial to this centrality was his ability to improvise his sermons. The measure of this improvisatory skill was the intensity of emotion that the preacher aroused within his listeners, who in turn would "bear [him] up" by various verbal and physical responses. Recently arrived southerners, fresh from religious experiences of this nature, came to old-line churches looking to the preacher as the focal point of the worship service. Northerners were not totally disinclined to centralize the preacher, for the minister among blacks—regardless of their regional orientation—held a "unique place" because of his "divine sanction." The difference between northerners' and southerners' relationships to their preachers lay chiefly in how much to "bear him up."[14]

When migrants first arrived, old-line ministers seem to have adopted the attitude that emotionalism, if tempered, would be tolerated. Around 1915, Elijah J. Fisher, pastor of Olivet Baptist Church, "believed in enthusiastic religion but did not countenance a church in demoniac pandemonium." By the end of the 1920s, Junius C. Austin, Sr., pastor of Pilgrim Baptist Church, believed his success hinged on keeping the congregation "dignified" but giving them "what they wanted in the pulpit." Thus he appears to have utilized the techniques of folk preaching while at the same time allowing only the response he thought appropriate to the urban church. According to his son, Junius C. Austin, Jr.:

> He was a university educated man, but he had the ability to make the people hang on his words. He had a voice that was [as] sharp as an eagle's call. He knew how to lift it and modulate it. He would scream; he was like a moving target. But he didn't let them [the congregation] holler; he kept them quiet.

By the late 1930s, Austin's strategy was the practice of "most of the very large congregations and many of the medium-sized churches" in black Chicago:

> To satisfy middle-class members, an astute pastor of a mixed-type church will present a "prepared message" with moral and ethical exhortation and intelligent allusions to current affairs; but he will also allow his lower-class members to shout a little. Such shouting is usually rigidly controlled, however, so that it does not dominate the service.[15]

Old-line pastors were forced to cultivate such conflicting roles because the pre-eminence of the ministry was increasingly threatened by the rise of an educated class. Even if a minister was a seminary or college graduate, or both, his education was usually less than that required for professions such as law, dentistry, or medicine. To old settlers their minister was to "win leadership by achievement, and not by virtue of his profession." The deference northerners gave a minister for his academic credentials was matched by the southerners' respect for his preaching. With migrants as the largest source of new members, and with a large membership "a measure of his status and influence, not to mention his control of economic resources," the northern preacher could afford to risk offending his old settlers by indulging—at least cautiously—the religious expression of his new settlers. Thus the position that old-line preachers occupied as the very sinews of compromise between competing ethoses and diverse publics was apparently cultivated to ensure not only congregational unity but a large following as well.[16]

Dorsey's uncertainties about the Sunday musicale are understandable when one considers this mixed religion of old-line churches. Most migrants were drawn into the old-line milieu by the social-welfare programs these churches conducted. But because of his music background, Dorsey discovered old-lineism through the musicale. It made little difference which entry he chose: to elevate one migrant like Dorsey by exposing him to Rossini and Beethoven was the analogue of feeding, clothing, and housing another. The churches—in their self-interest as well as in that of their newly arrived backward charges—proceeded gradually: they let newcomers shout a bit during worship and rock a bit during the musicale. The tasteful sermon and denatured spiritual alike were placebos administered to ease the pain of assimilation.

Migrants eagerly gulped down these doses of social and cultural medicine to the extent that they could be considered virtual co-conspirators in their deculturation. They flocked to the Sunday morning worship knowing that their praises would be all but silenced by the minister; a few hours later they stood in line for the chance to hear music they not only failed to understand but knew in advance they would not enjoy. Ambitious ones among them like Dorsey were flushed with gratitude when a J. Wesley Jones or Edward Boatner would deign to extend a hand. They intended for their arduous treks north to bypass the storefronts with their earnest moaners, continuing but for a few more blocks to the citadels of black urban religion, wherein dignity could be found basking in the strains of *All Hail the Power of Jesus' Name.*

For Dorsey, striking parallels existed between the standards old-line churches had set for migrants and the goals he had set for his own career. He would have come as close to a dead end in his quest to become an urban sophisticate had he continued to play downhome spirituals in New Hope Baptist church as he nearly did by crooning his downhome blues in wine rooms and at rent parties. Later he aspired to denature his blues and dress them up for the marketplace just as Work had succeeded in polishing up the original spiritual for the educated Negro. At about the same time he began to nimble up his fingers to play "jass" in the high-toned clubs, he started attending Metropolitan's musicales at Wendell Phillips High School. The ordeal of listening to Bach and Burleigh was no less than the strenuous practice it took to learn the "peppy" new riffs of "jass." Nor were the rewards less tangible: he could shake J. Wesley Jones's hand at Wendell Phillips on Sunday afternoon and Erskine Tate's at the Original Home of Jazz the next morning. Clearly, the resonance between Dorsey and the musicale echoed throughout many aspects of his life.

His return to downhome blues resounded just as clearly through his old-line experience. With the unexpected deflection of his career away from synthetic blues, Dorsey came to realize that many of his newfound values were similarly fabricated. This is the point at which he began to see the significance of blues in worship. The depth of feeling and the oneness between performer and audience that he helped create night after night with Ma Rainey were sadly missing from both the Sunday morning service and the musicale. The incongruity of his two lives as an aspiring urbanite feigning an appreciation for music and as an established bluesman pricking the hearts of his listeners was too glaring to continue, no matter what the benefit.

Clearly, there is a parallel between Dorsey's return to downhome secular blues and his advocacy of religious blues. But this return only caused him to reconsider his sycophancy to old-line values. It directly explains neither his motivation to write religious blues nor what emboldened him to take these blues into old-line churches. In order to understand why Dorsey confronted old-line churches instead of withdrawing, say, to a storefront, one should understand one of the most significant underpinnings of his religious conversion: his goal was not to alter the music of old-line churches but rather to dedicate his music talent to God. Dorsey assumed that the talent he had used—or misused—in order to become a blues musician was intended by God for the church. Talent was a gift from God and he was now God's instrument. Thus he felt that God, not Dorsey, was the perpetrator of change:

> No, I wasn't trying to change it [church music], but I was just struck with something that would change it over, something that the Lord gave me. *He* wanted it. *He* accepted it; I got my authority from God.[17]

But even this explanation belies somewhat the motivation Dorsey found to carry out what amounted to an outright change in church music. To attempt to restore blues to the church worship from which it had been expunged so effectively was nothing short of a revolutionary act. Within the first months of demonstrating his "gospels," Dorsey became well aware that he was in fact an agitator for change on such a fundamental level that the very standing order of old-line churches appeared to be threatened. Thus Dorsey's reference to divine assistance is in essence his attempt to explain the new harmony between blues and religion in his life, symbolizing the end of the conflict between his career and his religion.

As described earlier, this struggle was rooted in the two contrasting approaches to religion Dorsey saw as a child. His father, the preacher, practiced a theatrical, at times flamboyant, religion by carrying a cane and resorting to dramatic displays in the pulpit. His mother, as organist and Sunday school teacher, was as prominent in the church as his father. But her acts of kindness to strangers, her reading of the Bible, and her leadership of the family in daily worship made deeper impressions on him. He later summarized these qualities as her "quenchless fidelity."[18] Her image was a subtle, but powerful, beckoning to a life of piety.

That Dorsey favored his father's showy manner of devotion is evident in his conversion in 1921 when he was captivated by W. M. Nix's singing at the National Baptist Convention. Much of the significance Dorsey placed on Nix's singing can be traced to his childhood idolization of a similar role his father played in the pulpit. His father's preaching is among his most vivid memories of Villa Rica. The small cane his parents gave him when he was four to carry as his father did was certainly a symbol that they encouraged his enchantment with his father's vocation. Dorsey was further charmed by the pulpit because of his impressions of his father's prestige as a preacher and his own vicarious sense of importance as a preacher's son. Now as a young man in a burst of post-conversion euphoria, Dorsey became a pianist in a small Baptist church where he was able to captivate the congregation in much the same manner his father and Nix had. This experience he likened to his earlier blues playing in honky-tonks where, as pianist, he was "king of the night." For all intents and purposes, he was a preacher like Nix and his father, but at the piano, leading the congregation and ornamenting the hymns. He could compensate for having forsaken his blues by indulging in the same sort of dramatic display he had found attractive in a secular context, doing so now as a pianist in a sacred one. Such emulation, however, was apparently a weak foundation on which to build a religious commitment: Dorsey lost interest and accepted an invitation to join the Whispering Syncopators. Playing the piano in church lacked the pervasiveness of spirituality Dorsey idolized in his mother's practice of religion. Daily devotion was the essence of that religious commitment; he admitted as much when just before his conversion he said, "I thought more seriously about God than I had in many years, though I was a confessed believer and went to church."[19]

His second conversion in 1928 was brought on by a strong sense that he had to change his way of life. The resulting commitment to channel his compositional energies into religious music—even though the music itself was still blues—was tantamount to taking a vow of piety. Indeed, for Dorsey to refrain from the blues of the sort to which he had been practically wedded for most of his life signified his acquiescence to a form of musical celibacy. When he heeded the call by pledging to re-orient the message of his songs, his "trouble" was over:

> . . . I began to write songs. Not the blues and double-meaning songs that we played for the Saturday night parties, but songs of hope and faith, spiritual songs and gospel hymns. This was the turning point in my life.[20]

For all that his God required him to discard or alter fundamentally, Dorsey was able to hold fast to the blues as the stylistic medium for the texts of his songs. These in turn became expressions of his new outlook on life. Dorsey the showy pulpiteer and Dorsey the genuine devotee—though no less antithetical as personifications of the competing religious tendencies in his life—were now unified in purpose.

Now Dorsey could act on the notion that religion was both a way of life and the cultivation of an image. His practice of religion had been only a veiled recognition of the former and a troubled flirtation with the latter. In essence, his newfound "dedication" and "consecration" were his belated discovery that style and substance are not necessarily mutually exclusive components of religion. At last he understood that to maintain his psychic equilibrium, he would have to grant equal sway to both forces. The prospect of such inner harmony sent Dorsey almost headlong into his mission to bring gospel blues into old-line churches. At first armed with only two of his "gospels," he went to do battle with Rossini, Beethoven, and Mendelssohn, as well as Dett and Burleigh and all the institutional supports that were solidly in place by 1928 to protect and nurture the culture and religion of which Dorsey's gospel blues was the antithesis. Dorsey could have been inspired to undertake such a formidable challenge singlehandedly only if he were convinced that his life was in order and that he was at peace with himself, that is, that he had "authority from God."

If this religious truce can be said to have given Dorsey the courage to challenge the old-line music establishment, it was his earlier experience with the revitalization of downhome blues that provided him with the assurance that that style was an appropriate form of music for those churches. Dorsey could well remember that the strength of the resurgence of the older style of blues was a surprise to almost everyone in the business. Recordings by Bessie Smith and Ma Rainey exceeded all sales expectations. Because of the success of their records, Smith and Rainey now performed in the theaters and clubs that had been the exclusive domains of vaudeville blues artists who were considered the higher class singers. Dorsey knew, therefore, that downhome secular blues was a powerful medium even outside the rent parties, wine rooms, and honky-tonks in which it was usually performed. To Dorsey these traditional contexts for the older blues were comparable to the storefront for the older style of religion. As he had worked his way out of them and ultimately had been able to carry the music with him, he could now expect to remain in old-line churches and convince them of the virtues of the older music—no matter how formidable the challenge.

Dorsey's adaptation to the old-line environment also sheds light on this point. He found the deculturative process of old-lineism no less undesirable than most of the migrants who willingly subjected themselves to it. It was, nevertheless, the ticket to acceptance and a means of social advancement, both overarching goals since his first days in Atlanta. Surely the price of his religious conversion was not to have to lose the ground he had gained, be it in one of the fashionable theaters or the upscale churches. His music was no exception: if he could be dignified, why not his blues?

Armed with a divine decree, Dorsey should have been able to introduce his new old music with little difficulty. Instead, he failed miserably. In less than a year after he had sworn off secular blues, he was back in the business. Much of his lack of success can be traced to the seemingly inconsequential decision to write out his songs and print them for distribution.

The move to make printed copies of his music was rooted in Dorsey's previous blues experience. As an arranger, he was often engaged to write a version of a piece for copyright. Royalties on recorded songs could not be paid until the music or some arrangement of it had been copyrighted. As a composer, Dorsey knew to take the precaution of filing his pieces for copyright.[21] But Dorsey's composition and arranging skills were applied only as extensions of the sound recording process. The medium of distribution was the phonograph record, not printed music. Indeed, the rise of the recording industry had caused the near demise of the sheet-music industry.

As Dorsey recalls it, he accidentally came by the idea of notating and printing his songs especially in the one-page, single-side format with which he began:

> In 1925, Chas. H. Pace and his Pace Jubilee Singers made a Victor phonograph record of the song, "I'm Going Through Jesus," which became very popular and sold into the millions. The record company would not pay the royalties on the basis that the song was not published and there was no sheet music for it. Therefore, Mr. Pace made an arrangement and had a few one-sheet copies printed to collect the royalties. After the royalties were collected, the remainder of the copies were thrown into the waste basket. I got an idea. I retrieved the copies from the waste basket and said this is the type of copy on which I will publish my songs; I did. Not only did I, but hundreds of other writers [of gospel songs] did the same.[22]

There was a basic flaw in Dorsey's decision to go to print. In essence it constituted a rejection of a key element of his thought on both secular and sacred blues: he believed in the concept of "susceptibility," or the performer's right to alter the music according to the dictates of her feeling.[23] The sheet of music, therefore, was a faulty indicator of the actual sound of the music, and it was all but superfluous during performance.

But Dorsey was not acting solely on a whim after retrieving Pace's music from the wastebasket. He had at least two reasons to believe that printing his sacred music was a wise decision despite his earlier career and his new philosophy. For one, the publication of sacred music in Chicago was certainly not without precedent by 1928: Chicago was a major location of the sacred music industry. Indeed, between 1900 and the early 1920s, "gospel" publishers were the most prominent members of Chicago's music publishing industry.[24] Second, Dorsey's publication in 1922 of *If I Don't Get There* in *Gospel Pearls* and in 1924 of *We Will Meet Him in the Sweet By and By* in the *Baptist Hymnal* along with the broad circulation of those collections of songs amounted to firm evidence of the viability of printing and selling sacred music.

Had Dorsey recalled his reasons for ceasing to publish his blues in 1923, however, he might have initiated this venture more cautiously. His attempts then at packaging his Handy-style blues had come to naught as the sales of records, especially of the downhome variety, began to escalate. With his customary zeal, nevertheless, he began his gospel blues ministry by printing over 1000 copies of each of his first gospel blues, *If You See My Savior* and *Someday, Somewhere,* and going forth to "make a market" for them.[25]

No matter the ploy—including Dorsey's personal demonstration of his songs from church to church—purchasers failed to appear in adequate numbers for him to assume that he had started a trend. He mailed promotional copies of each piece to over 1000 churches listed in a Baptist publication called the *Foreign Mission Herald*. He enlisted a few ministers and musicians to go from door to door selling the songs. He even placed copies beside the cash register in his uncle's drugstore. Since Dorsey was not there to sell them, however, few were bought. In addition, the money from those sales was handled carelessly, leaving Dorsey justifiably open to the accusation, "You have something here, but you don't know what to do with it."[26]

These efforts amounted to little or no success in creating a demand for printed gospel blues. Indeed, Dorsey failed to gain a return on his initial investment:

> . . . many times I walked through the snow from church to church until my feet were soaked. . . . I was very thankful to God for a good day when I had a dollar and a half in my pockets to take home to Nettie. . . . After all of this distributing through the mail, all of the plugging away on the songs in different churches, giving out free copies for advertisement, it was over two years before I got an answer, order or reply of any kind. Then some churches sent in a few small orders for songs, but not enough to make a market trend or even to reimburse me for expenses.[27]

For all the qualities attributable to written gospel blues, it was still an inadequate medium. Ironically, Dorsey needed only to listen to his own thought about his sacred blues to understand why so few people who saw a copy of his music were impressed. The music as notated—especially without embellishments—was innocuous. Even a cursory comparison of Example 6-1, *If You See My Savior,* as printed, Example 6-2, as Dorsey recorded it in 1932 with his former blues partner, Hudson Whitaker, and Example 6-3, as he plays it alone, shows, as Dorsey believed, that the printed music, beyond the text, failed even to approximate that which was performed. Almost every quality that provided the animus of gospel blues was absent from its notated form. Even more serious, when he performed his written gospels according to the notation, he limited his own expressiveness. One can look at the ending of the first phrase in Example 6-1 (m. 6) and see that, compared with the same place in Example 6-3 (mm. 4-5), it is uneventful. The grace notes on "neighbor" and the three repetitions of the right-hand figure in the following measure are vintage downhome blues embellishments. Dorsey avoided these flights of improvisation and performed his new gospels more like Example 6-1. In playing Example 6-1, he had simply repressed his blues personality. In his days as a showman, Dorsey's blues music was but an extension of Dorsey the bluesman. He became "king of the night" *through* his "ivories." When he played for Ma Rainey, he realized that the sheer power of her personality was communicated through her songs in such a way that "she possessed her listeners." Even as an accompanist he felt the power to "sway" his audience.

Having tempered and perhaps even denied this element of self-projection when performing his written gospel blues—especially self-projection as a means of controlling his listeners—Dorsey then proceeded to hire a "sweet singer" named Louise Keller to demonstrate his songs. Dorsey chose this

Ex. 6-1

If You See My Saviour (original)

mm. 1-3

I was stand-ing by the bed-side of a neigh-bor,—Who was

mm. 4-6

Ex. 6-1 (cont.)

mm. 7-8

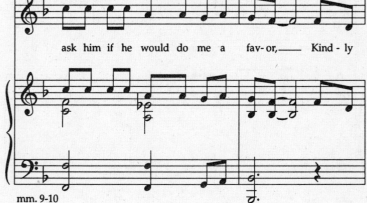

mm. 9-10

Ex. 6-1 (cont.)

mm. 11-12

mm. 13-14

Ex. 6-1 (cont.)

mm. 15-16

mm. 17-18

Ex. 6-1 (cont.)

I   am   com - ing   home   some   day.

mm. 19-20

woman because of his desire to blend his music with that in old-line churches. Keller sang in the "hymn style; she was one of them high-class singers—
had a lovely voice." This performance style complemented his written-out
gospel blues in that it was non-improvisational. She refused or was unable to
"beat them [gospel blues] out" or to put "those turns and moans and things
in there."[28] Her performances, as were Dorsey's with his notated music, were
insipid; they violated his principles of gospel blues. If she sang the notes as
written in Example 6-1, measures 8 and 9, one can clearly see that she could
not have generated the same feeling as compared with Dorsey's true blues
performance of the same part of the phrase in measures 9 through 12 in
Example 6-3. Dorsey's leap of a perfect fifth provides a dramatic underpin-
ning to the question being asked in the text. With Keller's unexpressive
style—at least unexpressive in a blues sense—Dorsey, as her accompanist,
was limited. He could work neither with her nor through her to "sway" his
audiences as he had been accustomed to do. The bluesman in him was
repressed.

Thus his failure to get his music accepted could have been expected with
the first stroke of his pen to write a gospel song. He so fundamentally
disguised his new music in both form and practice that it represented neither
an alternative to the prevailing musical fare of old-line churches nor a contrast to black traditional music. He followed this by obscuring the role of the
bluesman so much that the nexus between blues and religion that he had so

Ex. 6-2

If You See My Saviour (Dorsey and Whitaker)

Ex. 6-2 (cont.)

Ex. 6-2 (cont.)

Ex. 6-2 (cont.)

Ex. 6-2 (cont.)

m. 18

carefully forged with his conversion was now profoundly weakened. In essence, the old-line deculturative process had worked on this migrant. He stood too much in awe of it to proclaim through his gospel songs—with "authority from God"—the return to the true Afro-American religious song he knew old-line churches needed—especially with their ever-bulging migrant congregations.

For all of the negative qualities of Dorsey's notated gospel song, however, his initial decision to write down the music would ultimately prove problematic only because it was premature, not unwise. In Chicago, no publisher of black sacred music existed at the time Dorsey started; thus when he did begin to distribute his music as a business, he operated without competition.[29] The decision was wise because the songs, once written and copyrighted, were the sole property of Dorsey. He learned the value of this procedure from his popular blues experience and wasted no time in applying it to his gospel blues. From the beginning of the record of written gospel blues, therefore, particularly in old-line churches, Thomas A. Dorsey was the most significant name.

The most far-reaching benefit of Dorsey's decision to write gospel blues grew out of his decision to sell them; yet Dorsey could not have drawn on previous experience for this idea. The printing and distribution of popular music had been replaced by recordings. Possibly the only explanation for Dorsey's urge to market printed gospel blues was his awareness that he might be unsuccessful in his attempts to interest the recording industry in his new music. Although his gospel songs were blues, they were not to benefit from the results of blues' popularity, namely, a somewhat ready-made market and a medium of distribution. Thus Dorsey acted prudently in 1928 by making printed music the medium of distribution of gospel blues. Each person who heard a piece of gospel blues had an equal opportunity to own it. In years to come, when Dorsey would head a large gospel-publishing

Ex. 6-3

If You See My Saviour (Dorsey)

mm. 1-2

mm. 3-4

Ex. 6-3 (cont.)

Ex. 6-3 (cont.)

mm. 9-10

And— I asked him———— if he would do—

—— me a fa- vor,———

mm. 11-12

Ex. 6-3 (cont.)

mm. 13-14

mm. 15-16

Ex. 6-3 (cont.)

mm. 17-18

Now if you see my Sav - ior, tell

mm. 19-20

Him that you saw me,

Ex. 6-3 (cont.)

mm. 21-22

mm. 23-24

Ex. 6-3 (cont.)

mm. 25-26

mm. 27-28

Ex. 6-3 (cont.)

mm. 29-30

mm. 31-33 (8*vb*) loco

empire with an army of salespersons peddling his song sheets in most major cities across the United States and when he would see others copy and profit from his selling techniques, the simple but profound wisdom of printing and selling the music became evident. In essence Dorsey made the song sheet the currency of gospel music. The large money-making enterprise it became attests to the soundness of this move.

These long-range benefits aside, however, Dorsey's initial failure to make an impact was swift and overwhelming. So much so, that by September 1928, scarcely a year following his commitment to writing sacred blues, he was not only re-ensconced in his former career but was well into launching a related one as a recording artist. If copyright records are an indication, he returned to composition and arranging as early as August, when he registered *When You're in Love* (words by William Wilkin) on August 2, 1928. He wrote this song in the Tin Pan Alley, sentimental, popular style instead of the rural/urban blues style for which he was more widely known. Considering his copyrighting of this piece and the job he had recently obtained "arranging music for talent who came in to record their songs" at the Brunswick Recording Company, Dorsey not only had re-entered his blues career but had done so prominently: Brunswick was one of the six major companies issuing blues recordings during the "peak years" of the industry.[30]

Dorsey's return to secular blues was prompted not so much by the result of his failure to sell his gospels as it was by the opportunity to earn a quick dollar:

> One night a young man [Hudson Whitaker] came to my home. He had some words written down and wanted me to write the music and arrange a melody to his words. My wife cleared the dishes from the supper table and I looked over the words; the title of the song was "It's Tight Like That." I looked it over carefully and told him I did not do that kind of music anymore. I was now giving all of [my] time to gospel songs. But he prevailed with me to make a melody. After a long period of persuasion and much discussion, he said, "But there is big money in it if it clicks." I looked around at our poor furnishings and our limited wearing apparel. "Come on, once more won't matter," he said quietly with a smile.
>
> I reached over and took the lyrics from his hand. In no time I had written the harmony and melody and worked out a score ready to be played. We took it to Vocalion Recording Company the next day. We played and sang it for them and they were enthusiastic over the song and at once cut a wax record and rushed it through the finishing process.

The first check for royalties for *It's Tight Like That* amounted to $2,400.19. Over the next four months, Dorsey and Whitaker had recorded two more versions.[31] Dorsey's relapse into secular blues seemed even more justified to him when, as a result of his substantial earnings, he found himself able to provide more adequately for Nettie:

> I rushed home after we had cashed the check, gave my wife a couple of hundred dollars, then took her down to an exclusive vogue shop. There I bought her some new clothes in appreciation for the sacrifice she had made for me when I was ill and could not help myself.[32]

It's Tight Like That began Dorsey and Whitaker's recording success. The combination of Whitaker playing the guitar and Dorsey the piano was a new and apparently welcomed contrast to the piano or small wind ensembles that accompanied most blues. Since only one other identical instrumental combination had preceded that of Dorsey and Whitaker and numerous similar duos appeared within months, Georgia Tom and Tampa Red (their recording names) are credited with setting a precedent within the recording industry.[33]

More important than the new instrumental configuration was the double entendre of *It's Tight Like That*. Double meaning was a device long-noted for being abundant throughout the song literature of Afro-Americans. Two collectors of "negro songs" wrote about this genre just two years before Dorsey and Whitaker's recording of *It's Tight Like That:*

> It is to be regretted that a great mass of material cannot be published because of its vulgar and indecent content. . . . they [these songs] represent the superlative of the repulsive. The prevailing theme is that of sexual relations, and there is no restraint in expression. In comparison with the indecency that has come to light in the vulgar songs of other peoples, those of the Negro stand out undoubtedly in a class of their own.[34]

Until Dorsey and Whitaker's 1928 recording, however, these blues evidently remained in the recesses of black culture. Their status of being known but unrecorded can be traced most obviously to the question of taste and possibly to the fact that the traditional channels through which they were communicated were sufficient to keep them before the public that wanted to hear them. It is thus unclear why Vocalion would begin to record these songs except that the record companies dictated tastes by deciding what they would like to market. Whatever the reasons, the public "went wild" over *It's Tight Like That* and a host of other cunningly "erotic" blues, a number of which Dorsey wrote and recorded (for example, *Pat That Bread, You Got That Stuff, Where Did You Stay Last Night?, It's All Worn Out,* and *Somebody's Been Using That Thing*). Dorsey and Whitaker called their guitar/piano, suggestive blues style "hokum" and recorded under the name of the "Famous Hokum Boys" for Paramount and other recording companies. Between 1928 and 1932, Dorsey, as featured soloist or as part of the team of Georgia Tom and Tampa Red, made over sixty recordings.[35]

Something almost diabolical lurked beneath Dorsey's sudden rise to fame as a secular blues artist precisely at the time he had forsworn such music. From the night he granted sway to Whitaker's beguiling argument, "Come on, once more won't matter," and wrote the score to *It's Tight Like That,* Dorsey became entangled in a Faustian web of circumstances. The lure to leave gospel blues had been cast with fateful precision—indeed, within his grasp—and baited with the possible fulfillment of his deepest craving: to become a famous bluesman. As did the biblical Esau at the smell of a mess of lentils, Dorsey showed no restraint of his hunger to attain wealth and notoriety. In return for these apparent gains, he bartered his new birthright: his salvation through his God.

He could never feel comfortable with his new popularity, however, knowing that he had compromised his beliefs for it. Within a "few months," the bank in which Dorsey had deposited his first royalties "went broke and closed," thus causing him to lose most of his earnings from his new venture into blues. He had almost awaited such swift and justifiable retribution for his self-indulgent repudiation of his mission to establish gospel blues:

> . . . my wife came to console me after these great losses. She said, "My dear, you promised God that you would write only sacred music when you were ill and you have broken your promise when you wrote the song for Whitaker. It paid well. But God was displeased and suffered you to lose it all in the bank crash." I said, "That is right, dear, and I shall from this day dedicate my life to gospel songs only."[36]

But his penitence was short-lived. Dorsey recorded secular blues another four years until Nettie's unexpected death in August 1932. During this time, gospel blues became a secondary commitment. To some extent the problems inherent in selling printed gospel blues contributed to Dorsey's equivocation. But the financial stability and widespread fame that the blues world had granted him constituted gnawing temptations to compromise his earlier resolve. From the economic point of view, Dorsey could argue that gospel blues simply failed to support him and Nettie. In addition, he had written many blues that still "paid off": "I gave up writing, but I didn't give up what I had written." His reputation as an arranger, moreover, accounted for much of the pressure to lay aside his gospel blues: "I've had them to come to me and say, 'Can you help me out on this?' I'd say, 'Well I promised I wasn't gonna write anymore blues.'" Judging by his burgeoning blues career, he did little to hold himself to this promise.[37]

The Dorsey family in 1905. Thomas Madison Dorsey, seated; Etta Dorsey holding the youngest child, Lovie; standing beside Etta is Mr. Coefield, a boarder; in front, Thomas Andrew (left) and Lloyd. *From the Dorsey family papers.*

Nettie Harper in 1923, three years before her marriage to Dorsey. *From the Dorsey family papers.*

Gertrude "Ma" Rainey (center), Dorsey (far right), and unidentified musicians in her Georgia Band, a later variant of her Wild Cats Jazz Band which Dorsey organized for her in 1924. *From the Dorsey family papers.*

Dorsey in 1928, widely known by his recording name, Georgia Tom. *From the Dorsey family papers.*

Pilgrim Baptist Church Gospel Chorus soon after Dorsey founded it in February 1932. Mabel Mitchell Hamilton Davis (center front), the pianist; the Reverend Augustus A. Evans (Hamilton's left), assistant director; and Dorsey (Hamilton's right), director. *From the Dorsey family papers.*

Dorsey's Female Gospel Quartette which he organized in 1934. Standing, right to left: Sallie Martin, Mattie Wilson, Dettie Gay, and Bertha Armstrong. Dorsey is seated. *From the Dorsey family papers.*

Dorsey and Mahalia Jackson in 1939 in Dorsey's studio in Chicago. *From the Dorsey family papers.*

Dorsey, ca. 1982. *From the Dorsey family papers.*

7

Preachers
and Bluesmen:
1928–1931

If Dorsey had been the only source for gospel song, there might never have been a gospel blues movement—especially in old-line churches. He could never have mustered the extensive resources to bring about the radical change of tastes required for widespread acceptance of gospel blues. As it was, however, the practice of promoting the gospel through a musical medium was somewhat widespread before Dorsey adopted it. Other than his use of blues, Dorsey makes no claim to the term "gospel music":

> Now, I didn't originate the word gospel, I want you to know. I didn't originate that word. Gospel, the word "gospel" has been used down through the ages. But I took the word, took a group of singers, or one singer, as far as that's concerned, and I embellished [gospel], made it beautiful, more noticeable, more susceptible with runs and trills and moans in it. That's really one of the reasons my folk called it gospel music.

The phrase "gospel music" was used extensively by the end of the nineteenth century. Ira Sankey, music director of the revival campaigns conducted by the great late-nineteenth-century evangelist, Dwight L. Moody, claims to have witnessed the origination of the phrase "to sing the gospel" in Sunderland, England, in 1873.[1]

Especially among black Baptists, the term "gospel" was linked to music. In a broad sense the title of the first published song book of the National Baptist Convention, *Gospel Pearls*, indicates that the practice of conveying the gospel through song was accepted by the denomination's music leaders by 1921. More specifically, in the preface these same leaders wrote of *Gospel Pearls* as being a "boon to Gospel singers." The phrases "gospel singer" and "gospel solo" began to appear regularly in the minutes of the Convention as early as 1925. There in Baltimore, a "gospel solo, 'Happy with Jesus Alone,'" was sung by Miss E. V. McKinley of Georgia; furthermore, a

"Brother" William Lewis was noted in the minutes as being "the gospel singer." In general, the term was applied to any person whose singing was an integral part of her or his evangelism and who received a fair amount of notoriety as a singer at the Convention. Indeed, this evangelistic connotation of gospel singing among black Baptists comports with Dorsey's later application of it and thus may be considered evidence that his "gospels" had direct antecedents in the music hierarchy of the Baptist church, the denomination with which most of the old-line churches were affiliated.[2]

Ironically for Dorsey, the term was even more widely used in the race record industry. Since 1921 religious quartet singing had been recorded. Known at first as "jubilee" singers, the quartets—as they grew more popular—became known as "gospel quartets." In 1927, one year before Dorsey began writing his gospel music, more than 70 quartet records were issued, and with the exception of the Depression years, no less than 30 such records were produced almost every year until 1941. This makes the gospel quartet tradition one of the longest in recording history.[3]

Not only did the term "gospel" apply to quartets in a manner similar to the way Dorsey applied it to his songs, but their music reflected his philosophy of religious blues as closely. The thin line between blues and jubilee music is evident in the recorded works of the Norfolk Jubilee Quartet: they recorded as the Norfolk Jazz Singers as well. In their September 1927 recording of *His Eye Is on the Sparrow,* one can hear the same active bass line, tight syncopation, and close harmonies that are present in their March 1921 recording of *Monday Morning Blues.* Indeed, at a later session in July 1921, they recorded five blues songs including *Big Fat Mamma* and *Strut Miss Lizzie* and then two religious songs: *Who Built the Ark?* and *I Hope I May Join the Band.* The OKeh release of these sacred songs listed the Norfolk Jubilee Quartet, while the other songs were released under the quartet's jazz name. The significance here is that, with the exception of the text of their songs and the name on their records, the quartet's music differed little from sacred to secular pieces. Thus the melding of religious and popular song that Dorsey found so meaningful in 1928 had precedent not only within African American culture but also in the highly commercialized propagation of those styles of music found in the recording industry.[4]

Clearly, there was black "gospel music" and an accompanying notoriety for those who performed it both before and during the period Dorsey sought to introduce his gospel songs. Just as clearly, Dorsey's genteel performances with his "sweet" singer masked the very qualities of his gospel songs that would link them to what was currently known as gospel music. At some point, Dorsey realized the futility of this attempt to moderate his music before it was even recognized and before it could be identified as a part of the gospel song tradition. The key to gaining a more favorable reception for his songs, therefore, was for Dorsey to get a voice similar to the ones known for singing gospel songs—the itinerant evangelistic singer or the blues artist.

Thus it is in pursuit of the right singer that one finds Dorsey first trying to improve the acceptance of his music.

More than any other asset, including the ability to improvise, a blues singer had to possess a certain quality of voice:

> . . . smooth and heavy. I don't want a husky [voice] where you have those scratches in it. It takes a heavy voice. If you want to make a good blues singer, the texture of the voice, the heavier the voice, woman or man, the better the blues. If you goin' to be a good gospel singer, the choice of texture of the voice is heavy. The heavier the voice, the better singer you make.[5]

As one would expect, Dorsey first sought the most obvious person with this quality of voice, namely a professional blues vocalist. For a while, he worked with Rebecca Talbot, a singer who "used to be in show business." But his plan called not only for a blues type voice but, more important, for a person committed to the gospel message of his songs. For this reason, Talbot, as a blues singer, served more of a stop-gap role: someone to enhance the performance, if not the ideals, of his gospel music.

But there was a more obvious resource to which Dorsey could turn to find singers of and for the gospel: the Baptist church with its singing evangelists—the acknowledged "gospel singers" of his day. While demonstrating his songs at a meeting one night, Dorsey heard a Reverend E. H. Hall, a local singing preacher. As Dorsey remembers it, Hall "took the show." Dorsey was so impressed that he offered Hall the opportunity ". . . to come along with me, 'I play for you and you sing my songs for me.'" This chance meeting proved one of the most significant steps Dorsey would make toward gaining acceptance for his gospel blues, for in traditional Afro-American culture the association between the bluesman and the preacher has been mutually supportive.[6]

One can examine the roots of the preacher-bluesman relationship by understanding certain aspects of some earlier forms of black American music. Traditional Afro-American solo and group vocal music have served separate functions and thus, for the most part, were performed in different contexts. Beginning with slavery, most documentary evidence indicates that singing among black Americans was a "communal" activity—whether in work, social, or religious settings. This is not to say that slaves never sang alone. Rather, no genre of solo music has come to light. The work songs, spirituals, jubilees, and shouts—song types known among slaves—were choral forms. The solo singing that occurred, at least as the record shows, was almost invariably responsorial; that is, the soloist sang in a group in which he or she functioned as leader. This accounts for the prevalence of "call-response" slave music.[7]

As much as the record indicates that group music was the dominant musical expression of slavery, it also shows that solo black American song became a major form between Emancipation and the end of the first decade of the twentieth century. There is an obvious reason for the greater possibility of solo singing during this time: slavery was a group experience in which work, religion, living accommodations, and most of the other basic facets of one's life were communal. Freedom would have given greater vent to individualism. Freed slaves broke from the plantation and began shaping lives of their own. Thus not only could a new solo singer emerge but so could a vastly different subject matter to sing about: love, sadness, anger, frustration, guilt, remorse, pain, and suffering. All of these emotions could be expressed through the group, but not perhaps with the same sense of personal release. An alternative mode of expression was required. That alternative evolved as a solo style and most likely is what became known as the blues.[8]

From the perspective of the audience, the difference between the older music of slavery and the later solo blues involves more than the role of the soloist. In the former, the expression was collective, that is, declared *by* the group. No audience, in the sense of passive listeners, was presumed. In the latter, the expression was individual: one expresses and thereby declares feelings *to* the group. An audience as a group of listeners is presupposed.[9]

The blues soloist was the figure in traditional Afro-American culture responsible for emoting and otherwise expressing feeling to the group through music. Another individual, the preacher, was likewise responsible to a group, but he communicated through speech. Upon superficial investigation, one could conclude that these figures were the antithesis of one another. One sang in a secular setting; the other spoke in a religious setting. But the bluesman and the preacher, beyond surface distinctions, were cultural analogues of one another. The structure and delivery of sermons and blues songs bear more resemblance than dissimilarity. At the foundation of the art of each was a common creative mode: improvisation. The free use of chanting and other speech techniques by the bluesman and the preacher are but fragments of the considerable evidence of interchange between the two. Numerous observers, including Dorsey, have described the identical audience responses that the bluesman and preacher elicit.[10]

Indeed, even their most obvious dissimilarity, the respective secular and sacred settings for their performances, pales when placed in historical perspective. The contrast between sacred and secular grew along with post-Emancipation black culture. Before that time, for example, secular and sacred music sounded identical—except for the differentiation between texts. As with most groups without an indigenous notated music, slaves had one style of music for all applications. Thus the difference between sacred and secular was one of substance rather than sound. After slavery, the same commonality of sound prevailed, varied, of course, by solo or group delivery where customary.[11]

Only from the perspective of non-traditional Afro-American culture were the preacher and bluesman viewed as antitypes of one another. Their homologous development ceased when another strain of preacher began to evolve: the trained or educated minister. The trained ministry forged the newly emerged post-Emancipation black church into an agency of social control.[12] As an outgrowth of his education in white-supported schools, the trained minister stood for one ideal as the social foundation of the black America that he was committed to build: assimilation.[13] His goal was the eradication of all vestiges of traditional secular and sacred black culture where they were considered to be barriers to assimilation.

With the untrained minister and his church, the music and preaching of enslavement culture flourished. Thus it was in the folk church that the historic symbiotic relationship between the preacher and the bluesman remained intact. Indeed, the passage from the role of bluesman to that of preacher (and rarely vice versa) occurred frequently enough to be thought of as a rite.[14] The demarcation between worship and blues performance was for the most part synthetic; the interaction between bluesman/preacher or preacher/bluesman and his witnesses was, except perhaps for content, virtually identical. Thus, far from being antitypes of one another in this cultural context, the bluesman and preacher were joint solicitors of response and, with their common use of improvisation, co-conjurers of release. Church and blues performances in this culture were common experiences, for religious ecstasy and vicarious emotionalism were but different means to the same end. Only from a cross-cultural perspective were the bluesman and preacher seen as incongruous, for they represented an incongruity of cultures rather than roles.

At the time when Dorsey was making the effort to introduce his gospel blues, this mutuality was evident. Between 1926 and 1928, the downhome preacher enjoyed as much popularity through the recorded sermon as the downhome bluesman through his recordings. Indeed, much of the growth in popularity of the sermon record paralleled that of the blues recording. The first preaching record was made in 1925 by Reverend Calvin P. Dixon for Columbia Records. Not until the next year would the sermon record sell well, however. It was then that a Reverend J. M. Gates of Atlanta recorded two sermons followed by the most famous sermon record, *The Downfall of Nebuchadnezzar,* by Reverend J. C. Burnett from Kansas City. Other than the delivery of the preachers, the last two recordings differed from Dixon's only in that they contained singing at various points and responses by the singers to the preacher, much in the way congregations would react during a regular church service. These additions accounted for the tremendous popularity of the recorded sermon between 1926 and 1932. By the end of 1926, six preachers could be heard on record; that number grew to 30 the next year. By the end of the sermon era, over 750 sermons had been released.[15]

As did the bluesman, the preacher came to know that to practice his art in a less than authentic context would be to mask it to the point that black Americans would have little use for it. Thus Gates and Burnett can be compared to Bessie Smith and Ma Rainey: they restored the recorded sermon to its downhome prototype by engaging in practices the recording industry had not seen fit to encourage. They brought small groups with them to make the records. Not only did the additional persons provide the all-important verbal responses to the preacher, but they provided music as well. In a sermon recorded in April 1926, Gates has his "congregation" sing *Woe Be unto You* in a simple choral style to guitar accompaniment. He then preaches for a short time to their responses. This cycle repeats itself, after which the "congregation" closes with more singing. The Reverend J. C. Burnett in his famous *Nebuchadnezzar* recording begins lining out the hymn *I Heard the Voice of Jesus Say*. Throughout the ensuing sermon, several women hum constantly and utter words in the background. He used this same formula on his record *I've Even Heard of Thee*.

With the sermons of J. M. Gates, the sales of the sermon record increased greatly. Initially, 3,675 records were ordered when his *Death's Black Train Is Coming* was released by Columbia records in July 1926. By the following October, when the remainder of that recording session was issued, the initial order stood at 34,025. For Burnett, the sales "boom" amounted to no less: his *Nebuchadnezzar* sold 80,000 copies in 1926—four times the sales of a typical release of the leading blues singer that year, Bessie Smith.[16]

As with blues music, the recorded sermon—even with an intense attempt to shape it to traditional preaching—was fundamentally altered by the recording process. The limitation of time forced the most radical change in the classic black sermon. Most researchers agree that there is an underlying structure common to most black sermons. Though they disagree on the specific elements, these researchers have found, at least in a generic sense, introductory, developmental, and climactic parts to most sermons. Almost every preacher who recorded sermons shortened considerably or deleted the middle part in order to conform to the time allowed on one side of a record. The recorded sermon became, in essence, a climax preceded by a slightly extended introduction. At a time when the average income for black families in the South amounted to less than $300 per year and records sold at 75 cents each, the value of a short, pithy homily—one that would fit the three minutes allotted to one side of a record—was clearly measurable.[17]

Although Dorsey knew of the strong cultural link between himself as a bluesman and the preacher and although he must have sensed that the sermon record was as popular as his hokum blues, he was probably moved to begin working with Hall by a more personal coincidence: the sudden notoriety of the sermon records of the Reverend W. M. Nix (listed as "A. W. Nix" on recordings), the singing evangelist who inspired Dorsey at the 1921 National Baptist Convention. In 1927, Nix made seven recordings in New York City. His *Black Diamond Express to Hell* achieved the greatest notoriety. It was one of the few record sermons that extended beyond one side of a record, having been recorded in two parts for its first release in May 1927, two more parts in November 1929, and a final two parts in June 1930.[18]

It should be remembered that Dorsey first knew of Nix as an evangelistic singer. In 1921 Nix served on the music committee of the National Baptist Convention and was referred to then as the "popular evangelist." By 1927 he was also known for his preaching. Whether Nix formally switched from singer to preacher is almost a moot point inasmuch as one of the most distinctive traits of his sermons is the blues-like chanting he uses to deliver them. In other words, Nix carried many of the techniques of his singing over to his preaching. One of the best examples of this is his sermon *Watch Your Close Friend,* which is based on the biblical story of Samson and Delilah.

Watch Your Close Friend

My text this morning is found in Judges,
    sixteen' chapter and eighteen' verse.
"And when the Delilah saw that he had told her
    all of his heart, she sent and called
    for the lords of the Philistine' saying,   (5)
'Come, for he has told me all of his heart.' "
Watch your friends!
It is natural for all people to have someone
    whom they regard as their friend. *Amen!*
Everybody likes to have a friend, but a   (10)
    true friend *Amen!* is hard to find.
Amen, Amen!
Most of all the heartaches and disappointments and
    deception' and trouble of all kind come from
    people by their supposed friends. *All right!*   (15)
Great many people who have committed crimes have
    been turned up to the law by their supposed
    Amen! friends.
Sister, watch that woman that love you so well
    All right! that she's always at your house.   (20)
    Amen!
And just as soon as your back is turned, she's
    makin' love to your husband. *Amen!*
Brother, watch that friend that thinks so much of
    you until he won't room with nobody else   (25)
    but you. *All right!*
There are a great many widows in separation and
    breakin' up of families in the world
    today because of bosom friends *Well!*
    and roomers in your home. *Well!*   (30)
A great many homes have been robbed today are
    robbed by some friend who knows all about your
    house. *All right!*

Watch that friend that's in business with you. *Yeah!*

Watch that fast friend and pal of yours *All right!*   (35)
    that knows all about the secrets of your life.
    That's right!

Your enemy cannot harm you, but you must watch your
    friend. *All right!*

Your best supposed friend today may be your worst   (40)
    enemy tomorrow. *Amen!*

Just as soon as Sampson's wife ah got to him to tell her
    about all of his strength, why she went and called,
    "All of his hair!" *Well!* And she called
    his enemies and they rushed in and bound   (45)
    him *Yeah!* and put his eyes out and
    made a slave out of him. *All right!*

Brother, watch that close friend of yours.
    All right, Oh yeah!

I thank God that there are some true friends in the   (50)
    world today. *All right!*

Damon and Pickus were true friends. *Yes!*

Jonathan and David were true friends. *Amen!*
    All right!

Christ is a never failin' friend. *All right!*   (55)

He is a friend that sticketh closer than a brother.
    [*inaudible*]

He'll feed you when you're hungry *All right!*
    and when you' out doors, He, and, in
    the storm, *All right, Well!*, he'll   (60)
    take you in. *All right!*

When everybody's tryin' to press you down
    Well! and starve you out in
    the world, *Yeah!* He'll open a
    way for you. *Amen, All right!*   (65)

Won't He do it children? *Yes!*

Have you ever tried Him? *Yes!*

Have I got a witness here? *Yes!*

If you wan' ta true friend in the world, *Well!*
    Jesus will be your friend. *Well, All right!*   (70)

He'll stick to you 'til the evil shall end.

Amen![19]

As Nix opens with the obligatory introduction ("My text . . . is found in . . ."), he seems simultaneously to establish the tonal center of his sermon. He chants all but one word of the opening sentence on the "f" pitch below middle "c." As he continues into the scripture, he remains focused on the "f" but with one or two half-step inflections both above and below the principle "f." Only when he must assume Delilah's voice, as she calls out to Samson's enemies (line 6), does Nix make a significant departure from the "f." He leaps first up to a "g," the highest pitch up to that point in the sermon, and speaks Delilah's "Come!" only to fall seven half-steps on the next word ("for"); on the following word he returns to the "f" by leaping five half-steps. From there until the end of her statement, Nix gradually descends one half-step to an "e." To close the introduction, he announces the title of his sermon, *Watch Your Friends,* in a monotone on the "e."

As is evident, tonal modulation is an interpretive technique that Nix employs much as any other speaker would in rendering a text expressively. The difference between Nix's tonalization and that which others might use is that Nix's pitches are so clearly discernible. The chanting normally found in folk preaching has a singing quality to it. But unless the preacher is an experienced singer, the pitches are so intermingled with speech tones that they are indistinguishable for the most part. The lyricism in Nix's sermons is a recognizable melody that he seems to sing as much as speak.

The identifying traits of Nix's sermons, therefore, can be found in the dim nexus between the interpretive technique of the bluesman and that of the preacher. Each modulates his voice to drive home a message. Both personalities vary the voice spontaneously, even though the particular inflection may be different. Nix uses exact pitches where one might expect the preacher only to raise or lower the voice in volume. Indeed, from the point where he begins to develop the sermon through the climax, he chants mostly on either the "f" or the "a" flat. He uses the "a" flat, which is the higher pitch, to emphasize words and ideas. In lines 19–23, these are the two pitches Nix uses with the exception of a "b" flat for the first word, "Sister." If the words sung on the "a" flat are italicized, those lines read:

> Sister, *watch that* woman that *love you so well*
> that she's *always* at your house.
> And *just* as *soon as your* back is *turned,* she's
> *makin'* love to your husband.

One would think that a two-pitch melody might be uninteresting. Nix, as the bluesman/preacher, however, assigns roles to both pitches similar to those played by accents in metered speech: the "a" flat denotes stressed words or syllables, the "f" plain or weak ones. By employing the accents where he wants the listener to pay heed as opposed to using them in a predictable pattern or formula, Nix makes the pitches relatively inaudible, or at least he subordinates them to the point that the listener takes notice of them only in conjunction with the message. Thus the genius of Nix's sermons is that they are composed in melodic meter, the unit of which he forms while interpreting the text.

Nix's use of these randomly structured melodic feet, as they might be thought of, allows him to construct an intensely dramatic climax to his sermons. Such latitude is particularly advantageous to Nix since the recorded sermon formula consists mostly of climactic oratory. Other than the introduction, the divisions within *Watch Your Close Friend* are not readily discernible. This ambiguity may be intentional, since chanting is a technique most often used in the climax. But for Nix, who needs to maintain climactic levels of tension throughout, chanting is a readily available technique that he uses with more than its structural appropriateness in mind. With *Watch Your Close Friend* lasting only two minutes and 39 seconds, Nix has no time to build a climax on a carefully laid exposition. Within this long climax, there is a clear mounting of drama brought on by Nix's use of higher pitches and larger intervals. His warnings first to "Sister" (line 19) and then to "Brother" (line 24) each extend the upper range of his pitch by two half-steps ("b" flat and "c" respectively). Nix approaches each of the notes from the root pitch "f"; by doing so he uses increasingly larger intervals: five and seven half-steps, respectively. At lines 31 and 34 he moves up two more half-steps to "e" flat. Finally he reaches the highest note, "f'," 12 half-steps (an octave) above his principle "f" on line 48.

With the most climactic part of the sermon still to come—the part that demands the most intense melodic activity—and with Nix at the upper limit of his vocal range and therefore unable to resort to higher pitches for dramatic effect, he has little choice but to use melodic meter once again. Of the last six sentences (lines 62–71), the first word of all but the last begins on the "f'." All but sentences two and three (lines 66 and 67) end on his principle "f," meaning that he leaps a full octave to make three of his last six statements. Nix offsets these powerful undulations by locking onto the high "f'" in lines 66 and 67; these are the first two of the three questions he asks. Then in the third question he descends from the high "f'" down an octave, traversing no less than four pitch levels in the process. This giant leap plus the rapid barrage of new pitches may be considered the climactic moment of the sermon. He ascends an octave once more to begin the next sentence, falls for eight half-steps, reaches for the high "f'" again, then makes a final plunge to the low "f" where he remains, with one exception, until the end. Thus the last 12 lines read as follows (uppercase = "f'"; small print = "f"; normal print = any pitch other than "f'" or "f"; ↓ and ↑ = change of pitch, down or up respectively, other than between "f'" and "f" or either approaching or leaving "f'" and "f"):

> . . . take you in.
> WHEN EVERy ↓body's tryin' to press you down,
>   and starve you out in
>   the world, He'll open ↑a
> ↓way for you.

(65)

> WON'T HE DO IT CHILDREN?
> HAVE YOU EVER TRIED HIM?

HAVE I got ↓a ↓wit ↓ness here?
IF YOU WAN' TA true ↑friend in ↓the world,
    JESUS will ↓be your friend.   (70)
He'll stick to you 'til the evil shall end.
Amen.

Concerning congregational responses, Nix was no less creative and dramatic. His respondents included only women, perhaps no more than four. They "bear [him] up" in the traditional manner: "Amens" and "all rights" interrupting and punctuating his statements. In the text of the sermon, their replies are printed in italics. But Nix added a more appropriate response—actually, an accompaniment—to his song sermon: he had a member of his congregation sing her improvised response in the background. The result is a slow, haunting obbligato built on the same "f" (one octave higher) on which Nix chants most of the sermon. At times she merely sings the customary responses, as at the end of Example 7-1: "Well ["a'"], well ["a'" flat], well ["f'"]."

She is most effective, however, when she sings both a countermelody and countertext to Nix's chanted words. In Example 7-1, she improvises a melody to the opening of the 23rd Psalm, "The Lord is my shepherd; I shall not want." Her singing is as notable for its independence from Nix's chanting as for its harmony with it. She begins her phrase in the middle of Nix's, but cadences with him. Her pitches clash with his: for example, the "b'" she holds against the "c" he sings on "Brother." But they blend as well, as in her opening phrase, "Ah, the Lord is my . . . ." In essence, hers is the lesser voice of a sermon in two-part counterpoint. She is subordinate to, yet independent from, Nix in that his voice, as the principle one, is hers to embellish. Given that the inclusion of congregational responses—especially sung ones—counts as one of the major factors in the rise of the recorded sermon's popularity and given that the singing Nix included on his records was so spontaneous, one can see readily why the demand for his records soon exceeded that for Burnett's.

Nix had one more innovation that accounted for his popularity: he preached about everyday situations. In addition to *Watch Your Close Friend,* Nix recorded *The Prayer Meeting in Hell, Mind Your Own Business,* and *Pay Your Honest Debts.* He seemed to know no bounds in his effort to reach the common person. He even recorded *It Was Tight Like That* in October 1930 in apparent response to Dorsey's then-famous song.[20] Each of these, as its title suggests, addresses an issue likely to involve the common black American. Nix's sermons thus can be thought of as vernacular homilies: religious exhortations on mundane matters couched in simple language. For example, in *Watch Your Close Friend* he talks as a brother to a woman about the possibility that her good friend may be an adulterer with her husband. He continues by speaking about the crowded tenement situations in which

Ex. 7-1

Watch Your Close Friend (lines 22-28)

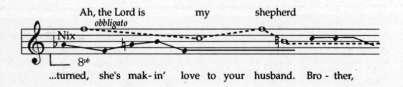

Ah, the Lord is   my   shepherd
obbligato
Nix
8ʋᵇ

...turned, she's mak-in' love to your husband. Bro-ther,

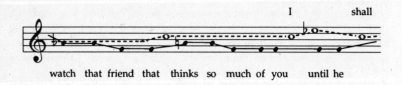

I   shall

watch that friend that thinks so much of you   until he

not   want.

won't room   with nobody else but you. There are great

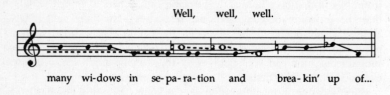

Well,   well,   well.

many wi-dows in se-pa-ra-tion and   brea-kin' up of...

(end of excerpt)

numbers of urban blacks then lived. Then he offers Jesus as the answer to
these and any other hardships his listeners might face.

Considering the tremendous appeal of Nix's records because of his
chanting, his respondents and singer, and his folksy theology, and considering as well that each of these innovations is rooted in black worship traditions, Nix may be thought of as the Bessie Smith or Ma Rainey of the
recorded sermon tradition. The most convincing indication that Smith and
Rainey had struck a highly resonant note with black Americans was found

in the sales figures for their records. The same is true for Nix. Black Americans had been signaling their desire for indigenous religious song by buying records of quartets singing both blues and "gospel" songs. They liked Gates and Burnett, but, apparently, neither of them rang as true as Nix. Even though the recording studio compromised the genuineness of Nix's sermons by requiring him to concentrate them into a small time frame and to synthesize his congregational interaction, it did not mute those basic sounds to which black Americans were attuned when their folk preachers held forth. Like Smith and Rainey, Nix was able to encapsulate the old so that it could be transmitted through a new medium without loss of its power to move. The analogy between Smith/Rainey and Nix extends further. Nix provided Dorsey—floundering with his spiritual blues—a salient link between his downhome and gospel blues. As the earthiness of Smith's and Rainey's singing had steered Dorsey from the trite ditties he had been publishing in 1923 and brought him back to pure blues, so would Nix's singing evangelism and quasi-blues chanting stand as the beacon to guide him from his half-hearted attempts at gospel blues performances.

Dorsey saw this light, although somewhat faintly at first, and followed it by bringing his gospel songs back into the blues performance tradition through the singing evangelist/recording preacher figure that he saw in Hall. Though Dorsey refers to it only in passing, this tradition loomed over bluesmen. The bluesman and preacher were not only linked through culture but, as recording artists, through the same business. Dorsey knew Gates, " . . . met him several times," and knew that Nix "was a [recording] preacher." Nix was too towering a figure for Dorsey not to notice, especially since Nix had played such a pivotal role in Dorsey's earlier return to the church. Though Dorsey may have been somewhat oblivious to his adoption of this tradition, the stylistic traits of his gospels, the path he took to gaining acceptance for them in old-line churches, and the role that the singer of Dorsey's gospels eventually assumed in the black church provide clear evidence that the singing evangelist/recording preacher, especially as epitomized by Nix, influenced Dorsey.[21]

Dorsey's move toward this tradition was eased somewhat by the presence of some Nix-like elements in his gospel songs. The most obvious of these was his use of the blues note. Although blues chanting and blues singing are similar, they differ enough so that any observations linking Nix's and Dorsey's blues must be made broadly. Also taking into consideration the major role of improvisation in both genres—and especially in Nix's and Dorsey's performances—patterns that one might note in one instance may vary considerably in the next. A comparison of Dorsey's performances of his *If You See My Savior* (Exs. 6-1, 6-2, and 6-3) illustrates this point.

With these words of caution in mind, one can discern as distinctive a use of the lowered third (blues note) in Dorsey's renderings of *If You See My Savior* as in Nix's application of the same pitch to parts of *Watch Your Close*

Friend. If You See My Savior offers a special opportunity for Dorsey to put the blues note to structural use: the piece is written in a major key in which the third by rule is in the raised position. When Dorsey lowers this third to make it a blues note, he not only introduces a new tonal color but quite possibly changes the mode of the piece from major to minor as well. He is constrained, therefore, in his use of the note more than a chanter like Nix, whose "piece" has no underlying harmonic structure.

In order to maintain modal uniformity and the simple chordal structure in which he writes his songs, Dorsey has only one chord in which he can use the blues note: the subdominant. Even here, however, the blues note does not belong. It is the optionally added—and, incidentally, lowered—seventh of the subdominant chord. Thus Dorsey's distinctive application of the blues note comes in a context in which the harmony is complete with or without it. This means that even though he is limited to one harmonic area in which the blues note's presence is appropriate, Dorsey can choose whether or not to add it.

The opportunities to make this choice are numerous. Because of its role in the harmonic scheme of Dorsey's gospels, the subdominant ends four of the eight phrases in *If You See My Savior*: measures 6, 10, 14, 18 in Example 6-1; 4, 8, 12, 16 in Example 6-2; and 4, 12, 20, and 28 in Example 6-3. The subdominant chord, then, is an effective ending or cadencing harmony. With or without its lowered seventh, it brings the music to a point of conclusion.

The choice to add the blues note is not Dorsey's on the basis of harmony alone, however. It is more than a coincidence that each of the points where the subdominant appears is also a rhyming point of the text: "neighbor," "favor," "me" and "me." As with the subdominant chord, these rhyming points contain enough innate emphasis that Dorsey's choice to add the blues note or not does not alter the textual structure.

An inherent conflict exists between Dorsey the composer, who, through chords and text, circumscribes the blues note's presence, and Dorsey the bluesman, who claims the right to sound it at will. Out of this tension between these two aspects of Dorsey's musical personality emerges the distinctive role of the blues note in his performances of his songs. There are points where he literally saturates the few beats in which the subdominant is active with the note. In measures 4 and 5 of Example 6-3, he not only embellishes the cadence and "neighbor" with the blues note, but, because the subdominant is active for another measure, he repeats it three more times in an accompaniment figure and then once again to begin the next line of text. The contrast with measures 12 and 13 of the same example is striking: except for a small hint of the note just before measure 12, Dorsey does not use it in measures 12 and 13, a point virtually identical textually and harmonically to measures 4 and 5.

The abundance and then paucity of the blues note show how Dorsey the bluesman improvises within the structure that Dorsey the composer has built. According to the music, Dorsey could have brought back the blues note in measures 12 and 13. But his permission to do so would have come from the music and words—Dorsey the composer. When he chooses not to use the note when he is allowed to, he not only alters the improvisatory pattern established by the music and words but wrests control of the music from Dorsey the composer. He sounds the blues note with all its meaning by silencing it. He improvises by not improvising.

Such disuse of the blues note is but one example of the extent to which Dorsey the bluesman gropes for maximum expressive effect within the narrow confines that Dorsey the composer allows. As a result, the blues note's appearance is unpredictable—almost erratic. For instance, in measure 4 of Example 6-2, the last note is the blues note—but misplaced. The chord in effect for that measure uses an "a" natural which is one-half step above the blues note. As if to confound his harmonic scheme further, Dorsey sings the "a" natural as the first note of the next measure. But the subdominant chord is in effect here; only "a" flats are allowed. Dorsey the bluesman again grabs the expected away from the music that Dorsey the composer has so well prepared by deliberately sounding an aberrant form of the blues note on the first—most prominent—syllable of the rhyming point. Dorsey makes use of the blues note in this teasing, capricious manner throughout this example. In measure 6 he sings it again on the first beat and once again with a chord that does not support either "a." On the word "kindly" in measure 8, he brings back both "a's" during the subdominant's tenure. Dorsey's juxtaposition of these mislaid notes, each at the spot the other is supposed to occupy, is evidence of the swagger with which the bluesman can commandeer both the music he has been given and that which the composer would keep to himself.

In Dorsey's gospels the blues note symbolizes the creative freedom that he demands regardless of the origin of the song—himself as composer included. As Nix marks meter with his blues note, Dorsey marks improvisational points with his. For each, his display of the note stamps his control over the expressive—rather than over the textual—message of his composition. Thus in the recorded sermon and in the gospel song, the bluesman's blues note is a whimsical utterance that takes on significance purely by its fleeting presence.

In addition to the blues note, Dorsey's improvisation includes varying the size of melodic intervals as a means of highlighting portions of the text. This is also Nix's most expressive tool in terms of pitch. Dorsey resorted to it less often, but for the same effect. The most dramatic leap occurs in measures 9–10 of Example 6-3. At the parallel point in the original (mm. 8–9, Ex. 6-1), the four "c's" state the question blandly. In Example 6-3, Dorsey begins the phrase identically, but upon reaching "him" adds a melisma during which he ascends seven half-steps and holds the note. Having risen so high, Dorsey sets up a cascade of melodic intervals—including a large eight-step leap downward ("he would")—in order to end on the pitch he had written originally. Thus he not only can place emphasis on "him" but can use the melodic wake generated by this accentuation to provide melodic interest to the remainder of the question.

But numerous melodic intervals of sizes proportional to the stress Dorsey wanted to place on certain words were not the only way he improvised melodically. He also controlled expression without these techniques. Measures 4–7 of Example 6-2 illustrate this point. In comparison with parallel measures in the original (mm. 6–8, Ex. 6-1), they contain fewer changes of pitch and a considerably shorter range. For the entire phrase, Dorsey changes pitch six times in Example 6-2 and eight in the original. These numbers alone are insignificant until the distance between the highest and lowest of the notes is considered. When Dorsey is free to use wide-ranging pitches in order to put certain words in melodic relief, he chooses instead to sing the phrase within four half-steps. In the notated version, where Dorsey aims for simplicity, his melody ranges over eight half-steps. This breadth of range has its effect. In Example 7-2, the melodic contour of the original (top staff) with its short descent followed by a long ascent with a plateau in the middle and a slight drop off at the conclusion contrasts significantly with the improvised version (bottom staff) with its straight line with upturns on either end. Indeed, were the two blues notes absent, these ends would be even less pronounced.

This reduction of melodic improvisation calls attention once more to one of the ingenious aspects of Dorsey's improvisational technique. As with the blues note when he silences it to give both it and his bluesman role more prominence, Dorsey's compression of the melodic range serves to seize con-

Ex. 7-2

If You See My Saviour

(Melodic Contour Comparison)

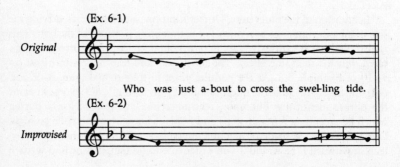

(Ex. 6-1)

Original

Who   was   just   a-bout   to   cross   the   swel-ling   tide.

(Ex. 6-2)

Improvised

Comparison of Melodic Improvisation

Phrase	Starting Text	Range	Changes of Pitch	Range	Changes of Pitch
		(Ex. 6-1)		(Ex. 6-2)	
1	I was . . .	7	7	7	6
2	who was . . .	8	7	4	5
3	And I . . .	7	7	8	9
4	kindly take . . .	8	7	4	7
5	If you . . .	7	7	8	9
6	when you . . .	8	7	4	3
7	You may . . .	7	7	8	9
8	tell Him . . .	8	8	4	7

trol of a key point in a way contrary to the design of Dorsey the composer. As the table shows, the written version alternates between seven and eight half-steps per phrase and, with the exception of the last, changes pitch seven times per phrase. Predictable variability like this is to be expected in a notated version of Dorsey's songs; it is also the one aspect of the composed gospel that Dorsey the bluesman is pledged to change—but not completely. He also sets a pattern for range variability. With one exception, it is consistent throughout the piece. But he reverses the placement of small and large ranges (Ex. 6-2). This difference coupled with the greater degree of variance between these phrases (50 percent average versus 12 percent in original) makes the contrast between them more striking than in the original.

If less may be said to mean more as concerns the blues note and range, Dorsey the bluesman all but obscures this point when it comes to the use of different pitches within phrases. In the original, Dorsey almost always calls for one change of pitch for each degree of range. When improvising, he establishes no consistent ratio except in the smaller ranges, where, with the exception of phrases two and six, he uses an average of two pitches per degree of range for all four of the smaller-ranged phrases (2, 4, 6, and 8). Already cut in half from their original ranges, all but one of these phrases are now filled with as many notes as their originals. In this instance less has been enhanced by more notes. The greater amount of melodic activity within the smaller area makes more pronounced the already striking contrast Dorsey built into these phrases by contracting them. He seems to be juggling less with more and then more with less; for example, seven changes within four half-steps (phrase 8) preceded by only nine within eight. Once again Dorsey the bluesman's improvisational strategy knows no tactical bounds. He can embellish a line in one place only to denude it in another—both maneuvers in the cause of communicating most effectively the message of the moment.

Through the bluesman's techniques, Dorsey's gospels clearly shared common sounds with the singing evangelist/recorded sermon traditions—particularly as practiced by Nix. But Dorsey's gospels had an even more conspicuous similarity that connected them to the sermon whether or not they were sung: their subject matter. Dorsey's *If You See My Savior,* for example, amounts to an affirmation of life after death—an assurance the Christian could expect to hear over and over in scripturally based homilies. His presentation of this familiar concept in the context of the death of a friend is analogous to Nix's framing of the Samson and Delilah story in the context of the betrayal of a friend. It allows Dorsey to personalize one of the basic tenets of Christianity, to speak of it in terms of *"my* Savior," who knows *"I am coming home some day,"* and to refer to his mother, father, sister, and brother as sharing in the same good fortune. In the other gospel song he had written at this time, *How About You?,* Dorsey adopts the same mode of presentation. The same personalization of broad doctrines with references to everyday life is evident:

How About You?

I

How well do I remember how Jesus brought me through.
I prayed and walked the floor a night or two.
I said, "Lord, take and use me; that's all that I can do."
And I gave my heart to Jesus, how about you?

I I

When shadows overtake me and trouble starts to brew,
And when I've done the best that I can do.
My best friends talk about me; sometime my kinfolks, too.
But I take it all to Jesus; how about you?

I I I

When I press my dying pillow and I know my life is through,
And there's no more that earthly friends can do.
When my sight begins to fail me and my fingernails turn blue,
Then He'll take me home to glory, how about you?

I V

Over there I'll meet my mother and see my father too;
And we'll talk about the things we used to do.
And then someone will ask me, "How did you make it through?"
I came through tribulations, how about you?

CHORUS

How about you, how about you?
I hope my Savior is your Savior, too.
I said, "Lord, take and use me; that's all that I can do."
And I gave my heart to Jesus; how about you?

By some standards, this text would be considered little more than religious doggerel. But it was precisely this profound simplification—almost trans-parency—of doctrinal concepts that allowed Dorsey's songs—like Nix's ser-mons—to speak to virtually anyone who would listen.

Dorsey's gospel songs virtually mirror Nix's sermons in terms of their structure. By default they tend toward the pithy climaxes that marked Nix's sermons. Dorsey takes two minutes and 30 seconds to perform his im-provised version of *If You See My Savior*, roughly the same amount of time Nix had for one of his sermons if it was recorded for one side of a record. Thus each quatrain-chorus unit of Dorsey's songs is equal in time to one sermon (or one part of those sermons recorded over multiple sides). Indeed, since Dorsey could not expect all verses of his songs to be performed each time, he had to write each unit as if it were the only text to which the song would be sung. This means that each quatrain introduces a thought, devel-ops it, and then begins a climax that reaches its peak in the chorus. In verse III of *How About You*, for example, Dorsey introduces the idea of death ("When I press my dying pillow"), continues it with two additional subordi-nate clauses, and concludes by declaring that death leads one "home to glory."

When approaching and executing the climax, Dorsey's songs depart from the Nix model but have the same goal of enhancing the dramatic effect of their high points as Nix's sermons had. The one trait that most consistently marks the climax of a black sermon, be it recorded or otherwise delivered, is the shift from "objective fact to subjective testimony." In sermons where the climax is extended, as it was in most sermon records, this shift occurs in successive levels of greater subjectivity. For example, after reading his scrip-ture, Nix makes two observations on true friendship through line 10 of *Watch Your Close Friend*. He then introduces his first testimonial thought, "but a true friend is hard to find" (lines 10–11). On this precautionary note about friendship, the remainder of the sermon is built. His admonishment to be alert for betrayal is based on experiences—perhaps personal ones—to which Nix testifies for the remainder of his sermon: "Most all of the heart-aches and disappointments and deception' and trouble of all kind come from people by their supposed friends"; "many homes have been robbed . . . by some friends"; "Your best supposed friend today may be your worst enemy tomorrow." Since he is already in the testimonial mode but still needs to increase the tension, Nix has to resort to more dramatic testimony. To do so, he introduces the first person pronoun, the most subjective point from which to testify: "I thank God that there are some true friends in the world today." So powerful is this shift of standpoint that Nix uses it explicitly only once more—"Have I got a witness here?"—at the climax of his sermon. Between his first and second "I," Nix can offer his most personal testimony: his belief that Jesus is one's most trustworthy friend.[22]

Dorsey's shift of standpoint is the opposite: he begins with "I." "How well do I remember" opens *How About You,* and "I was standing by the bedside of a neighbor" starts *If You See My Savior.* But as both titles suggest, and so does Nix's *Watch Your Close Friend,* the text that follows not only presumes a listener, the second person, but involves her as well. Thus, through his verses, Dorsey is an intimist, baring the "I's" innermost worries, doubts, and expectations and—most essentially—the whispered sentiments between the "I" and the "Lord." In gradually exposing the "I," Dorsey intends for it more and more to reflect the concerns and spiritual confidences of the listener, for once stripped of its façade, his "I" emerges as "you." One can paraphrase his definition of the blues to express this notion: "blues ain't nothin' but a good woman or man—[or "I"]—feelin' bad." As did Nix, Dorsey went to a well of shared experiences to find a message for his listener—but while Nix drew from the Bible, Dorsey dipped from everyday life.

Since he implies the "you" all along, Dorsey cannot just shift to it in order to make the climax; he has to sculpt it into sharp relief against the "I" in which it has been submerged. In *If You See My Savior,* his "you" has been the dying neighbor. But the "you" rises triumphantly, not only claiming the next life but, in doing so, conveying the hopes of the "I" it left behind: "Take this message to the other side"; "Tell Him I am coming home some day." In the chorus, in particular, in *How About You,* Dorsey is more overt: he directs the same question to "you" four times each iteration (once at the close of each verse and three times during the chorus). These are rhetorical questions. Without allowing the "you" to respond, the "I" taunts the "you" subtly: "I hope my Savior is your Savior, too" and "I gave my heart to Jesus." By gently goading the "you," Dorsey keeps the "I" in control, but with the "you" still the focus of attention. In each stanza and in the chorus, therefore, the shift is deceptive—rather than from the "I" to the "you," it is from the "I" to the tension between the "I" and the "you." This tension marks each cycle of the climax.

In light of these marked similarities between Dorsey's gospels and the recorded sermons and in light of the widespread popularity of the sermon and the utter failure of his gospels, Dorsey could sense as compelling a need to change his presentation of the gospels as he had his earlier Tin Pan Alley blues songs. Exactly when Dorsey began to conceive of his songs as sermons cannot be pinpointed, although it seems most likely between 1928, after his successful recording of *It's Tight Like That,* and 1930, when he was introduced at the National Baptist Convention as the composer of *If You See My Savior*. If the precise moment is undiscernible, Dorsey's first step is not: he found a Reverend Nix type to preach his gospels by making a deal with the Reverend E. H. Hall, who "took the show" at a meeting during which Dorsey had demonstrated his songs. Hall's voice struck Dorsey as having the same quality and impact as Nix's. And Dorsey's response to it was no less immediate and forthcoming than it had been to Nix's in 1921 when he sang *I Do, Don't You:*

> I was somewhere one night, in the gospel now, and Hall sang and took the show and I went to him, I think, to give him my card. I thought maybe he wanted some music or something like that. I liked his singing and I asked him to come along with me, go along with me, "I play for you and you sing my songs for me" and we did very good at it.[23]

Of all the moves Dorsey would or could make to refashion his songs, establishing a partnership between himself the bluesman and Hall the preacher would be the most significant. Dorsey knew the preacher's sound was powerful, but he had never thought to use the preacher to perform his songs. His quest for popularizing his gospels was always in the direction of the right singer, whom he had found, supposedly, in Rebecca Talbot. The night he heard Hall, he had just finished demonstrating one of his gospels—probably with the "smooth, heavy" voice of Rebecca Talbot. Even if he got his gospel song as low-down as he could, however, Dorsey knew that Hall "took the show" with something like his blues, but quite different just the same. Perhaps the congregation shouted and moaned to his music, but it did so even more fervently to Hall's singing/preaching.

Most likely the difference he sensed was rooted in the slight variance that existed between the audience's response to the bluesman and to the preacher. For all the similarities one can find between the bluesman and the preacher, there is a difference in how each relates to the audience. Either one can evoke impassioned replies from his listeners, but for distinctly different reasons. The bluesman's role evolved out of his relation to his audience as the cultural figure delegated the responsibility to declare his emotions before the group and in doing so to prompt them to emote with him. The preacher, on the other hand, could make it his duty to elicit emotion, but he could depend as well on his audience's sensing its equally compelling duty to "bear [him] up." This is apparent in the type of audience improvisation on the Nix records. In some instances it follows his lead, virtually punctuating his phrases. In others it is independent, as with the woman extemporizing both music and text along with his preaching. Both types are supportive of Nix as the primary figure, but both types evolve without Nix's direction other than as lead enunciator of the text they follow. Any support Dorsey would have from the audience would come at his behest and would indicate the effectiveness of his control. Thus no one would dare improvise a countermelody to his blues song while he was performing it. As "king of the night," he needs no one to bear him up; indeed, he is there to bear up his audience.[24]

If this was the difference Dorsey sensed, it would have weighed upon him considerably. Supposedly, by putting the real blues back into his gospels and by getting a real blues singer to moan them, he gave them the kind of cultural integrity they needed to ring true to his listeners. But Hall's "gospel" rang even truer. For Dorsey's to do so, he needed to relinquish his control and accept the free-will support that church audiences usually gave. The problem was that by neither instinct nor training did he or a Talbot-like singer perform with this goal in mind. The congregation must have sensed this. No doubt Dorsey was as deft at pricking their hearts that night as at any other time, but when they responded it was to indicate whether or not they shared the mood Dorsey created and whether or not they felt as *he* wanted them to. When Hall sang, he created a mood for his listeners, too; but it was the cue for them to preach and sing back to him as well as along with him. Thus it was not Hall alone, but Hall in consort with his bearers, who "took the show" that night.

But it was not only this noticeable difference in audience response that kindled Dorsey's interest in forming a partnership with a Nix-like preacher. To a great extent Dorsey was predisposed to yielding to the preacher's charisma. He had held a deep fascination for this figure stemming from his childhood idolization of his father as a preacher. The allure of Thomas Madison's pulpitry manifested itself in young Dorsey's imitation of the preacher under the front porch of his home. He witnessed first-hand the congregation's response to the preacher not only through its "amens" and "hallelujahs" but through the admiration, good food, and status it heaped upon him for merely being the preacher's son.

If this latent fixation had any expression, it was in Dorsey's gospel blues. In essence, he had been a preacher of the sort he revered since returning to religion. Indeed, his justification for writing blues songs with sacred texts was that the music in either its sacred or secular guise served the same function: to prick the heart, to get "low-down." As he had seen his father prick and get low-down with his voice and pulpit histrionics, so he had set out to do the same, first with his ivories and stage actions and now with his gospels and Rebecca Talbot. Comparisons with the recorded sermon illustrate that when Dorsey sat down to compose a gospel song, he in essence wrote a sermonette to blues accompaniment. He had come as close as he could to merging his music profession and religious beliefs through the bluesman/preacher he considered himself to be.

But there was a special quality about Dorsey the bluesman/preacher that made him uniquely eligible for a partnership with Hall. With the exception of the early rent parties and bordellos at which he had crooned, and with the exception of his years as Georgia Tom the blues singer, Dorsey's blues career had been made as an accompanist. He could sing—although he almost bragged about not being able to "a lick"—but the brunt of his artistry was funneled through the piano as a backup for a vocalist. He firmly believed in the subordinate role of the accompanist:

> Accompaniment is just accompaniment. The accompanist is just what it says, an accompanist. The singer is the one supposed to stand out, always. The voice stands out, even in opera, even in blues or whatever it is.[25]

Even with his gospel music, Dorsey continued to cultivate the accompanist's role. Indeed, it was his search for a better singer that drove him to approach Hall that night.

Underlying this almost constant quest for a singer was Dorsey's conviction that the mood of the song was established by the singer with the help of the accompanist:

> And it's okay to stay behind, stay under the singer, what I mean [by] behind the singer is, let the singer make the first [move]; you anticipate what's going to happen, see.

The supportive role of the pianist is really one in which she or he amplifies or otherwise strengthens the vocalist's expressions—taking care not to overpower or otherwise usurp the creative leadership of the singer:

> Now, the piano can show off [in] an introduction; that's the way I get them with the introduction, see. Now, you can embellish all you want to up here with the right hand, see. In your mind you do anything up here, see, but don't kill the singer.

In his own way, Dorsey saw himself as bearing up his singers much in the way a congregation would bear up a preacher. As it was theirs, so was it his duty to follow—even to anticipate—the singer's feelings, but never to take over. Even when he embellished, he worked within parameters similar to the singer on Nix's record: he was free to do as much musical extemporizing as he wanted without overpowering the singer. Nix's singer soared all around him, her melodic flight one of fancy. But she never obscured his voice.[26]

Considering the structure and content of his gospels and his accompanist role, Dorsey was a preacher, but only vicariously. As a composer, he created the message. As an accompanist, he was somewhat of a one-person congregation bearing up his singer. In neither of these roles, however, did Dorsey preach the message himself. Indeed, in both functions, he saw it as his duty to subordinate himself to the more overt preacher. He wrote the text and melody of the sermon. But knowing that the preacher/singer had to be "susceptible" at the time of delivery, Dorsey held back from notating all of the expressions and nuances. He could endure this denial of creative freedom knowing that as the accompanist he would assist in the rebirth of his creation. But even then he was no more than an attentive midwife, preparing for the great moment with a flourishing introduction only to have to stay behind the singer through it all as a mere preventive against artistic stillbirth. Small wonder that when he encountered the weak sweetness of a Louise Keller, he recoiled at her inability to "beat" out his songs. What little pianistic preaching he allowed himself was all the more suppressed by his accompanist's pledge to stay under her timid voice. With the smooth professionalism of a Rebecca Talbot, on the other hand, he could show all of his keyboard pulpitry, but only to have the congregation hold back its customary approval— perhaps questioning the sincerity of such polished blues artistry amidst the rawer utterances of spontaneous worship.

Three Dorseys rushed up to Hall that night, each of whom saw Hall as the preacher he wanted to be. Thomas Madison, for years lurking about as a dramatic impulse, longed for Hall's pulpit from which he could once again mesmerize his congregation. Thomas Andrew, for years the writer of blues songs, needed Hall to preach and thereby authenticate the blues sermons he now composed. And Georgia Tom, wishing to put his honky-tonk days behind him, wanted to use his ivories to bear Hall up so that he could be the king of the worship hour as he once was of the night. In Hall, Dorsey found one alter ego for the parts of himself that at various times in his life had ravaged his well-being with their warfare. As he asked Hall to "come along with me, go along with me," each part of him was signaling a willingness to vent itself through Hall.

From the perspective of Dorsey's personality, therefore, the deal he made with Hall was more than "I play for you and you sing my songs for me." It was a pledge of support from the bluesman/preacher/composer Dorsey: we will bear you up musically and dramatically as you preach our sermons for us. With one decision, Dorsey had consolidated his theatrical, compositional, and performing talents into one religious persona. When he walked away from the meeting that night, Dorsey must have had a premonition that he and Hall would make the gospel blues he had always wanted. As he would put it many years later, "we did very good at it."

The "good" Dorsey speaks of refers to the more tangible effects of their partnership on his efforts to popularize his songs. Dorsey's primary concern after composing gospel blues was to "make a market" for them. His search for the right voice to sing them was brought on by his realization that the "market" already existed through the efforts of the singing evangelist and recording preacher traditions. Upon hearing Hall, Dorsey certainly reacted on the basis of the preacher antecedents in his life. But the more concrete benefits of an association with Hall as a singer with direct access to the "market" that Dorsey needed were just as surely at the root of his rush to team up with Hall.

This is clearly illustrated by Hall's role in bringing Dorsey to the seat of singing evangelists and recording preachers, the National Baptist Convention. In 1930 the Baptists held their annual convention in Chicago. This was not just an ordinary meeting but a celebration of the Convention's Jubilee Anniversary. In many respects, however, the fractiousness that had characterized the National Baptist Convention since its inception was so pronounced as to mar the grandeur of the occasion. There were challenges to the leadership of President L. K. Williams and charges of fraud and mismanagement of the Sunday School Publishing Board. The Board's problems received national attention because of the indictment of its director, Dr. A. M. Townsend, in connection with the murder of Edward Pierson, a Convention auditor who had recently checked the Board's records. The Convention was aswarm with protest pamphlets and rumors of various conspiracies. Only 1,034 of the 15,000 delegates registered, meaning that the election of the president and most other business matters were suspected of being controlled by Williams loyalists.[27]

In spite of these problems, however, the Convention's pageantry was conducted as usual and only as it could have been under the sponsorship of the black Baptist churches of Chicago. Old-line choir directors assembled a chorus of 1000 voices that was described as "a rare treat for all." The church drama clubs and professional actors and musicians throughout the city presented a musical about Baptist history in America with the 1000-voice chorus and a 50-piece orchestra. Even Chicago musicians with national reputations and no connection to the Convention took part. These included J. Wesley Jones, the choir director at Metropolitan Community Church, Anita Patti Brown, the internationally known singer, and Florence Price, the first black American woman to achieve notoriety as a composer.[28]

Amidst the classical music and musicians were performances of the more familiar hymns and "gospels" by the congregation and church musicians. The Convention opened with a song service that included *My Hope Is Built on Nothing Less, What a Fellowship,* and *Am I a Soldier of the Cross.* Various soloists—including some singing evangelists—sang traditional hymns such as *Old Ship of Zion* as well as the newer "gospels" such as Tindley's *Take Your Burdens to the Lord.* These musicians also introduced new music to the Convention. One of them, a Mrs. Willie Mae Fisher, sang Dorsey's *If You See My Savior* during the morning devotions on August 23.[29]

Had it not been for Hall, the National Baptist Convention premiere of Dorsey's song might have occurred without Dorsey's notice and without benefit to him. By the time Dorsey heard about Fisher's performance, *If You See My Savior* was a "hit." Indeed, as Dorsey recalls, "every man, woman and child was singing or humming the tune." Hall went in search of Dorsey, knowing, evidently, that Dorsey would be unaware of the new popularity of his first gospel blues:

This National Baptist Convention met here at the coliseum. I didn't bother about it. Reverend Hall had attended this convention. Now before I go further, I had written about three or four gospel songs. This Reverend Hall came out to my house to see me and says, "Dorsey, come on, man, you've got to go on down here. It's a woman down there from," I think he said, "St. Louis, or Kansas City, somewhere in Missouri, man. She's got that 'If You See My Savior.' She's laying them out in the aisle and the folk are just jumping and going on. Man, you got to see them." I said, "Oh, I ain't got time." He said, "No, come on, get ready, get ready; I'll be back at such and such a time. They kind of out for dinner now; you get ready and come and go." I did.[30]

Dorsey had good reason not to want to "bother with" the Convention:

I wasn't giving all my time to the church, see. I was kind of straddling the fence—making money out there on the outside, you know, in the band business and then going to church Sunday morning helping what I could do for them for they wasn't able to pay nothing. I could make money out there.

"Out there," especially in 1930, meant the record business. This was one of the best years of his recording career. Since the beginning of 1930, Dorsey had made sixteen recordings, most of which he published under his own name, his Paramount name, George Ramsey, as the other member of the now famous duet, Tampa Red and Georgia Tom, or as a member of the ensemble, the Famous Hokum Boys. In addition, he accompanied Big Bill Broonzy, Kansas City Kitty, Jane Lucas (also known as Hannah May), and Frank Brasswell. In no way had Dorsey altered the suggestive content of his songs: a mere week or so before he appeared at the Convention, he recorded She Can Love So Good and You Rascal You with Tampa Red.[31]

Even if it had occurred to Dorsey to "bother with" the Convention, he would have been skeptical about his chances for promoting his music there. The hierarchy among the Convention's musicians would make introducing new music virtually impossible for an unknown composer such as Dorsey. National Baptist Convention music giants such as "Professor" E. W. D. Isaacs and Mrs. Lucie Campbell, from their positions as "director general" and "pianist," respectively, of the Baptist Young People's Union, exercised considerable authority over the music of the Convention. To Dorsey, these were the "bigwigs" whom he knew only through "books and in the papers." Even though Isaacs had been the one to send Hall to find Dorsey, Dorsey was no more encouraged to attend. Isaacs and Campbell had been the sources of much of Dorsey's disillusionment with the Convention. They were two of the people to whom he had sent his songs and from whom he had gotten neither an order nor even an acknowledgment that they had received his music. If anyone could have helped the fledgling gospel writer, it was Isaacs and Campbell. As head of the Convention's youth organization, Isaacs managed a large network of pastors and youth leaders; to a great extent these people composed the market that Dorsey was finding so elusive. Even more significant, Isaacs and Campbell served on the National Baptist Convention's Music Committee. In this capacity they could control the introduction of music into Baptist churches across the nation. Campbell, in particular, was an ideal conduit for new music. Since becoming active in the Convention in 1916, she had published many songs and was well known because of them.[32]

Ironically, it was this sense of the elitism of the Convention that drew Dorsey to follow Hall back there:

> The gig at that time was to grab what you could while you could, for if it went away, you never saw it anymore. If you got a chance to perform in any organization, do it right then, for God only knows when you reach them again.

This was Dorsey the shrewd opportunist thinking as much as it was Dorsey the unknown gospel songwriter grateful for the chance to gain exposure for his songs. One of Hall's most persuasive arguments was his description of the audience's response to *If You See My Savior*. Dorsey knew, therefore, that in spite of its closed membership, the Convention was already open to him as a result of the demand for his song. He had, in effect, leaped over the music committee and other such bureaucratic barriers to capture the hearts of the conventioneers. Thus when Dorsey thought about it, Isaacs's summons was not for the composer who had been sending him the songs; it was for Thomas A. Dorsey, the composer whose song had slipped by him. While Dorsey could not be sure that he would actually be accepted as one of the Isaacs and Campbells of the Convention, he could be certain that he had become as well known as one of them:

> No, no, they wasn't letting them [other composers] in. But I just happened to have what they didn't have. The people liked it and I got in.[33]

While Dorsey's recruitment of Hall as a surrogate preacher benefited him psychologically, his introduction to the Convention signaled the first tangible success of his gospel song venture. The actual event in which he participated, however, was rather insignificant: it was a rehearsal after one of the meetings. After being introduced to Campbell and "some of the big preachers," Dorsey met Willie Mae Fisher, who once again performed Dorsey's song. Isaacs then introduced Dorsey as the composer of *If You See My Savior* and asked him to say a few words:

> I got in and they had a rehearsal after the meeting was out, and someone took me in and introduced me. They said, "Are you the Dorsey that writes the songs?" They didn't say what kind of songs. I said, "Oh, yes, sir. I write all kinds of songs." I had several words to say. I told them about my music. I guess they liked my talk, and they wanted to hear some of the songs. That's all I wanted.

Dorsey, with Hall's singing, took advantage of the opportunity for all he could:

> Isaacs said, "Go and bring your music down here and set you up a stand over there in the corner." And I did. "Bring some of—all your music." I did. "Put it there." And I been in the music business ever since, ever since. That was the big moment right there.

By the time the Convention ended, Dorsey recalls selling 4000 copies of his music. Moreover, he made a lasting impression on the major musicians of the Convention. Both Isaacs and Campbell helped him with his music from then on, often arranging demonstrations and concerts for him and inviting him to participate in each of the Conventions thereafter. He had every reason to feel that he "had made the grade and was a success as a gospel song writer."[34]

Hall had demonstrated his worth well. Not only had he been the unifying agent of Dorsey's contentious personalities, but now he was the means to Dorsey's newfound "success" and to his becoming an esteemed new member of the National Baptist Convention musicians' elite. Hall had spent two days searching for Dorsey and then humoring him to come to a Convention Dorsey "wasn't much bothered about."[35] If Hall's purpose had been just to boost his own reputation, he would have had no need to put such effort into finding Dorsey. As Willie Mae Fisher and her pianist had shown convincingly, Hall could have gained considerable notice just by singing one of Dorsey's songs without Dorsey as the accompanist. Hall certainly had the performance ability, inasmuch as it was he who sang the songs Dorsey demonstrated for the Convention. Thus, much of the enthusiasm Isaacs and Campbell had for Dorsey's gospels was generated not only by the music itself but by the way Hall rendered it. Indeed, there is as much reason as not to believe that they were drawn to *If You See My Savior* by the same qualities in Hall's performance as Dorsey had been when he first enlisted Hall's assistance. Hall clearly had filled the role Dorsey, the shrewd showman, had anticipated. With several hundred dollars in his pocket and the National Baptist Convention taken by his song and abuzz with his name, Dorsey had Hall to thank in particular for having "made the grade."

But the debt was not only Dorsey's. Whatever each man endeavored to accomplish professionally seemed to accrue to the ambitions of the other. When Hall could track down "the man that writes the songs," the Isaacses and Campbells appreciated him all the more for his contacts. All the while Dorsey gained access to the market he so desperately wanted. As Hall sang other Dorsey songs during their demonstration, he was helping Dorsey show that he was not a fly-by-night, perhaps lucky, writer of the most popular song of the Convention; rather he was a serious composer with an established repertoire of songs. All the while Hall was identifying himself as the singing evangelist/preacher riding the crest of what was clearly a new wave in black sacred music. In essence, the historical symbiosis between them as bluesman and preacher was complemented by the delicate symmetry of their individual professional strivings. The National Baptist Convention was just one of the many episodes in which their cross-purposes would yield mutual benefits. As the Convention closed, they both had many reasons to think that "we did very good at it."

By the end of the Convention, Dorsey can be said to have undergone all of the personal development that he would in the cause of the advent of gospel blues. He had decided to present his songs as sermons. From that decision had ensued the personal and professional benefits of his relationship with Hall, the popularity of his gospels, and the new collegial and business contacts he was poised to exploit in order to market his music. From the success he was enjoying—all of it occurring in an aura of inner reconciliation—Dorsey could well conclude that his choice to set the gospel to blues and market the result was a mission he should continue to pursue seriously.

8

The Emergence
of Gospel Blues:
1931–1932

James Mundy, an old-line choir director, explains the sweep of Dorsey's gospels through Chicago's black churches allegorically:

> The Negro people liked gospel 'cause it goes back to Africa. That's why it got a hold of them. It's indigenous. The teacher told a story about an eagle and an eaglet. The mother eagle laid her egg down on a farm, you know, and then she went scouting way out somewheres. So the eaglet hatched out of the egg and went along with the little chickens; couldn't tell the difference. So the mother screamed, "Wah, wah." To hear that scream, there is no chicken no more. It ran on up to its mother and they went off together. So that's the way it is with the American Negroes; there's an awakening. This mother is Africa. They were sort of going along with the chickens and they heard that cry. Eagles running with chickens. But this scream had something innate within it; [the eaglet] went on up to its mother where it belonged.[1]

At each of the critical points in Dorsey's career a cry—perhaps to him like the mother eagle's—sounded for him to alter his life significantly. The cry from Bessie Smith's downhome blues awakened him to the fact that he had been running with the Tin Pan Alley "chickens." Her cry brought him back to traditional blues and into his blues-making with Ma Rainey and then into his recording career as Georgia Tom. Next the cry came in the preaching/singing of the Reverends Nix and Hall and the other recording preachers. They summoned him to a more effective presentation of his gospel songs and to a unification of the disparate parts of his religious personality.

Given the critical role of the downhome blues cry in his life, Dorsey could be counted on to let it figure prominently in his gospel blues. In many ways the cry itself was the hallmark of the blues in that, along with the moan, it signaled the singer's ability to get lowdown. Dorsey was "pricked" by it and thus aimed to use it to get deep into his gospel listeners:

. . . it's those turns, that's the thing that sells the music and that's the thing that comes from the soul. They cry it out. You can go up or you can drop; [you] can moan, see, you beg, then you express it. Let the folk wonder what the next thing is gonna be. It isn't the tune that makes it; it's what you put in the tune.[2]

Even though the cry comes from the soul, it is a technique that the blues singer, secular or religious, has to learn to execute:

There is a trick in it. I use that more than I do the piano, for people can't, even singers can't do that [naturally]. That is something you got to practice in the throat and that is why I can get over. You cry a little bit. [You] teach them how to say their words in a way, in a moanful way and more of a crying way, more to show the sadness and the weight that was upon them, the burden.[3]

Thus the cry was foremost in Dorsey's mind when he sought out the most effective singer for his gospels. He had to reject Louise Keller because she lacked it. Although he could depend on Rebecca Talbot to produce it, he often cringed at the professionalism with which she performed it. In Hall, Dorsey at last found the cry he needed, probably because Hall used some variant of it in his preaching and thus carried it over to his singing.

The cry was important to Dorsey from more than the performer's perspective, however. Although it was the singer's responsibility to initiate it, the cry was a shared reaction. The singer cued her audience with her cry:

[The singer] got to give enough attention for what is being conveyed to go inside of the individual, and then if there is something that touches them, if there is something in them, they holler out, "Hallelujah" or "Amen" in church. In the theater, they holler "Sing it again" or "Do it again" something like that.

Optimally, therefore, the cry invoked communal emotionalism:

Here is a man or woman singing blues and a certain strain in the blues touched somebody out there in the audience. I have seen them holler out. I have seen women and men jump up and, well, they wasn't shouting—we can't call it shouting in the theater—but they would holler, whoop, jump up, and wring and shout just like folk do in church.[4]

This was the ambience—one in which the performer and listener fueled one another's fervor—that Dorsey pursued relentlessly. Each time he discovered it, he felt that he had reached a new plateau in his struggle to introduce his music. When Hall "took the show," Dorsey knew he had found the right voice to deliver his gospels. After hearing that Willie Mae Fisher was "laying them out in the aisle" and had the National Baptist Convention "jumping and going on," Dorsey overcame his reluctance to participate in the Convention.

The cry or the scream is deeply rooted in the black religious experience. Slaves used blankets and inverted pots to muffle it during their secret "hush harbor" meetings. Charles Grandy recalls that during his days as a slave in Hampton, Virginia, his fellow slaves lined up to get the chance to holler into the pot at worship services:

> Whites in our section used to have a service fo' us slaves ev'y fo'th Sunday, but da twasn't 'nuf fo' dem who wanted to talk wid Jesus. Used to go 'cross de fields nights to a old tobacco barn on de side of a hill. Do' was on de ground flo', an' you could climb up a ladder an' step out de winder to de ground on de other side. Had a old pot hid dere to catch de sound. Sometimes would stick yo' haid down in de pot if you got to shout awful loud. 'Member ole Sister Miller Jeffries. Would stick her haid in de pot an' shout an' pray all night whilst de others was bustin' to take dere turn. Sometimes de slaves would have to pull her haid out dat pot so's de others could shout.

Writing in 1950, Willis Laurence James traced African American "'whoops,' 'hollers,' [and] 'calls'" back "hundreds of years." They reside today, he stated, in African American song patterns and account for "the great pull these songs exert on Negroes."[5]

Dorsey should have been able to perform in any church—old-line churches included—knowing that the cries of his gospels had such historical precedence. But it was precisely the latency of this tradition that kept old-line ministers alerted to any signs of its resurgence. As the modern Bishop Daniel Paynes, as the ideological progeny of the white missionaries, and as the guardians of progressive blackness, they traced their opposition to the cry back to such nineteenth-century black intellectual giants as William Wells Brown. Upon witnessing folk religion, Brown wrote:

> It will be difficult to erase from the mind of the negro of the South, the prevailing idea that outward demonstrations, such as, shouting, the loud "amen," and the most boisterous noise in prayer, are not necessary adjuncts to piety.[6]

By putting deacons' prayer services in the basements of their churches and anthem-singing choirs in their pulpits and by smothering the spontaneous singing of their congregations with formal hymns, old-line ministers had rid their churches of the very uncontrolled outbursts Dorsey looked forward to re-introducing. Thus Dorsey was roundly rebuked when he brought his gospels into their churches. Some rejected his music with the excuse that it was theologically inappropriate:

> This thing of gospel, it was something new; they didn't take to it well. Preacher don't want you singing no gospel. The preacher'd get up there and say, "You can't sing no gospel, only preach the gospel." I've been thrown out of some of the best churches in the country for that. 'Course that just made

me angry. And I wanted to challenge him there, then. There's no need of me arguing with them in their own churches.

Others thought he was inconsequential and "forgot" or, as the case may be, ignored him:

> I shall never forget the embarrassment I suffered one Sunday morning when I had made arrangements with a minister to sing and introduce one of my songs in the morning service in one of the largest churches in the city. I arrived that morning about thirty minutes before service time with my singer Rebecca Talbot. The minister greeted us and gave us a seat on the front row of pews and said, "I will call for you to sing just after the morning message." Was I beaming over with joy to know my song would be sung in this church which had over 2000 people worshipping that morning! But something happened or there was a change of mind. The choir marched in, the minister preached, extended the invitation for members, lifted the offering, dismissed the congregation, and left me and my singer sitting on the front row seats without a word of explanation.[7]

In other instances, the rebuke was neither as mild nor as subtle. Augustus Evans, one of the earliest singers to introduce gospel blues independently of Dorsey, tells of an occasion when he experienced a direct reprimand for singing the "gospel":

> I recall very, very plainly a very sophisticated church, very, very professional, the minister highly sophisticated. I sang this Sunday morning, at the morning service. I carried on; so one lady hollered when I was singing one of these songs. Immediately the usher rushed to her and got her and carried her out of the seat. The preacher got up and caught me by the arm and then just that quick at the bottom of the steps coming off the rostrum, there the treasurer was with a check in his hands. He handed it to me and said, "Come on man, get out."

When Evans says that he "carried on," he probably means that he sang in a more traditional style than was customary. He was allowed to sing at this church only because of his reputation as a fine singer. Moreover, as an old-line choir director, he was known to his counterpart there:

> . . . otherwise, they wouldn't have let me in in the first place to do this. They had heard me before. [There was] a highly sophisticated and very well trained musician there and we worked together and we knew each other. So there was no problem with that [until] that lady shouted.[8]

More than any of Dorsey's summary dismissals, Evans's experience illustrates the volatile tension that existed between Dorsey's music and old-line ministers. Once Evans, who had not previously been singing blues, adopted Dorsey's music and performance style and thus "carried on," he provoked the classic response—the one old-line ministers thought they had heard the last of. With the first ecstatic cry from a member of the congregation, Evans became an outcast among those who had been his colleagues:

> These gospel songs created a spontaneous response. It reached out there and it touched the heart. People would shout and people would say "Amen." In some of these churches you didn't say "Amen." And this was one of them and I knew it. But they had no idea that this was going to happen; otherwise they wouldn't have let me in. They got me out of there and her out of there very, very quickly. I looked at the check afterwards and I said, "I wonder what did he pay me for?"[9]

There is something over-reactive, almost jittery, in these responses to Dorsey's music. After all, gospel song and singers were not new. Given the recording preachers, itinerant evangelists and singers, and the officially designated "gospel" singers of the day, there should have been numerous antecedents for Dorsey's songs. But it was precisely because this music was prevalent that old-line ministers were so overbearing in their reactions. They knew of this music, but only in contexts vastly different from the worship hours at which they officiated. A Nix preached and sang his gospel on the record player in a home. A Hall sang his in a special meeting such as a revival. A. J. H. Smiley or Willie Mae Fisher was featured at a large assembly like the National Baptist Convention annual meetings. Even at the Convention where Dorsey's songs had been well received "by every man, woman and child," a contextual orthodoxy of sorts dictated where his music could be performed. The pageant, the thousand-voice chorus, and the solos by old-line directors such as Edward Boatner occurred at special sessions which were held in the Coliseum away from the Convention headquarters at Olivet Baptist Church. Although some "gospel" singers performed in these special sessions, none of the Boatners or other classical music performers appeared in the regular sessions. The Convention, it seems, would put on its musical airs when it went out into the public and then take them off when it returned home. The Sunday School and Baptist Young People's Congress at which Fisher introduced *If You See My Savior* met as a "departmental" meeting, adjunct as such to the Convention. Here a Dorsey or a Hall could perform under the watchful eyes of Isaacs and Campbell, members of the Convention's music establishment.[10]

Not even the cry itself, however, should have aroused old-line ministers to act as precipitously as they did upon hearing Dorsey's music. The "mixed" worship that they conducted required the measured use of traditional black preaching techniques. Indeed, eclecticism of this sort lay at the foundation of the old-line dialectic. The balance between old and new in the old-line sermon was a device to prompt the same in congregational demeanor. Thus there was a place even in old-line churches for an oratorical technique such as the cry. "University" educated preachers like Pilgrim's J. C. Austin could "scream" while at the same time disapprove of shouting from the congregation.[11]

At first glance, therefore, old-line ministers' indignation at Dorsey's songs appears to be rooted in their notion of territoriality. Dorsey's gospels were no more to be judged as theologically askew, or to be ignored, or to be thrown out than any of the other music that could be identified under the same rubric. He simply misjudged where they were to be heard. But this analysis focuses on the effect instead of the cause. Old-line ministers' sense of territoriality stemmed from their growing awareness that they were being besieged by Dorsey's kind of music. They could see the records of the Nixes and his singers selling by the thousands. They could see unknown singing evangelists like Hall and upstart gospel composers like Dorsey walk into the National Baptist Convention and sell 4000 copies of music in two days. And they could observe their congregations swelling week by week with the very people whose desire for this type of music seemed palpable enough to bring the Nixes, Halls, and Dorseys ever-increasing fame and fortune.

Even more alarming to old-line ministers than the growing popularity of this music was the sense that Dorsey's songs and his singers posed a greater threat than the other gospel singers. Although Dorsey may have been converted, he was still a practicing bluesman whose identity as Georgia Tom, one of the most popular blues artists of the time, loomed over that of most old-line ministers. As one notorious for his suggestive blues, Dorsey appeared as a highly visible symbol—beyond and within old-line churches—of the literal and figurative lowdownness of blues. And as if to fuel old-line ministers' suspicions even further, Dorsey arrived in their churches with a blues show-woman or a preacher of similar ilk. Even if they were unfamiliar with his recording name, ministers must have detected a certain pruriency in the cries of Dorsey, Talbot, and Hall. Next to its use by some old-line ministers as a gesture of compromise, the cry of these bluespeople shattered the fragile formalism of old-line churches with an unexpected, virulent sincerity. These were professionals committed to the black church as the proper place to "get lowdown" and to "prick" the very response old-line ministers were pledged to quell.

One more fundamental reason existed for old-line ministers to react so irritably to Dorsey's songs: he threatened their control over their congregations. The symbolic importance of Dorsey's conversion was that it re-unified the bluesman and the traditional black preacher. As a bluesman/preacher, Dorsey, through his ivories and with Hall as his surrogate voice, assumed the role in church that he had cultivated so well in the hole-in-the-wall blues joints—that of eliciting a collective response through the declaration of his personal feelings. Old-line ministers, on the other hand, specialized in suppressing audience reaction. Even when they resorted to traditional preaching techniques such as the cry, they used them artificially in that they discouraged the complementary congregational, that is, collective, reply. Thus with the first lone cry of the bluesman—from Evans, when he "carried on," from Talbot and Hall with their "moans and turns," and from Dorsey with his "ivories"—old-line ministers instinctively recoiled: their antitype was unexpectedly and inexplicably in their midst, engaged in an expressive dialogue with their congregations. These audiences overflowed with recent southern migrants who, for the most part, hailed from the culture and religion where the bluesman in his most primordial function was the preacher—the exact preacher that old-line ministers had been educated not to be. What little crying and screaming they allowed themselves paled in comparison to the bluesman when he "carried on" and the church shouted back. To those new settlers long nurtured in the southern ethos, the sound of this bluesman's gospel song exposed old-line preaching as an imposture; its cry, a mockery.

Ironically, at least some old-line ministers had made allowances for communal interaction of the sort Dorsey provoked. As now seems characteristic of old-line religion, its rigid assimilationist bent was often blunted by the ever-mounting presence of southerners. Just as ministers had been forced to mimic some aspects of traditional preaching in order to draw more migrants into their congregations, they were equally pressed to provide some semblance of the traditional communal worship environment in order to keep these new settlers.

As early as 1921, migrants had clearly shown their desire for more participatory worship. The *Chicago Defender* noted that, in spite of the "large number of fine and expensive churches" with their pulpits occupied by ministers of "marked intelligence and of more than ordinary ability," some members still insisted on converting their residences "into places of public worship":

> These religious enthusiasts do not seem to realize that residential neighborhoods are liable to have people living there who do not share with them in their demonstrative manifestations of religious devotion. Loud and noisy declamations and moans and groans from sisters and brothers until a late hour in the night are not only annoying but an unmistakable nuisance. . . .

Throughout the 1920s and '30s, black religious cults and non-traditionally organized Christian groups multiplied, especially in cities with large migrant populations such as Philadelphia, New York, and Chicago. Writing in 1936 about this phenomenon, Miles Mark Fisher observed that not all people who took part in the services of the cults and the alternative churches were actually members of those groups:

> A pastor in a cult center facetiously remarked to me: "If you want to see my folks on a Sunday night, go to Elder Lucy Smith's." It is not accidental that church attendance, particularly on Sunday nights, has decreased while cult attendance has increased, that cult meetings become crowded on Sundays after the churches have about dismissed and that the cults hold meetings during the week at times when the churches have no worship services.

Evidently, like the slaves who felt the need to slip behind the tobacco barn in order "to talk wid Jesus" by hollering into a pot, recent migrants just as compulsively sought out the traditional collective religious experience to compensate for the passivity expected of them in old-line churches.[12]

Old-line ministers seem to have made a token effort to address the need for responsive worship. Ironically, they stumbled on the opportunity for this type of gathering by allowing groups devoted to indigenous singing to form. The precedent for such an organization is found in the early 1920s at Bethel AME, one of the oldest of old-line Methodist churches. The minister requested the senior choir to sing throughout an upcoming revival, but some of them balked at the idea because they would have to sing traditional songs in a traditional manner. Not to be defeated, the minister went to his congregation:

> Well, then, he called for volunteers and people to come in. People from the audience who liked to sing and [who liked] spontaneity [said], "I'll come up and help him out. I'll come up and help him out." So he went through that whole revival meeting with this volunteer choir.[13]

In true old-line spirit, the first indigenous singing group was created out of condescension for traditional black music.

Evidently this chorus rekindled more than revival sentiments: "They just made such a fine go of it, see, they said, 'Let's keep this thing going.' And after this they started up the gospel chorus." At Quinn Chapel, the same type of group was organized under similar circumstances.[14] The absence of records of the formation of either of these choruses such as those available for the choirs of Bethel and Quinn indicates a lower regard for the chorus compared with the choir. The lack of documentation is not, however, conclusive evidence that either chorus became extinct. Indeed, the above account indicates the opposite: chorus members wanted to "keep this thing going" by getting the gospel chorus "started up."

Almost eight years later, at the point the record resumes, organized indigenous singing became more formalized. At Metropolitan Community Church, a chorus was organized in 1928; Dr. William D. Cook, the pastor, requested Mrs. Magnolia Lewis (Butts) to form the group in order to "sing for funerals, because the Senior Choir's repertoire wasn't funeral music." Later, they "began to sing according to the dictates of Magnolia's heart and mind; they moved to the gospel area." As their popularity grew, they took responsibility for music at the Friday night evangelistic service: "The Friday night service was singing by the gospel choir, testimony by the people of the congregation; it was called fellowship night." Although the reason was never explained to them—especially curious considering their successful evangelism, the chorus was not invited to sing during the Sunday morning worship: "All that we knew was that we never sang on Sunday morning."[15]

On one hand, with the formation of the chorus at Metropolitan, the contours of indigenous musical expression within old-line religion were out-lined. Any means by which the fervor associated with traditional Afro-American religion could be expressed without threat to the stability and prestige of old-line religion were encouraged. With this policy, the chorus could indulge in its quaint manner of singing, praying, and testifying. Just as apparent was the sanctity of the Sunday morning worship as the hour in which old-line religion shone forth in strictest purity. With its foundations unchallenged and its weekly ascent to high church customs untethered by the earthiness of its past, old-line religion could tolerate and even foster the institutionalizing of the very form of expression to which it was diametrically opposed.

On the other hand, the existence of the chorus in old-line churches while in the heat of their rush to abandon traditional religion is perhaps the clearest indication of the intrinsic duality of old-line religion up to 1931. The presence at Metropolitan, Bethel, and Quinn Chapel of some of the city's finest black choirs, the most lauded Sunday afternoon musicales, and the best-trained and most noted directors of music did little to dissuade the longing for traditional songs. The chorus showed irrefutably that the prac-tice of the old religion—southern and truly black—could be curtailed but not denied.

This duality was made even more explicit by the positions that Bethel, Quinn Chapel, and Metropolitan occupied on the spectrum of old-line re-ligious values. Old-line religion ranged from the dogmatic formality of its acculturative goals to the friendly warmth of its social ones. Quinn was known as a "'swank' church, not for the 'common herd.'" It was an impos-ing, "commodious" structure located in a neighborhood in which few blacks lived. Early in its history, Bethel was widely known to cater only to intellec-tuals, in part because of its Sunday forums and other cultural events. Collec-tively, along with other AME churches, Bethel and Quinn Chapel were generally "passed up" by the recently migrated "Southern Negro" because they were oriented to "the more intelligent type."[16]

By virtue of its history and origins, Metropolitan occupied the opposite end of the spectrum. It began as an experiment in "seeking a greater demo-cracy in religious worship." Metropolitan's pastor, Dr. William D. Cook, formerly of Bethel, refused to accept the AME Bishop's assignment to an-other church. He and a large number of followers left Bethel and established Metropolitan in September 1920, in order "'to preach the Gospel without dictation'":

> The case here was that the Community movement was brand new and it gave to the people from the Methodist church a certain freedom. They were not involved where they came from and so this gave them a sense of belonging. They came from other churches, because they just sat. Many of them testified here on Friday night that they just sat in Bethel because they didn't seem a

part of the organized thing. But this Community movement gave everybody freedom to become involved.

As a need-oriented church, Metropolitan shaped its mission not to the tenets of a theology "but according to the present-day experiences and needs of its people." Even its physical plan was shaped around its social goals: there were several buildings with facilities for clubs, relief for the poor, and even employment services. The gospel chorus was but another opportunity to fulfill a social need: it served "the people, if they wanted, to make an individual contribution." The Friday night service was the central event of "fellowship night," the most participatory worship experience Metropolitan offered. During this service the chorus could fulfill its real goals:

> "I can't read music; I'm going into the gospel choir." And, for no other purpose or for no other feeling than "I'm helping this church move, because this is it as far as I am concerned." Everybody was so bent on helping the movement until they didn't have any motive than maybe, perhaps "I was shut out here, or there, or yonder."[17]

Regardless of the leanings of an old-line church, organized indigenous music seemed to benefit the congregation. In the old-line churches where the emphasis was on acculturation, indigenous music thrived only slightly less than in those churches where social goals were stressed. And yet social concern could not absolve any old-line church from upholding the acculturative elements of the Sunday worship. Clearly, the duality of old-line religion was equally binding on all of its institutions.

Perhaps in its deepest sense, the duality lay with each member of these old-line churches, but especially with the new settlers because of their overwhelming presence. By the single fact that they filled the pews in increasing numbers, migrants encouraged the development of old-line religion. Those old settlers who were truly alienated by the vestiges of downhome worship in old-line churches left to organize Presbyterian, Episcopalian, and other such churches in denominations that were not traditionally black. New settlers likewise departed to storefront churches or completely severed their ties with the church when old-line services failed to stir them. Each person who stayed behind despite the availability of such clear alternatives helped to nurture the "mixed-type" religion that old-line values had become.[18] In doing so, each individual acknowledged the sometimes subliminal cultural ambivalence that smoldered within.

This duality, at least on the personal level, contained a strong element of duplicity. A clear rejection by the congregation of any of the cultural principles of old-line religion would have sufficed to alter it. But prior to 1931, migrants never signaled their wholehearted dislike of the choir; neither did old settlers show their total disdain of the chorus—in its proper place. By sitting Sunday after Sunday listening to Mendelssohn, Mozart, and concert arrangements of black spirituals, each recent southerner demonstrated a deep desire to leave "medieval America for modern"—to grow beyond the old religion. So did each northerner, by singing and shouting at the Friday night service, acknowledge the need for at least marginal adherence to old-time religion.[19]

Given the visceral response of old-line ministers to his gospels, Dorsey could have reasonably expected their hostility to continue were it not for these indigenous singing groups—especially Metropolitan's. He virtually happened upon Metropolitan's usefulness to his cause:

> There were no gospel choirs that were active; the word was just a name and very few groups had the name. I stumbled into a political meeting one night at the Eighth Regiment Armory in Chicago and there was a slight short brown-skinned woman with a big voice singing my song, "How About You." I wanted to know who she was. I found out she was Magnolia Lewis who was soloist in the great Metropolitan Community Church Choir directed by the late J. Wesley Jones. She invited me to come over to the church and hear her choir, the W. D. Cook Gospel Choir.

Evidently, Dorsey not only listened to the chorus but, true to his calling, led its members through his songs. The response was so favorable that he was able to sell them some of his music, and they in turn performed it regularly:

> This choir was the first choir in Chicago to use the Dorsey songs. They sang only twice a month. But they would have a large crowd each time they sang, because these gospel songs were something new and the people would come out to hear them.[20]

The choral performance of his songs marked the most significant change in his strategies to create a "market" for his music and to set the stage for the acceptance of gospel blues in old-line churches. Dorsey, along with his soloists, stood as a highly profiled representation of the classic black preacher. He so clearly violated the standards of old-line worship because his blues persona so explicity contrasted with that of the old-line leadership character. Moreover, he was easily expelled from old-line churches because he was a transient presence. With his expressed monetary incentive for attending these churches, he would have appeared to have little regard for their values, against which he so passionately crooned. Old-line ministers risked little or no backlash for turning out this musical mercenary.

The chorus, on the other hand, in addition to being a ready-made "market," had a place in old-line churches. It gave legitimacy to Dorsey's music if for no other reason than the fact that its members composed significant parts of old-line congregations and thus would not appear to want to violate old-line principles. Most important, with its place rigidly defined by the paternalistic impulse of old-line ministers toward their less cultured brothers and sisters, the chorus was never in a position to challenge the old-line preacher during the most important Sunday morning worship hour. Holler, shout, and sing as it may to Dorsey's music, the old-line chorus knew well that such deportment would not be tolerated outside of the revivals, funerals, prayer services, and Friday night testimony meetings.

Dorsey still might not have known the full benefits of the chorus had he not been called to organize one at Ebenezer Baptist Church in 1931. Indeed, it is within the context of the chorus's role as an old-line compromise and as a potential medium for gospel song that the Ebenezer Gospel Chorus was first formed. Theoretically, the decline—or at least the reshaping—of classic old-line religion would begin once indigenous singing and the demeanor that accompanied it joined the choir in the activity that most exemplified old-line religion: Sunday morning worship. Such juxtaposition of the familiar and the foreign elements of old-line religion would produce a mixed religion of truly equal proportions. The formation of the chorus at Ebenezer in 1931 brought about this mixture.

Ebenezer adopted a profile that advocated acculturative excess in the degrees that Bethel and Quinn Chapel were known for. Indeed, Ebenezer, as a Baptist church, may have leaned uncharacteristically toward their persuasion. Baptist churches were known to tolerate more of the traditional worship responses than did the Methodists.[21] Even if Ebenezer allowed such demeanor, however, the full expression of it was tempered by the Ebenezer Senior Choir, one of the most noted of old-line choirs. One could tell just by the training and experience of the organist and choir director, Mabel Sanford Lewis, that the music at Ebenezer met or exceeded old-line standards. Known as one who "has been placed just below the immortals" in her talent, Lewis studied with such notables as Felix Borowski in Chicago, Isadore Phillip in London, and Vincent d'Indy in Paris. For several years she accompanied the famous black singer Anita Patti Brown ("Black Patti"). She came to Ebenezer in 1926 and remained until 1938, at first as its organist and later as its organist/choir director. So imposing was the choir music, in fact, that congregational singing was limited to familiar old songs; Ebenezer provided no hymnals for its congregation.[22]

Ebenezer was one of the first of the Baptist churches that split from Olivet and formed the core group of old-line institutions. From its beginning as an Olivet splinter group through 1930, Ebenezer followed the classic old-line rites of passage. In 1902, the Reverend John Francis Thomas (perhaps a former pastor from the South) organized a group of thirty members of Olivet; they began meeting informally at "Arlington Hall." A short while later, because of their rapid growth, they purchased a building and, in 1920, a former synagogue. In short, nothing exists in Ebenezer's recorded history to indicate that it would depart so drastically from old-line norms by establishing a place for indigenous singing in the Sunday morning worship—until October 2, 1930. On that date "the church met in a business conference and accepted the resignation of Reverend Clark." Ten years into an apparently illustrious pastorate—a period in which Ebenezer experienced great growth and even "burned" its mortgage three years before it was due—something apparently forced Clark to leave Ebenezer:

> There was something about this period of Ebenezer's history that resembles the history of the devasting Chicago fire. Despite her period of chagrin, the wide, hideous and exaggerated publicity her struggles were given . . . her restoration to placidity and her membership growth can only be measured in terms of the rehabilitation of Chicago after its great fire.

The key to Ebenezer's "restoration" lies in the appointment of Dr. James Howard Lorenzo Smith, Clark's replacement:

> Its [Ebenezer's] name became an attraction and its multitude of curiosity seekers, through the power of God and sincerity of Rev. Smith, were transformed into loyal, Ebenezer faithful members. . . . The church took on new life under its new leader.[23]

Most, if not all, of the "changes . . . in the order of the church" Smith made from the time he assumed his duties in August 1931 at least until the organization of the gospel chorus in December came in response to the dearth of spirituality following Clark's resignation. Moreover, since one of those "changes" involved the chorus, one may infer that the music of the Sunday morning worship—though of the highest old-line order—had failed to maintain Ebenezer's vitality:

> A lot of people here who remembered what singing was like down home liked Smith, Lord, yes. The music the Senior Choir was singing was not what Reverend Smith nor the congregation was used to. And then them old songs that they had been used to hearing, like "This Rock I'm Standing On" or "Bye and Bye," see, the Senior Choir didn't sing them then. They sang ooh, ah, way up high and the anthems.

Thus it was out of a sense of nearly desperate frustration that Smith dramatically declared to his congregation one Sunday in December 1931, clapping his hands for emphasis:

> I have a vision of a group singing the good old-fashioned songs that were born in the hearts of our forefathers down in the southland. I want those [clap, clap, clap] songs that my old forefathers and mothers sing down in, way down in the southland. I want this group sitting behind *me* [emphasis added].[24]

As an educated minister with most of his professional background in a southern church, the Reverend Doctor J. H. L. Smith was uniquely qualified to break the impasse between old-line ministers and the bluesman figure that Dorsey symbolized. By 1932, when Dorsey and Smith met, Dorsey had ceased all but a negligible amount of gospel blues work in old-line churches.

Old-line ministers' defense of their positions posed an impregnable barrier to gospel blues and the aesthetic it represented. Only one of their peers, unintimidated by the bluesman, could convince them to realign themselves with their congregations and delegate part of their liturgical authority to the bluesman.[25]

From information on Smith's organization of the gospel chorus, a profile of him, significantly different from that of other old-line ministers, can be extrapolated. Old-line ministers felt it their duty to extol black cultural progress beyond the confines of worship and the church. Their involvement in social problems was one such extension. When an L. K. Williams set up kindergartens at Olivet and a J. C. Austin sent workers into the homes of the poor to make sure children were fed, old-line ministers were attempting to make converts to old-line cultural goals through social channels. Even these ministers' life-styles seemed bound to an unwavering allegiance to the northern ethos. The Reverend Reverdy C. Ransom, whose Institutional Church had a pronounced political and cultural emphasis, was too embarrassed to allow poet Paul Laurence Dunbar, his neighbor and good friend, to join him in a meal of pork chitterlings because this dish was a staple of black traditional cooking:

> We did not serve them while he was there, but he had sensed them because of their smell. He finally left, but soon returned with a bowl in his hand. When Mrs. Ransom admitted him, he held out the bowl and pleaded, "Mrs. Ransom, please give me just one gut.[26]

With the standard of old-line cultural progress embracing such integral facets of its preachers' lives, they were hardly able to partake of the blues culture—especially that in the "black and tan" joints. Beyond the obvious secular purposes of those places, they harbored a culture with which the old-line minister was reluctant to identify. The old-line minister would have been as uncomfortable with the bluesman in the bluesman's habitat as he was intimidated by the bluesman when he performed in the old-line worship. He seemed to avoid the bluesman's presence out of not only a fear of his cry but also a disdain for his ways.

Contrary to the feelings of his colleagues, Smith seemed at ease with the bluesman, almost to the point of fraternizing with him, as indicated by his association with one of Dorsey's colleagues, Theodore Frye, an urban evangelist like Hall. Frye sang frequently at Ebenezer between Smith's arrival in August and his call for the chorus in December 1931. And it was Frye whom Smith asked to direct the chorus. Considering Frye's background and his collaboration with Dorsey, Frye was a unique combination of the classic bluesman and the traditional preacher.

In many ways, Frye was Dorsey's second Hall, except that Dorsey and Frye worked together for different reasons than did Dorsey and Hall. Whereas Dorsey had chosen to work with Hall out of frustration at finding the right voice to enunciate his music, Dorsey chose to work with Frye because of his demonstrated potential to sell his songs. Dorsey first heard Frye at the 1930 Baptist Convention, where Frye had made his reputation as "'a ball of fire.'" More than any other singer who worked with Dorsey, Frye exuded the blend of sacred and secular that Dorsey thought ideal for gospel blues. Like Dorsey, he had been born and raised in the South (Mississippi). He had been a preacher in Vicksburg, Mississippi, before moving to Chicago, and apparently while still in Mississippi, he began singing solos in churches. Dorsey credits himself with making Frye a gospel singer by training him in many blues stage techniques, one of which, "strutting," Frye became famous for:

> We teamed up and traveled through the South, East, and Midwest making the national meetings and winning the acclaim of every audience we sang and played to. He was doin' it [walking] in Mississippi, but he didn't have the right material to walk to 'til he found me. [He] was known as the "Walking Gospel Singer."

A typical performance with Frye and Dorsey resembled any other blues event. Indeed, Dorsey employed the same stage actions that he had used in Ma Rainey's show:

> They got to the place if Frye didn't walk, they'd holler at him, "Walk, Frye, walk!!" Then Frye'd start struttin'. He would walk and sing; I would stand up at the piano and pound the beat out to his marching steps. Frye would strut; women would fall out—don't know whether he looked good or they were just happy. Frye could get over anywhere with anything.[27]

Such din and bedlam were the bane of any old-line church except for Smith's Ebenezer. To one like Smith, who was so steeped in the southern ethos and who had come to a northern urban church plagued with strife and devoid of spirituality, the hollers and cries, the ecstatic prostrations, and the pompous "strut" of the singing preacher constituted the celebration of black worship in its most unadulterated and unbridled form. He was an old-line minister who could chant and scream in this mêlée without worry that it would be seen as mimicry. He suffered no waning of his power over the congregation when the bluesman sang; he and the bluesman were partners.

Smith had one problem, however, with this type of worship: it occurred infrequently. He had to depend on itinerant musicians to provide the usual complement to his preaching. The choir, moreover, was unable to sing traditional music when he requested it:

> Well, they used to sing a few Dr. Watts once in awhile. We had a lovely senior choir. [But] it wasn't what he wanted. It wasn't what he had, in other words, it wasn't what he'd been used to. Because he was from Alabama, you know. And when he came here, of course he'd been used to that old-time singing down there and he wanted the same thing here at Ebenezer.

When Frye sang for Ebenezer on the second Sunday in October 1931, Smith asked to have a conference with him afterward. Smith's "vision" was born in that meeting. On the second Sunday in January 1932, Smith heard the "old-time singing" that he wanted at Ebenezer.[28]

The literal and symbolic import of the chorus was apparent at its debut. With Smith in position to make and execute policy at Ebenezer and with the chorus as the fulfillment of his quest for a new mode of worship, gospel singing enjoyed a prominence not even granted the choir. Smith's "behind me" was literal; it meant constructing a choir stand behind the pulpit complete with "brass rods and velvet curtains." Since the choir had always sung from the balcony, Smith's partiality toward the chorus and its music was blatant and, therefore, precipitous:

> Some of the [Senior Choir] members [would say], "Oh Lord! Why in the world they come up here with that old stuff?" And sometimes you could hear whispering, you know; they would grin at us, "Oh, y'all just sing, y'all sure do." But then we would hear what they was saying, you know: "Old ignorant folks; wasn't singing nothing." Some of them didn't want it. But whether they wanted it or not, we stayed there—the Senior Choir was in the balcony and the Gospel Chorus sits behind the Pastor.[29]

Smith ignored the bickering and condescension. In doing so, he demonstrated not only his allegiance to traditional worship music but his equally strong support of Dorsey's and Frye's unique performances of it:

> [Frye] would strut, you know, strut all the way across the [stage]. Dorsey would stand up a while and then he'd sit down a while.

If the initial reaction to the chorus was any indication, the choir's jealousy had little effect. As it marched down the aisle for its debut, the chorus "seemed to give new life to the whole church":

> We made our first appearance on the second Sunday in January, 1932. We had to be taught everything, even how to march. The church was filled to capacity. Everyone was endowed with the Holy Spirit, ready to do their best. We received so much encouragement from our members and friends, needless to say, which helped tremendously at a time like that.

With each successive performance, the chorus's fame increased. Smith had them sing every Sunday morning and evening, and also for revivals. The popularity of the chorus grew so much that folding chairs had to be purchased, and "they had to have deacons usher us in and push the people back out of our way." Even the *Chicago Defender* announced the group and published a photograph. Word of the chorus traveled about Chicago quickly:

> Everybody at that time was pulling at the chorus, because nobody had a gospel chorus but Ebenezer. And every church wanted them to come, because

wherever we went we drew a crowd and I mean a crowd. You didn't have standing room no place. So with our pastor, and sometimes alone, we were invited to sing at many different churches in our city and other cities as well.[30]

The second chorus in old-line churches was formed in the wake of a performance by Ebenezer's chorus in February 1932 at Pilgrim Baptist Church. The Reverend Junius C. Austin invited Smith and the chorus to help celebrate his sixth "anniversary" as pastor of Pilgrim. Second only to Olivet Baptist Church in size, Pilgrim was among the most influential of the old-line churches, especially under the leadership of Austin. Its worship was among the most decorus of old-line churches. Thus when Smith, Frye, and Dorsey decided to take the chorus to Pilgrim, they had to consider carefully whether or not to go "wild" as they did routinely at Ebenezer. Apparently, however, they were unwavering in their customary display of emotion:

> In February 1932, the chorus was invited to visit the great Pilgrim Baptist Church, pastored by Dr. J. C. Austin to sing while Rev. J. H. Smith preached the sermon for the anniversary service. We had our songs well worked up and knew every cue. When we got to the middle of the chorus of "I'm on the Battlefield for My Lord," I would stand up at the piano and Professor Frye would walk across the choir stand and sing the verses, then we would go wild. When we had finished, the church was all worked up and the spirit was at its highest pitch.[31]

Considering Austin's exceptional adherence to old-line worship norms—for example, moving the pre-worship prayer service to the basement, reducing the number of congregational hymns that were sung during the service, and engaging a twenty-seven-piece orchestra—his reaction to the chorus was unexpected:

> Reverend Austin was very, very comical. He got up and looked over the rostrum and he spoke about how the chorus sang and how pleased he was. [Then] he said, "Tell me this; what I want to know is where did you get that little black man [pointing to Dorsey] from?"

Austin's query about Dorsey and his seeming fascination with Dorsey's performance went further than the remark made jokingly from the pulpit:

> A few days after this, Dr. Austin called and engaged me to organize a gospel chorus at Pilgrim Church and be its director.[32]

To the same extent that Smith's efforts to organize a chorus can be traced to a heartfelt belief in the efficacy of traditional worship practices, Austin's were rooted in a shrewd calculation of their benefit to his ministry. Having demonstrated an unstinting devotion to old-line worship standards, Austin was caught in a dilemma upon seeing the reaction of his congregation to the

chorus. On the one hand, the chorus's music and the pandemonium following it threatened to reduce the decorum of Pilgrim's membership to that of
any storefront following on State Street. On the other, the unmuffled enthusiasm for the chorus shown by the majority of the congregation revealed a
source of attraction for Pilgrim that Austin would not have anticipated or, if
he had, would probably have found repugnant. If he wished to emulate
Smith by resurrecting the icons of traditional black worship, he had to
remove many that he himself had erected in the name of old-line worship.

In the "few days" that passed before his meeting with Dorsey, Austin
moved adroitly to prepare for the chorus. His first task was rather pro-
cedural: he had to ask for the approval of his Board of Deacons. The idea
was foreign:

> Black Baptist folk, they liked, in those days, a solemn type of religious back-
> ground. Nothing with a great crescendo, you know, shaking and wobbling
> your hips, you know and hollering out. They wanted it soft and refined, you
> know, but still uplifting. They still loved the classical music. And they didn't
> want anything that appeared to be what folks might call, "That's alley junk."
> See, and the gospel chorus music has a swing to it, you know.

The board consented, but reluctantly, as indicated by its refusal to pay
Dorsey. They were accustomed to compensating choir directors handsomely.
After all, Pilgrim's Senior Choir director, Edward Boatner, was one of the
highest paid old-line directors, having been won over from Olivet Baptist
(black Chicago's largest) by Austin's offer of a generous salary.[33]

Boatner's privileged status—at Austin's doing, no less—was the major
obstacle in the way of organizing the chorus. Austin approached Boatner
about the idea obliquely, almost as if the chorus were merely a vehicle for
congregational hymn singing:

> He said this man wanted to come there and organize a gospel choir. I said,
> "What's a gospel choir for? You've got hymns already. You've got hymn
> books."

Boatner's mere bewilderment became consternation when he first heard Dorsey's piano playing:

> At that time I never knew what a gospel choir was. But I knew that when I
> heard him play the piano, I knew what was happening. He was sitting in the
> church one day and he was playing a gospel hymn or song for some lady who
> was sitting there. And it was nothing but jazz, the rhythm of jazz. You can
> look at any of them today, any of the gospel songs. They have that same jazz
> type of form.[34]

Boatner had two reasons to resist and perhaps even fear Dorsey and his
gospels, each of which made Austin all the more pressed to pursue the matter
delicately. For one, Boatner was trained in the western European classical

tradition and was a composer/arranger of anthem spirituals. What tolerance he could muster for indigenous black music, therefore, was not ample enough to condone "mixing" it with styles he would have considered more ennobling:

> I felt it was degrading. How can something that's jazzy give a religious feeling? If you're in a club downtown, a nightclub, that's all right. That's where it belongs. But how can you associate that with God's word? It's a desecration. The only people who think it isn't a desecration are the people who haven't had any training, any musical training—people who haven't heard fine religious anthems, cantatas, oratorios.

In true old-line fashion, he equated the embracing of non-black cultural values with an adherence to religious principles. He despaired of what he considered a weakness of blacks for their music:

> People sing, get happy. You know the black race is a rhythmic race. They can be moved just by hearing rhythm, rhythm songs. It don't have to have no religious words to it. You just want to tap your feet and say, "Amen."[35]

His second objection to Dorsey was hardly as philosophical. He, like Austin, sensed an underlying threat not only to his status as choir director but to the concept itself of the choir and its pre-eminent role in old-line worship. He knew, however, that Austin's decision in favor of Dorsey was inevitable. His defense, therefore, was reduced to a petty play for turf:

> If he wants to have it, that's his church. He can do with it what he wants. You can't overstep the preacher. Then if he wants that man to come there, let him come and do what he wants. But I wasn't going to let him sit on my choir [rostrum]. I said, "Where would you put them?" He said, "I'll put one on one side of the altar from the other." I said, "That'll never be as long as I'm here." I said, "If you want them here, put them up there in the back of the church." And that's where they were until I left.[36]

Only one who was driven by the anticipation of success would wrangle and cajole as did Austin and finally accept the ultimatum that Boatner gave. Whether the chorus was positioned in the back balcony or on the rostrum was of secondary importance to its presence in the sanctuary on Sunday morning. While one part of Austin could listen sympathetically to Boatner's protests and even agree with his assessment of gospel blues, the other could not ignore what Austin correctly perceived as a mass sentiment for such music. Austin's preaching style and social activism had already resulted in Pilgrim's good reputation among recent migrants; now he sought its un-rivaled popularity:

> He was an outstanding pulpiteer, a great orator, a master preacher. Back in those days, the preacher had to have a great attraction to himself. My dad

could see times changing and people desiring another type of music. He tried it [gospel music] in his church and, because of his preaching *and* the music, folk crowded out that church.[37]

At Ebenezer, the October 1931 meeting between Smith, Frye, and Dorsey to organize the chorus represented the confluence of gospel blues and the movement to encourage indigenous singing in old-line churches. Since Ebenezer up to the time of that meeting had no active choral group singing traditional music, the idea of a gospel chorus must have originated with those three participants. This could be expected, considering the commonality of their cultural roles. Each was a southerner who evolved into a professional role particularly reflective of the southern ethos. Smith and Frye were southern preachers and Dorsey was a downhome bluesman. Each of their roles was altered, however, by its recontextualization in Chicago. Smith assumed an old-line pulpit; to some extent he must have had to reshape his delivery to conform to the unique mixture of preaching styles old-line congregations had come to expect of their ministers. Frye moved to Chicago and recast his preaching into gospel blues singing under the tutelage of a bluesman. Dorsey experienced a musical and religious metamorphosis caused by his determination to infuse his northern worship experience with his southern blues background.

Little else but the gospel chorus could have been born in the October meeting, considering the commonality of origins, the parity of experiences, and the unity of outlook among these participants. They shared a nostalgia for the traditional religious group singing of the South that was tempered by the realization that this former practice had to be re-bred in the North just as each of their lives had been. Ebenezer's chorus was the product of indigenous choral singing and gospel blues because those who conceived of it represented a similar concrescence of culturally related minds. The southern—now old-line—preacher, the preacher/bluesman, and the gospel bluesman each craved his traditional counterpart, someone who could "bear him up." If the great orators of old-line religion were complemented by the refined warbling of their choirs, then the displaced criers of downhome worship no less required the raw shouting and wailing of the chorus.

Thus Ebenezer's chorus occupied a unique place among the indigenous choral groups in old-line churches. Far from being the reluctant accommodation of backward tastes banished to the nether parts of the church, Ebenezer's chorus represented the viability of the past as a check on old-line excesses of the present. Smith's December "vision" was in fact the October proclamation by a one-of-a-kind troika of interrelated black cultural figures. Among these three improvisators was the authority and talent necessary to give Ebenezer's chorus a status (within Ebenezer) and sound unthought and unheard of in old-line churches.

These same attributes served to isolate Ebenezer's chorus and make it irreplicable. The qualities of its creators were rare. Even if there were other old-line preachers who hailed from the South as recently as did Smith, they camouflaged, if they utilized at all, the practices of their southern churches. Frye's fame was based almost solely on his histrionics; no other "strutting" gospel singer was known around Chicago's churches. Nor does another composer/recording artist of both raunchy and sacred blues seem to have been known around old-line churches during the years Dorsey was struggling to disseminate his gospel blues. Smith, Frye, Dorsey, and company could have torn up and gone "wild" at Ebenezer indefinitely. With the exception of sporadic forays into temporarily receptive old-line churches, Smith's chorus would have been regarded as a band of misguided outcasts who yearned for the quaint babbling of religion gone by. He and his congregation could have continued to be seen as romanticizing the antics of a best-forgotten past to their hearts content with no more than mild amusement from the other churches.

Because of the idiosyncrasy of the Ebenezer chorus, one can assume that had Austin not organized a chorus at Pilgrim, the advent of gospel blues in old-line churches would have stagnated in derision and for want of serious regard from the old-line establishment. Smith and his followers provided the form, substance, and medium of old-line gospel blues, but only an old-line preacher and church of the stature of Austin and Pilgrim could have imparted respect to gospel blues' notoriety. From this perspective, the February 1932 meeting between Dorsey and Austin marked a turning point in the emergence of gospel blues in old-line churches.

For all of their obvious differences, Dorsey and Austin shared at least two traits. For one, each was a master showman, especially in manipulating an audience. As with Dorsey's "ivories" and his standing while playing the piano, Austin, too, resorted to such crowd-pleasing tactics in the pulpit:

> Men in this day and generation who heard my daddy are still talkin' about him. He was university trained. He wasn't one of those dumb preachers that put his finger in his ear and moan. Brother, he was saying something, building a scaffold, and dramatizing all the time. And he had a voice that was sharp as the eagle's call. And he knew how to lift it and how to modulate it. And when he would scream and walk off, people'd go crazy. He was what you call a preacher's preacher.

Counterbalancing these actions, however, were the orchestra, the lack of hymn singing, and the anthem-singing senior choir, each carefully cultivated by Austin as if to keep his congregation from over-responding to his preaching. Dorsey did the same when, in the midst of the moans and shouts of his listeners, he would "never give them all they want."[38]

But the trait they shared that was to have a major impact on the advent of gospel blues can only be defined as opportunism, though not necessarily in a pejorative sense; each had a demonstrated will to achieve that was not always counterbalanced by a consideration of the means by which he achieved. Throughout his life, Dorsey exhibited a penchant for seizing an opportunity with not much thought of the consequences or principles involved. His present dual career as a popular performer of double entendre and gospel blues was but one instance of the opportunistic tinge present in numerous progressions in his life. Lacking all but the most sparse biographical information, one can infer the same about Austin—especially in reference to his organization of the gospel chorus. During the performance of Ebenezer's chorus at Pilgrim, he seemed to take note of Dorsey's showmanship as much as the chorus's appeal to his congregation. When he was ready to organize his chorus, he called on "that little black man," perhaps realizing that his church had gone "wild" almost as if on cue when Dorsey stood while playing the piano. Austin recognized a kinship between himself and one who could prompt such mass excitability so effortlessly. When thinking of ways to maintain Pilgrim's popularity and competitive edge, Austin clearly saw the value of a skillful crowd-pleaser such as Dorsey. Dorsey was just as aware of Austin's motives, even though he had not been witness to Austin's hectic activities during the "few days" between the chorus's appearance and his meeting with Austin:

> Austin called me and wanted me and engaged me to organize a gospel chorus in Pilgrim Baptist Church. He sat onto the side of the desk and says, "Brother Dorsey, I want you to do this for me." I said, "What is it?" "I want you to get me together one of those things like Smith had down here." He didn't say "chorus." He said "one of them things" that we had down here. I said, "That was the Gospel Chorus." "All right, well and good. I want you to bring your gospel chorus." I got it there for him.[39]

Because of the kindredness of their characters, the "hokum"/gospel bluesman and the old-line master pulpiteer met with extraordinary accord at their February 1932 meeting. Far from the wariness and antagonism that generally characterized the interaction between these antitypes, the relationship between Austin and Dorsey was moored to the deep-seated, powerful drive of each to succeed without undue consideration of the costs. Dorsey seized the opportunity to leave Ebenezer and establish his fledgling movement at Pilgrim, even though he was deposed to the balcony, held in disdain by the choir director, and "it wasn't payin' nothin'." Austin's need for Dorsey was no less self-serving:

> My dad was farsighted, I think. He could see times changing and people desiring another type of music. He said, "Dorsey's music's going to sweep the country. And I want it in Pilgrim Church!" And he tried it in his church. And when they started liking it, brother, it just went like wildfire, like a fire in your house. When the fire started, he didn't have a thing to do but just let the good times roll.[40]

The traits of showmanship and opportunism that Austin shared with Dorsey may be considered to no small extent inherent in the conduct of old-line ministry. For one to succeed while adhering to old-line preaching tenets, one had to utilize the techniques of the southern preacher, whose values the old-line preacher eschewed. Indeed, the old-line preacher's popularity was predicated on his successful execution, week after week, of a paradox. Master orators such as Austin finely tuned their homiletical duplicity, especially as the migrant population in the congregations increased.

Dorsey and other southern-bred blues artists such as Bessie Smith had experienced a similar pressure to succeed in the North by performing down-home music in a vaudeville style. Save for the reassertion of southern performance practices spurred by the mass sales of recordings by traditional singers, Dorsey and a number of southern blues singers would have been compelled to sing the very paradox that old-line ministers preached. As it was, Dorsey and other such blues persons could switch back and forth at will, performing the most backwoods blues one time and the slickest urban ones the next. Not only were blues singers able to perform with such flexibility, however, but they seemed as free to evoke and otherwise encourage responses from the audience. The cornerstone of old-line religion, on the other hand, blocked the demeanor that complemented downhome preaching.

As the traditional solo bluesman, Dorsey threatened further to circumscribe the few expressive options left to old-line preachers by exposing their mimicry of the most popular one, the cry. But as a traditional *and* urban bluesman along with a chorus, Dorsey enhanced the old-line preacher's expressive capability. At the 1932 meeting, this, more than any other understanding between Austin and Dorsey—explicit or implicit—paved the way for the new rapprochement between the bluesman and old-line preacher. The swift pace at which the other old-line churches copied Pilgrim's chorus attests to the lack of any more antagonism between the bluesman and either guise of the old-line preacher. As with Austin, each minister could "sit back and let the good times roll," knowing that whichever preaching mode he wanted to adopt, its complement—the choir or the chorus—was conveniently and controllably there to respond. By August 1933, old-line ministers had accepted the preaching, music, and demeanor of both worship styles under one roof. They did so knowing that their authority to preside over as well as to partake of either was unchallenged.

At the time of his appointment as director of the chorus at Pilgrim, Dorsey might not have been aware of the chorus as the medium through which he would now bring blues, or at least blues-like music, into mainline black worship. As his experience with Magnolia Butts's group at Metropolitan indicates, Dorsey knew of the existence of the choral groups that had been formed to sing traditional black religious music in old-line churches. He also knew that they were organized to placate the desire of recent migrants to sing downhome church music. That he had to be convinced of the potential of these choruses as a medium for his music, however, is evident by the lack of interest he showed in working with them before he was brought to Ebenezer at the invitation of Smith and Frye. Thus the idea of a chorus of singers of his songs was as much a revelation to him as it was to numerous persons who first heard it in old-line churches. Indeed, it is the notion of *choral* gospel blues as opposed to the more likely *solo* gospel blues that provides the most significant twist to Dorsey's effort to bring his music into old-line churches.

Beginning with his first meeting with the chorus, Dorsey seemed to de-emphasize his music. Austin issued his call for the chorus at a meeting on the Thursday evening following his Monday conference with Dorsey. Apparently, the music of Ebenezer's chorus had whetted the desire of a large number of Pilgrim's members to sing in such a group: "over a hundred" people volunteered to join the new chorus. Dorsey's first impulse at seeing a hundred chorus members normally would have been to sell copies of his music as he had done when he stumbled onto Metropolitan's chorus. Instead, he "sang a song for them" and then "carried them through a song or two." More than likely, in order to have "carried" the chorus through music, Dorsey would not have been able to use any of his gospels: at that time none of them was arranged for choral performance. Moreover, since it was he who sang a solo before working with the chorus that night, he obviously had none of his soloists with him. One could conclude from this that he thought his solo-oriented gospel blues was inappropriate for his new chorus to rehearse at its introductory meeting. He admitted as much when he decided not to sell his songs then:

No, I didn't bother about carrying music around. I'd just catch them another night when I had them all together when they had some money. I didn't go in it to make money. I was making money.[41]

To no small degree, Dorsey's previous work with Frye at Ebenezer prompted his avoidance of his own music. He had written at most only four gospel songs, including *If I Don't Get There* in *Gospel Pearls*. With the exception of this song, all of his gospels were written for solo voice with piano accompaniment. Although neither he nor Frye needed the Ebenezer chorus to further his burgeoning gospel blues career, each found the chorus to be a showcase for his dramatic gospel performances, especially in the church. Frye was able to walk while singing and Dorsey to stand while playing the piano. Significantly, they could perform in the gospel blues manner while singing traditional songs such as *He's the Lily of the Valley* and *I'm on the Battlefield*. Given Dorsey's improvisational skills and Frye's bluesman/preacher singing style, neither needed a specially composed gospel song such as Dorsey's gospel blues to "prick" the listener. Thus Ebenezer's chorus under the Frye/Dorsey team was not the medium for Dorsey's composed gospel blues. Indeed, the chorus seemed to flourish because Dorsey and Frye took "the songs that were born in the hearts of [the] forefathers down in the southland" and made them sound like the gospel blues that Dorsey wrote.

It is clear that by not "carrying music around" with him, especially the night he went to organize the Pilgrim chorus, Dorsey intended to work with the Pilgrim chorus as he had with Ebenezer's. After all, he had the same twofold opportunity here as he had had at Ebenezer: he could make gospel blues out of traditional songs while increasing his reputation as a gospel bluesman by using the chorus to perform these re-composed songs in old-line churches. One of the most convincing pieces of evidence in support of this point is Dorsey's choice of pianist for the Pilgrim chorus. As the accompanist at Ebenezer, Dorsey had control over the improvisation with which he made the songs into blues. But as the director at Pilgrim, he needed a pianist who, like himself, had blues-playing experience and could apply it to sacred songs.

As apparent as this need was to Dorsey, it was not so to Austin when he thought of a pianist for the chorus. Austin took it on himself to appoint his daughter, Dorothy, who had been taking piano lessons and playing for various organizations around Pilgrim such as the Sunday school. Not having had any advanced training, she was not the caliber of musician to work with Boatner and the choir. But she was destined to be, at least as far as her training went:

> I had been taking piano and I was down at Chicago Music College. Everything that I was working with was classic. That was what I was into with a French teacher down at Chicago Music College.

Either Austin misunderstood or disregarded the stylistic traits of gospel blues; otherwise he would have realized that his daughter could not play for the chorus. Ignoring both her novice classical ability and her lack of exposure to blues, Austin told her to "go down and help" the fledgling chorus with little thought as to what she would encounter:

> I went there. And I found it difficult to read the music. In gospel chorus music, you know that you can set a piece on the piano and play it like it's written, just exactly like it's written. [But] it doesn't give anybody any sort of emotional effect, . . . no mood in it. That's the way I would play it because I didn't play by ear and I had never practiced any sort of swing. I didn't feel at ease doing it. I had heard someone else at another time playing one of the songs and they could sort of swing it along. Just because it's 4/4 time you don't play it that way. You syncopate. Gradually I got sort of on to it. But I was really just waiting until somebody else would come along.[42]

Dorsey was probably "waiting" as well. Unable to "beat" the music with her as he had been unable to with Louise Keller—the other too-properly

trained musician he had tried to teach to play his gospel blues—Dorsey
engaged another pianist for the chorus, Mabel Mitchell. Even a scant look
into her background reveals why Dorsey would find her preferable to Dorothy Austin. Mitchell had studied piano—"the basics . . . the high stuff"—in
her native Birmingham, Alabama, for "eight or nine years." When her family
moved to Chicago, her lessons continued. She played well enough that her
parents and teachers thought she would become a concert pianist, but, as she
likes to recall, "I fooled them":

> Some of the fellows around in the neighborhood got together and decided
> they wanted to have an orchestra. And they got one and I played the piano.

The group became well known, enough so that it played "all around Chicago," not at house parties but at established dance places such as Mallox
Mallon at 37th and State. As a small four-piece ensemble consisting of a
drummer, saxophonist, trumpeter, and pianist, the band played music that
"would possibly be classified as jazz."[43]

The similarity of musical backgrounds and training between Dorsey and
Mitchell was significant. In addition to being born in the South, each had
attempted enough classical piano so that the playing technique and reading
skills of each exceeded those of the typical downhome folk pianist. Although
her "jazz" ("jass?") or blues band-playing was not as widely known as
Dorsey's, it was comparable to his work with the Whispering Sycopators
and Ma Rainey's Wild Cats Jazz Band. These small ensembles of accomplished, but amateur, musicians began by playing dances or, as in the case of
the Wild Cats, by offering to play the road shows—a less than desirable job
for an established artist. Moreover, through a group of this sort, Mitchell,
like Dorsey, brought non-Afro-American popular music to blacks by playing
improvisations and arrangements of it in black social spots such as dance
halls. Dorsey had accomplished much the same, for example, when he played
A Good Man Is Hard to Find in the out-of-the-way "black and tan joints"
frequented by urban migrants.

Because of the parallels between the musical aspects of their backgrounds, Mitchell and Dorsey were logical partners in the launching of
Pilgrim's chorus. Mitchell had no problem playing her Saturday night dance-
hall music at the Sunday morning worship hour:

> That type of playing was a lot of good experience for me when it came to
> playing gospel music. That's exactly where Mr. Dorsey got his. I mean he
> took it right from pop music. Other than the words of the music, there was no
> difference, none at all. You could just play from one to another.[44]

The significance of her being able to play in a popular music style becomes
even more apparent when one considers that Dorsey had composed no more
than four of his gospel blues songs at this time. Taking familiar songs—

probably from hymnals—and improvising on them enough to make them into the sacred blues he normally wrote would be Dorsey's way of making the Pilgrim chorus shimmer with the excitement that he and Frye generated when they gospel-blued traditional songs at Ebenezer. Mitchell's experience of musically recontextualizing non-indigenous, popular music allowed her to hold up the keyboard aspect of this job while Dorsey directed the choral parts:

> Before the church really accepted gospel music, [people] were saying it wasn't nothing but the blues—playing all the blues and stuff in the church—especially the older heads. But of course it didn't phase me one way or the other. I enjoyed playing. Whatever they said play, I'd play it and get enjoyment out of it. I never thought to compare whether this is right for church, because the music carries words or praises. It's still gospel music, whether it's an anthem or spiritual. It's still the gospel being sung.[45]

Mitchell's blues background and the use she found for it at Pilgrim, combined with her ideas concerning the place of blues in worship, indicate that Dorsey had the Pilgrim chorus singing the gospel blues that he had conceived of in 1928. Clearly, the connection between gospel blues and the Pilgrim chorus is obvious when Mitchell can state that her blues playing "was a lot of good experience . . . when it came to playing gospel music." Still, one is somewhat hard put to think how Dorsey, with his vast number of solo blues—including his new gospel solo blues that were now being preached successfully by solo singers—would find the notion of choral gospel blues acceptable. Yet the Pilgrim chorus became, in essence, a group of bluespersons acting in concert to declare communal feelings to the congregation.

If there was anything around which the gospel chorus at Pilgrim seemed united, it was a sense of community. Most Pilgrimites who thought of themselves as musicians and who wanted to participate in worship could join the choir. But there were some who could have been participating in worship through groups such as the choir who, for a variety of reasons, felt disinclined to do so. Lillian Reescer, a charter member of the chorus, had been active around Pilgrim since joining in 1918. She sang "in the missionary work and Sunday school" but refused to become a member of the choir because she "didn't care for Mr. Boatner." Mabel Craft, another charter member, remembers her active participation in the singing in New Hopewell Baptist Church in her native Bernice, Louisiana. But she found little incentive to join Pilgrim's choir—in part because she often worked on Sundays. Yet when she heard talk of the Ebenezer chorus and then heard that Dorsey was going to organize a similar group at Pilgrim, she decided to join:

> I had heard some of the . . . different ones talking about Professor Dorsey singing at some other church. In fact, it was the talk all over about his

singing. So, I just hadn't joined no choir and I just decided that I'd just join the chorus. It was something different.[46]

Unlike Boatner and his choir, Dorsey from the beginning sought to de-emphasize musicianship as a standard for the chorus. Instead, he stressed the one quality that he knew would make a good chorus as it would a good blues singer: expressiveness. At the first rehearsal, Dorsey announced that he wanted to "express himself in song and that was the way he was going to express himself, in singing." He assured his newly formed chorus members that he would "help . . . anyway that he could" to have them express themselves as he did.

The emphasis that he placed on the idea of group expression considered along with the attraction that the chorus seemed to have for recent—and somewhat alienated—migrants provides the key to understanding Dorsey's unexpected turn to choral blues. Dorsey knew that any widespread accep-tance of his songs by old-line ministers would occur only if they could be assured that the emotionalism of the chorus could be contained. Dorsey, therefore, needed a self-contained group, the control over which he could maintain so as to convince old-line ministers to share their services with him. This challenge for Dorsey, combined with the displacement that many of his new members felt at Pilgrim, created an almost instantaneous symbi-otic relationship: the very community that newly arrived migrants needed to cultivate was the very one that Dorsey could mold into the self-contained congregation needed as the backdrop for his gospel blues.

To understand this more fully, one need only look to the "'Praying and Singing Bands'" that Bishop Daniel Payne criticized so sharply. It was the practice of these groups to carry on their shouting, clapping, and ring danc-ing after the sermon or as an appendage to the formal worship. Bishop Payne's annoyance with them stemmed not so much from a dislike of the ritual itself as from the practice of that ritual in the church, where it had no place. Payne knew there were the "ignorant masses," for whom the "'Bands'" comprised "the essence of religion." They were not, however, supposed to be found in the churches over which Payne officiated—churches pledged to eradicate the vestiges of slave culture. Payne's frustration was mounted against the old-line AME churches of his day that should have grown beyond the Bands' "strange delusion."[47]

Dorsey's newly formed gospel chorus could be considered a new singing Band, but in a resurrected version: as the gospel chorus it had become an institution within the very church in which it had been considered not to have a part. The desire among black Americans, it seemed, had never been to assimilate non-traditional worship practices to the point that they would obliterate the root black religious experience, slavery. The early membership of the Pilgrim gospel chorus illustrates this point well. Although the gospel blues movement was known for attracting a large number of recent migrants, a significant number of old settlers, some of whom were professionals, also joined the chorus:

> That first chorus [at Pilgrim] had lawyers, doctors, and nurses. When you sat
> and looked at people with their degrees—bachelors and masters—going to
> sit where they could clap their hands and sway their bodies and go on, you
> wondered what had happened![48]

The chorus offered to many black Americans the same ultimate resolution of black religious duality that gospel blues had offered Thomas Andrew Dorsey: it became the means by which black Americans could hold fast to their former religion in the face of the powerful urgings to plunge into mainstream America, as Dorsey had remained anchored to downhome blues in the face of pressure to grab mainstream popularity.

The central role of gospel blues as sung by the gospel chorus in black churches recalls the well-known statement by Du Bois:

> One ever feels his twoness—an American, a Negro; two souls, two thoughts,
> two unreconciled strivings; two warring ideals in one dark body, whose
> dogged strength alone keeps it from being torn asunder.[49]

As he directed the first performance of his chorus at Pilgrim Baptist Church in the spring of 1932, Dorsey must have been reminded of a similar occasion at the Grand Theater in 1924. There, with Ma Rainey, her husky contralto bellowing out some lonesome blues, the audience moaning and sobbing, Dorsey could claim a major role in bringing downhome music to black Chicago's premier entertainment establishment. There, as at Pilgrim, black Americans who had been walking with the chickens heard that "scream" and "went on up." As he stood at the piano and watched doctors, lawyers, and his fellow new migrants "go wild," he could claim some of the credit that "all that [learning] flew out of the window."[50] Dorsey's "dogged strength" had kept old-line churches from possibly being torn asunder. After February 1932, they sang a strangely familiar, comforting new song that acknowledged their "twoness": old-line gospel blues.

9

Giving the Gospel
a Blues Voice:
1932

By early spring 1932, two forms of gospel blues had emerged and were becoming acceptable as modes of music in old-line black churches. For the first of these, solo gospel blues, Dorsey was the most prominent in shaping it—especially its notated and printed forms—and in bringing it out before the public. This form also evolved most clearly out of Dorsey's life history and thus may be considered more the product of Dorsey's creation than any style of music he played with the exception of the soft, rhythmic party blues he was well known for during his early professional years in Atlanta. The second form, choral gospel blues, emerged out of circumstances in which Dorsey was at most peripherally involved. Although this form clearly helped to resolve some of the lingering conflicts that had dogged Dorsey since childhood, the reasons underlying its growth were unrelated to Dorsey's life to the extent that choral gospel blues cannot be considered a logical development of Dorsey's biographical history.

Considering the establishment of two forms of gospel blues and Dorsey's asymmetrical involvement in them, one has to rethink Dorsey's role in the emergence of gospel blues, especially the characterization of Dorsey as the "father" of the song form. He is careful to point out that he took an existing concept, "gospel," and merged it with his blues performance practices:

> Now, I didn't originate the word gospel, I want you to know. I didn't originate that word. Gospel, the word "gospel" has been used down through the ages. But I took the word, took a group of singers, or one singer, as far as that's concerned, and I embellished [gospel], made it beautiful, more noticeable, more susceptible with runs and trills and moans in it. That's really one of the reasons my folk called it gospel music.[1]

Clearly, Dorsey crafted this solo form. But he points out forthrightly that, rather than any innovation or intention on his part, the "idea" of the chorus was Frye's, prompted by Smith's desire for different singing. Even though Smith had a realistic vision of the chorus he wanted, based on his ministry in the South, he had not conceived of the version of it that Frye and Dorsey were capable of producing. Indeed, "until [Smith] heard [the chorus], he didn't know what he was going to get."[2] In short, Dorsey's performance techniques alone constitute his unique contribution to gospel blues and define the solo form.

In the spring of 1932, however, with Dorsey recently appointed to organize and direct the chorus at one of the most prestigious old-line churches, his role in the emergence of both forms concerned him little. There was enough of a symbiosis between them for Dorsey to see that he benefited no matter in which mode or context gospel blues was presented. But it is precisely because of the generic difference between the two forms—one related to a set of performance practices and the other to a context—that Dorsey would come to see the need to involve himself equally in the presentation of both. Indeed, it was this realization that prompted the particular gospel blues movement—as opposed to form—of which Dorsey can be thought of as "the father."

As was often the case in his career, especially his former secular blues career, Dorsey was quick to discern an advantageous trend and seize upon it for his professional good. Thus he realized that choral gospel blues constituted more of an opportunity to advance gospel blues in general than his own solo form. At first, the opposite had seemed true. Dorsey and Frye had heard of a "gospel chorus" at a small church in Chicago. They visited the church one Sunday to perform some of Dorsey's pieces and to satisfy their curiosity as to what a gospel chorus—a choral gospel group—was. As it turns out, there were only four people "singing hymns." Their response to Frye and Dorsey's performance amounted to evidence to Dorsey that solo gospel blues was the more effective medium for the gospel in song:

> This group heard [the songs]. Frye got to walkin' round there, and folk forgot there was a gospel chorus or choir, or whatever they called it there . . . and turned their attention to us. Then we were the show.

Dorsey believed so much that blues performance techniques alone accounted for the success of both solo and choral gospel that he attributed the uniqueness of the Ebenezer chorus's fame to them. Dorsey found Ebenezer's singing better, for example, than the indigenous singing group at Metropolitan Community Church, the W. D. Cook Gospel Singers, because of the way he and Frye had the Ebenezer Chorus perform:

> See, they didn't shout the gospel like we did. See, they was kind of a reserved group. They sang; they gave [a] message. But they didn't jump up and shout, run, and holler "Amen" and all the stuff we put in it.

He found the same at another old-line church, Monumental Baptist, where "Professor" Luscha Allen was directing an indigenous song group similar to Butts's at Metropolitan: "I'd go in and help them get their stuff down, 'cause they didn't know how to do it."[3]

To a great extent, Dorsey's assessment of the effect of his performance practices on the success of choral gospel blues has merit. His position at Pilgrim in no small part arose out of Austin's desire for "one of those things like Smith had" with Frye strutting through the aisles, Dorsey standing at the piano, and the chorus clapping and singing the gospel—all standard accoutrements of a downhome blues performance. Just as well, however, Dorsey's assessment is overdrawn. With the exception of the National Baptist Convention in 1930, no combination of his well-rehearsed techniques and well-suited gospel blues singers and preachers had brought his unique style of solo gospel blues into even marginal acceptance in old-line churches. After all, for over two years he and Frye had traveled around as a team, "winning the acclaim of every audience but not enough evidently to be accepted in churches." The same was true when Dorsey toured with each of his female gospel blues singers and then Hall. Even after Frye and Dorsey had begun working steadily at Ebenezer, Dorsey was still not convinced of the value of the choruses. He once again teamed up with a male church singer, Luscha Allen, who was the director of the indigenous song choir at Monumental Baptist Church. They, too, as Frye and Dorsey were doing, toured through neighboring states "with marked success," according to Dorsey—more, he could presume, than they would have had with Allen's chorus.[4]

Dorsey had reason to become even less sanguine about solo gospel blues' progress when choruses singing choral blues began to appear at a phenomenal rate. Although isolated from one another, these groups all thought of themselves as engaged in the choral performance of gospel music. They came into being, moreover, without the aid of anyone—including Dorsey—actively involved in the rise of gospel blues or even, apparently, in the rise of indigenous choral song. Although no records seem to exist, Dorsey is consistent enough throughout various sources for one to be able to conclude that gospel choruses began forming at a noticeable pace throughout the spring of 1933. He states in an interview that he considered Allen's chorus to be "number three," after which "we stopped counting"—an indication that at a certain point the appearance of a chorus was no longer an unusual event. He mentions in two presidential addresses, given ten and thirteen years after the fact, respectively, that a Convention of choruses first met in 1932: "My Dear Co-Workers, we have come to the tenth session of our convention . . ." and "In these thirteen years I have been with this convention . . . ."[5] This is further evidence that as many as several choruses existed by then.

Two aspects of this 1932 convention point to its being pivotal in Dorsey's decision to become as involved in establishing choral gospel blues as he was in developing solo gospel blues. For one, the idea of a convocation of these groups was itself an acknowledgment of the potential drawing power of choral indigenous song groups in their own right. The participants included the three groups with which Dorsey had had direct involvement, Ebenezer's and Pilgrim's gospel choruses and Metropolitan's W. D. Cook indigenous singing choir: ". . . we got together in a big musicale . . . the three churches." Dorsey was unlikely to have taken part in this convention solely because he wanted to market his solo blues, since he had quite possibly written no more than seven gospel blues at that time.[6] Furthermore, he was more successful selling these as a two-person team than through choral performances. The key to understanding the significance for Dorsey of a convocation of gospel choruses lies in his involvement with these three particular groups up to August 1932: he had been coaching them in blues performance practices—how to holler, clap, jump, and say, "Amen." Both the Ebenezer and Pilgrim choruses were unique for their use of these techniques, not for singing Dorsey's songs or any other songs generically known as gospel. One good example of this is the song that the Ebenezer chorus sang at Pilgrim that convinced Austin to start a chorus, *I'm on the Battlefield for My Lord*. Austin and his congregation were brought to their feet by the chorus's histrionics, especially Frye's "walking" and Dorsey's standing at the piano. Thus it was apparently not in hopes that his style of gospel music would find favor so much as that his style of singing might catch on that Dorsey saw the convening of these ensembles as advantageous to his efforts to popularize the gospel in blues. In this sense, Dorsey helped to spawn the choral gospel blues style before he actually composed for it.[7]

The significance of this gospel chorus convocation lies in the structure of the performance itself. As a musicale, this concert was the traditional showcase for old-line vocal ensembles. Indeed, Dorsey and the other directors had selected what might have been the seat of the tradition, Metropolitan Community Church, as the place to present their groups. Here, J. Wesley Jones, possibly the most pre-eminent of the old-line choir directors, had put on one of the most popular monthly musicales. Even Butts's indigenous singing chorus, though it was an accepted performing group in the Metropolitan music community, was seen only at Friday night services and on special occasions such as funerals. The reasoning for not permitting it to sing at the Sunday morning service applied as well to its not being considered an appropriate monthly musicale performing ensemble, especially in a place where the musicale was so venerated. Nor do records suggest that either the Ebenezer or Pilgrim group had been presented in musicales. Indeed, for the Ebenezer chorus—even with the wholehearted support of Smith, the chief officer of the church—performance opportunities outside of the Sunday worship came only during revivals.[8]

Considering their previous status even in the churches in which they were accepted, these choruses could be considered presumptuous for gathering together for a musicale at Metropolitan on that Sunday in August 1932. Because of this very presumptuousness, however, choral gospel blues began to seem more viable to Dorsey. The musicale was specifically founded to provide a non-liturgical context for the choir whose *raison d'être* was liturgical. It was an opportunity to present music for music's sake and to have the choir heard for its ability to perform western European classical anthems rather than to enhance the worship hour. The impetus for this non-liturgical performance opportunity came from the choir directors who, as a result of their professional training, wanted a truly professional context in which to display their talents. And it was in this context that their talents competed, literally at times, and built their reputations. This musicale, thus, was intrinsically a Dorsey opportunity, for his whole approach to gospel blues was molded around his experience as a professional bluesman. This was literally the case when he wrote his first gospel blues song: he wedded sacred texts to secular blues music. He followed this by introducing his new secular/sacred synthesis through both the blues singer and the bluesman-type preacher. But what was implied in these actions was explicit in his work with the Ebenezer and Pilgrim choruses. Dorsey's major contribution to the performance practices of each was to impart to them the same distinct style of showmanship that he had insisted on with the singers who performed his solo gospel blues. "Everything is a show," he insists, "but you got to know how to do your show":

I try and train my choir[s], I says, "Now you got to be able to capture the people. You got to be able to show yourself, show what you can do." This music with all of this moan and roll in it that gospel's got, that's the thing that got the people.[9]

Religious showmanship, moreover, had deep roots in Dorsey's life, back to his childhood imitation of his father's pulpiteering. His commitment to his religious conversion hinged on this nexus between supposedly secular and sacred histrionics—a transparent difference, he believed, because the blues world and traditional African American sacred world had, since his conversion, become one. It is quite reasonable to assume, therefore, that Dorsey sought the same venue for his talents that old-line choir directors had for theirs: a place for the chorus to be heard in its own right, a non-liturgical context for choral blues to be moaned and rolled, and a platform on which he could build his reputation as a leading old-line choral gospel blues director. The Dorsey who had stood in line at Metropolitan with other recent migrants just to have the chance to shake the great J. Wesley Jones's hand now extended his to those recent converts to choral gospel blues who were awestruck not only by Dorsey but by the recent arrival of their downhome religious song in a major old-line concert hall. The significance of choral gospel blues in bringing this moment about was not lost on Dorsey, the old-line choral bluesman for whom "everything is a show."

If the circumstances themselves of the musicale can be argued to have been momentous in Dorsey's decision to give his attention to choral gospel blues, an actual event at the close of that meeting pushed him further toward that decision. This was his "election" as president of what was to become the National Convention of Gospel Choirs and Choruses. As one might expect, given the popularity of these groups in their respective churches and the general enthusiasm—particularly among recent migrants—for choral gospel blues, the August 1932 musicale "went over . . . great." In the aftermath of being received so well, the three directors were chatting in a group when Butts asked, "How come we can't have a convention?" Dorsey was taken by surprise: "What do you mean, convention?" "A national convention," she said. Speaking out of his solo gospel experience until then, Dorsey thought Butts too visionary and impractical: "Well, we are not national; we are just here." Although his various travels throughout the Midwest to sell his songs had already convinced him that there was a market beyond Chicago for them, the chorus, even though it was now a more attractive medium to develop for his gospels, was still something he could only conceive of in individual church contexts. Groups of choruses could come together to give something like a musicale in some epicycle, but only to keep choral blues before wider than congregational audiences. Butts, however, was giving Dorsey even more of a reason to see the chorus as an endeavor worth as much of his time and energy as his solo blues: "But we'll go around and get others and make a national convention out of it." Even if Butts's idea did merit consideration, Dorsey knew it was nothing to take up on a whim. Having spent most of his professional life directing, stage managing, and organizing groups and presently spending an inordinate amount of time doing the same with his new chorus while still traveling extensively to sell his solo songs, Dorsey knew only too well all that Butts's plan entailed. Thus he was willing to give it thought, but certainly not effort: "It's all right with me, [but] I don't want all that work." At this point, Frye joined with Butts, not only agreeing with her basic idea but rejecting Dorsey's refusal to get involved. He and Butts "dumped it right in [Dorsey's] lap": "You've got to take it; we're going to make you the president." Butts and Frye then proceeded to elect themselves vice president and treasurer, respectively. If there was something prophetic about their trust in Dorsey, it might be found in his musing over that election: "I've been president ever since."[10]

As much as the August 1932 concert was a pivotal point in his decision to turn to choral gospel blues, a personal tragedy at the end of that month brought Dorsey to make that decision. On August 26, Nettie died while giving birth to their first child. Early the next morning, the child died too.

Dorsey left the concert little more than mildly aware that choral gospels could serve as an alternative mode for his solo gospels and little more than slightly bemused at the prospect that the choruses could be organized, perhaps even nationally, by someone other than himself. But the deaths—as did his two earlier nervous breakdowns and the religious conversions that followed—shook Dorsey so profoundly that he was forced to rethink his commitment to gospel blues, particularly the chorus: ". . . I guess that made me work more. I got into that chorus. . . ."[11]

Ironically, the tragedy was made somewhat more painful by Dorsey's involvement in one of the first national convention efforts. Augustus Evans, the assistant director of the Pilgrim chorus, saw wisdom enough in Butts's idea of a nationwide organization that he decided to move to St. Louis to begin organizing choruses. Through previous contacts there, he arranged for a concert "series" lasting "three or four nights or maybe a week" not only in St. Louis but in several locations in southern Illinois and southern Missouri. One of the major features of the St. Louis series was to be a mass chorus—modeled, one would presume, after the musicale in Chicago earlier in that month. He would have Dorsey direct this chorus, and by doing so he called himself "singing up the convention."[12]

Evans was the first itinerant salesperson of Dorsey's solo gospels other than Dorsey. Since the Sunday musicale, he had spent time in St. Louis selling the "two numbers" Dorsey had printed at that time:

> . . . believe it or not, I'd get up mornings, just like I was punching a time clock and I'd knock doors, just like a salesman. I became known over St. Louis in a very short time as "the singing man," because I knocked doors in all . . . communities—white and black.

Evans's knocking all over was just the beginning of his efforts. He would actually demonstrate the songs if the person had a piano. He also had to explain the music:

> I'd say who I am and I said, "Do you have a piano?" Maybe the person had a piano and says, "yes." I said, "Well now, I've got some gospel music here." Well, when you say gospel music, "What in the world is that? Never heard of that before!" "Let me sing this for you. Let me play this for you."

Outfitted with the only two printed songs that Dorsey had at that time—both "only selling for 10 cents a copy"—Evans was undoubtedly dedicated to gospel blues, especially given that he had to live off this music: "You know how many copies and how many doors I had to knock."[13]

Obviously the demonstration concerts that he planned with Dorsey required less effort and, with the composer there, were more lucrative occasions. For this reason, Evans took great pains to plan this series of concerts.

Dorsey would bring one of his best singers, Luscha Allen, and the two would make a ringing impression:

> I thought quite a bit of Luscha because he had the kind of "it" in the voice and all. . . . with Dorsey's style of playing, with those long fingers . . . and Luscha, I said, "Now . . . this is it."[14]

For Dorsey, who usually had all the responsibility for arranging to perform his songs, Evans's St. Louis series represented a rare opportunity simply to reap the economic and professional benefits of performing a gospel concert.

For all that the St. Louis series could mean to Dorsey's struggle to earn both a living and a reputation with his gospels, he was not all that enthusiastic about going, at least at that time. Nettie was due to give birth at almost any moment. He was "happy and carefree" both because of the rising popularity of his songs, several of which "were going great," and the expectation of becoming a father. Having had no previous tour like Evans had planned, Dorsey was not eager at that time to explore new sales strategies. Then, too, Evans was pushing the convention idea; already on record as being less sanguine about its success than the other directors, Dorsey was even more unwilling to become engaged in it at the expense of being away from Nettie. One more minor but persistent problem was a summer cold, one "he didn't like traveling . . . with."[15]

Nettie was mainly a "homemaker" and thus was never directly involved in either Dorsey's earlier blues profession (with the exception of once touring with Dorsey as Ma Rainey's wardrobe mistress) or his present gospel blues career. But she had always been a subtle inspiration to Dorsey, especially when he composed: "I['d] sing them to her. She liked everything I did." She also followed his work closely, often giving him advice. Thus when she encouraged him to go to St. Louis and promised him that she would "have a present" for him when he returned, he had less of an excuse not to go. Nettie's pregnancy, moreover, had been routine. She had good medical attention: her sister was a nurse, and she and Dorsey lived at the home of his uncle Joshua, the pharmacist. Despite a "deep down . . . uneasiness," therefore, Dorsey and Allen left for St. Louis, only to have to return after traveling for thirty miles to pick up Dorsey's briefcase with all of his music. At the house, Nettie was asleep. Not wanting to disturb her, Dorsey crept into their bedroom to pick up the music. He would never see her alive again. When Dorsey returned to his car, his singer decided to stay home. Dorsey would later consider these events more fatalistically:

> God was trying to tell me something when He had me return to the house for the case, but I didn't understand. [The singer] riding with me suddenly changed his mind; got out of the car. . . . I went alone. But [I] learned later that it was I God wanted to get out of the car and not leave town.[16]

Dorsey's uncle Joshua was the first person in the family to suspect that Nettie's delivery was becoming complicated: "He didn't like her breathing." Dorsey and Nettie had a pre-paid arrangement for Nettie to deliver at a hospital. But when she went there on August 25 after beginning labor, no beds were available. Her doctor offered to admit her elsewhere, but she asked to have the baby at home with the doctor and a nurse present. Thus Joshua had the opportunity to be closely in touch with Nettie's birthing. And thus it was he who had to bring the news to the rest of the family waiting downstairs in his house: Nettie died "during delivery of child" on August 26.[17]

Dorsey first heard of Nettie's difficulties via a telegram from one of her sisters. It was delivered during one of his concerts: "Hurry home. Your wife is very sick. She is going to have the baby." With the assurance that the baby was still to come, Dorsey decided to telephone home after the concert, perhaps not thinking that Nettie was fighting for survival and "not wanting to disturb the meeting by leaving immediately." When he made that call, he heard a great amount of "confusion and disturbance" and then, "when things did come to order," the words that "took the run out": "Nettie's dead! Nettie's dead! Hurry home!" Evans cancelled the remaining concerts and drove the two of them back to Chicago in Dorsey's car:

> It just numbed him. It numbed both of us. There was hardly anything said. We were both stung. The trip was just the two of us just riding along. So there was very little talking being done then.[18]

When they arrived, Dorsey "just fell out of the car."

> That day became a long hot summer day. The white pillared clouds lay in huge sheets across the heavenly blue. Some looked like temples; some looked to me like castles. Something seemed to say to me, the spirit of your wife dwells within the walls of those beautiful clouds. I arrived home about 6:00 p.m. I ran into the house, fainted and fell.

Perhaps anticipating Dorsey's grief, Joshua had a doctor awaiting Dorsey's arrival. The family had arranged with the undertaker not to remove the body before Dorsey arrived, but also not to allow him to see it. This added to his shock to the point that the doctor had to give him a sedative.[19]

Dorsey awoke several hours later to find a nurse who was showing him Thomas Andrew Dorsey, Jr., "that's what we were going to call him." He was a large—almost nine-pound—baby, very much alive and healthy:

> The baby was pronounced healthy in every respect. I looked at it and vowed to give it the best a father could: the best training, the best of home care, the best schooling from kindergarten through college. Then I gave it to God. I realized that there was joy in the midst of sorrow: joy on the first floor of the house and sorrow on the second floor, for the mortician had not yet come to move the body of my wife from the bedroom. The house was crowded with

friends and neighbors. After Nettie was taken away, my relatives in some way managed to get me off to bed in a little quiet room. I struggled through the night, thoughts of sorrow for my wife and thoughts of joy for my newborn son. . . .

It was left to Joshua once again to be the bearer of bad news by closing even this door of hope: little Thomas Andrew died in the night. The agony of this ordeal came to a climax as Dorsey arrived at the church where the funeral was to be held:

> . . . I entered the Pilgrim Baptist Church and looked down that long aisle which led to the altar where my wife and baby lay in the same casket. I started the walk in the procession and the aisle grew longer and longer before me. My legs got weak, my knees would not work right, my eyes became blind with a flood of tears. There Nettie lay, cold, unmoving, unspeaking.[20]

Whereas most of Dorsey's secular blues career can be characterized as opportunistic—the grab for notoriety with any style of blues that seemed popular at a given time—his gospel blues career for the most part seemed prompted by tragic ordeals out of which Dorsey made some significant—though not always sustained—commitment to the style even when gospel blues seemed professionally unattractive. After both nervous breakdowns, he became actively involved in religious music. He composed his first gospel blues, moreover, out of the sudden, unexplained death of a neighbor. And his current commitment had been spurred by the loss of all of his blues earnings from *It's Tight Like That.*

That each of these ties into the religious conflict that dogged Dorsey all of his life is obvious. A more intriguing meaning to the relationship between tragedy and religious commitment in Dorsey's life, however, lies in the nature of tragedy itself: it is most often unpredictable, and it victimizes by rendering one apparently powerless. Dorsey's quest to be a famous blues-man was quite the opposite: his ambition—whether realized or not—in many ways functioned as the illusion of his control over events that were happening and were yet to happen. Simply by grabbing at what he wanted in the present, Dorsey thought he was achieving what he would need beyond then. Thus his rent party blues, then his Tin Pan Alley blues, then his rejuvenated downhome blues, and finally his double-meaning blues all amounted to little more than professional opportunities that, in his most candid moments with himself, he would regard more as career ephemera than as professional accomplishments. In gospel blues, however, he seldom longed for or pursued success in this way. He knew from his initial involvement that there was only a limited market for it and thus virtually no fame connected with it. Instead, he usually sought out the gospel blues music itself as a refuge from the terror of random misfortune that seemed to stalk him and then strike at will. There was a long history of this musical haven in Dorsey's life: it began with his first religious song published in *Gospel Pearls* follow-ing his first nervous breakdown and conversion. He tried to make this shelter a sturdier presence in his life by accompanying at New Hope Baptist Church. He rebuilt it after his second nervous breakdown by composing *If You See My Savior*. And now he was strengthening it by giving his full time to trying to get his gospel blues heard and appreciated.

Dorsey's response to the sudden, unexplained deaths of Nettie and their child indicates that this dichotomy between styles and their function in his life had become blurred. His first impulse was to return to secular blues. He felt that "God had been unfair . . . " and that he wanted to "quit the work." But to do so would mean more than walking out on his commitment: it would mean as well not availing himself of the customary succor of his religious songs. Although the blues recording industry was in a slump be-cause of the economic depression that was just beginning to be widely felt, Dorsey still had reason to believe that his return to that music was a viable alternative, simply because he had made three blues records between Febru-ary and April of 1932 but only a single gospel one. Thus it seemed that despite the antithetical nature of these styles and the disparate ways they seemed to play themselves out in his life, both had the potential to provide the emotional resuscitation that Dorsey needed now. This was because his mourning was tinged with bitterness; he was struck by misfortune, but he also wanted to strike back. With Dorsey, the victim, and Dorsey, the ag-gressor, simultaneously asserting themselves and with each threatening to sweep him into its exclusive psychic realm, Dorsey was experiencing some manner of acute dialectical tension the likes of which he had never before known. If he was to find relief both from his recent tragedy and from this stress of competing responses to it, he would have to surrender himself in some degree to both tendencies and hope in the process to remain one person.[21]

With an understanding of the binary nature of the stress that Dorsey was undergoing and his desire to regain control over his life by obliging the two competing impulses simultaneously, one can gain a critical perspective on the actions Dorsey took immediately following this crisis. Part of this per-spective is the realization that Dorsey's behavior must be analyzed not only for its obvious biographical significance but for its import on the emergence of gospel blues as a popular, organized religious movement. Indeed, because they stem from the unique circumstances of his life, Dorsey's actions con-stitute his greatest individual, and thus most distinct, contribution to the emergence of gospel blues. These actions can be subsumed under two broad categories: one, to give his solo gospel blues a new voice, and the other, to build the chorus into an institution.

The most perplexing element of Dorsey's dilemma was the possibility of having to go back to secular blues in order to achieve part of the emotional equilibrium he sought. Since he made no blues records after April 1932 and since there is no indication that he wrote secular blues songs thereafter, however, Dorsey appears to have found in gospel blues that which he would have customarily sought from secular blues. Dorsey had been gradually moving in this direction by engaging in the development of gospel blues both as an artist and as an entrepreneur. This latter involvement can be attributed, of course, to his desire to make a living from gospel blues. But clearly the effort that he was making to travel widely and, even though he was not enthused about it, to develop choral gospel blues through the convention mechanism indicates that he could conceive of the economic benefits of gospel blues beyond the simple goal of subsistence. This adoption of sacred blues at a time when he thought only secular blues could meet his needs is the most critical of the actions Dorsey took after his crisis because it determined the characteristic voice of his gospel blues from there on out.

Until Dorsey wrote *Take My Hand, Precious Lord* in response to the deaths of Nettie and Thomas, Jr., he had set the textual voice of his religious songs—all in solo form—in personal evangelical terms. These early texts concentrate on three evangelical themes: salvation, personal conversion, and preaching. For example, in *If I Don't Get There,* his first published religious composition (1922), the words speak to salvation in the sense of the threat of not gaining it by not getting "there," or to heaven. The members of one's family and one's friends who have made it "there" will each be "disappointed" if "I" fail to follow:

> Dear friends and kindreds have gone from this world,
> To dwell in that city so fair,
> Hard trials and troubles no longer they share,
> They'll be disappointed if I don't get there.

> *REFRAIN*
> If I don't get there, if I don't get there,
> They'll be disappointed with hearts in despair,
> Dear father and mother, sweet sister and brother,
> They'll be disappointed if I don't get there.

Even when his song was prompted by tragedy and depression such as the sudden death of his neighbor during his second nervous breakdown, Dorsey casts his remorse in terms of a pilgrimage toward redemption, the course of which necessarily winds through unexpected, unexplained misfortunes. The dying neighbor thus becomes a messenger, assuring Dorsey's "savior" that he is making progress on his journey to salvation:

> I was standing by the beside of a neighbor,
> Who was just about to cross the swelling tide.

And I ask[ed] him if he would do me a favor,
Kindly take this message to the other side.

CHORUS

If you see my savior tell him that you saw me,
When you saw me I was on my way.
You may meet some old friend who may ask you for me,
Tell them I am coming home some day.

Later, after Dorsey had passed through his period of torment and had resolved to write gospel songs full time, both of his next gospels, *Someday Somewhere* and *How About You,* are less plaintive. When he wrote *Someday,* he was beginning to feel "more and more inspiration":

> It was a beautiful morning as I sat by the open window writing the words to my song "Someday Somewhere." The new spring breeze seemed to speak and sing with such beauty of expression and the sun shown with such unusual brightness, that I could almost see the buds bursting and the twigs growing on the trees.[22]

The song gushes with so much confidence that it barely alludes to any earthly troubles; instead, it presumes salvation to the point that Dorsey merely tries to imagine what his new home will be like:

CHORUS

Someday somewhere in a city so fair,
Far away from these burdens and cares
There'll be peace, there'll be joy
There'll be riches I'll share
When I reach that city over there.

Similarly, in *How About You,* "Jesus" has "brought me through." The voice is one of the saved, testifying how salvation came about and chiding the listener to give serious thought to it:

CHORUS

How about you? How about you?
I hope my Savior is your Savior too;
I said Lord take and use me
That's all that I can do
And I gave my heart to Jesus
How about you?

Dorsey's evangelical message focuses on salvation almost to the exclusion of conversion. Indeed, Dorsey renders the act of conversion abstruse. In all four songs, he only implies conversion by suggesting that everyone he knows has gained salvation by going "there" or "home." Presumably, each has done so by becoming converted, that is, resolving to believe in the gospel message. Only in *How About You* does he become explicit about some condition for going home: ". . . I gave my heart to Jesus, How about you?" The difference between the three earlier songs and this one rests on the point at which Dorsey wrote them—immediately following versus in the midst of a period of crisis, respectively. Even given the strain under which it was written, *How About You* does not detail Dorsey's need to convert; rather it offers a retrospective on having gained salvation. Composing this piece, as he found with the act of religious composition in general, constituted the building of an emotional haven. Conversion, therefore, was the process of arriving at that location. He usually casts it as "home," using the alias "there" only in his first religious song. Particularly for Dorsey, conversion was the struggle for spiritual stasis, a struggle marked by the mental vexation and physical agony he had experienced. By the time he wrote *How About You,* his aim was to draw attention to the process of his conversion as opposed to the conditions prompting it, since those conditions which were present during the writing of the other three songs no longer existed in his life. Also he could assume that his listeners wanted to know more of the process in general—from the traditional evangelical perspective—than of his personal narrative. The concept of conversion thus evolved, in Dorsey's mind, into one deserving to be addressed only because Dorsey had likewise passed on to the next logical stage beyond it.

But the implied linearity of this evolution cannot be explained completely by Dorsey's history of conversion. It is at least equally explained by the third aspect of his evangelical voicing, an aspect on which Dorsey's perspective seems to have undergone a progressive transformation similar to that of his conversion, preaching. In the first three songs, Dorsey is simply giving testimony to the fact that he believes in the gospel message. His belief was spawned by tribulations in his life, especially death. The gospel he believed promised him a "home" that was "far from this world of despair." He had a right to live there if he "gave his heart to Jesus." These songs, therefore, amounted to testimonial evangelism—Dorsey's spreading of the gospel as he experienced it. But by the time he turned to composing *How About You,* Dorsey no longer saw his mission as one of writing the musical version of his own spiritual narrative. His purpose now was to evangelize; to do so, he had to become an evangelist, one who had grown beyond preaching the gospel for how it had benefited him. His burden now was to enable the gospel to be sung for the message itself, to objectify it by rendering his personal acceptance of it transparent to his newly adopted role as presenter of it. Dorsey assumed the preaching voice directly by establishing two persons.

The first is the converted one, speaking of being ready to be "used" and of already having been redeemed: "How well do I remember, How Jesus brought me through." The second person could quite possibly be unconverted; more important, she is silent. Dorsey uses her voiceless presence only to receive his rhetorical question, "How about you?" His purpose is to tell this news, not to discuss it. By late 1928 or early 1929, after "Jesus" had brought him through his depression, he was ready to declare this happening to others—not just to acquaint them with an event in his life but to convince them that they could experience something as profound.

His other compositions that appeared after these three written by 1929 but before *Take My Hand, Precious Lord,* written in September 1932, indicate that Dorsey had settled on these three evangelical constructs—salvation, personal conversion, and preaching—as the standard theological concepts of his sacred texts. During these years, Dorsey wrote and copyrighted at least five gospel blues. But none of these pieces seems to have appeared in print or, if so, not in any significant quantities in this period. Augustus Evans, who sold Dorsey's songs beginning in 1932, speaks of only a "couple" of pieces that Dorsey had available to sell at this time. Dorsey, too, recalls only having "two or three songs" right at the time he turned to gospel blues full time. One can assume that these included *If You See My Savior,* because he registered it in 1929. Although he registered the other two, *Someday Somewhere* and *How About You,* in 1941, he writes of having mailed out copies of the former with *If You See My Savior* sometime between 1928 and the 1930 Baptist Convention and of hearing Magnolia Butts singing the latter after having "stumbled into a political meeting one night" in 1930. Also he recorded *If You See My Savior* and *How About You* in March 1932.[23]

In many ways, the fact that Dorsey failed to publicize these five songs between 1929 and 1932 indicates that he had arrived at a plateau with the evangelical thrust of *How About You.* Beginning with *Trusting in My Jesus* in 1929, continuing through *He'll Know Me Over Yonder* in 1930, and ending with *Jesus, My Comforter, Right Now,* and *Treasures in Heaven* in 1931, Dorsey not only maintained his emphasis on salvation, his careful contextualization of conversion, and his evangelist role, but he became markedly sanguine as well. He presents Jesus as a day-to-day companion in *Trusting in My Jesus* and *Jesus, My Comforter:*

> When I am lonesome and my heart is feeling sad,
> He moves all my burdens and it makes my soul feel glad.

> Ev'ry time you send a message,
> He will answer your pray'r,
> Keep the way clear before you,
> His blessings you will share[.]

His previous speculative stance regarding his Christian afterlife as expressed in *If You See My Savior* and *Someday Somewhere* has evaporated into self-assured salvation and a preoccupation with heavenly amenities in *He'll Know Me Over Yonder* and *Treasures in Heaven:*

> Yes He'll know me, yes He'll know me,
> When I cross that great divide[.]
> (Chorus)
> I am building my treasures in heaven,
> Where the trials of this live can never come.
> (Chorus)

As still more evidence of his strengthened evangelism, the Dorsey—now preacher—who was satisfied merely with posing an interrogative in *How About You* now feels he must confront the still silent "you" with an imperative in *Right Now* (Ex. 9-6):

> Right now, Right now
> Let the Savior bless your soul right now[.]
> Don't put off till tomorrow
> What you can do today,
> Let the Savior bless your soul right now.
> (Chorus)

In essence, Dorsey's earlier, halting other-worldliness becomes a celestial this-worldliness during this compositional period. Not only does he seem to have found the spiritual haven he sought, but he now writes of it with the complacency of one ensconced in it. Apparently, however, this self-possessed spirituality had too much of a peculiar, even hollow, ring to it for these gospels to catch on with either his soloists' or his choruses' performances. Perhaps the gospels closer to the times of his torment resonated more in harmony with the strife and affliction of those new migrants and other downtrodden who preferred to listen to or sing his songs.

In general, this group of gospels is analogous to the 1923 set of Tin Pan Alley ditties that Dorsey composed. Then, too, he had endured a setback and had resolved to pursue a new career path. At some point in the process, however, his drive to produce eclipsed his creative genius and his stylistic integrity. The result was musical drivel quite unrepresentative of the lowdown blues that he wrote expressly to "prick" his listeners' hearts. Right at the time of his National Baptist Convention success in 1930 with *If You See My Savior*—not with any of these other songs—Dorsey switches to producing his gospels with professional as opposed to his earlier personal, circumstantial motivation: now he wanted "to beat the depression" and "make a name" for himself. He felt that "it was up to me to make [gospel music] a success" and that he had to give himself "fully to the task of writing gospel songs."[24] Although one can never accurately critique a Dorsey song by its notation, some of these five songs do show uncharacteristic problems. For example, in *Trusting in My Jesus* (Ex. 9-1), the melody consists of a fragment that Dorsey repeats three times to make a phrase; then he uses this phrase three more times, or for roughly three-fourths of the song. Dorsey relieves this monotony only by injecting what amounts to a melodic episode or "B" section of almost four measures between the second and third iterations of the phrase. Despite a gospel singer's proclivity to improvise freely, she would consider the demand to vary nine repetitions of a fragment enough to sustain her listeners' interest not only excessive but almost impossible. Another example is the chorus of *He'll Know Me Over Yonder* (Ex. 9-2). The natural accentuation of the text fails to fit with that of the music. In measures 3, 5, and 17, Dorsey has the singer holding a long note on "that" or "the." By virtue of each of those long notes being three times longer than the value of the preceding note, there is natural rhythmic accentuation coming at a point where there is no comparable text of consequence. In all, Dorsey's gospel blues were most genuine, as were his secular downhome blues, when spawned by personal despair and written to make a declaration to listeners who could empathize with the desolation that such a loss of hope brings. His composition of sacred blues for career purposes would exact its toll only by causing him to lower his artistic standards and, in the short run, shunt him away from religious song as an expression of his basic emotional needs. This is the realization he came to shortly after the deaths of Nettie and Thomas, Jr.

Thus Dorsey faced a dilemma in coping with this tragedy. He would normally turn to blues for the aggressiveness with which he could pursue success. And he would normally turn to sacred composing for the solace it provided him from emotional despondency. This dilemma had one more complex dimension in that the distinction between what he could get out of either music had become blurred by his pursuit of career goals with his gospel blues. Furthermore, the strong evangelical voice of his gospels—a voice that sprang from his earlier song writing in response to tragedy—now sounded more like the blathering of a naïve proselyte.

These problems help to explain two striking features about *Take My Hand, Precious Lord,* the gospel song that Dorsey wrote in response to his wife's and child's deaths. One is the melody itself: it is not his alone. It nearly matches note for note *Must Jesus Bear the Cross Alone?*, composed by George Nelson Allen in 1852. Dorsey would have heard it often in old-line Baptist churches, for it appears in the *National Baptist Hymnal.* Dorsey readily admits that he borrowed an "old tune." The circumstances surround-

Ex. 9-1

Trusting In My Jesus (excerpts)

♩ = c. 60

Opening phrase

mm. 4-6   Trust-ing in my Je-sus_ Trust-ing in my Je-sus_ Find my jour-ney

mm. 7-8

eas-y_____ Just trust-ing in my Je-sus,_____

"B" section

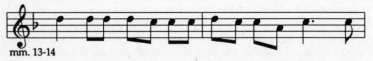

mm. 13-14

Night   in my slum-ber I can hear his ten-der   voice   He

mm. 15-16

speaks words of kind-ness and it makes my soul re-joice.

Ex. 9-2

He'll Know Me Over Yonder (excerpts)

♩ = c. 58

Verse excerpt

mm. 1-2

There's a Sav - ior   that will know me,

mm. 3-4

For the work that   I have done,

mm. 5-6

When I reach that   gold - en ci - ty...

Chorus excerpt

mm. 15-16

Yes He'll know me,   yes He'll know me,

mm. 17-18

When I cross the   great di - vide,...

ing Dorsey's initial creation of *Take My Hand* establish the link between this "old tune" and Dorsey's crisis. He was still deeply wracked and "beat up" by the deaths:

> We never really miss anyone until they are gone for good. I missed Nettie on every turn of the way. When I came in after a hard day, there was no one to greet me at the door. When I sat to the table to eat, there was no smiling face across the table and I had to eat alone. When I retired for the night, there was no goodnight kiss. I became so lonely I did not feel that I could go on alone. I needed help; my friends and relations had done all they could for me. I was failing and did not see how I could live.[25]

In this state of utter despondency, Theodore Frye urged Dorsey to "get away from home . . . and kind of get [himself] together." The two walked over to the "Poro" college, a beauty-training school. There was a community function room at the school with a piano that was easily accessible: "You could go down there and rehearse or practice or whatever you want." In this melancholy mood, Dorsey was unable to summon any creative energy: "I plunked 'round on the piano . . . played a song or two, a hymn." He was simply "fumbling" around at the keyboard with "an old tune . . . that's sung to many songs, many sets of lyrics." While it appears that Dorsey had no intention of composing at that moment, he clearly was seeking out the soothing effect of religious song, in this instance traditional Anglo-Protestant hymnody.[26]

The genesis of *Must Jesus Bear the Cross Alone* foretells somewhat Dorsey's use of it in his present crisis. The words were composed by Thomas Shepherd (1665–1739), a minister of the Church of England, who in 1694 withdrew to become pastor of the Castle Hill Meeting House, an Independent or Nonconformist sect in Nottingham. The poem first appeared in Shepherd's *Penitential Cries,* which was published along with John Mason's *Songs of Praise* in 1693. The year is significant because the Independents first began using hymns—as opposed to psalms—in worship during 1690. Indeed, Mason's collection was one of the few issued and in use before Sir Isaac Watts brought notoriety to the movement with his *Hymns and Spiritual Songs* in 1707. The classic difference between these genres is that the hymn, a religious, metrical composition, is spiritual, but not biblical like the psalm which is either verbatim or paraphrased scriptural text. Early Protestants debated the use of human-generated texts for worship music versus divine words. Thus the appearance of hymns introduced a humanistic voice into liturgical practices in which only biblical expression had been considered appropriate. Mason was one of the Independents who spearheaded this movement, compiling, among other works, Shepherd's texts which treat exclusively repentance as a state of grief or pain. Thus at the root of *Must Jesus Bear the Cross Alone* is the "feeling of despondency and the withdrawal of God's favour," a feeling that gripped Dorsey as he "fumbled" over the keys.[27]

But Dorsey discarded Shepherd's text at some point while he "plunked" out *Must Jesus*. This switch from reflecting on his tragedy through Shepherd's text to composing his own while keeping Allen's melody amounts to a key departure by Dorsey from his usual compositional practice. Although Shepherd's text, written in common meter, could have been sung to any number of tunes, given the practice of singing all varieties of religious texts to secular melodies at the time Shepherd wrote his hymn, there is no record of a tune for *Must Jesus Bear the Cross Alone* until Allen put it to his *Maitland*. But from simply a professional standpoint, Allen—a professor of sacred music at Oberlin and a composer/compiler of hymns—was as likely as Dorsey to seek to image the feelings evoked by Shepherd's hymn in music. Indeed, there is speculation that he, like Dorsey, might have felt the need to rework the text inasmuch as the three stanzas varied substantially in certain lines from the original by the time the newly composed *Must Jesus* appeared in 1844 in *The Oberlin Social and Sabbath School Hymn Book,* compiled by Geo. N. Allen, Professor of Music in O. C. Institute. Evidently, he successfully captured the sentiment of Shepherd's text (as altered) in his melody, for no one has altered Allen's setting musically or textually—at least not as a customarily accepted arrangement. Unlike a large number of the notable Anglo-Protestant hymns like it, *Must Jesus Bear the Cross Alone* has appeared in its original setting throughout its long, popular history—one that includes publication in widely disseminated collections beginning with Henry Ward Beecher's *Plymouth Collection* in 1855, where it gained its first notoriety, and lasting until as late as 1979 in 26 of the 78 compilations used by major religious groups in the United States in their "chief services of worship."[28]

Out with Frye just to "get away from home," Dorsey had no plans to compose that evening. His plunking away at an "old hymn" amounted to musical meandering, perhaps just trying to numb some of the persistent pain. Thus something about Allen's setting of *Must Jesus Bear the Cross Alone* must have shaken Dorsey out of his melancholia. Identifying just what it was that lodged itself in Dorsey's ear lies only within the realm of speculation. But there is some evidence in Dorsey's music itself that would indicate what Dorsey might have been alert, perhaps even susceptible, to in Allen's tune. It can be found in *Someday Somewhere,* his second gospel blues: with minor exceptions, its melodic material is identical to the B section of Allen's melody. In Example 9-3, beginning with the last beat of measure 8 and ending at the second beat of measure 16 is Allen's single iteration of the B phrase. In Example 9-4, the first eight measures are virtually identical to Allen's B section. Dorsey uses this material, however, as both the A and B sections. In each of these sections, the melody line is nearly

Ex. 9-3

Must Jesus Bear the Cross Alone? (original)

music by George N. Allen

mm. 1-4 Must— Je - sus bear the cross a - lone,— And

mm. 5-8 all the world go free?——————— No:—

mm. 9-12 There's a cross for ev - 'ry one,—— And

mm. 13-16 there's a cross for me.—————————

mm. 17-18 A - MEN.

identical except for the last two and one-third measures, during which he varies the line at the end of the A section so that he can cadence on the dominant (V) chord and then repeat the phrase once more with the same material up to the same point but then cadence on the tonic (I) chord. With the exception of these harmonic structural points, *Someday Somewhere* consists of four and a half iterations of material identical to the B section of *Must Jesus Bear the Cross Alone.*

But there is a more subtle aspect to this similarity of melodic material than the suggestion that Dorsey may have previously borrowed Allen's material. The similarity has less to do with pitches than with a certain structure around which Dorsey had been building his gospels. With the exception of *Trusting in My Jesus,* Dorsey had composed each of his songs in two sections, one for the verses, the other for the refrain. By its repetitiveness alone, the refrain implies the musical emphasis of a textual point. Given the increasingly evangelical voice of Dorsey's songs, this emphasis could well be characterized as didactic. For example, in *Right Now,* his verses for the most part speak to the benefits of letting "the Savior bless your soul right now." The evangelical—particularly preaching—voice of this song, however, holds forth in the chorus, conveying, even instructing, the message "right now." Dorsey's means of crafting a corresponding moral, or lesson, for the expositional music of his verse section—particularly when he has to limit the amount and complexity of his melodic material—is to raise the overall melodic level as a means of creating musically tensional significance. Almost without fail, each of the refrain sections of Dorsey's songs up to 1932 (and virtually with no exception thereafter) contains a melody line with a generally elevated tessitura. Indeed, the greatest number of the highest pitches found in a Dorsey gospel as written are located in the B section. For example, in *Treasures in Heaven* (Ex. 9-5), Dorsey uses "e-flat‴" four times in the chorus; the next most frequently used note is a "g′," which lies six pitches lower. Moreover, Dorsey uses three pitches ("e flat″," "c″," and "b flat‴") above the "g′" a total of twelve times in the chorus. Even when the highest pitch can be found in the verse section, Dorsey will do something with the highest pitch in the refrain section to give it greater emphasis. In *If You See My Savior* (Ex. 6-1), for example, the two sections do not vary from one another. But in the Dorsey/Hudson Whitaker performance (Ex. 6-2), they vary by singing the "d‴" twice, once in each cycle of the chorus melody (mm.

Ex. 9-4

Someday Somewhere (introduction)

mm. 1-3

mm. 4-8

Ex. 9-5

Treasures in Heaven (chorus)

mm. 8-10

I am build- ing my trea- sures in heav- en,— Where the

mm. 11-12

tri - als of this life can nev- er come. I will

mm. 13-14

find peace and joy there for - ev- er,———— When my

mm. 15-16

life's work on earth here is done.————

11 and 15) and only once in the verse melody (m. 7), in the second strophe. In Dorsey's solo version (Ex. 6-3), the highest note is present in each section (at mm. 10 and 25–26, respectively), but for nine beats in the chorus versus five in the verse.

The manner in which Dorsey elevates the tessitura accounts for much of the drama of the refrain section and in many ways represents the signature of the evangelical voice. Often Dorsey calls for a wide melodic leap usually at the beginning and often within the chorus section. For example, in *Treasures in Heaven* (Ex. 9-5, m. 8), he has a minor seventh leap to make the declaration "I am building my treasures in heaven." And beginning with the last beat of measure 12 in *Right Now* (Ex. 9-6), Dorsey writes a melodic sequence that ascends steadily the interval of an eleventh over six and a half beats. These melodic acrobatics are not merely instances in which Dorsey is calling for musical agility. Dorsey, as any good composer would, avoids a display of technique simply for the feat of it. Instead, the refrain uses melodic drama to reinforce the homiletic climax of the text. Like Nix's and the other recording preachers' sermons, Dorsey's gospel blues are fashioned to make their point at the end, where, in the black preaching style in particular, the model calls for the tension to rise to its peak by the speaker's shift of voice from "objective fact" to "objective testimony."[29] While the texts of Dorsey's songs do not always indicate this substantive shift, they do follow the rhetorical structure of black preaching, that is, the ending must burst forth with oratorical flourish. Even as banal as Dorsey's evangelical voice had become by 1932, it never shrugged off this expectation. For certain, Dorsey at times resorted to trite musical devices to create and sustain the concluding tension, but he never wavered in his commitment to the form.

An examination of Dorsey's adaptation of Allen's *Maitland* to *Take My Hand, Precious Lord* indicates that while he seems to have tapped into the suitability of Allen's tune as a melodic image of contrition, he had to rework it as a melodic sermon. As he did with the similar tonal material for *Someday Somewhere*, Dorsey expands the small amount available by calling for it to be repeated. In this instance, he takes Allen's complete melody and uses one iteration of it for the two verses and another for the refrain. This structure requires that Dorsey embellish the melody distinctly, so that the listener, even though she hears it twice, understands the contrasting role that each cycle plays. Dorsey accomplishes this by switching one of his most familiar refrain devices to the verse: there he calls for the highest pitch and the most elaborate ornamentation. In Example 9-7, he writes only an "f'" as the highest note in the refrain (m. 13), while at the parallel point in the verse he writes an "a flat'"" (m. 29). His frequent use of greater leaps in the refrain has been transferred to the verse section as well. From the second eighth note of measure 25 to the last one of the following measure, Dorsey calls for the melody to ascend one octave. He follows this in measure 28 with an ascen-

Ex. 9-6

Right Now (excerpt)

mm. 12-13

Don't— put off till to-mor-row, What

mm. 14-16

you can do to-day, Let the Sav-ior bless your soul right now.—

Ex. 9-7

Take My Hand, Precious Lord (original)

Ex. 9-7 (cont.)

mm. 20-22   When my way grows—— drear, Pre-cious

mm. 23-25   Lord, lin-ger near,—— When my life—— is——

mm. 26-28   al - most—— gone,——————— *cresc.* Hear my

mm. 29-31   cry, hear my— call,—— *dim.* Hold— my hand lest I

mm. 32-34   fall,—— Take- my hand,— Pre-cious Lord,— lead me

D. C. al Fine

mm. 35-36   home.———————————————

sion of a minor seventh to the highest note of the verse section and then with a quick cascade of pitches down one octave to "a flat'" (m. 28 through second eighth note of m. 30). The interval activity in the corresponding part of the refrain traverses only a perfect fifth (mm. 11–15).

The need to recast Allen's tune into sermonic structure was not the only urging Dorsey had to rely on these devices. Much of the aptness of Allen's melody for the feeling of Shepherd's penitential poem derives from the careful placement of high notes, well-crafted melodic ascents and descents, and intervallic leaps. A student of Lowell Mason, the mid-nineteenth-century hymn reformer, Allen was well disposed to the "science" of composing suitable melodies to hymns in the growing effort, spearheaded by Mason, to wean the public off the secular tunes or "'light music'" so frequently resorted to for hymn settings.[30] For example, the opening seven beats of Allen's tune rise one octave (Ex. 9-3). The final pitch of the ascent, a "d"," comes on the definite article "the" in order to emphasize the fact that there is only one cross. The following phrase, although it has a shorter ascent, is basically melodically redundant. Because Shepherd's text takes a dramatic turn after the first two strophes of each verse, Allen had to compose something as musically emphatic. It is at this point that he makes skillful use of the melodic leap by repeating the opening three notes an octave higher. Thus as Shepherd (as revised) asks the two questions,

> Must Jesus bear the cross alone,
> And all the world go free?

Allen sets it to the opening two matched melodic lines. Then when Shepherd answers the question,

> No: there's a cross for ev'ry one,
> And there's a cross for me,

Allen responds to "No: there's" with the octave transposition of the opening notes. Facing such an ingenious usage of the devices he would have used were he writing a setting of Shepherd's text, Dorsey relies more heavily on ornamentation, so much so that he writes it into the music more than he had previously. In *If You See My Savior,* which has the same duplication of material between the verse and refrain sections, Dorsey writes in no embellishments (Ex. 6-1), even though he performs them in two versions (Exs. 6-2 and 6-3). But in *Take My Hand,* he writes in grace notes (e.g., mm. 11 and 12), cascading embellishments (mm. 29–30), and even a blues note (mm. 24 and 32).

While Dorsey was urged on by his desire to reshape the piece to fit his sermonic mold, his switching of compositional devices between the principal sections does not account for the most surprising alteration he made: he put the refrain at the beginning of *Take My Hand* instead of after the verse section. The hint as to why this occurred is found in Dorsey's account of his shift from "browsing over the keys" with *Must Jesus* to composing from it—from simply sharing in Shepherd's penitence to issuing his own cry for divine assurance:

> Now the melody's an old melody, but they couldn't turn it around, twist it as much as I could. They can't handle it with the embellishments and the beauty, you know, the trills and the turns that I put in it, see?

Dorsey seems to have begun playing *Must Jesus* in an improvisatory mode, adding his ornamentation to Allen's song. By doing so he was already assuming compositional control and thereby filtering both Shepherd's feelings and Allen's melodic representation of them through his familiar blues "trills" and "turns." More important, he was channeling his own sense of despair into the partnership forged by Allen with Shepherd's text. Allen's melodic "science," as expressive a melody as it yielded, was too ready-made and pristine perhaps for Dorsey, who normally re-composed even his own melodies according to the circumstances in which he was performing. Dorsey, who so often used his "ivories" to get "lowdown" and to "prick" the hearts of others, was now in the act of becoming "susceptible" to himself. Thus Dorsey's "browsing" became a sort of musical squirming; he needed to do more than "twist" the melody:

> I called Mr. Frye. I said, "Come on Frye! Listen to this. Come over here to this piano! I got this tune and I'm trying to put words with it."[31]

With the difference between the bluesman and the preacher culturally insignificant and, especially in Dorsey's case, existing virtually in name only now that he was a sacred bluesman, Dorsey had made the step from attempting to represent Shepherd's emotions through music to presenting his own through words with the first two words he tried to "put with it"—"blessed Lord":

> . . . take my hand." I needed somebody there to hold me up. I just couldn't. [That's] why I went down there to get away from everybody, just [Frye] and I.

The weight of all that had recently happened to Dorsey pressed in on him heavily in that moment. The need for "somebody" caused him to grope first melodically and then verbally for the right plea:

> I played [it] for [Frye]: "What'd you think about it?"
> "It's all right, sounds good." I went over it again. He said, "No man, no. Call Him 'precious Lord.' Don't call him 'blessed Lord'; call him 'precious Lord.' "
> "Why, why? He *is* a blessing."

"Call Him 'precious Lord.' "

And that thing like something hit me and went all over me, see. I said, "That does sound better! That's it." And that hooked right in there. The words dropped just like drops of water . . . from the crevice of a rock. [I sat] right there and I wrote out half of the song . . . part of the song right then and there. I finished the other in the next day or two.[32]

Dorsey's moment of catharsis pivoted on that turn of phrase from "blessed" to "precious" Lord—from a Lord whose holiness he proclaimed to one whose worthiness he cherished. Dorsey had begun to compose the song at its homiletic climax—its refrain. The verses followed this rush of self-enlightenment "in the next day or two" because they were reflections on how he had arrived at the realization that Jesus was "precious," that he held Him dear. This was not just another didactic chorus, a theological point to reinforce. Although it followed on the heels of the conditions that led to its creation, this refrain was to be enshrined as a moment of epiphany. By reversing the order of the verse/refrain structure, Dorsey made the words that "hooked" him into the song's epigraph: whenever it was sung, Dorsey's affection for his "precious Lord" would make the first impression.

This reverse compositional sequence explains in great part the switching of melodic devices between the verse and refrain sections. Dorsey's arrival at the words for the refrain represented the conclusion of his quest for relief from his torment and assurance that he could still expect God's blessing, including the ultimate one, salvation. The refrain makes its point musically, therefore, by being less ornamented and less melodically elevated than the verse section. In the latter, Dorsey is vexed and in agony: "When my way grows drear'," "When the darkness appears," and "Hear my cry, hear my call." In the refrain, the dominant theme is the certainty of being led "home" even though "I am tired . . . weak . . . worn" and must be led "Thru the storm" and the "night."

For all the significance of these melodic and structural aspects of Dorsey's creation of *Take My Hand, Precious Lord,* none of them speaks to the one element of the piece that solved the dilemma that Dorsey faced in responding to Nettie's and Thomas Andrew's deaths. Dorsey wanted to strike back through the secular blues, both for the career success and the greater expressive latitude that the style seemed to offer him. Instead, with the title of this gospel song of contrition, Dorsey fundamentally altered the voice of his gospel blues. He found at last a way to speak as forthrightly with his gospel blues as he had so routinely done with his lowdown, secular blues. Dorsey's practice up to *Take My Hand, Precious Lord* had been to entitle his gospel blues with the opening phrase of the refrain. This procedure ensures that the person who sees the music will be acquainted with the homiletic focus of the piece even before she hears or performs it. Dorsey, moreover, usually called for the title to be the most repeated phrase, almost always writing it in the verse section as well. At the root of his textual voice change is his abandoning of these habits. "Precious Lord," for example, is sung three times in the verse section but only twice in the refrain.

The standard evangelical voice that Dorsey had used until *Precious Lord* called for him to preach the gospel, the good news. The ultimate message of each of Dorsey's gospel blues, therefore, was salvation. Even when he wrote a song out of painful circumstances, Dorsey was careful to hone its meaning down to a redemptive essence, leaving the personal difficulties reduced to virtual musical asides. Thus he could suffer great anguish at the sudden death of his neighbor in *If You See My Savior,* but he would enshroud those feelings in the expectation that the neighbor not only will "cross the swelling tide" and will see the "Savior," but will tell Him that when he last "saw me, I was on my way" there, too. Had it not been muted by events so grave as the deaths of his wife and child, Dorsey's evangelical voice would have continued to preach redemptive drivel of the sort that had trivialized his recent compositions.

While he wants to stress the preciousness of his Lord and so maintain the evangelical stance of this song, Dorsey desires even more to stress what he *needs* from that precious Lord in order to endure his present hardship. Thus "Precious Lord" is a salutation initially—especially as Dorsey was inspired by it the night he composed the song. But in the remainder of the song, he shifts it into apposition to the "you," who is the silent subject of the imperatives with which he saturates the text: "take my hand," "linger near," "hear my cry," "hear my call," "guide my feet." When he turns at last to the evangelical theme, even then he retains the voice that commands need: "lead me on to the light," "lead me home." With this new voice, Dorsey still makes the gospel message stand out, but now in subjective relief: it garners attention only against the backdrop of his grief and turmoil.

In essence, Dorsey finally had given his gospel blues music a truly complementary blues text. Whereas previously he had only been able to cower away from sorrow in his gospels, he had always been able to cry out about it in his blues. The evangelical message was intended to provide a refuge: to guide one along the path to divine submission. Blues, on the other hand, was intrinsically declarative: "a good man or woman, feeling bad," as Dorsey so often defined it. Up until "precious Lord" "hooked" Dorsey that night, his gospel blues consisted of lowdown blues "twists" and "turns," but without their verbal "prick," their articulation of sorrow. With *Take My Hand, Precious Lord,* Dorsey allowed himself to wail, to get "lowdown," to purge—rather than just soothe—his grief. Thus that moment in which he joined his divine pleadings to his lowdown blues assumed a near mystical aura. No longer masquerading as evangelical platitudes, his needs began to gasp for some suitable expression. He "fumbled" for it with his "trills" and "turns," casting aside as irrelevant the question "Must Jesus bear the cross alone?" Now deep within the "crevice" of his bluesman's "embellishments," he continued his groping. There, in one last, wrenching, lowdown "twist," he moaned out those needs through words and music that seeped like "drops of water" through his voice and fingers: "Precious Lord, take my hand."

10

A Place for Gospel Blues in Old-Line Religion: 1932–1937

The marriage of Dorsey's musical and textual voices, as represented by the composition of *Take My Hand, Precious Lord,* amounted to the final resolution of the warring interpersonal dualities in Dorsey's life. It ultimately would offer a similar resolution of the deep conflicts between old-line and indigenous African American religion. The first hint of this broader cultural impact came the following week when Frye and Dorsey introduced the song at Ebenezer:

> The folk went wild. They went wild. They broke up the church. Folk were shouting everywhere.

Dorsey was initially befuddled by this response. He had found his song deeply moving, but only, he thought, because of his personal connection to it through tragedy:

> I don't know what they were shouting for. I was the one who should be shouting . . . or sorry.

Dorsey and Frye, moreover, usually elicited similar responses from their performances. There was good reason not to think of this particular "wild" reaction as being prompted by anything new. Frye had strutted as he often did:

> He sang it that morning, I mean he sang. He walked two or three steps and braced himself and wow![1]

In one sense the response of old-line congregations to Dorsey's gospel blues in both solo and choral forms mirrored his feeling in 1928 when he began to set his sacred texts to blues: they rejoiced simply at the use of blues idioms in conjunction with worship. Indeed, one could reason that they were as much incited to "go wild" by sacred blues as a novelty as they were moved by the feelings that the music-text combination evoked. Dorsey had spent the last four years composing and performing under a similar illusion. The mere fact of singing his blues to sacred words of any sort had become his mission. Instead of placing his effort on getting his gospel texts accepted, he spent time training singers and choruses how to "moan and roll." The Ebenezers and Pilgrims went wild because the bluesman stirred them with his music, quite possibly more than with his words. The new migrants who rushed to join the choruses did so to celebrate the arrival of their former demonstrative ways at the 11 a.m. Sunday worship hours, not really to "get lowdown" because the words evoked some pain or sorrow. They would seem as likely to be "hooked" as Dorsey, therefore, if the right words were to tumble out of the "crevice" of truly indigenous black religion.

Not only did old-line worshippers seem to mirror his earlier feelings, but they were beginning to develop a corresponding theological perspective as well. In an extensive study of the idea of God among black Americans in two "epochs," 1760 to the Civil War and the Civil War to 1914, Benjamin E. Mays notes that in "'mass'" literature there is a generally otherworldly, compensatory conceptualization of God: "[These views] make God influential chiefly in the beyond, in preparing a home for the faithful—a home where His suffering servants will be free of the trials and tribulations which beset them on the earth." This clearly describes the evangelical vision Dorsey preaches in his gospels up to *Take My Hand*. A new conception of God began to appear in the "third period" of Mays's study, 1914 to 1937; the same genre of literature "reveals . . . a desire to be protected from danger, sickness, disease, death, hell, and enemies." There is a deep desire for "security." It evolves out of "the fear that comes to one who is afraid of life generally because of experiences that make life a precarious and hazardous undertaking."[2] This shift resonates with Dorsey's new declaration of his desire for his precious Lord to "hold my hand lest I fall"; it is as well a recognition that his Lord *can* keep him from falling.

For those more recent old-liners from the South, the attraction to Dorsey's new voice was quite likely not rooted in literary representations of this- or other-worldliness. Dorsey's *Take My Hand* harked back to the relation between God and the believer in traditional worship. Zora Neale Hurston, who was an astute observer of the black church in the 1920s and '30s, characterized this voice as emanating from Africanisms in African American culture, a major one being "spirit possession." She describes religious ritual in these congregations as being a "protest against the high-brow tendency" that marks some Protestant churches as "Negroes gain more education and wealth." To the outsider, this protesting "Sanctified Church" is "barbaric." But Hurston sees it as the persistence of the "African 'Possession' by the gods." The role of music, she continues, is central in that "the service is really drama with music. And since music without motion is unnatural among

Negroes[,] there is always something that approaches dancing—in fact *IS* dancing—in such a ceremony. So the congregation is restored to its primitive altars under the new name of Christ."[3]

If the sanctifieds and the upper crust worshipped in different modes, they did not always do so in different places, as Hurston implies. The large migrations during the years of Mays's "third epoch" blurred the distinction between both groups. The old-line God, now more this-worldly, was active in the social programs sponsored by the middle-class churches. The two groups, moreover, intermingled regularly: old-liners made weekly pilgrimages to the sanctified temples. They even divided their donations between the two institutions so much so that many of the old-line churches became "practically bankrupt," not just because they suffered from an economic depression at the time "but also because they did not compete successfully with the cults [Holiness and Pentecostal groups] which generally thrived all during the period." Clearly, two sets of African American religious ears were straining to hear something like Dorsey's new gospel blues voice. Just as clearly evident was the fact that each culture was susceptible to such a variant articulation of that voice that Dorsey would find it difficult to sing his newfound words of solace in such a way as to have them heard with the same impact on both groups. This situation echoed back to the difficulty that the early post-Emancipation black churches faced. The young man who told Payne "Sinners won't get converted unless there is a ring [shout]" had become today's sanctified preacher. Similarly, Daniel Payne's successors, "practical Christians," were still wagging their heads and echoing his sentiments to the modern bush-meeting adherents: "You might sing till you fell down dead, and you would fail to convert a single sinner."[4]

Thus Dorsey's confusion at the response to *Take My Hand, Precious Lord* on the Sunday morning of its rousing debut was understandable. Unbeknownst to him, his song had been the cue for a more unified spirituality in old-line churches. But the resounding affirmation which the Ebenezer congregation gave that spirituality contained the dissonance of several generations of cultural conflict. In the cacophony of going "wild," some old-liners were shouting approval at the more assertive relationship with God that was signified by "take my hand"; it matched their new conception of a God concerned as they were about their social condition. Others, quickened by the "turns" of sacred blues, were shouting approval at being, of all things, "possessed" in an old-line church. This disharmony amidst such unified elation at hearing *Take My Hand* was the extraneous sound that Dorsey could pick up on but not comprehend. Over the next few months its persistence became apparent by the mixed responses he received. The day after introducing *Take My Hand,* Dorsey prepared the manuscript and had it "printed up," thinking that the song would sell easily. But it took "about two years before it came on": "it wasn't sellin' nothin'." Not until the end of the

'30s did it become well known. On the other hand, "[Frye and I] got out, started singing that thing. . . . Any church we [went] in had folks shouting and jumping before we got out."[5]

As confusing initially as these mixed responses were, they ultimately led to the rise of gospel blues as an established song form in old-line churches. The reason for this apparent anomaly lies in the common point between the two responses: both were coping tactics. One need only glance into slavery to find the precedent for communal-oriented means of adaptation to oppression.

Much of the commentary on the spirituals has noted that, despite their other-worldly, "compensatory" message, they were really survival texts. Mays suggests that they "were born of necessity in order that the slave might more adequately adjust himself to the new conditions in the world." The very theology of the spiritual evolves out of the black experience, argues James Cone. This experience "created the spiritual," and one of its components is "survival in the land of death." The tendency to over-emphasize the escapism in these songs is traceable to the slaves' encrypting of the texts with multiple meanings. This imparted both "mask and symbol" dimensions to the songs. They contained a means of expression that was masked for "protection against whites," and they avoided "direct language" so that the "messages of assurance" would speak to the group at large, regardless of the localized experiences of individuals. This need to speak universally to the community in a shared language was facilitated by the call-and-response pattern of performing the spirituals. The leader or caller, in many cases the "Negro preacher" or a similar figure, was the agent of symbolic unity, concludes James Weldon Johnson: "It was through him that the people of diverse languages and customs who were brought here from diverse parts of Africa and thrown into slavery were given their first sense of unity and solidarity." This unity was suggested by the performance configuration itself: the caller was responsible for providing texts that consisted of ideas that were shared widely enough for the remainder of the community to feel inspired to respond back. In this sense the slave "priesthood" developed as a key part of the survival ethic. So strong was its influence, indeed, that it may be said to have given birth to a "black national sensibility."[6]

The other widely documented coping tactic of slavery was the secret meeting. Although its purpose was not always religious, the meeting does seem by its nature to have been the forum for unmonitored—and, given the oppression of enslavement, one could say unleashed—communal expression. Thus slaves could be found gathering for activities as varied as simple recreation or socializing such as "'frolics'" to unmistakable debauchery such as drinking or "'a shootin' craps.'" The most common references to these gatherings, however, is that they were convened around the desire for religious ritual, varying from small prayer meetings to full preaching services. In Virginia, for example, ex-slaves who were interviewed separately and by different interviewers provided consistent testimony to the widespread presence of the "hush" or "bush" "harbor" or "arbor" (hereinafter, these terms will be used interchangeably). They are as consistent about details such as the constant threat of being discovered by "patterollers [patrollers]" and about setting up elaborate warning systems and camouflage networks:

> An' when they was havin' a meetin' an' de patterollers come, Uncle Jackson
> wouldn't never let them slip up an' break up a meetin'. Used to station
> niggers in relays from the trail to the meetin' place an' when the patterollers
> would show up, Uncle Jackson who was always the one farthest out, would
> whistle like a bob-cat to warn the others. Sometimes they would stretch
> grape-vines across the path, ef they was an important meetin', an' Uncle
> Jackson would go up an' bait the patteroller. An' when they come ridin' down
> the path tryin' to catch Uncle Jackson, he would crouch down an' run under
> the grape vine' an' the fust patteroller would come ridin' into it an' git
> thowed offen his horse.

The most striking part of these meetings, according to numerous participants, was their noisiness; they were not meditational, introspective events. They were times to "praise God in de way we knowd." Indeed, numerous accounts correlate on the fact that slaves had to use various devices such as an inverted pot to dampen the sound:

> . . . some of the masters didn't like the way we slaves carried on [when] we
> turn pots down, and tubs to keep the sound from going out. Den we would
> have a good time, shouting, singing, and praying just like we pleased.

Clearly, the operative idea here is "just like we pleased," for in this case the person was enslaved in a comparatively congenial situation. Her master was very religious, treated his slaves virtually as equals as far as, for example, not allowing them even to serve dinner or to do any work on Sundays. He prayed with his slaves, but "if they wanted to pray by dem selves they could." Even with this unsupervised, sanctioned opportunity to have their own prayer meetings, however, these slaves sneaked off to hold secret ones.[7]

Significantly, the "preacher" figure is rarely mentioned in these accounts of the meetings: "everyone was so anxious to have a word to say that a preacher did not have a chance. All of them would sing and pray."[8] Obviously, if there were singing, there would have to be a functioning leader even if it were as transitory as the person who did the "call" during a spiritual. Thus the absence of a ritualistic leadership role seems to imply that communal catharsis of the sort that flourished in slavery was so participatory that even the "priesthood" could not contribute in its customary manner. Secret slave communal activities seem to have been self-therapeutic sessions. They were so intrapersonal that an external presence, even one with an acknowledged spiritual role such as a preacher, would be considered an interference. In essence, a preacher "did not have a chance" because the specialized fellowship among those who, ironically, were normally disposed to defer to him prohibited him from exercising his authority.

But leadership of a facilitating sort did exist in these meetings. By virtue of the performance structure of the spiritual, this leadership surfaced in the caller of the call-and-response pattern of the spiritual. But this was a special role, unique to the song style. The caller, an individual presence, differed from the respondents only as the other component of an antiphonal ensemble. The performer ratio of one to many implied neither a diminished role for group members nor a structurally dominant role for the caller. The caller's distinct purpose was to improvise, or spontaneously compose, text. The fresh words, in turn, were taken up and amplified through repetition by the respondents. Caught up in their inner therapy, these persons accepted the caller's words as embellishments of their inner feelings and thus as guides in group-aided self-catharsis. Even though an individual answered back in a chorus of other releasing selves, she was answering first and foremost for herself and as someone signaling approval of the caller's selection of words to enhance her own therapeutic expression. The description of singing and praying in a meeting "just as we pleased" can be read, therefore, as a chorus of selves, each of whom did just as he or she "pleased," thanks to the caller.

From a purely abstract point of analysis, these two coping strategies emerge as generic complements of one another: the spiritual is a means and the meeting is an end. Simply by virtue of its call-and-response singing pattern, the spiritual—even when its text was not religious—was the slave's instrument for declaring and eliciting feeling, whether it was this- or other-worldly, whether it encouraged accommodation or resistance. Simply by virtue of its communal purgative function, on the other hand, the secret meeting, or "brush harbor," was more than anything a feeling in and of itself. While an individual or group of slaves could always declare feelings, encoded if necessary, and more often than not receive back a response in kind when singing the spiritual, being able to act on them or actually feel them was not always possible. Thus one finds even masters able to encourage singing. It was one of several "innocent amusements [that], when under proper regulations and when partaken of with moderation, conduce to morality and virtue."[9] This is why the spiritual was virtually ubiquitous, why it seemed to serve so many ends no matter how varied they were. On the other hand, the highly behaviorally proscribed "bush arbor" had to be clandestine. Slaves went there to feel the forbidden. As a priestless temple with an old, upturned pot for its altar, the bush meeting provided for a fundamental alteration of the slave psyche. Hidden away behind a veil of old blankets and protected by a welt of carefully placed grapevines, the "hush harbor" took on the allure of a salutary vice: few slaves, regardless of the condition of their enslavement, seemed to want to resist it. Risking death, they returned to it surreptitiously again and again simply to administer to themselves—in all-too-fleeting but ever more addictive doses—the therapeutic narcotic of doing, alas, "just as we pleased."

In Ebenezer Baptist Church nearly seventy years after the abolition of chattel enslavement, Dorsey was caught in the crossfire of what had become an almost antagonistic complementarity between these two slave survival strategies, the call-and-response spiritual singing and the "bush arbor." Even though the spiritual could be masked and sung in the most anti-survivalist of circumstances, its very versatility assured that it could always complement the special demands of the "bush harbor." Hence there existed the seamless unity between the spiritual performance as a mere means to survive and the fellowship of unleashed expressivity as survival itself. By the time Bishop Payne encountered this union in its post-Emancipation guise as the after-church ring shout, it already showed signs of being shattered by the newly Protestantized African American who could "sit down and sing in a rational manner." The more institutionalized the black church became, the more marginalized its "bush harbor" survivals became. The spiritual, however, because of its chameleon-like adaptivity, continued its partnership with the meeting. But it also took on another life and identity with the "jubilee" singing tradition and with the Works, Burleighs, and Detts who sought to "dress it up" as an appropriate song form for the "new" Negro.

By the time both of these strategies had migrated to the northern urban centers, they were no less tactics of coping with a hostile world than they had been during enslavement. But because they each thrived in opposite wings of the urban African American church, they appeared to be mutually exclusive of one another even though, as Mays would find, they were both compensatory in nature as far as they conceptualized a God of the Negro experience in the 1930s. The Payne/ring shout encounter took place when the divided church was in its embryonic stage. By the mid-1920s, the AME denomination was an established, old-line presence throughout black areas of the urban North with its counterpart in each of the major denominations. The "intelligence" and "refinement" that Payne wanted were institutionalized; they were musically represented by the new spiritual as it was celebrated along with the western European anthem in the Sunday morning worship hour and the monthly musicale. The spiritual's use as a coping mechanism now was highly circumspect—what with its powerful creative texts now frozen and its call-and-response structure replaced by chordal, Anglophonic harmony. But even in this disguise it served nobly in the accommodation of the African American presence in the strange land of white mainline Protestantism. The black old-line Protestant could take comfort that such a crucial link to the slavery past could still reverberate in aid to the new survival imperative, dignity.

Because of its deeply personal and uniquely communal nature, the "bush harbor" did not evolve along such an obvious and linear path. After the ring shouters whom Payne encountered had ceased their "dancing and clapping of hands," they "remained singing and rocking their bodies to and fro" for "about fifteen minutes." This was a clear sign that something like the "bush arbor" psyche had all but enveloped these shouters. But since they had just come out of church, there is as well a sign that the shouters were resorting to the ring shout in its classic context: away, secreted from daily life, even from aspects of that life that were religious. The urban "bush harbor" of the 1920s seemed to have lost none of those characteristics. Furthermore, in the back "winerooms" and in the "hole-in-the-wall" tawdry joints in which lowdown blues flourished over and against the upscale "jass" clubs, there existed that deep, introspective ambience that had been the hallmark of the secret meeting. The caller, now most often a downhome piano player like Dorsey, set the mood as much with his "ivories" as with his no longer dampened voice. The same caller, later a Ma Rainey or Bessie Smith, could transform large theaters into "hush arbors" by singing to the weariness of the migrant masses. These callers later revolutionized the recording industry by displacing the vaudeville singers and packaging the "bush harbor's" medicinal shout in two and a half minute, seventy-five-cent doses.

The "bush arbor's" most distinct survival in the urban setting, however, appears in the church. In one of two guises it became the worship hour itself. This is seen most clearly in the "cult," or Holiness, groups described by Miles M. Fisher and the "possession" ceremonies described by Zora Hurston. Here the "bush arbor" was institutionalized and openly celebrated until it became a form of black Protestantism. As an urban form of Protestantism, it was as syncretic as the slave "invisible institution" had been: a blend of African, Afro-American, and evangelical Christian rites and theology. In the second guise, it struck a more traditional profile. This "bush harbor" existed on the periphery of old-line churches, first as the house meetings held by migrant groups and, later on, as the split-offs from old-line churches that became over time newer old-line congregations such as Olivet Baptist. The urban "hush arbor" continued to thrive in old-line churches—whether newly spawned or original—in the para-liturgical settings such as the mid-week testimony meetings and the Friday night services in which the early prototypes of the gospel choruses first flourished. Eventually, this special communal gathering actually crept into the high worship hour itself in Baptist old-line churches, particularly with the deacons' prayer and song service that was held just prior to the high worship hour. But such a literal echo of the "bush arbor" prayer and shout threatened the new old-line aesthetic so much that a church like Pilgrim Baptist had to move it out of the main sanctuary into the basement—perhaps unaware that the cellar was a more authentic setting than the upstairs formal meeting hall by any stretch of one's imagination.

Given the dressing up of the slave caller and her text to become the refined spiritual and given the metamorphosis of the secret meeting along with its caller into a virtual symbiotic relationship with old-line organizations and liturgies, the notion of an antagonistic complementarity between these enslavement coping tactics seems conceivable. Indeed, it is one to the extent that it reflected the fundamental duality of the old-line religious ethos. In essence, this was a protestantism built on the notion of the appropriateness of cultural survivals of African American enslavement in the progressive religious institutions of northern urban African Americans of the early twentieth century. As long as the premise of black socially progressive Protestantism held to the mainline white Protestant worship aesthetic as its liturgical norm, its enslavement roots would seem anomalous. From the earliest days of Emancipation, progress meant leaving slavery in the past. Protestantism, indeed, had its greatest growth among formerly enslaved African Americans who adopted it as the post-enslavement Christianity benefiting their status as freedpeople deserving of a place in mainline society. Even when Protestantism came at the hands of black Americans such as Payne, the linkage between one's right to freedom and one's deserving of that right by assimilating dominant social and religious ways was never challenged. The subtle but pervasive presence of this motivation cannot be overstated. Beginning with such disparate developments as the reluctance of former slaves to sing the spirituals of enslavement, passing on through the changes in African American family structures, continuing on with the waves of the southern and then northern urban in-migration during the early years of the twentieth century, and taking due note of the creation of the "new Negro" in the early 1920s, one can see how African American social progressiveness seemed always to chart a course that presupposed the necessity to distance oneself from the cultural survivals of African American enslavement. Old-line religion, therefore, was simply another vehicle for a deep-seated African American cultural ambiguity with a long history that was inextricably bound up with mainline white Protestantism.

The persistence in some cases within the hallowed halls of old-line Protestantism of the "brush harbor" spirit—that demonstrative need to separate the therapeutic exercise of seeking individual solace from the communal behavioral patterns of enslavement—posed the antagonism of what, in fact, were complementary forces. During slavery the pull of doing "just as we pleased" seemed to cut across the varieties of slave experience and to draw many repeatedly—and at risk—to the forested sanctuary. Now in the late 1930s, the same desire persisted, motivated perhaps by a comparable sense among both old and new urban settlers of having less and less control over their circumstances. The storefront churches and other similar sites were insignificant as far as causing the antagonism. If there was any enmity, it evolved out of the competition old-line churches felt from these smaller churches' pull on the purses and hearts of old-line members. The real source of irritation lay in the indomitability of the "bush harbor" spirit within the walls of old-line churches. It was volatile and unpredictable. It seemed to seep into remote corners where it would ignite under the most forbidding of circumstances. Most often it manifested itself in individual demonstrative eruptions such as the characteristic verbal "bear him up" responses like "amen," "yes, Lord," and "preach it." But as often it would explode in spontaneous group brush fires, as one might view it. These were the demonstrations most feared by old-line ministers. Some like Pilgrim's Austin cautioned their congregations in advance against such behavior or made sure that the conditions could not exist by, for example, severely curtailing congregational hymn singing, or, in a pre-emptive move, sending praying and singing deacons into the basement.

If any event explains the nature of the antagonism, it is the appearance of the first gospel blues soloists and choruses in old-line churches. They burst on the scene in an old-line Baptist church in which the pastor intentionally wanted to rekindle the "bush arbor" ambience. The intentionality is noteworthy here because Smith wanted to utilize this slave practice as an antidote for a lack of morale at Ebenezer. Nothing from the old-line Protestant aesthetic had worked. He first employed a team of vintage callers, Frye and Dorsey. Noting their success he specifically forged ahead to give them an authentic call-and-response context by asking them to form a group to sing the music of enslavement. Frye's strutting, Dorsey's keyboard theatrics, and the chorus's clapping and shouting constituted enough "just as we pleased" ethos to induce the warmth and conviviality Smith needed.

Thus, from its very introduction into old-line worship, gospel blues functioned as a powerful witness to the usefulness of one of the principal coping strategies of enslavement. As such, it became a powerful means of beckoning old-line Protestantism to adopt a less antagonistic encounter with its enslavement roots. The antagonism, then, that still pierced the clamor accompanying the premier of *Take My Hand, Precious Lord* was no longer a challenge to the appropriateness of the "hush harbor" spirit. The ease with which Frye and Dorsey gained admission to church after church to sing this and other gospels and the wide enough acceptance of the gospel chorus for a group of them to have met for a musicale attest to this. What remained to contend with—what, in essence, was not providing for sales of the song commensurate with the "wild" response to its performance—was a sense of frustration over the placement and, therefore, containment of the powerful "bush arbor" spirit. In short, a new old-line religious ethos with its accompanying aesthetic was aborning. The problem was neither with the elements of the new thinking nor its inevitability. The problem involved, instead, the fit of the old and new. To some, the new order was itself a threat, while to others it was a tolerable—perhaps even benign—inconvenience. For this reason, gospels all along had received such disparate responses. Evans, for example, was asked to leave the church when a member cried out in response to his singing, and Dorsey "was thrown out of some of the best churches." Yet these instances were matched by Ebenezer's, Metropolitan's, and Pilgrim's peripheral accommodation of bush-meeting ardor in the choruses, Evans's successful forays into new territory in St. Louis, and Dorsey's and Frye's acceptance in some of the other "best churches."

At last, in the institutionalization of the urbanized "bush arbor" within old-line religion, the emotional survival of one Thomas Andrew Dorsey, gospel blues composer and artist, and the organizational survival of urban mainline black churches became one quest briefly beginning in the fall of 1932 and lasting through the late spring of 1933. In essence, Dorsey's decision to vent his aggressive response to his wife's and child's deaths and to seek solace for the pain of these tragedies in gospel blues virtually necessitated his reconfiguration of gospel blues in such a way as to make a place for the bush-meeting aesthetic in old-line worship. Dorsey accomplished this by appropriating the format of the basic bush gathering—the caller and the community of respondents—for his gospel blues. Beyond its implications for old-line religious aesthetics, Dorsey's new design for gospel blues would constitute his most distinct and lasting contribution to gospel music as it is known up to the present.

Given the traditional role of the preacher and the emergence of the new singer of the "Negro spiritual," the classic slave caller had a high profile across the liturgical expanse of old-line religion. These roles, moreover, were so integral to the "mixed" aesthetic of old-line religion that they were firmly entrenched. The preacher could regularly parse out folk elements in his preaching—perhaps even a "scream" now and then—with the assurance that his congregation knew not to take them as a cue to revert to the characteristic folk response. The revised voice of the spiritual soloist could word all of the familiar texts of enslavement songs but only to music from another culture and, like the preacher, only with the tacit agreement that traditional responses were inappropriate. Dorsey's major effort to cast the caller in her truly classical mode and yet maintain the "mixed" character of the old-line aesthetic mainly involved continuing to compose in the new voice that he found with *Take My Hand, Precious Lord*.

Throughout the remainder of 1932 and 1933, Dorsey dispersed the caller's voice in various ways among the five songs that he composed and registered. In two of them, *You Can't Go Through This World by Yourself* and *I Got Heaven in My View*, he further exploits his reversal of the refrain and verse parts of his gospel compositions, announcing the title line of each song in the first phrase of the chorus. But as the two titles indicate, the caller is used differently. In the first, she is the preacher voice that Dorsey developed in his songs with a strong evangelical thrust. Nothing better indicates this than the single, mere passing mention of the first person singular; otherwise, all the text is directed at a "you":

> You may have some kindred a thousand miles away,
> You may have some good friends and see them ev'ry day,
> I'm recommending Jesus, He'll guide you all the way,
> O you can't go thro' this world by your-self.

This neglect of any reference to a personal experience represents Dorsey in his most stridently evangelistic mode. But it is a strongly declarative evangelist who is singing—one who can put the blues assertiveness to as much use as the individual who wants to moan out her feelings to her listeners.

In the other song, the caller begins in the voice of the other-worldly centered proclaimer of Dorsey's earlier songs:

> I got heaven in my view
> And my journey I pursue
> I'm on my way to the city
> I got heaven in my view.

This is vintage, post-recommitment Dorsey, but only for refrain purposes: in the verses he casts the caller in the traditional blues-voiced "I" that he recently found in *Take My Hand, Precious Lord*:

> I went up on the mountain
> And I fell down on my knees
> I cried to my savior
> To save me if you please.

This abject subjectivity, the beseeching quality of the text, comes through by virtue of the natural declarative stance of the blues singer. Dorsey makes it prevail even more, however, by juxtaposing it next to the most insipid of his evangelical voices. The correlation of these voices with the refrain-verse structure of the song gives musical emphasis to what would otherwise have been simply textual shifts.

Dorsey thus continued the use of his evangelical voices in his post-1932 gospels, but he did so by allowing the blues declarative caller to assume those voices much as the blues note itself appeared so whimsically in his gospel improvisations. At times he would cast an entire song in the blues voice or *Take My Hand* mode. As the title suggests, his 1937 *I'm Just a Sinner Saved by Grace* takes this stance, but with a significant departure from his usual form: he dispenses with the refrain by interspersing it throughout the verse strophes:

(3rd verse)
Give me a heart of love, teach me to pray
I'm just a sinner saved by grace[,]
I'll serve Thee more and more, work day by day
I'm just a sinner saved by grace,
Take Thy spirit not from me, keep me free from pain,
If I stumble, if I fall, let me rise again
Now when my end is near, show me thy face
I'm just a sinner saved by grace.

Clearly, Dorsey does not feel himself wedded to any single form to utilize his blues voice to its fullest. The combination of contrition and pleading gives this song its gospel blues stance despite its lack of the customary structural chorus.

In other songs, he would couch the blues voice in a strongly affirmative evangelical statement. His 1943 *God Is Good to Me* begins with the refrain describing an assurance of God's goodness:

God is good to me, God is good to me,
God is good to me, He is the same to you.
God is good to me, His blessings I can see,
And on Him I depend, And trust Him as a friend,
When trouble starts to brew[,] He sees me safely through
God is good to me, He's the same to you.

The self-centered text is moderated by placing God as the source of the self's well-being. This self becomes much more focused in the second verse, however, by turning to the troubles that led her to God. Here she speaks of turmoil in the pleading that marks the blues voice:

(2nd verse)
When I'd given all my strength, and had no more to give,
The doctor said I'd surely die, the Master let me live;
Not for good that I had done, but mercy heard my plea,
And lifted me from my despair and now He's part of me.

This mixing of voice modes allowed Dorsey's new caller to fit most conveniently into the bush arbor that he would help build in old-line churches. For the caller to sing consistently of her personal plight would risk isolating the bush arbor as it had been during enslavement and in its early northern urban existence. Such communal commiseration—with its corresponding group groanings and other verbal gestures—at the behest of a moaning caller would threaten the decorum of typical old-line worship. Yet given the "wild" responses to the first performances of *Take My Hand*, some recognition of an individual's predicament was precisely what large segments of old-line congregations were desiring. This was precisely the shift in the "Negro's God" that Mays found in his study. The otherworldly expression was strong, but it was accompanied by as prominent an air of troubled presentism. Dorsey's decision to maintain the strong preaching voice of his evangelical texts directed the listener to redemption and an afterlife as a placebo for the tribulation and sinfulness of this one. But he always gave the caller some means to address her circumstances in his solo gospel texts. At times he let his caller do only a small amount of cajoling or wrangling with God about life as it pressed on her now; this was the blues voice that darted about in his new textual twists and turns. At other times he let her outright plead and wail by writing the text in a full blues voice.

These varied combinations and even the melding of evangelical and subjective voices—in this case literally those of the preacher and the bluesman—accounted for a great amount of the "wild" response that Dorsey describes his songs receiving. Members of the congregation, especially those who were experiencing pain and sorrow, found themselves in Dorsey's predicament in which he bemoaned his sorrow while also seeking reassurance that he was not in disfavor with his God. The use to which one of Dorsey's charter chorus members at Pilgrim put *Take My Hand, Precious Lord* illustrates this point. Lillian Reescer's five-year-old daughter received third-degree burns in an accident involving a cooking stove. During her recovery, the child and her mother would stay up on Sunday nights to hear a weekly performance of *Take My Hand* on the radio:

> Yeah, I'll never forget that—never forget that song. I'd stay up and she would stay up. The song wouldn't come on until eleven o'clock and we got so much out of it. Five months we sat there at night, on Sunday night, and listened at that song. It did me so much good. Look like it did her a lot of good too.

The therapeutic potential of the blues voicing in Dorsey's *Take My Hand* is no less recognized even by theologians and psychologists today. A Los Angeles therapist, for example, has used the song to help a male patient overcome disorders relating to stress and identity:

> . . . the song "Precious Lord, Take My Hand" affirmed Harvey's present dependency, but it moved on to say "let me *stand*," which spoke right to his area of need.[10]

Whatever can be said about the compositional merits of Dorsey's gospel blues and the attraction of congregations to them pales considerably in the face of his most visible contribution to the placement of the bush harbor in old-line religion, the cultivation of the caller herself. If the caller as Dorsey developed her can be considered the twentieth-century urban descendent of the bush harbor leader, then the connection between secular blues as Dorsey practiced it and the old-line gospel blues tradition as he nurtured it is embodied in her. Dorsey is clear about the origins of this effort:

> See, I got it out of show business. I got a lot of my gospel training out of show business . . . used it over here for the gospel. Made it help gospel where the gospel didn't have much to help itself.[11]

Thinking of himself as the promoter of the show-business blues performance style guided most of Dorsey's dealings with his singers. This is the reason he had to let go of his first "sweet" singer, Louise Keller, and hire Rebecca Talbot, a "stout, . . . madam-looking," genuinely blues vocalist. Indeed, Dorsey seemed constantly in search of the right caller, settling most recently on male preachers, such as Allen and Frye, who, despite their pulpit careers, were effective at engendering the communal spirit that one expected from a blues performance.

One suspects that, with *Take My Hand, Precious Lord*-style gospels now flowing from his pen, Dorsey would need more of a Ma Rainey type gospel singer than either of his males could provide. The best evidence for this is the blues voice itself; its role is to declare feelings themselves to those who listen to it. If it does this well, its listeners emote with those feelings and usually respond in kind. The blues voice is thus a more direct descendent of the bush harbor caller than the preacher voice. There are enough accounts of the secret meeting to show that the preacher figure, even if involved, was not singly responsible for the ambience characterized as doing "just as we pleased." Moreover, the singing, praying, and general noisiness of these meetings (even though they could be life-threatening) indicate they were not solely occasions for the quiet contemplation of the gospel. While a Frye could "strut" or "walk" as he sang/preached a Dorsey gospel, he, like the slave preacher, was not seen as the person whose religious display was in and of itself to be mirrored in his audience. Indeed, in his priestly role, the preacher was expected to engender a sense of his own uniqueness; in doing so, he built a wall of deference between him and his hearers—just the opposite of the caller whose role it was to bridge together her feelings with those of her responders. As long as Dorsey wrote gospels in his strongly homiletical voice, a Reverend Allen or Frye, with Dorsey at the keyboard bearing him up, constituted an authentic and persuasive evangelical duo. But the new old-line caller needed to be developed more as the classic blues caller, the communal moaner.

With these criteria in mind and "show business" blues his goal, Dorsey went seeking after a culturally ancestoral figure, the likes of which were extant, but fragmented and, most often, miscontextualized. He needed someone with the blues background of Talbot and the religious orientation of Allen and Frye. His first success in finding a workable combination of blues techniques and religion in a singer occurred when he perchance walked into a "music class" in which Sallie Martin was performing a dramatic reading. Her performance was so effective that Dorsey "never would have associated her with gospel singing." Martin's speaking ability had a certain quality to it, however, that struck Dorsey as appropriate for the new gospel blues he was composing. Perhaps this was rooted in her desire "for the ministry." At any rate, she "had not given much time and study to singing" up to that time, and she apparently was not enthusiastic about doing so. Indeed, she had gone to the music class because she had heard that she could buy Dorsey's *How About You* there. She found that the music "wasn't so much different [than] we were accustomed to." But the words "were so different": "The words was the biggest thing. I said, 'I want to find that. Where can I get it?'"[12]

Martin's focus on Dorsey's text joined her to his mission to fashion the caller into someone who could turn the emotion-laden words of his gospels into a highly charged sermonic presentation. Indeed, in 1929, when Martin recalls first buying Dorsey's song, Dorsey had just begun crafting his homiletical voice. Her aspiration for the ministry over her desire to sing would seem to sensitize her to Dorsey, the evangelical songwriter. Her apparent disregard for the music can be explained by the fact that the woman who told her where to buy Dorsey's music had sung *How About You* at her church. Given how much improvisational and stylistic latitude the gospel blues singer has and given the presence of a distinct style of music in the Holiness church to which Martin and the woman belonged, the song would most likely have been sung in a manner that "wasn't so much different" than much of the music Martin was accustomed to hearing. Dorsey and Martin, therefore, had become one in purpose before they became one in fact by virtue of their being two preachers in search of musical sermons and pulpits.

This unusual unity both bound them together as performers and ultimately rendered their partnership unfulfilling to each other. To Dorsey, Martin was "a diamond in the rough." Thus their initial collaboration consisted of his encouraging her "to sing and study more." Martin willingly complied by joining the first radio singing group of four women that he had formed, "The University Radio Singers." In 1932, some four years after their first meeting, she joined his gospel chorus at Pilgrim—not, however, as a soloist. In fact, Martin never seemed to develop the singing aspect of her sermonic performance to the extent that she exemplified all that Dorsey envisioned in a caller. This did not harm her career, however. Indeed, she became known for a unique, speaking style of gospel singing:

> Right . . . in Pilgrim, when I started with Mr. Dorsey, they said, "Oh, she can't sing; she just talks and pat her foot." I said, "So, I'm still patting it and I'm still talking."

Possessed with a deep voice and a gripping presence, Martin had little trouble holding her audiences when performing her special speech song:

"Sallie can't sing a lick, but she can get over anywhere in the world." Dorsey worked with her to develop this style. From the beginning of their work with one another, he recognized that he would have to take special measures to enhance what could be considered a fault. During their first conversation, which took place after he heard Martin's dramatic reading, Dorsey as much as admitted that her husky voice—"one of them low contralto [singers]"—would have to be dealt with: ". . . everything will have to be transposed for you."[13]

Thus it is clear that the nature of Martin's style as it concerns the caller whom Dorsey sought after 1932 ran counter to his expectations. But it is just as clear that he found Martin's singing useful in the propagation of his new blues voice, for it was after 1932 that they began touring as a team. So pivotal was Martin's solo work with Dorsey after the tragedy of 1932, in fact, that he credits her as "being responsible for much of the success of gospel songs and gospel singing":

> We met singers and contacted ministers to offer our programs all over the country. We were favorites in New York, Washington, Baltimore, Pittsburgh, Philadelphia . . . and many other cities where folk were hungry for gospel singing. So were the travels of our efforts to establish gospel songs and gospel singing in [the] beginning.[14]

The success that Dorsey refers to was not so much musical as it was organizational. Martin became an agent like Evans and traveled widely, establishing choruses in churches. It was she who first pointed out to Dorsey that he was squandering the business opportunity that his songs had made for him by selling them only to persons who happened to stop to buy them in his uncle's drugstore. No sooner than the two of them had begun work together in 1929, Martin, in her characteristic brusque manner, took one look at the brown bag of dimes that had accumulated in the cash drawer and said: "You know, you have something here but you don't know what to do with it." In short, her solo work was more effective in terms of building the choral network that Dorsey needed than nurturing the bush harbor spirit in old-line churches. They worked together until 1939, when Martin, seeing the gospel music business beginning to grow beyond the market that Dorsey had built, founded her own music publishing company with Kenneth Morris, another writer and arranger:

> It was a great loss to me for her to go, but in this period I had come from a one-room studio, where I had my desk, my bed, and my shipping table, to a five-room studio with a private office, reception room, shipping department, and five people on my payroll.[15]

During most of the nine years in which Dorsey worked with Martin, he would actively seek out and train other soloists. Not until he heard the voice of seventeen-year-old Mahalia Jackson sometime in 1928, however, did it occur to him that he could find the blend of blues presence and spirituality that would convey the sentiment of his new, more emotive gospels. In his collaboration with Jackson, Dorsey distilled the essence of both singer types and then crafted it into the old-line caller who became the classic gospel blues soloist.

Jackson had two distinct ways of working a crowd that attracted Dorsey to her. The first involved her personable manner:

> I met Mahalia way back when I was a jazz musician. She was a good mix- er . . . and she loved everybody, at least she acted like she loved everybody. She called everybody "baby, honey, darling." . . . She made a wonderful [impression].

The second involved her powerful performance techniques:

> Mahalia, I think, was the only woman in [a] group at that time. [They] were really rocking them everywhere they went. Mahalia was with this group and was going and killing them off, I mean she was laying them out.

Jackson describes this group as "the first organized gospel group to circulate the city." It was the Johnson Singers, composed of Jackson and three brothers whom she met at her aunt's church shortly after moving to Chicago from New Orleans in 1927. The group first began by performing religious plays that the brothers wrote and in which Jackson acted female roles. Both Dorsey and Jackson describe the group in terms that suggest it was known for performing indigenous black religious song in a downhome manner. In the urban North, where such singing was repressed in old-line churches, Jackson and the Johnson Singers elicited the same response from new settlers as did Dorsey with his singers. One pastor was so offended by the group's singing that he threw them out of his church, saying "Get that twisting and jazz out of the church." On her way out of the door, Jackson replied, "This is the way we *sing* down South!"[16]

Jackson's appeal, therefore, rested on her adherence to the deeply emotive manner of singing that one finds referred to among enslaved African Americans as being heard in their secret meetings. She was now becoming widely known for it even among old-line ministers. At Pilgrim, for example, she was used for revival services and for the home and hospital visitation ministries. Jackson's singing was especially welcomed among the recent settlers. She and the Johnson Singers regularly performed at storefronts, the most common sites for the new settlers' urban bush harbor meetings. There, where she was literally among her own, she helped them retain the old spirituality: "Halie was a fresh wind from the down-home religion."[17]

In Jackson, Dorsey thus found two of the caller's major attributes: her sense of oneness with her respondents and her ability to capture the communal spirit of a performance so as to play it out virtually at will. Jackson's possession of these traits clearly emerged from her grounding in the urban brush arbor experience. In the sense that she could lead out in the bush harbor, she could be said to embody the priestly function of bush arbor leadership. Dorsey, on the other hand, wanted a singer more like the hush arbor caller, who could evoke shared emotion while she maintained an aura as leader. Thus he found Jackson wanting even as she "was laying them out." He thought of Jackson as "one of them coon-shoutin' singers"; she was "hollering" and could get her audiences to "patting their hands." Yet even though she seemed able to excite her audiences, she was not able to do so in a manner that could "prick" them as Dorsey knew blues singers could. While acknowledging that Jackson was "fiery and *exciting*," one listener recalls that there was concern for the intense energy that marked her style: "She sang so hard, and she so small, people used to say, 'That woman sing too *hard*, she going to have TB!'" Contributing to this shortcoming was her dependence on music, at least when she performed with the Johnson Singers. Jackson sang out of *Gospel Pearls* and other "books." Doing so, it seemed to Dorsey, imposed some kind of constraint on Jackson's performances: "Mahalia's almost in a class to herself. She could do it, but used to sing the gospel songs on the books."[18]

From the beginning of his professional encounter with Jackson, therefore, Dorsey seized the opportunity to build on her talent and natural appeal in order to transform her into a caller:

> She had it [talent] naturally. But you have a lot of things naturally, but you don't know how to use it, to exhibit it. [I wanted her] to get them trills and the turns and the moans and expression.

According to Dorsey, Jackson first approached him with a request for him to become her coach: "Dorsey, I want some of these gospel songs. I want to learn some of these gospel songs of yours." His training began with "studying her voice and style." As she requested, he taught her his songs: "I worked hard training her and teaching her new songs. I took two months out to train her." In addition to building her repertoire, Dorsey spent time revamping her performance technique. Her timing concerned him most. She had a tendency to "start off shoutin'" and to sing her songs in an upbeat or faster tempo than Dorsey wanted:

> I wanted to train her how to do my numbers and do them with the beat— shake at the right time; shout at the right time. [You] don't get up to start off shoutin'. You lose yourself.

His suggested cure was to get her "to breathe correctly, and to use her voice with ease . . . and to smooth the roughness out of her singing . . . ."[19]

The most significant aspect of this training is not whether or not it occurred as Dorsey claims (Jackson tells no such story), but that it reveals his ideal gospel singer and ideal performance techniques. His work with Jackson was reminiscent of his coaching of blues singers who came to Paramount's studios during the years when Dorsey was employed there as an accompanist. As a consequence, Dorsey could easily make the connection between blues show business and his new gospel blues caller. But technique was only the beginning: Dorsey also counted on an evangelical spirituality that was rooted in downhome religious culture. Jackson's tendency to shout too early, to breath in the middle of phrases, and to begin her songs too quickly and at a highly excitable emotional point represented gospel singing as she knew it. In many ways, at the stage Dorsey began working with Jackson, she was the analogue of Dorsey in his gospel music career prior to *Take My Hand, Precious Lord,* especially to the extent that he had then developed a pronounced homiletical voice with texts and performance practices that were basically antithetical to the gospel blues that he now composed and coached. Jackson clapped her hands and patted her feet in response to the inspiration of the gospel message. These actions had been a part of her Christian experience since her childhood in New Orleans. Indeed, she was so accustomed to this sort of bush arbor behavior that when she walked into her first church service in Chicago in 1927, Jackson stood up and gave her testimony in an old spiritual, *Hand Me Down,* the way she would have done in "any church back home." The problem, as she would come to know it in Chicago, was that such a spontaneous outpouring was forbidden where Jackson chose to release it that Sunday: the 11 a.m. worship hour at Greater Salem Baptist, one of Chicago's five major old-line churches. Dorsey's plan was neither to dislodge her from her commitment to the gospel nor to muffle her sincere—and now quaint seeming—expression of it. Instead, he wanted to build on these by joining her religious enthusiasm to her emotional being. Thus the last phase of his training concerned her concert programming: "I taught her a number of slow, gentle, sentimental songs, so that her full program would not be all of the fast shouting types of songs." Dorsey clearly had his newly voiced songs in mind: one of the first he taught Jackson and one she became widely known for was *Take My Hand, Precious Lord.*[20]

Dorsey's ideal caller thus became a moaning preacher who would seek more to evoke deep emotion from within the listener than simply to exhibit it before her. The common denominator between the new old-line caller and both the old-line preacher and his predecessor, the folk preacher, would be only the act of verbalizing the gospel either through speech or music or some combination of the two. While Dorsey could put either performance persona to effective use—witness his successful collaboration with Allen, Frye, and Martin—he would from now on prefer the former, now that his new gospels had the great possibility of voice in Jackson. His caller might be regarded as a priest, but only in the context of the new bush harbor, where the caller functioned in tandem and on par with her respondents. His pedagogical sculpting of Jackson into his hybrid of the two consisted of smoothing out the verbal assertiveness of the preacher while chiseling into sharper relief the affective presence of the bush caller. The more Dorsey could get Jackson to begin her performances at a lower level of excitement, the more he could assure that she would commence her empathizing from a common emotional baseline with her respondents. The less she shouted and clapped her hands before her listeners wanted her to, the less she would risk sealing off her spirituality from the community's. The more he challenged her to include his "slow, gentle, sentimental" songs in her concerts, the more he could guarantee that she would be transformed into the lowdown, pricking hush harbor icon who would entreat old-liners who especially desired to do "just as we pleased."

Whether all that Mahalia Jackson became can be laid exclusively to Dorsey's craftsmanship or not remains between them. But her rise to virtual mystical status as a gospel singer—caller to many—undoubtedly rests between them in his texts as they have been brought to life by her voice. She became a major presence in Chicago throughout the 1930s. Often along with the Johnson Singers and Dorsey, she raised the new northern urban gospel singer to unprecedented status—so much so that she was used by politicians for their election campaigns and was even regularly hired to sing at funerals, an almost unheard-of professionalization of one's sacred calling. As late as 1963, when he would publish his classic study, *The Negro Church*, the noted black sociologist E. Franklin Frazier would devote considerable space to a discussion of the symbolic role of "the Gospel Singer." When he listed the ones most representative of his analysis, Jackson's name appeared first.[21]

Aside from carving a place for the caller and shaping her performance profile, Dorsey can claim another distinctive contribution to the development of the caller in the old-line bush harbor: beginning in 1932, one could assume the caller to be female. Even though he had worked as early as 1928 with women soloists such as Louise Keller, Rebecca Talbot, and Sallie Martin, Dorsey himself had credited his male singers, Luscha Allen and Theodore Frye, with providing him his greatest boosts in crucial times. To an extent he could be expected to think this, given that women's leadership in old-line churches had been almost non-existent. "Here and there" a woman could be found on the local church board among the Baptists. Within the Methodist denomination, a woman could rise to an "evangelist" position. But by the 1930s, observers could clearly see a trend in which the primacy of the role of old-line Protestantism in African American society was being challenged by "cults" and groups of supposed lower status because of the greater opportunity the latter offered women. The range of women's involvement in these alternative religious organizations encompassed many roles. In Holiness or "sanctified" churches, for example, Drake and Cayton found that "ambitious women [could] rise to the top." Sallie Martin was engrossed in this pursuit when Dorsey first heard her. The legendary Elder Lucy Smith founded and presided over one of Chicago's largest black Holiness congregations, the All Nations Pentecostal Church. Her rise to national prominence occurred during the 1930s and was symbolized by the growth of several branches of her church in the South and West. Mother Rosa Horne's Mount Calvary Assembly Hall of the Pentecostal Faith of All Nations in New York City's Harlem rose during this period as well. And the role of women in Father Divine's Peace Mission Movement was undisputably one of the most public during the 1930s with stories such as the conversion of former prostitute Viola Wilson into Faithful Mary, his "most honored disciple during the mid-thirties," being widely told.[22]

Even with systemic marginalization of women in old-line churches, however, Dorsey's appearance with female vocalists to introduce his new songs would hardly have raised many eyebrows. The role of woman as an aid to worship ritual has precedent as far back as the early Christian churches and the creation of the role of deaconess. In old-line churches, especially with music, women enjoyed unchallenged authority and were considered the co-equals of male musicians. But in the context of the classic bush arbor that Dorsey sought to establish in old-line churches, the female singer could be perceived as challenging the preacher. The possibility of being understood as such was even greater since more often than not Dorsey and his vocalist appeared as a duo. Thus when she began to moan out her gospel or preach it, if she was a Sallie Martin, the female caller addressed the congregation as directly as did the regular, male preacher of the church. If she sang as Dorsey expected her to, moreover, she would elicit responses from that congregation as least as fervent as the preacher would. She possibly could conjure up even deeper sentiment if she succeeded in transforming the worship experience into the bush harbor. It was this threat that led an old-line minister to rebuke Dorsey for attempting to usurp his, or any preacher's, role:

> The church[es], some of them were favorable toward [gospel] and some didn't like it. I had one preacher, he [got] up after [we] had sung the song, and the folk had felt good and shouted. This guy got up and said, "You can't sing no gospel; you can only preach the gospel."

In fact, soon after Sallie Martin had begun singing and organizing in Cincinnati, ministers attempted to call her in: "'Let's see what is this, what all this singing [is] about.'" With a zeal all too customary for Martin, she ignored them, saying that "she was doing Kingdom work and got her authority from God."[23]

The female caller's competition with the preacher would have continued to run athwart the male order of old-line religion had not Dorsey's purpose from the start been to re-establish the arena in which her leadership was structurally appropriate and in which the preacher accepted that his role as priest was limited. Thus to a great extent Dorsey was destined to go back to the idea of choral gospel blues and the viability of the chorus, if for no other reason than to institutionalize the bush harbor in such a way that old-line ministers would not be threatened by the gender of his gospel blues singers.

It is in the context of the fundamental change called for by the appearance of a figure who was at once as focal as the preacher but who was at the same time virtually his antithesis, in both role and gender, that Dorsey's work to institutionalize the gospel chorus must be seen as his second most distinctive contribution to the rise of gospel blues. Already gathering momentum by late 1932, the chorus movement was destined to collide with the preacher and to suffer consequences as dire as its demise if its proponents failed to channel the movement into a well-demarcated and unquestionably ancillary realm.

Dorsey had little sense of this set of conditions in the fall of 1932, however. Then, his chorus at Pilgrim sang for Nettie's "funeral, baby and all."[24] If the chorus had come to mean anything to him, therefore, it was as a source of communal support, the very function that its prototype had served during enslavement. Had Dorsey continued to see it in this light, he would have confined his gospel blues efforts to cultivating the soloist. But even in this respect Dorsey had to acknowledge the ever-increasing plausibility of institutionalized choral gospel blues: his soloists—especially Evans and Martin—lived off their earnings from organizing choruses and then selling Dorsey's songs to them. Moreover, his soloists—with the exception of one with the rare voice and presence of Jackson—could realistically expect to find regular performance opportunities as callers only within the urban bush harbor context, the chorus. They never gained (nor seemed to want to gain) notoriety as singers—particularly from a blues perspective—who performed before an audience that wanted to hear them sing for their singing talent alone. Still, Dorsey was on record as not having any interest in the choral gospel movement other than his directorship at Pilgrim: he had done nothing with the presidency of the convention that Frye and Butts had bestowed on him. But Dorsey now had reasons ranging from emotional comfort to economic potential to cause him to rethink his commitment to choral gospel blues after Nettie's and Thomas, Jr.'s, deaths.

As is so often the case throughout Dorsey's life when he made a major move, the rewards of which he could scarcely have known at the time, Dorsey was unaware of developments concerning the chorus movement when he made his decision to "work more" and to get "into that chorus" in the fall of 1932. Several months later, the inexorable spread of the chorus quickened to the point that one observer characterized the movement as spreading "like wild-fire[,] invading every type and kind of church." Evidently the sheer contagion of the earlier groups prompted old-line churches and even Holiness churches to move aside any barriers. Choruses were "invading . . . every Baptist, Sanctified and Church of God in Christ" throughout the "entire Negro districts of Chicago." Perhaps the most surprising aspect of the emergence of the chorus is the apparent shift of the ministers away from dependence on their choirs:

> In many churches the gospel choirs have supplanted the regular choirs. In these churches few of the pastors give preliminary lectures to get their hearers in a receptive mood for their sermons, for the gospel songs have done it for them.

Although the movement seemed to have widespread acceptance, one could still hear of a scattered word or two decrying the use of "jazz gospel hymns." Reluctantly, however, detractors of gospel blues, in either its solo or choral forms, were witnessing a fundamental shift in the aesthetics of old-line religion.[25]

While it is clear that Dorsey would have benefitted from this surge in the number of choruses by being able to sell more of his music, what role he actually played in this phase of the expansion of the gospel choral movement is less evident. This was the time when he and either Frye, Martin, or—ever more frequently—Jackson were traveling throughout the Midwest giving gospel blues concerts and organizing choruses in other cities. By the spring, however, Dorsey was aware that there was something phenomenal happening:

> By March 1933 many other churches in Chicago and throughout the country began organizing gospel choirs to serve simultaneously with the so-called Senior Choir. . . . Then gospel singing began to spread like wildfire to other churches and in twelve months almost every church throughout the country had a gospel choir or wanted one.[26]

Whether the records bear out the geographical sweep Dorsey claims is less relevant than his noting, as did the observer above, the zeal—even near-craze—that drove the movement.

Dorsey's involvement in the movement was no longer reluctant or administratively marginal by April 1933. Noting the existence of over "20 churches . . . with organizations dedicated to the singing of gospel only," the *Chicago Defender* credits Dorsey along with Butts and Frye for initiating the chorus movement:

> The gospel chorus movement had its beginning April 1, 1932, when Prof. Thomas A. Dorsey, eminent gospel song writer; Mme. Magnolia Lewis [Butts], directoress, Metropolitan Community Church Gospel chorus; Prof. Theodore Frye, director, Ebenezer Baptist chorus, launched a drive advocating a renaissance of gospel singing in the churches of Chicago.

The paper continues by pointing out that Dorsey's travels and those of "his executive committee" came in response to the demands of gospel singers in neighboring states. These efforts led first to the gathering of the Chicago choruses into a "union" of over 1500 members. This organization was the "convention" over which Dorsey had been voted president by Frye and Butts. Dorsey and *his* committee's travels prompted the organization of individual choruses in 24 states. Dorsey, Butts, and Frye called for these groups to come to Chicago to meet with the Chicago union "to map plans and programs for their expansion of the organization throughout the country."[27]

One can assume that Dorsey's organizational role was rooted in something greater than either his emotional attachment to the chorus or his economic interest in it as a market. Had he wanted to continue to rely on the bush harbor for his personal benefit, Dorsey would not have needed to travel widely to stitch together a protective net of interstate proportions. His Pilgrim arbor fulfilled his emotional needs in the aftermath of his recent tragedy without the assistance of either the Ebenezer or Metropolitan choruses, ones he was close to. Similarly, though greatly aided by the growing network of choruses, the sales of his songs could have continued to increase without Dorsey's assumption of greater choral organizational responsibilities. Thus one finds that by the spring of 1933, more than having grabbed for the leadership of the burgeoning gospel choral movement out of some personal need or gain, Dorsey had abruptly switched from its titular leader to its major organizing force, even though six or so months earlier he had refused the task, muttering, "I don't want all that work."

Dorsey indicates why he was motivated to involve himself in the movement more prominently with his description of one of the more troubling responses to the appearance of the chorus:

> This gospel choir movement was not accepted by all and was not taken well by many of the Senior Choirs and their directors. There was much jealousy, envy, rivalry, and displeasure among singers and directors.

The source of this animosity lay most obviously in the chorus's challenge to old-line order, especially the preacher's sense that he was the main attraction: "He's a gospel preacher and couldn't draw the crowd. We could draw with the gospel singing, a gospel program." But beneath this more visceral response was a deeper uneasiness with the new sense of bonding among the socially invisible in old-line congregations:

> . . . the people who make up the membership of the gospel choirs were people who had otherwise nothing active to do in the church. The senior choir would not take them in. And many of the other clubs or units of the church could not offer a place for their enthusiastic outlet.[28]

From his start with the Pilgrim chorus, Dorsey directed as much attention to the non-musical dimension of his singers as he did to their vocal development. Indeed, it was this sense of having a place to belong along with the making of pleasant music that accounted for the closely knit communality of the chorus. When Fannie P. Hunt stood up along with her three

THE RISE OF GOSPEL BLUES

friends to answer Austin's call for the chorus, she had resigned herself to sitting in the congregation: "I just figured I couldn't sing." She was not admitting that she "had no voice to sing": "I just didn't want to be in the choir." Dorsey, however, was so steadfast in his desire to see the chorus function more as a hush arbor than as a formal music group that he refused to audition prospective members:

> And there'd be [one] thing he would ask you if you wanted to sing. He'd ask you did you belong to the church? Was you religious? And if you had religion, that's all it was. Just come on in because he said he could train you.[29]

For Dorsey to have a chorus in which one entered "by the Spirit," yet which met his performance standards, he had to provide the training that he assured his members. This he accomplished by conducting rehearsals with classroom rigor:

> Well when it first started we just like [it] was school. You had to look and listen to see what was going on and how it was going on. One thing about it, you had to be really on your feet. You had to do the right thing. He was strict. He could really see and hear.

For those like Lillian Reescer, who had their afternoons free, Dorsey held special music classes "to have you read it" and to learn key signatures. Here the voices of his unauditioned—sometimes reticent—singers received careful and what seemed intimidating attention. Sometimes, recalls Reescer, "He'd try your voice. I'd be scared to death." Much of this effort was prompted by Dorsey's music showmanship and the need to develop the chorus's image in such a way as to counter the condescension many of the chorus members felt, especially from the supposedly more musically trained choir. Thus the spirituality had to be girded up by musicianship. At times Dorsey might have even seemed overly concerned that the "monkey" epithet that some wanted to attach to his chorus members would not stick. For example, no choir director would insist that all of the music for a monthly musicale be sung by memory. But Dorsey had his chorus sing without music for his hour-long musicales: "It looks so much better if we can memorize. . . ."[30]

For one who did not "want all that work," Dorsey had assumed an inordinate amount of responsibility, much of it apparently to keep this choral hush arbor available to those who wanted it and, in turn, to have it serve as the wellspring for indigenous African American spirituality in old-line churches. His pedagogical drive thus had one goal:

> In gospel singing we tried to awaken an immediate response in our listeners by allowing them to participate with us through the rhythm of our songs. Some of the more reserved members of the church have felt that jubilation was not proper within church walls. It has been up to the singers to show how praise to Him can be joyous as well as somber.

Years later, when the pressures of World War II were grating on old-line congregations, Dorsey's desire for communal participation was evidently well ensconced and living up to his expectations:

> . . . just during the war, people were looking for something that they weren't getting. They were looking for some more spirit, more spirit in the church and in the singing and everything else. And that's what they got out of the chorus.[31]

It is with this clarity of the chorus's purpose, honed out of his rededication to the movement in the aftermath of his tragedy and now driven by his desire to make it a respected, self-sustaining organization, that Dorsey—the "eminent gospel song writer"—strode into the forefront of the fledgling national gospel choral movement in the first months of 1933. By August of that year, he was no longer just one of the leaders of the movement; he was "the Race's greatest gospel song writer." Neither was his nor the other Chicago choruses only tenuously bound together in the Gospel Choral Union of Chicago: Dorsey was elected the founding "national president" of the National Convention of Gospel Choirs and Choruses. In his "splendid" inaugural address, Dorsey outlined his major objective for the Convention. Without equivocation, he virtually restated the goals that he had pursued at Pilgrim. He recommended that the Convention establish a headquarters that would institutionalize the functions of his chorus: "I recommend that the gospel singers of this national convention have a home or headquarters, with departments to study, rehearse and develop the highest type of gospel singing with the very best interpretation of the spirituals and heart songs." The headquarters was to balance its music mission with a steadfast commitment to the religious life of both its inhabitants and the singers throughout the Convention's ranks:

> [I recommend] that the headquarters be a place for gospel singers to stop over when traveling through the city and that the place be kept free from any activity or doings unbecoming for a Christian home; a place to reach the young singer and help the older one to reach the highest accomplishment along this line.[32]

This meeting of the national organization can be said to represent the end of Dorsey's quest for acceptance of gospel blues in both its solo and choral forms in old-line churches. The appearance of Ebenezer's and Pilgrim's choruses in the winter of 1932 indicated a popular need for a new spirituality that would be rooted in the culture and behavioral norms of historical African American Protestant Christianity. The performances of the solo gospel singer had by that time been received with stunning approval, precisely because old-line congregants had finally been re-awakened to her call. Thus Dorsey came out of the infancy (as it might be termed) of the choral gospel blues movement aware of it as a mechanism for implanting the new spirituality, but not aware that it could actually be a movement. Aside from his work with the Pilgrim chorus and his continuing concertizing with his soloists, Dorsey's activities do not reveal how he actually switched to this new awareness; there simply was no single trajectory from the Pilgrim chorus to the head of the Convention. This indecipherability results from the fact that Dorsey's purposes and the growing presence of choral gospel organizations had merged into one. Indeed, that August 1933 meeting serves as the melding point of the man and the movement. To extricate one from the other is to dismiss the obvious symbolic import of the events of the first annual Convention meeting.

If there was any reason for the *Defender* to introduce the meeting as "a new epoch in the musical world," it was because of the extraordinary uniting of the disparate parties on all sides of the gospel blues issue. The opening concert signaled a rapprochement between old-line choirs and choruses, their musics, and their directors. Dorsey led the combined choruses of Chicago, now 600 strong, "in true choral style," indicating that his choral gospel standards matched what was perceived as "true." No one had reason to call Dorsey's band of untutored singers "monkeys" any longer. But the actual selections reveal even more the blurring of distinctions between choruses and choirs. The Choral Union's program consisted of a mixture of traditional "Negro" spirituals such as *Nobody Knows the Trouble I['ve] See[n]* and well-known gospels such as *He's the Lily of the Valley*. This mixture represents Dorsey's and the other gospel directors' attempts to show that their choruses could sing Anglicized spirituals as well as choral gospel blues. Complementing the appearance of the spirituals on the program was the performance of them by at least one well-known solo choir singer, "Mrs. Willie Jones," who sang Boatner's *City Called Heaven*. In addition to being a member of Metropolitan's Senior Choir, Jones had recently performed at the annual citywide Chicagoland music festival with "telling success." The most symbolic of unifying events, however, came during the next night's concert when, following the singing of the St. Paul C. M. E. gospel chorus, J. Wesley Jones, black Chicago's premier old-line choir director, addressed the convention. Although he pointed out some "defects" in their singing, Jones welcomed the gospel singers into the old-line music fold with "the greatest encouragement" and "profuse . . . congratulations." This uniting extended even beyond the music realm. Old-line ministers—among them, Austin of Pilgrim, Evans of Metropolitan, Hindon of Morning Star Baptist, and McDowell of Mt. Vernon Baptist—spoke in a variety of capacities from welcoming remarks to major sermons. Even the political dimension was accounted for by the welcoming speech of William L. Dawson, one of Chicago's black city aldermen.[33]

The prominence of women throughout the meeting constitutes the most telling evidence that the choral gospel movement had secured its place in old-line churches to the extent that its most visible figure, the female gospel singer, could preside over it without fear of intimidation by the ministers. Beginning with the first group of national officers, the National Convention became for all intents a women's movement. Nine of the thirteen officers elected were women. This included three of the five vice presidents and all but one of the lower elected officials. Photographs of the Ebenezer, Pilgrim, and Chicago Union choruses show women in far greater numbers than men. These developments along with the growing personal popularity during this time of Martin and Jackson argue that, although greatly circumscribed by male dominance of the denominational and local organizations, women's leadership in Protestant African American churches had found an undisputed sphere of influence and locus of operation. As of this writing, the gospel singer and chorus are virtually synonymous with woman, while the administrative and pastoral ranks of most old-line denominations remain overly represented by men.[34]

In the afterglow of this August 1933 triumph, however, the ghost of Bishop Payne returned to remind old-line ministers, choirs, choristers, and their music directors that the bush-meeting aesthetic should not overshadow the urban assimilationist orientation of old-line worship. Within two weeks following the National Convention, Ebenezer's monthly senior choir musicale was addressed by "Professor" H. B. P. Johnson, music director of the smaller "unincorporated" National Baptist Convention. His purpose was to caution against "gospel singing ministers and a predominating jazz age environment" that worked together to change the "complexion" of church music. Negro church musicians, he claimed, had less respect for the slave songs than "the Caucasian race," which "in many cases" was "beating Negroes" at singing their own songs. He proceeded by demonstrating "the right and the wrong" ways to play the spirituals. In essence, he advocated that accompanists and singers avoid any "attempt to improve the author's work by playing additional notes [improvising] of their own choosing." To the interruption of applause "several times," Johnson acknowledged the popularity of gospel music and the dilemma that many churches faced by being forced to have it if they were to remain. He must have known, though, that those seeking the new spirituality would go to the non-mainline churches to find it: "But we must be careful . . . because if we fail to give the fish some of the kind of bait he wants he will seek it elsewhere."[35]

If the events of the previous two years indicate how far black Protestantism had come toward accommodating the hush arbor spirit and the assimilationist aesthetic, they lead to the moment when the Reverend J. H. L. Smith rose to reply to Professor Johnson. Whereas the power of the African Methodist Episcopal church was embodied in Payne, its Bishop, and whereas throughout much of the post-Emancipation history of African American Protestantism the force behind assimilationism rested with the denominational leadership, on this night in September 1933 the defense of a more indigenous spirituality emanated from a lowly pastor. In what must have been a calm but defiant manner, Smith "voiced his approval" of the very improvisatory methods that Johnson "classified as wrong." Then, in reaffirmation of his earlier call for a group to sing the "good old-fashion[ed] songs that were born in the hearts of our forefathers," Smith reminded his audience that "emotion and spirit are much so akin that one could hardly be far removed from the other."[36]

By 1937, old-line churches and their leaders throughout the United States had come to share Smith's conviction. The largest black denomination in the United States, the National Baptist Convention, installed a mass gospel chorus at its annual meeting in Los Angeles with Dorsey as director. Yet as early as 1935, at the National Baptist Convention in New York, Dorsey's prominence within the Convention was already growing both through his rising popularity and through his most well-known song then, *Take My Hand, Precious Lord*. At the 1935 convention in New York, his song was sung four times, as recorded in the minutes, more than any song during the meeting. It was performed three times by soloists and once in a choral arrangement, led by Isaacs, who had urged Dorsey to sell his *If You See My Savior* at the 1930 convention. Isaacs presented Dorsey as the "composer" and then let him lead "several selections." Two of the solo renditions came from persons located outside of Chicago: one from Memphis and the other from Ohio.

No longer recognized only in Chicago circles, Dorsey and his gospel blues were well on their way to gaining national recognition. In a sense, therefore, the 1937 convention stands both as the curtain call of the emergence of gospel blues and the opening act of its nationwide institutionalization. Mahalia Jackson, Sallie Martin, Dorsey, and a host of "gospel singers" peppered the convention with Dorsey songs, the most often heard of which was *Take My Hand, Precious Lord*. They were closing out the era in which they went about as renegades, crusading for the right to sing the gospel message to blues music. Their presence itself at the 1937 convention signaled their new status. Jackson had joined the ranks of the Convention's solo evangelists. Two years later, Dorsey, so swept away by her singing at one of their concerts, would rise from his piano after and proclaim Jackson "the Empress of gospel singers." In 1934, Martin was voted "National Organizer" of the National Convention of Gospel Choirs and Choruses. What had been regarded as her guerrilla tactics had evolved into a carefully orchestrated strategy, under her direction, to bring every gospel chorus in the country into a supportive network of institutionalized old-line bush harbors under the auspices of the gospel chorus Convention. Dorsey, since the 1934 meeting of the gospel chorus Convention, was President of the National Convention of Gospel Choirs and Choruses, *Incorporated*. The gospel singers' "home" he called for in his address to the Chicago Union in 1933 would become a reality in 1945. Even now he and the gospel Convention were already operating out of a busy headquarters on Oakwood Avenue in Chicago. Dorsey had appeared first at the 1930 convention as a bewildered songwriter, somewhat shocked by the sudden demand for one of his songs. Now, as a result of his compositional output and his control over the Baptist Convention's gospel music program, he had become one of music directors' aristocracy.[37]

Because it sang each day of the convention and functioned as the devotional music group, the mass gospel chorus best symbolized the end of one era of gospel blues and the beginning of another. As persistent as it had been in its right to sing "just as we pleased" from its hush arbor birth, on through its early Emancipation ringshout adolescence, continuing through its choral movement young adulthood, and now into its choral bureaucracy maturity, the chorus was about to take its place in the very theology of old-line Protestantism. It was to become a spiritual reminder that modern, old-line Christianity had roots in the enslaved religion of the African in the United States. In the words of a speaker at the convention, the chorus was charged with becoming an "instrumentality" for developing "soulforce." Through its choral gospel blues it must keep black old-liners everywhere connected to their past. Then, in the most ringing endorsement of the function of gospel music in old-line religion and the role of the chorus in maintaining it, the speaker placed the mantle of responsibility where it had been from the bush harbor to the gospel chorus: "Our worship would gain immensely if the choirs would spend less time in the preparation of anthems and special musical numbers, and devote more time to the music of the gospel songs and the hymn tunes. These belong preeminently to the people. . . ."[38]

Notes

Introduction

1. Bishop Daniel E. Payne, *History of the African Methodist Episcopal Church,* ed., C. S. Smith (1891, rpt. New York: Johnson Reprint, 1968), 457.

2. Alan H. Spear, *Black Chicago: The Making of a Negro Ghetto: 1890–1920* (Chicago: Univ. of Chicago Press, 1967), 178.

3. See this point well-argued in Alain Locke's *The New Negro* (1925, rpt. New York: Atheneum, 1968), 6.

4. St. Clair Drake and Horace Cayton, *Black Metropolis: A Study of Negro Life in a Northern City,* Vol. II (1945, rev. enlarged New York: Harper and Row, 1962), 673.

5. Interviews with Chicago choir directors, James A. Mundy (Chicago), April 2, 1976, Edward H. S. Boatner (New York), Sept. 26, 1977, and the Reverend Augustus A. Evans (Memphis), March 24 and Dec. 13, 1976.

6. George D. Lewis, "Spirituals of Today," WPA Illinois Writers Project, Microfilm 5, MS 89, p. 10.

7. E. Franklin Frazier, *The Negro Church in America* (1963, rpt. Schocken, 1974), 77–79; Drake and Cayton, Vol. II, pp. 670–79; Lawrence W. Levine, *Black Culture and Black Consciousness: Afro-American Folk Thought from Slavery to Freedom* (New York: Oxford Univ. Press, 1977), 174–89.

8. Photograph of Ebenezer Baptist Church "Gospel Chorus" in the *Chicago Defender,* Feb. 6, 1932, p. 22; also "Gospel Singers Close National Meeting," *Chicago Defender,* Sept. 9, 1933, p. 15.

9. W. E. B. Du Bois: "One ever feels his twoness,—an American, a Negro . . ." in *The Souls of Black Folk* (1903, rpt. Millwood, N.Y.: Kraus-Thomson, 1973), 3.

10. Corrie M. Hindsman, *Inspirational Songs* (Atlanta, Ga.: pub. by author, n.d.).

Chapter 1

Religion and Blackness in Rural Georgia

1. *Recollections of Seventy Years* (1888, rpt. New York: Arno Press and the New York Times, 1968), 253–54. Payne served as bishop from 1852 until his death in November 1892. For a biographical sketch that focuses on his work in the AME church, see R. R. Wright, Jr., *The Bishops of the African Methodist Episcopal Church* (n.p.: A.M.E. Sunday School Union, 1963), 266–79.

2. This topic has been written about extensively. For the most comprehensive critique, see James M. McPherson, *The Abolitionist Legacy: From Reconstruction to the NAACP* (Princeton: Princeton Univ. Press, 1975), especially Chapter 4, "Time, Education, and Bootstraps," and Chapter 9, "The Roots of Freedmen's Education," pp. 53–80 and 143–60, respectively. For a detailed view of the interactions between northern missionaries and freedpersons, see Chapter 6, "'To Teach Them How to Live,'" in Jacqueline Jones, *Soldiers of Light and Love: Northern Teachers and Georgia Blacks, 1865–1873* (Chapel Hill: Univ. of North Carolina Press, 1980), 140–66.

3. Passage quoted from Lewis G. Jordan, *Negro Baptist History U.S.A.: 1750[-]1930* (Nashville: Sunday School Publishing Board, N.B.C. [National Baptist Convention], [1930]), 294–95. On early black colleges see "Laying the Foundations," pp. 3–20, and "Founding the First Colleges," pp. 21–33, in Willard Range, *The Rise and Progress of Negro Colleges in Georgia: 1865–1949* (Athens: Univ. of Georgia Press, 1951), 3–33, and W. A. Daniel, *The Education of Negro Ministers* (1925, rpt. New York: Negro Universities Press, 1969), 27, 32, 101, and passim. The following are among the institutions the Society established that today remain prestigious black schools of higher education: Richmond Institute (1865), now Virginia Union University; Shaw University (1865); Spelman Seminary (1862), later Spelman College; and Benedict Institute (1870), later Benedict College (1894).

4. Resolution no. 7 passed at the Annual Meeting of the American Missionary Association in November 1864, published in the *American Missionary Magazine* 8 (1864): 284.

5. McPherson, *The Abolitionist Legacy*, 151.

6. [Richard Allen], *The Life Experience and Gospel Labors of the Rt. Rev. Richard Allen* (n.d., rpt. Nashville: Abingdon Press, 1960), 24 and 35. For a general chronology of the walkout at St. George's and a complete discussion of the movement and of Richard Allen, see Carol V. R. George, *Segregated Sabbaths: Richard Allen and the Emergence of Independent Black Churches 1760–1840* (New York: Oxford Univ. Press, 1973), esp. 55–71.

7. John Thompson, *The Life of John Thompson, A Fugitive Slave: Containing His History of 25 Years in Bondage and His Providential Escape* (1856, rpt. New York: Negro Universities Press, 1968), 18–19. For discussion of slaves' preferences for certain denominations, see Albert J. Raboteau, *Slave Religion: The "Invisible Institution" in the Antebellum South* (New York: Oxford Univ. Press, 1978), 128–38; also see Chapter 4, "The Appeal of Methodism to Black Americans," in William B. McClain, *Black People in the Methodist Church: Whither Thou Goest?* (Cambridge, Mass.: Schenkman, 1984), 19–37. This account is useful for its compilation of a wide range of sources on the subject of black Methodists more than for its critique of this relationship.

8. Allen, *Life Experience and Gospel Labors,* 29–30.

9. Ibid., 64. A full account of the yellow fever outbreak, written by Absalom Jones and Richard Allen, is published on pp. 48–65.

10. Quoted from the "Introduction" of *Doctrines and Discipline of the African Methodist Episcopal Church* (Philadelphia: J. H. Cunningham, 1817), which was signed by Richard Allen, Daniel Coker, and James Champion (printed in Eileen Southern, "Musical Practices in Black Churches of Philadelphia and New York, ca. 1800–1844," *Journal of the American Musicological Society* 30 (1977) no. 2: 301). See George, *Segregated Sabbaths,* for discussion of the journal manuscript and various entries, especially pp. 93–97. For a thorough analysis and discussion of AME hymnals see Eileen Southern, *The Music of Black Americans: A History,* 2nd ed. (New York: W. W. Norton, 1983), 80–81, and Southern, "Musical Practices," 296–312.

11. Payne, *Recollections,* 93–94. For Payne's role in bringing European classical instrumental music and choirs to AME churches, see his *History of the A. M. E. Church,* 452-64, quoted passage on p. 12.

12. Payne, *Recollections,* 254–256.

13. Carter G. Woodson, "The Conservative and Progressive," Chapter 12 in *The History of the Negro Church,* 2nd ed. (Washington, D.C.: Associated Publishers, 1945), 224–41. The most notable example of a conservative-progressive debate leading to the formation of a denomination is the organization of the National Baptist Convention in 1895.

14. *International Journal of Ethics* 14 (1904): 298.

15. Interviews: Carrie Lee Hindsman Phillips (Atlanta), July 10, 1976, p. 13; Thomas Andrew Dorsey (Chicago), Jan. 30, 1976, ll. 207–8. Information on Silvey's household is located on lines 64–69, Sheet 6B, Enumeration District One, Carroll County, Vol. 9, State of Georgia, Twelfth Decennial United States Census (1900). Four children, a grandchild, and a boarder are listed as living with Silvey: "Mollie, Gennie, Phillip, and Alice" are the children, Carrie L. Hindsman, the granddaughter, and Daniel B. Moon, the boarder. Carrie Lee is listed as a Hindsman, but Jennie Plant did not marry Corrie M. Hindsman until April 9, 1905, according to the "Colored Marriage Book," State of Georgia, County of Carroll, p. 511. To add more mystery to the parentage of Carrie Lee, see line 45, Sheet 8A, Enumeration District 2, Villa Rica, County of Carroll, State of Georgia, Thirteenth Decennial United States Census: "Corry Lee" is listed as "Corry" Hindsman's "step daughter."

16. Du Bois, "The Development of a People," 305–6.

17. As listed on lines 5–11, Sheet 19, Enumeration District 6, Vol. 18, County of Columbia, State of Georgia, Twelfth Decennial United States Census, Andrew and Lucy Dorsey had been married for 37 years. They lived in a "rented farm" with three of the twelve children they had (eight were living then), "John S., Isaiah S., and Rebecca D." Rebecca was noted as having had two children, "Susie and Tarsus," listed as granddaughter and grandson, respectively, of Andrew and Lucy.

18. "The Work of Negro Women in Society," *Spelman Messenger* 18 (Feb. 1902): 1. Du Bois, who studied in Germany, not only held as an ideal the *kaffeeklatsch* (p. 3) but admired the way German parents let their children socialize (p. 184 in "The Problem of Amusement," *Southern Workman* 26 [Sept. 1897]: 181–84). Du Bois, "The Development of a People," 306.

19. Du Bois, "The Development of a People," 306 and 307–8.

20. Payne, *Recollections,* 256. For his role in establishing Wilberforce University, see *History of the A.M.E. Church,* 393–401. Scholarly biographies of Du Bois, dating back to Francis Broderick's *W. E. B. Du Bois: Negro Leader in a Time of Crisis* (Stanford, Calif.: Stanford Univ. Press, 1959), devote much attention to Du Bois's education at Fisk and Harvard, to name just the principal schools he attended. His idea that education provided "essential humanity" is found in "Caste: That Is the Root of Trouble," *Des Moines Register and Leader,* Oct. 19, 1904, p. 5.

21. McPherson, *Abolitionist Legacy,* 187 and 288. For the most comprehensive and accurate assessment of the divisions among black Baptists, especially between Emancipation and 1900, see James M. Washington, *Frustrated Fellowship: The Black Baptist Quest for Social Power* (Macon, Ga.: Mercer Univ. Press, 1986), especially the epilogue, "The Enduring Legacy of Separatism," 187–207. On Gaston, see Edwin S. Redkey, *Black Exodus: Black Nationalist and Back-to-Africa Movements, 1890–1910* (New Haven: Yale Univ. Press, 1969), 152–69.

22. On Baptist training of black preachers and establishing schools, see American Baptist Home Missionary Society *Annual Report,* 1866, pp. 31–32, quoted in Dwight O. W. Holmes, *The Evolution of the Negro College* (1934, rpt. New York: Arno Press and the New York Times, 1969), 122. Also see 120–23 for general discussion of these activities. On Joshua Dorsey, see Thirteenth Decennial Census, State of Illinois, County of Cook, Vol. 096, Enumeration District 1313, Family Visitation Number 0045: "Joshua L. Dorsey . . . Druggist, Drugstore, Is An Employer." See also "Registration Card," Order Number 3662, card number 2340, for World War I draft for Joshua S. Dorsey, signed "9/12/1918." Joshua indicates that he was a "druggist" and that his employer's name was "self." Joshua received his training for this profession working as a "porter" in an Atlanta drugstore owned by A. L. Curtis from 1897 through 1903 (with the exception of 1902). This information was located in the *Atlanta City Directory for 1897,* Vol. XXI, p. 632; . . . *for 1898,* Vol. XXII, p. 602; . . . *for 1899,* [no Vol. #], p. 641; . . . *for 1900,* [no Vol. #], p. 1123; . . . *for 1901,* [no Vol. #], p. 1421; . . . *for 1903,* Vol. XXVII, p. 610 (no listing for A. L. Curtis in this edition). James is variously listed in the *Directory* as a "barber" (. . . *1900,* p. 1123), a "grocer" (. . . *1901,* p. 1421), a "drayman" (. . . *1903,* p. 610), and a "Reverend" (e.g., . . . *1910, 1913, 1916,* p. 716, 746, and 769, respectively). On the changes at Atlanta Baptist Seminary, see Jordan, *Negro Baptist History,* 295.

23. On Thomas's graduation from Atlanta Baptist College, see letter from Nathaniel C. Veale, Jr., Director of Office of Alumni Affairs, Morehouse College to Michael W. Harris: "Alumnus Thomas Madison Dorsey . . . graduated from this institution in 1894." Quote from Dorsey interview (Jan. 29, 1976), 4 and 32–33.

24. In addition to Du Bois, see, for example, E. Franklin Frazier, *The Negro Family in the United States* (1939, rev. and abr. 1948, rpt., Chicago: Univ. of Chicago Press, 1969), 92, 98, and Chapter 6, "Unfettered Motherhood," passim; Frazier, *Negro Church in America,* 35–40; also Herbert G. Gutman, *The Black Family in Slavery and Freedom, 1750–1925* (New York: Vintage, 1976), 363–450.

25. Information on Charles and Phillip Plant was gathered from an interview with Thomas A. Dorsey, Jan. 30, 1976, ll. 256–356 and 1585–1606; also from Silvey's (referred to as "Kit") listing in the Tenth Decennial United States Census (no volume or district references), in which Charles is listed as Silvey's son and 18 years of age, and her listing in the "Twelfth" Census (Volume G, Enumeration District 1, Sheet 6B, lines 64–68), in which Phillip is listed as being born to Silvey in 1883. On Mollie

Plant, see Mary Tally Anderson, *The History of Villa Rica: [City of Gold]* (Villa Rica, Ga.: Georgia Bicentennial Committee, 1976), 118: "As we stroll down memory lane, we are reminded that many of the older people [Villa Rica's older blacks] were well known for their cooking art and special trades, such as . . . Mollie Plant. . . ." On Jennie, see interview with Carrie Lee Hindsman Phillips, her daughter, July 10, 1976, p. 1. Also on Jennie and Corrie Hindsman, see "State of Georgia, County of Carroll, Colored Marriage Book," pp. 396 and 511. The "Marriage Book" indicates that "Corry" and Jennie received a marriage license on Sept. 20, 1902, but did not marry at that time. On March 18, 1905, they obtained another license and were married by Thomas Madison Dorsey, "MG [Minister of the Gospel]," on April 9.

26. For Etta's birthdate see "The Thomas A. Dorsey Story: From Blues-Jazz to Gospel Song" (unpublished TS, c. 1961), 11, hereinafter designated as TADS: "[My mother] died July 19, 1961. She was 90 years of age"; see also the Tenth Decennial United States Census, District 1281, Lutherville, Meriwether County, State of Georgia, in which Etta is listed as ten years old. Other information for this paragraph comes from TADS, 10, and the following interviews: Carrie L. Phillips, July 10, 1976, p. 10; Leon Plant (Villa Rica, Ga.), July 18, 1976, pp. 2–3; and Velma Johnson Butler, daughter of Bernice Dorsey Johnson, Dorsey's sister (Atlanta), June 7, 1976, pp. 14–15.

27. "Carroll County, Georgia, Superior Court General Index to Deeds and Mortgages: Grantees L-Z—1828–1934" and "Book of Deeds: Book Y," p. 224, entry dated Nov. 30, 1894, show that Etta paid $100 for two acres "more or less" of town lots one and four in block two of land lot #162. On p. 225 is an entry showing that Etta paid $480 for "50 acres of land more or less" of lots 95 and 98 of the fifth section of the sixth district of Carroll County on Nov. 22, 1894. For information on black land-ownership in Georgia, see Du Bois, "Georgia Negroes and Their Fifty Millions of Savings," in *World's Work* 18 (May 1908): 11553.

28. On p. 10 of TADS, Dorsey writes that his parents were married in 1898. The "Colored Marriage Book," however, lists their marriage on Oct. 15, 1895 (p. 94). Material for the description of Etta and Thomas's meeting and marriage was gathered from interviews with Velma Johnson Butler, June 7, 1976, pp. 3–4 and 14–15 and Leon Plant, July 18, 1976, pp. 3–4; also TADS, 10.

29. TADS, 10.

30. On agriculture and general financial conditions in Georgia, see William F. Holmes, "Economic Developments: 1890–1940," in *A History of Georgia*, Kenneth Coleman, gen. ed. (Athens: Univ. of Georgia Press, 1977), 257–76. The "oldest bank in Carroll County," the Bank of Villa Rica, was chartered and began business May 4, 1899. See Anderson, *History of Villa Rica*, 73.

31. Du Bois, "Georgia Negroes and Their Fifty Millions of Savings," 11551.

32. "Index to Deeds and Mortgages," 94. Twelfth Decennial Census, Vol. 31, Enumeration District 79, Sheet 22b, lines 57–62, show a Stephen Dorsey living with his wife Etta, son Thomas A. (born "7/1899"), brothers James and Joshua, and sister Hattie. There is little doubt that this is a record of *Thomas Madison* Dorsey and not anyone else. In addition to the correct names for his brothers, sister, wife, and son, Thomas is listed as being married to Etta for five years which would agree with information on their certificate in the Carroll County "Colored Marriage Book." Also Thomas's occupation is listed as "Minister," and his son's birthdate as July 1899; moreover, the address for them matches that listed for both James and Joshua

in the *Atlanta City Directory for 1900*, p. 1123. One simply cannot ascertain whether Thomas Wood, the census taker, made an error or was misinformed. There is an indication, however, that he was slightly careless: though he recorded Thomas A.'s birthdate as being "July 1899," he recorded his age as being "10/12." By June 15, 1900, when Wood visited the Dorseys, Thomas Andrew was eleven months old. On the location of Forsyth, see Marion R. Hemperley, comp., *Cities, Towns and Communities of Georgia Between 1847 [and] 1962, 8500 Places and the County in Which Located* (Easley, S.C.: Southern Historical Press, 1980), 55. The 1901 "Defaulters" list for District 649 shows "T. M. Dorsey." There is no way to ascertain his tax status in 1902, as the "A–G" pages of the "Colored" listing of the Villa Rica district are missing from the Tax Digest. On Samuel E. J. Dorsey, see TADS, 11, and interview, Jan. 29, 1976, l. 260.

33. "Carroll County General Index to Mortgages and Deeds," 198. Carroll County Tax Digests show the Dorseys' aggregate value at $163 in 1903, $146 in 1904, $160 in 1905, $293 in 1906, and $410 in 1907. The last figure seems to be an error. Since the entry lists $200 for the value of the Dorseys' city property, $10 for their household goods, $90 for their livestock, and $10 for "plantation, mechanical" items, the aggregate should be $310. On crop prices, sharecropping, and other financial systems in Georgia between 1890 and 1930, see Holmes, "Economic Developments," 259–63.

34. TADS, 10.

35. In Vol. 9 on line 11 of Sheet 13 of Enumeration District 1, Villa Rica, County of Carroll, of the Twelfth Decennial Census, a 59-year-old ("b. 5/1841") white male, James M. Taylor, is listed as a "landlord" who owns a "farm house." Dorsey's description of Taylor is found in interview, Jan. 15, 1977, pp. 27–28. Also see TADS, 13–14, for description of crops.

36. Interviews: Jan. 29, 1976, pp. 13 and 33; Feb. 3, 1976, p. 6; Jan. 15, 1977, pp. 9 and 34; Jan. 17, 1977, p. 2; also TADS, 10 and 14.

37. TADS, 12; interviews: Jan. 29, 1976, p. 9, and Jan. 15, 1977, p. 24.

38. This type of educational cycle was common for rural children, white or black, and for ministers as well. See James C. Bonner, *Georgia's Last Frontier: The Development of Carroll County* (Athens, Ga.: Univ. of Georgia Press, 1971), 165. Interviews: Jan. 29, 1976, p. 4; Jan. 30, 1976, p. 16; Jan. 15, 1977, p. 3; TADS, 11.

39. Interviews: Jan. 29, 1976, pp. 12 and 13; Jan. 30, 1976, pp. 14–15. A walking cane along with "beaver hat [and] kid gloves" were evidently the accessories of educated black men. This image did not always provoke favorable reactions, however. Booker T. Washington described a man so dressed (and presumably so educated) as "the proud fop," who needed to be "brought down to something practical and useful." Quoted in Louis R. Harlan, ed., *The Booker T. Washington Papers*, Vol. II (Urbana: Univ. of Illinois Press, 1972), 260–61. Du Bois thought just the opposite, of course. Liberal education "freed the spirit to find its true, lofty level." See Arnold Rampersad, *The Art and Imagination of W. E. B. Du Bois* (Cambridge: Harvard Univ. Press, 1976), 86.

40. Thomas A. Dorsey, *Inspirational Thoughts* (Chicago: pub. by author, 1935), 59–60. Interview, Jan. 29, 1976, p. 16.

41. Interview, Jan. 29, 1976, p. 8. TADS, 12–13. Feeding tramps was not an unusual occurrence in Villa Rica. See interview with Lucious and Leila Plant (no relation to Etta) in Anderson, *History of Villa Rica*, 181–83.

42. Interviews: Jan. 29, 1976, p. 10; Feb. 2, 1976, pp. 24–25; Jan. 29, 1976, p. 1.

43. Washington, *Up from Slavery* (1902, rpt. New York: Avon, 1965), 89. William E. B. Du Bois, ed., *The Negro American Family*, [Atlanta University Publications No. 13] (1908, rpt. New York: Negro Universities Press, 1969), 117. Interviews: Jan. 30, 1976, p. 15; Jan. 15, 1977, p. 24; Velma Johnson Butler, June 7, 1976, p. 15. TADS, 11.

44. Interview, Jan. 29, 1976, pp. 2, 8, and 10.

45. Interview, Bessie Jones (St. Simons Island, Ga.), June 1976, ll. 359–79. Miss Jones's description of "picking" is the source for this discussion. As a child, her grandfather told her about slave and post-slavery musical practices of Georgia and the Georgia Sea Islands. Between 1977 and 1978, she worked with John Stewart on tape-recording her memoirs; in the book that was published from these interviews, she describes "picking" briefly (Bessie Jones, *For the Ancestors: Autobiographical Memories*, John Stewart, collector and ed. [Urbana: Univ. of Illinois Press, 1983], 9 and 30). She performed regularly for the Smithsonian Institution's annual Festival of American Folklife and has recorded extensively. She was one of the major informants for Lydia Parrish's *Slave Songs of the Georgia Sea Islands* (1942, rpt. Hatboro, Penn.: Folklore Associates, 1965) and co-author with Bess Lomax Hawes of *Step It Down: Games, Plays, Songs, and Stories from the Afro-American Heritage* (New York: Harper & Row, 1972). Dorsey quote from interview, Jan. 30, 1976, p. 8.

46. Anderson, *History of Villa Rica*, 117. Hindsman, *Inspirational Songs*. C[orrie] M. Hindsman, *The History of Mt. Prospect Baptist Church of Villa Rica, Ga[.]* ([Villa Rica]: n.p., 1949), 2–3.

47. On stylistic features of shaped note singing, see Dorothy D. Horn, *Sing to Me of Heaven: A Study of Folk and Early American Materials in Three Old Harp Books* (Gainesville: Univ. of Florida Press, 1970), 90–116. On the harmonic texture of slave spirituals, George R. Ricks notes: "In the jubilee style, full harmony is not used in strict homophonic idiom of Western church music. . . . The use of full harmony in this folk idiom is influenced by the pre-existing interest in rhythm, improvisation, and leader-chorus patterning" (*Some Aspects of the Religious Music of the United States Negro: An Ethnomusicological Study with Special Emphasis on the Gospel Tradition* [Ph.D. diss., Northwestern University, 1960, rpt. New York: Arno Press, 1977], 392). See also Lydia Parrish, *Slave Songs of the Georgia Sea Islands,* passim. Also see the foreword in Natalie C. Burlin, *Negro Folk Songs*, Hampton Series, Nos. 6716, 6726, 6756, and 6766 (New York: G. Schirmer, 1918), 5–6. Studies on spirituals as slave songs and/or post-emancipation African American music are numerous. In most instances, however, the music, if and when included, is an incomplete transcription or outright arrangement. Parrish and Burlin have transcribed and included in their works all the parts, presented so far as possible in the way in which they were performed. The term "polyphonic homophony" is a descriptive phrase this writer has found useful based on his analysis of Rick's, Parrish's, and Burlin's transcriptions. Quote from Dorsey interview, Jan. 29, 1976, pp. 1 and 9–11.

48. Interview, Jan. 29, 1976, p. 11.

49. Interview, Feb. 2, 1976, pp. 24 and 33–35.

50. Interview, Feb. 2, 1976, pp. 24–25 and 33.

51. Thomas A Dorsey, *Songs With a Message: With My Ups and Downs* (Chicago: pub. by author, 1941), 11.

Chapter 2

Music, Literacy, and Society in Atlanta

1. Interviews: Jan. 17, 1977, pp. 2–4, and Jan. 29, 1976, p. 22. *Atlanta City Directory . . . for 1909*, p. 880; . . . *for 1912*, p. 674; . . . *for 1913*, p. 747; . . . *for 1914*, p. 823; . . . *for 1915*, p. 832; for sample listing of minister and church, see *Atlanta City Directory for 1913* for James Dorsey, Thomas's brother, "pastor Zion Baptist Church" (p. 746). *Annual Catalogue of Morehouse College* (Atlanta: Morehouse College).

2. TADS, 14; interview, Jan. 29, 1976, p. 23.

3. John Dittmer, *Black Georgia in the Progressive Era, 1900–1920* (Urbana: Univ. of Illinois Press, 1977), 27.

4. Interview, Jan. 29, 1976, p. 32.

5. Ibid.

6. Advertisement for Dr. Palmer's Skin Whitener manufactured by Jacobs' Pharmacy in Atlanta in *Atlanta Independent,* Aug. 27, 1910, p. 7, and for Her-Tru-Line in same newspaper, Dec. 17, 1910, p. 5.

7. TADS, 16–17.

8. TADS, 16, and interview, Jan. 30, 1976, ll. 939–74.

9. For information on the founding and early history of the Carrie Steele Orphanage see Mrs. Gussie Mims Logan, "The Carrie Steele Orphanage," *The Voice* 1 (Nov. 11, 1904): 538–40. "Double Sessions Must Go," *Atlanta Independent,* Oct. 24, 1914, p. 4; Melvin W. Ecke, *From Ivy Street to Kennedy Center: Centennial History of the Atlanta Public School System* ([Atlanta]: Atlanta Board of Education, 1972), 79 and 143–44; TADS, 15.

10. Interview, Jan. 15, 1977, l. 1512. U.S. Bureau of the Census, *Negro Population in the United States: 1790–1915* (1918, rpt. New York: Arno Press and the New York Times, 1968), 432.

11. Interviews: Jan. 29, 1976, p. 47; Jan. 30, 1976, pp. 40–42; Jan. 17, 1977, p. 4.

12. TADS, 17; interview, Jan. 29, 1976, p. 24. For information on the conditions of black urban migrants during this period, see Du Bois, *Negro American Family,* 58–64.

13. TADS, 15; interview, Jan. 17, 1977, p. 10. About Decatur Street, see "Saturday on Decatur St.," in the *Atlanta Journal,* May 18, 1913, p. 2: "The Champs Elysees of Paris and the Strand of London are celebrated for their glitter and gorgeousness; Broadway . . . and the Bowery . . . are known as widely as the city which mothers them; Canal Street in Mardi Gras season is the highest spot of color in New Orleans; tourists to San Francisco seek Chinatown before they do Knob Hill. But there is not one of those whose romance matches that of Decatur Street, whose habitues are quainter or more original." On movie theaters of this era, see Q. David Bowers, *Nickelodeon Theatres and Their Music* (Vestal, N.Y.: Vestal Press, 1986), passim. For typical shows at three other black theaters in Atlanta (New Auditorium, Majestic, and Dixie), see "Sports and Theatre News," *Atlanta Independent,* May 16, 1914, p. 5. On the early touring shows see Derrick Stewart-Baxter, *Ma Rainey and the Classic Blues Singers* (New York: Stein and Day, 1970), 35–44, and Paul Oliver, "The Long-Tailed Blue: Songsters of the Road Shows," in *Songsters and Saints: Vocal*

Traditions on Race Records (Cambridge, Eng.: Cambridge Univ. Press, 1984), 78–108.

14. TADS, 17; interview, Jan. 17, 1977, p. 32. In the Atlanta City Directories for 1910–16, James is listed as a pastor: *Atlanta City Directory . . . for 1910*, p. 716; . . . *for 1911*, p. 708; . . . *for 1912*, p. 673; . . . *for 1913*, p. 746; . . . *for 1914*, p. 823; . . . *for 1915*, p. 832; . . . *for 1916*, p. 769.

15. Interview, Jan. 30, 1976, p. 36.

16. Interview, Jan. 29, 1976, p. 40.

17. TADS, 17; interview, Jan. 29, 1976, p. 31. Carrie Lee Phillips, Dorsey's cousin who lived with his family for several years in Atlanta, recalls that Dorsey played the organ late at night "almost every night" (Interview, July 10, 1976, p. 9).

18. Interviews: Jan. 30, 1976, p. 32, and Jan. 17, 1977, p. 13.

19. Interviews: Jan. 29, 1976, p. 41, and Jan. 30, 1976, p. 31.

20. Interview, Jan. 29, 1976, p. 36.

21. Interview, Jan. 30, 1976, p. 32.

22. Measures 9–12 are more intricate, Dorsey says, but because of the present arthritic condition of his hands, he is unable to perform them accurately.

23. TADS, 17–18. Interviews: Feb. 2, 1976, p. 5; Jan. 30, 1976, p. 38; Jan. 17, 1977, pp. 9 and 15–18.

24. Interviews: Jan. 30, 1976, p. 31; Jan. 29, 1976, pp. 27 and 33; Jan. 17, 1977, p. 17; and Jan. 15, 1977, p. 44.

25. Interviews: Jan. 29, 1976, p. 27; Jan. 30, 1976, p. 34; and Jan. 17, 1977, p. 30.

26. Interviews: Jan. 30, 1976, pp. 32 and 35, and Jan. 17, 1977, p. 9. TADS, 17.

27. Interview, Jan. 30, 1976, p. 32.

28. Interview, Jan. 30, 1976, pp. 20 and 33–35.

29. Ibid.

30. Interviews: Jan. 17, 1977, p. 18, and Jan. 15, 1977, pp. 13 and 38.

31. Interview, Feb. 2, 1976, pp. 4–5.

32. Interviews: Jan. 29, 1976, p. 45, and Jan. 30, 1976, p. 32. On Smith at the Eighty-One, see Chris Albertson, *Bessie* (New York: Stein and Day, 1972), 27–28.

33. Interview, Jan. 30, 1976, p. 40.

34. Interviews: Jan. 15, 1977, p. 49, and Feb. 2, 1976, p. 1.

35. Interviews: Jan. 30, 1976, pp. 21–22, and Jan. 17, 1977, pp. 33–43. *Atlanta Independent,* June 19, 1915, p. 1, announcing "grand opening" of Odd Fellows Roof Garden, Tuesday, June 29.

36. Interview, Feb. 2, 1976, pp. 1–2. On prohibition see the Dec. 27, 1907, edition of the *Atlanta Constitution,* which announced that on Jan. 1, 1908, as a result of a vote of the Georgia state legislature, Atlanta "will go absolutely dry." Although national repeal of prohibition took place in 1933, Georgia waited until Feb. 3, 1938, to legalize alcoholic consumption on the state level and Atlanta until March 30, 1938, on the city level. See also Dittmer, *Black Georgia,* 111–14, for a discussion on the racial factors in Georgia's 1907 prohibition law.

37. Interviews: Jan. 29, 1976, p. 43; Jan. 30, 1976, p. 30; and Feb. 2, 1976, p. 2.

38. Interview, Feb. 2, 1976, p. 1.

39. TADS, 17 and 23.

Chapter 3

Blues—From "Lowdown" to "Jass"

1. Emmett J. Scott, *Negro Migration During the War* ([1920], rpt. New York: Arno Press, 1969), 29–30.

2. For a thorough discussion of the role of the *Chicago Defender* in the migration movement before and during World War I, see Roi Ottley, *The Lonely Warrior: The Life and Times of Robert S. Abbott* (Chicago: Henry Regnery, 1955), Chapter 10, "The Uneasy Exodus," passim.

3. Scott, *Negro Migration*, 29–30; Drake and Cayton, *Black Metropolis*, 59. Interview, Jan. 30, 1976, p. 44.

4. Interview, Jan. 17, 1977, p. 25.

5. Interviews: Jan. 30, 1976, pp. 44–45; Feb. 2, 1976, pp. 27–29; Jan. 17, 1977, pp. 34–36; also TADS, 23–24. Draft registration information comes from Dorsey's card, Order Number 5341, card number 2343 (National Archives, Atlanta Branch, Atlanta, Ga.). Dorsey registered at the Local Board for Division No. 3 in Chicago.

6. Scott, *Negro Migration*, 7; Chicago Commission on Race Relations, *The Negro in Chicago: A Study of Race Relations and a Race Riot* (Chicago: Univ. of Chicago Press, 1922), 1–52 and 79–105; E. Franklin Frazier, *The Negro Family in Chicago*, (1932; rpt. Chicago: Univ. of Illinois Press, 1966), 88–90; Arvarh E. Strickland, *History of the Chicago Urban League* (Urbana: Univ. of Illinois Press, 1966), 261; William S. Rossiter, *Increase of Population in the United States: 1910–1920: A Study of Changes in the Population of Divisions, States, Counties, and Rural and Urban Areas, and in Sex, Color, and Nativity, at the Fourteenth Census*, Census Monographs I (Washington, D.C.: Government Printing Office, 1922), 128–31. These works represent but a sampling of the social and statistical analyses of the black migration between 1910 and 1920 and its effect on Chicago.

7. Frazier, *Negro Family in Chicago*, 95. Unidentified "Old Settler" quoted in Drake and Cayton, *Black Metropolis*, Vol. I, pp. 73–74. See also Allan H. Spear, "The Impact of the Migration: Negro Community Life," in *Black Chicago*, 167–79.

8. Eileen Southern, *The Music of Black Americans*, 308–30. Spear, *Black Chicago*, 76. The Pekin theater may have been black-run, but apparently not attended by Blacks too much: the Pekin "outclasses . . . the Grand and Monogram," but still slanted its presentations toward white audiences (*Chicago Defender,* April 23, 1910, p. 4). Gilbert Chase, *America's Music from the Pilgrims to the Present*, Rev. 2nd ed. (New York: McGraw-Hill, 1966), 445–47; Alfons M. Dauer, *Der Jazz: Seine Ursprünge und Seine Entwicklung* (Kassel, Germany: Erich Röth-Verlag, 1958), 108.

9. Chase, *America's Music*, 434 and 469.

10. TADS, 25; Southern, *Music of Black Americans*, 342. See also Samuel B. Charters IV, *Jazz: New Orleans*[,] *1885–1963: An Index to the Negro Musicians of New Orleans* (1958, rev. New York: Oak Publications, 1963), 18–19. Charters implies that a midnight curfew in the "red-light district" may have accounted for some of the use of unusual mutes (e.g., a derby hat), pp. 18–19.

11. TADS, 23.

12. Interviews: Feb. 2, 1976, pp. 7–8; March 29, 1976, p. 4; Jan. 17, 1977, pp. 37–8; also TADS, 23.

13. TADS, 23 and 25; Albertson, *Bessie*, 122.

14. Interview, Feb. 2, 1976, pp. 35–36.

15. TADS, 25; also interview, Jan. 18, 1977, p. 4.

16. Interviews: Jan. 17, 1977, pp. 14–15; Jan. 18, 1977, pp. 3 and 23; Feb. 2, 1976, p. 11.

17. Interviews: Jan. 17, 1977, p. 7, and Jan. 18, 1977, pp. 10–12; also TADS, 27.

18. Southern, *Music of Black Americans*, 347–49; Charters, *Jazz: New Orleans*, 18; interview, Jan. 17, 1977, pp. 3–4 and 21; TADS, 25.

19. *A Good Man is Hard to Find* by Eddie Green (New York: E. H. Morris & Co., 1917); interview, Jan. 17, 1977, pp. 6 and 7.

20. W[illiam] C. Handy, *Father of the Blues: An Autobiography by W. C. Handy*, Arna Bontemps, ed. (New York: Macmillan, 1941), 186. Interviews: Jan. 17, 1977, part 2, p. 5; and Jan. 30, 1976, p. 30. Ricks makes similar conclusions about migrants' reticence to expose themselves to new forms of culture by stating that this group, "composed largely of parents and children of the southern, rural migrant group," can be characterized "by a low degree of adherence to American cultural standards" (*Aspects of Religious Music*, 100).

21. TADS, 40–41; interview, Jan. 18, 1977, pp. 10–13.

22. Southern, *Music of Black Americans*, 337–38; and Handy, *Father of the Blues*, 99.

23. Johnson quoted in Levine's *Black Culture and Black Consciousness*, 224. Willie the Lion Smith, *Music on My Mind: The Memoirs of an American Pianist* (Garden City, N.Y.: Doubleday, 1964), 66. Perry Bradford, *Born With the Blues: Perry Bradford's Own Story: The True Story of the Pioneering Blues Singers and Musicians in the Early Days of Jazz* (New York: Oak Publications, 1965), 122 and 97.

24. TADS, 24 and 27. Interviews: Feb. 2, 1976, pp. 7 and 14, and March 29, 1976, p. 4.

25. Interview, Feb. 2, 1976, p. 8.

26. TADS, 30–31. Considerable investigation of music schools in Chicago from 1916 through 1923 has yielded no institution named Chicago School of Composition and Arranging, nor any record of Dorsey's attendance at any of the music schools now in existence. One "Chicago University of Music" announced its opening in the *Chicago Defender* (July 8, 1922, pp. 2 and 5). The "faculty" was to consist of local black musicians and number around "33." From all indications from the opening night program, however, no instruction in jazz composition and arranging would have been available. The debut night consisted solely of opera excerpts (p. 5). No more information was found about this school. Dorsey did compose, arrange, and publish music, however, and was known to be hired for such functions by Paramount Records and the Brunswick Recording Company. Plausible explanations are either that he might have picked up the skills as he did in Atlanta by asking arrangers to teach him or that the Chicago School of Composition and Arranging existed but not as a formally established institution.

27. Interview, Jan. 17, 1977, pp. 6 and 43. Jim and Amy O'Neal, "Living Blues Interview: Georgia Tom Dorsey," in *Living Blues: A Journal of the Black American Blues Tradition* 20 (March–April, 1975): 23–24. TADS, 24.

28. Bradford, *Born With the Blues*, 98–100.

29. John Godrich and Robert M. W. Dixon, comps. in *Blues and Gospel Records: 1902–1943*, 3d ed., fully rev. (Essex, Eng.: Storyville Publications, 1982), place the date of the recording as Feb. 14, 1920 (p. 679). Robert M. W. Dixon and John Godrich, *Recording the Blues* (New York: Stein and Day, 1970), 7–8; Bradford, *Born With the Blues,* 48–49, 118–19, 121, and 123–24. "Making Records," *Chicago Defender,* March 13, 1920, p. 6. OKeh advertisement, July 31, 1920, p. 5. "Pace & Handy," *Chicago Defender,* July 31, 1920, p. 4.

30. Bradford, *Born With the Blues,* 100, 119, 121, 124, and 125.

31. Godrich and Dixon, *Blues and Gospel Records,* 680; Bradford, *Born With the Blues,* 48 (Bradford quotes Handy, *Father of the Blues,* p. 207, on the $53,000 figure), 119, and 122–25. Some disagreement exists over the members of the Jazz Hounds. Bradford says he was the pianist for the group. Godrich and Dixon list "probably Willie the Lion Smith, piano" (*Blues and Gospel Records,* 680). Willie "The Lion" Smith in his biography says not only that he played piano on the recording but that Addington Major was the cornetist. He claims that he left the group and that Bradford filled the opening for its tour through the South because "It has always been the Lion's policy to stay away from climates that don't fit my clothes" (pp. 103–6). Smith's account is of dubious accuracy for at least two reasons: (1) He claims to have made arrangements with Ralph Peer at OKeh. Hager, as Bradford writes and as Godrich and Dixon confirm (*Blues and Gospel Records,* p. 680), was manager at OKeh; (2) Smith claims to have taken Mamie Smith "for her audition" to make *Crazy Blues,* her "first record," but seems unaware of her earlier recording in February.

32. Stewart-Baxter in *Ma Rainey and the Classic Blues Singers* (New York, Stein and Day, 1970) defines the "classic" blues singer as "a stage performer who came up with the glorious music hall tradition" (p. 8). See also his chapters: "Classic Blues—Vaudeville Style" (pp. 10–31) and "Classic Blues—Southern Style" (pp. 35–52). Dixon and Godrich concur: "The classic blues singers [were] professional vaudeville and cabaret performers, almost exclusively female, who sang 12-bar blues interspersed with a few traditional and pop numbers . . . often [accompanied by] a small hot jazz band" (*Recording the Blues,* pp. 20–21).

33. TADS, 30. Registration E4911668, registered on Oct. 9, 1920.

34. TADS, 23; interview, Velma Johnson Butler, June 7, 1976, p. 7.

Chapter 4

Blues—From "Jass" to "Lowdown"

1. Interview, Jan. 18, 1977, p. 23.

2. Ibid.

3. National Baptist Convention, *Proceedings of the 41st Annual Meeting* (Nashville: National Baptist Convention, 1921), 136, 211. Interview, Jan. 21, 1977, p. 38. Dorsey, *Songs With a Message,* 18–20. Convention description in "Baptist End Most Remarkable Meeting," *Chicago Defender,* Sept. 17, 1921, p. 3.

4. Music Committee of the Sunday School Publishing Board, *Gospel Pearls* (Nashville: Sunday School Publishing Board [of the] National Baptist Convention, U.S.A., [1921]), [1–2]. Mrs. A. M. Townsend, ed., *The Baptist Standard Hymnal, with Responsive Readings: A New Book for All Services* (Nashville: Sunday School

Publishing Board [of the] National Baptist Convention, U.S.A., 1924), 4. Evidently, *Gospel Pearls* was designated as a "songbook" because it was compiled for use at any religious event, whereas the "hymnal" was written specifically for church worship.

5. Townsend, *Baptists Standard Hymnal,* 4. Music Committee, *Gospel Pearls,* p. [4]. For a thorough discussion of the white gospel tradition in the United States, see Robert Stevenson, *Protestant Church Music in America: A Short Survey of Men and Movements from 1564 to the Present* (New York: W. W. Norton, 1966), Chapter 10, "Diverging Currents, 1850–Present," 106–32. For the gospel hymn from the perspective of the Anglo-American hymn and gospel song tradition, see Louis F. Benson, *The English Hymn: Its Development and Use in Worship* (New York: Hodder and Stoughton, 1915), 482–92. C. A. Tindley composed black "gospel" songs and ministered in Philadelphia during the early 1900s (Tony Heilbut, *The Gospel Sound: Good News and Bad Times* [New York: Simon and Schuster, 1971], 58–61). In 1915, John Wesley Work published a classic study of black folk music, *Folk Song of the American Negro* (1915, rpt. New York: Negro Universities Press, 1969). For more discussion on *Gospel Pearls* and on Work's and Tindley's publications, see Southern, *Music of Black Americans,* 277 and 450–51. The presence of the Work brothers and Dr. J. D. Bushnell, another composer/arranger of spirituals, on the music committee of the Sunday School Board and the inclusion of the section "Spirituals" in *Gospel Pearls* raise a number of questions regarding the use of spirituals in the black church at that time; some of these will be discussed in the following chapter.

6. National Baptist Convention, *Proceedings,* 136; *Gospel Pearls,* "Preface," p. [4]. The phrase "Gospel singers" as it appears in the preface of *Gospel Pearls* may be considered evidence of its usage among black Baptists as early as 1921, but not conclusively so. The Sunday School Publishing Board was lax in indicating reprints and revisions of *Gospel Pearls.* As an example, the edition on which this analysis was based has only the 1921 copyright notice; but it contains an advertisement for *The Standard Baptist Hymnal* which was not published until 1924. As with much terminology, attempting to establish the origin of the term "gospel singer" will prove to be an exercise in futility. One may hazard a tentative conclusion, however, about the usage of "gospel singer" among members of the National Baptist Convention: if the preface to the edition of *Gospel Pearls* used here is from the 1921 original, then at least among the committee members the phrase was in use in 1921. For the purposes of this biography, the post-1924 preface will be considered the original one.

7. Interview, Jan. 21, 1977, pp. 39–41. On improvisation in black preaching, see for example Chapter 3, "Sermon Content and Structure," in Bruce A. Rosenberg's *The Art of the American Folk Preacher* (New York: Oxford Univ. Press, 1970), 27–34.

8. Interview, Jan. 21, 1977, pp. 38–40. On the central role of improvisation in black religious music, see George Ricks, *Some Aspects of the Religious Music,* 387 and passim: "Close correlations among spirituals, jubilees and gospels are seen in the . . . prominence of improvisation."

9. See discussion on "blues notes" in Southern, *Music of Black Americans,* 334.

10. Interview, March 29, 1976, pp. 33–34. Dorsey's tempo, ♩ = c. 72, is so slow that, with the melodic ornamentation, the transcription of his performance was best notated in 6/4 rather than in 6/8 as in the original.

11. With neither external evidence of "moaning" nor more than a written de-

scription of Nix's singing at the Convention, the close relationship between "moaning" and Nix's singing is conjectural. If this writer is assured of anything, however, it is Dorsey's acute sensitivity to stylistic variances. Despite his arthritic hands and thus his inability to play certain technically demanding passages, Dorsey during interviews would demonstrate over and over the distinctive elements of styles as he remembered playing them. Thus internal similarities should not be summarily dismissed as unreliable or coincidental, as may be the tendency when they are alleged to exist between Examples 1-1 and 4-2. With respect to these two examples, in particular, Dorsey's accuracy is hard to question since he played them during interviews conducted almost a year apart (Feb. 2, 1976, and Jan. 21, 1977) and in the context of different subject matter.

12. Charles E. Hall, *Negroes in the United States: 1920–1932* (1935, rpt. New York: Arno Press, 1969), 530. One of the most comprehensive private compilations of black church statistics can be found in Benjamin E. Mays and Joseph W. Nicholson, *The Negro's Church* (1933, rpt. New York: Arno Press, 1969). On p. 220 see: "As in the South, the Baptists lead. Of the 1,029 churches in the five northern cities, 466, or 45.3 per cent [sic], are Baptist." This is the earliest published study with statistical information on black churches in the United States. On the different types of black churches, both assimilated and unassimilated, see, for example, Robert L. Sutherland's "An Analysis of Negro Churches in Chicago" (Ph.D. diss., Univ. of Chicago, 1930): Sutherland has developed a typology for the 278 churches he found in Chicago in 1928, 47.8% of which were Baptist (pp. 44 and 55). Of the five types, one and two represent those where "rural religious practices" dominate, several qualities of which are: the absence of hymnals, the singing of mostly spirituals and jubilees, and the tendency of these churches to be housed in non-church structures, e.g., storefronts, houses, rooms, etc. (pp. 4–6). Over 60% of his sample conformed to these two types (p. 47). Chicago, then, had a large number of the "hole-in-the-wall" churches in which Nix's singing would have been welcome. See also Ricks, *Some Aspects of the Religious Music,* 110–23 and passim.

13. Interview, Jan. 19, 1977, pp. 12–17.

14. TADS, 45–46.

15. For a discussion of the history of these groups, see Southern, *Music of Black Americans,* esp. pp. 343–48. For names of bands, see: Feb. 18, 1922, Pt. I, pp. 6 and 7; July 1, 1922, p. 6; Nov. 25, 1922, p. 7; Dec. 2, 1922, p. 6; and Jan. 27, 1923, p. 7.

16. This salary figure appears commensurate with the rate of pay for professional theater musicians, judging by figures in the Oct. 9, 1920, edition of the *Chicago Defender,* p. 5. The South Side Theater Managers Association was attempting to garner public support for its opposition to a threatened strike by musicians by placing a large announcement in the paper stating that admission prices would rise proportionate to the 40% pay increase for which the theater musicians of Local 208 of the Musicians' Protective Union were asking. Average salaries, the announcement continued, were $30 through $33 per week per person and $65 per week for band leaders. By the Oct. 16 edition (p. 5), the musicians had prevailed. An advertisement by the association reported that the pay increase had been granted.

17. Interview, Jan. 18, 1977, p. 30. TADS, 31–32. See also Bradford, *Born With the Blues,* 130: "Before the end of 1923, Clarence Williams had sold out his music stores in Chicago, and opened a music publishing firm on the fourth floor [Gaiety

Theatre Building, 1547 Broadway, New York]." Dixon and Godrich, *Recording the Blues,* 13.

18. Dixon and Godrich, *Recording the Blues,* 10. On Black Swan and its failure to promote a wider variety of styles, see the *Chicago Defender,* Jan. 15, 1921, p. 1: "[Harry Pace's] new corporation proposes to furnish . . . sacred and spiritual songs, the popular songs of the day and the high class ballads and operatic selections." Also see June 4 edition, pp. 6 and 7. In Handy, *Father of the Blues,* see p. 210: "In The Black Swan Company, Pace had scored heavily with a recording of Ethel Waters singing *Down Home Blues.* In fact, he had started a stampede." Waters's recording was made in May 1921; *Oh Daddy* was included (Godrich and Dixon, *Blues and Gospel Records,* 809).

19. Chase, *America's Music,* 414. The personnel for "The Whispering Syncopators" is impossible to ascertain from information Dorsey supplies. He speaks of instrumentalists who later became noted jazz players who were members of the group—Lionel Hampton, Les Hite, George Orendorff—but in conflicting ways. In *Songs With a Message,* p. 20, he says, ". . . some of the outstanding musicians of this present day . . . were in that band with me" and then lists the names above. In his memoirs he lists "some of the musicians Harney hired in addition to 'The Whispering Syncopators,' " giving the same names. The point is that Dorsey played with musicians of a caliber to be hired by a nationally famous musician. See also TADS, 46.

20. Interview, Jan. 18, 1977, p. 27. Dixon and Godrich, *Recording the Blues,* 20–22. About Williams, Dixon and Godrich write that he was hired by Paramount in 1924. They contradict themselves, however, by saying that Williams recruited Ma Rainey for Paramount after he was hired as their talent scout in 1924; Ma Rainey began recording for Paramount in December 1923 (Godrich and Dixon, *Blues and Gospel Records,* 605). According to Dorsey, Williams was working at this business in 1923, since he arranged for Monette Moore and Clarence M. Jones to record one of Dorsey's songs in January 1923 for Paramount (see TADS, 32). Possibly he was a free agent before 1924 and under some contractual arrangement, especially given the contacts he could have developed by the beginning of 1924.

21. Dixon and Godrich, *Recording the Blues,* 16, 18, 24, and 27; TADS, 32–33.

22. William C. Handy, ed., *Blues: An Anthology* (New York: Albert and Charles Boni, 1926), 71–74; Handy, *Father of the Blues,* 153–54.

23. Godrich and Dixon, *Blues and Gospel Records,* 545; TADS, 32.

24. Interview, Jan. 18, 1977, p. 30.

25. Godrich and Dixon, *Blues and Gospel Records,* 545; Brian Rust, ed., *Jazz Records: 1897–1942,* 4th rev. and enlarged ed., 2 vols. (New Rochelle, N.Y.: Arlington House, 1978), 1166.

26. Dorsey's application for *A Heart There Was for You* was granted Feb. 17 (No. E558124). The description of Smith is that of Frank Walker, Columbia's supervisor of "race" records. Apparently his observation that she was "scared" was not exaggerated; none of the recordings she made that day was released. The first record Columbia issued was from the session of the following day (Albertson, *Bessie,* 43–44). Interview, Jan. 29, 1976, p. 45; see also Albertson, *Bessie,* 27–28, 30, 32, 40, and 42.

27. Albertson, *Bessie,* 37–39 and 43. Bradford, *Born With the Blues,* 13 and 119.

28. Stewart-Baxter, *Ma Rainey,* 8, 35, passim; Dixon and Godrich, *Recording the Blues,* 10, 21, passim.

29. Dixon and Godrich, *Recording the Blues,* 20–22; Albertson, *Bessie,* 42–43.

30. Albertson, *Bessie,* 42, 46–51.

31. See "W. C. Handy In," *Chicago Defender,* Oct. 23, 1920, p. 4 (refers to *Beale Street Blues* and *A Good Man Is Hard to Find*); also "Pace and Handy," Nov. 13, 1920, p. 5, and "Loveless Love," Nov. 13, 1920, p. 5. On sales of Smith's record and Hunter's *Downhearted Blues,* see Albertson, *Bessie,* 46.

32. Albertson, *Bessie,* 46, 65. Dixon and Godrich, *Recording the Blues,* 21, 41, 59–60.

33. TADS, 37. Southern, *Music of Black Americans,* 374 and 375. *Chicago Defender,* "Dorsey Busy," March 1, 1924, Pt. I, p. 7.

34. *Chicago Defender,* Feb. 2, 1924, Pt. II, p. 10.

35. For a thorough discussion of the differences between "downhome" and classic vaudeville blues singers, see Jeff Todd Titon, *Early Downhome Blues: A Musical and Cultural Analysis* (Urbana: Univ. of Illinois Press, 1977), xv-xvi. Titon classifies Smith and Rainey as vaudeville professionals, as were Mamie Smith and Alberta Hunter, on the basis of their show experience. Given, however, the marked difference of their styles (Titon admits the difference; see p. 209), and the fact that both women developed as artists in the South rather than the North, any similarity they had to their northern counterparts grew out of their comparable roles as professional entertainers. Otherwise, neither Rainey nor Smith would have made the profound impact she did. This impact—a consequence of their distinctive singing style—is demonstrated by the sales of their records, sales greater than those of other vaudeville blues singers.

36. "Lead-sheet" is defined as "a song as written down in its simplest form—melody line and lyric" in Arnold Shaw, "The Vocabulary of Tin-Pan Alley Explained," *Music Library Association Notes,* Dec. 12, 1949, p. 46.

37. Dixon and Godrich, *Recording the Blues,* 22–24. TADS, 47; interview, Jan. 18, 1977, pp. 30–31.

38. Williams's company was evidently one of a number that engaged in this questionable practice. See Alan Lomax, *Mister Jelly Roll: The Fortunes of Jelly Roll Morton, New Orleans Creole and "Inventor of Jazz"* (1950, 2d ed., Berkeley: Univ. of California Press, 1973). Lomax writes of this copyrighting scheme as the "accepted practice" (p. 187). Dorsey quoted in O'Neal and O'Neal, "Georgia Tom Dorsey," 23.

39. Interview, Jan. 18, 1977, pp. 30–31.

40. Dixon and Godrich, *Recording the Blues,* 34; Sterling Brown on Rainey's "moaning" as quoted in Stewart-Baxter, *Ma Rainey,* 42; TADS, 48.

41. "Points Particular," *Chicago Defender,* Dec. 14, 1912, p. 5.

42. Interview, Jan. 19, 1977, pp. 21–22; TADS, 49.

43. *Chicago Defender,* April 12, 1924, p. 6, and May 10, 1924, Pt. I, p. 6; Albertson, *Bessie,* 57.

44. TADS, 49; interview, Jan. 19, 1977, p. 22.

45. TADS, 41–43.

Chapter 5

Old-Line Religion and Musicians

1. On the emerging importance of "moanin'" blues, see Dixon and Godrich, *Recording the Blues,* 26–33; also Stewart-Baxter, *Ma Rainey,* 35–44. TADS, 48–49 and 59.

2. See Bradford, *Born with the Blues,* 100 and 121–29; Albertson, *Bessie,* 60; and Stewart-Baxter, *Ma Rainey,* 22 and 38–44, for use of instrumental accompaniment with classic blues female vocalists. Interview, Jan. 19, 1977, pp. 24–25. Also see discussion of "jass" and "low-down" blues in Chapter 3, pp. 49 and 50–51.

3. Barry McRae, "The Ma Rainey and Bessie Smith Accompaniments: A Survey," *Jazz Journal* 14 (no. 3): 6 and 8.

4. TADS, 48–49.

5. TADS, 49–51.

6. In the Thirteenth Decennial Census, State of Illinois, County of Cooke, Vol. 096, Enumeration District 1313, Family Visitation Number 0045, Joshua L. Dorsey is listed as a "druggist" and an "employer." Interview, Jan. 21, 1977, pp. 1–3 and 10–13. TADS, 55–56; also certified copy of State of Illinois, Cook County, Marriage License and Marriage Certificate #1079865 issued to Dorsey on July 31, 1925.

7. Interview, Jan. 19, 1977, pp. 20–21. On the T.O.B.A., see Smith, *Music on My Mind,* 105; Giles Oakley, *The Devil's Music: A History of the Blues* (New York: Taplinger, 1976), 104, and Albertson, *Bessie,* 66.

8. TADS, 57–58.

9. Interviews: Jan. 21, 1977, p. 22, and Jan. 21, 1977, pp. 6–7; TADS, 59–60.

10. TADS, 60–61; interview, Jan. 21, 1977, p. 25a.

11. TADS, 62.

12. TADS, 42; interview, Jan. 19, 1977, pp. 5–8.

13. Interview, Jan. 21, 1977, p. 42. Dorsey is not alone in his thought on the insignificant distinction between the sacred and secular in black culture. See, for example, Levine, *Black Culture and Black Consciousness:* "Neither the slaves nor their African forebears ever drew modernity's clear line between the sacred and the secular" (p. 30).

14. Interview, Jan. 22, 1977, p. 6.

15. TADS, 43; interview, Jan. 19, 1977, pp. 1 and 13.

16. Interview, Jan. 19, 1977, pp. 21–23.

17. James H. Cone, *The Spirituals and the Blues: An Interpretation* (San Francisco: Harper and Row, 1972). Throughout Chapter 6, "The Blues: A Secular Spiritual," Cone writes of the misinterpretation of the blues by the black church. Interview, Jan. 19, 1977, pp. 21–23.

18. Interviews: Jan. 19, 1977, p. 7, and Jan. 22, 1977, p. 4.

19. Interviews: Jan. 19, 1977, pp. 2 and 18; Jan. 30, 1976, p. 31; and Jan. 29, 1976, p. 41.

20. Interview, Feb. 2, 1976, p. 52.

21. Interview, Jan. 19, 1977, p. 10.

22. Interview, Jan. 19, 1977, p. 9.

23. Interview, Jan. 19, 1977, pp. 2–3.

24. Ibid.

25. See, for example, George Pullen Jackson, ed., *Spiritual Folk-Songs of Early*

America: Two Hundred and Fifty Tunes and Texts With an Introduction and Notes (1937, rpt. New York: Dover, 1964), 153. Jackson prints the original version of the source tune, *New Britain,* and an embellished version he recorded in Nashville, Tennessee, in 1936. See also Townsend, *Baptist Standard Hymnal,* p. 427. The original tune here is *Willa;* as it is ornamented, however, it bears striking resemblance to the embellished version of *New Britain* in Jackson's *Spiritual Folk-Songs.* Of even more note though is the printing of the ornamented version in the hymnal. Since Dr. A. M. Townsend, husband of the editor, is recorded as the "arranger" of the ornamented version, the implicit message is that both Townsends wanted to encourage embellishment of at least this hymn and perhaps similar treatment of others.

26. Ann Williams and E. Jennings, "Churches and Voluntary Associations in Chicago: Earliest Baptist Negro Community," in Historical Letters and Records of the Hall Library Branch of the Chicago Public Library, Microfilm No. 2, pp. [4–5]; also Perry J. Stackhouse, *Chicago and the Baptists: A Century of Progress* (Chicago: Univ. of Chicago Press, 1933), 49; Spear, *Black Chicago,* 91–97, 174–78. Spear's term "old-line" will be used to designate the group of original and original-split Baptist and Methodist churches in black Chicago. This usage varies slightly from Spear's because his classification of "old-line" churches seems inconsistent with his definition of the term. He speaks of most of the original-split churches (Pilgrim, Progressive, Monumental, etc.) as having an average membership of 500 and as being "primarily migrant churches [that] provided a middle ground between the formal, old-line northern congregations and the emotional, uninhibited storefronts" (p. 178). Among those churches he classifies as "old-line," however, he mentions Olivet Baptist Church and Quinn Chapel, both of whose memberships were substantially larger than 500. These two churches, he continues, experienced the largest growth of membership among black churches during the migration period (1915–20). Such a large growth is evidence that these "old-line" churches were themselves "migrant" churches at least as much as those he designates. "Old-line" here will include, therefore, Olivet and Quinn as well as Pilgrim, Progressive, and so on, especially since the two other principal studies on black churches in Chicago (Sutherland, and Drake and Cayton) classify all these churches together.

27. Frazier, *The Negro Church.* See Chapter 3, "The Negro Church: A Nation within a Nation," and Chapter 5, "The Negro Church and Assimilation." Quote from Payne, *History of the A. M. E. Church,* 457.

28. George D. Lewis, "The Chicago Choral Study Club," MS 89, Illinois Writers Project, p. 1. Various sources disagree on the date of organization of the club. Lewis says the club was organized "sometime between 1895 and 1898." In an article in the *Inter Ocean* (May 24, 1908, p. 9), "The Negro in Music in Chicago," Glenn Dillard Gunn writes that the club was organized in 1902. Louise Henry, writing for the Illinois Writers Project ("History of Negro Music and Musicians: Data on Early Chicago and the Negro," MS 101, p. 4), asserts that the club was organized in 1900. For the purposes of this study, the consensus among sources that the club was organized around the turn of the century is sufficient.

29. Interview, James Ahlyn Mundy (Chicago), April 2, 1976, pp. 13–14. Next to Dorsey, Mundy was the most informative interviewee on a broad range of subjects central to this study, mostly because he lived in Chicago since 1906 and was recognized as one of the most noted and accomplished among Chicago's black musicians trained in the classical music tradition. He was one of the first accompanists of the

Olivet Choral Study Club from 1906 until 1920, after which he assumed the directorship of the Bethel AME Church choir. In 1925, he switched from there to Pilgrim Baptist Church where, as at Bethel, he led the choir in a number of large choral works among which was Mendelssohn's *Elijah.* His last post, until his death in 1982, was as director of the Senior Choir at Olivet Baptist Church. See also Illinois Writers Project, MS 99, "Negro Music and Musicians in Chicago: James A. Mundy," by George D. Lewis, pp. 1–3.

30. Interview, the Reverend Augustus A. Evans (Memphis), March 24, 1976, p. 12. Mr. Evans was assistant choir director under Edward Boatner at Pilgrim and later an assistant under Dorsey there.

31. Interviews: Edward H. S. Boatner (New York), Sept. 26, 1977, pp. 16–18, 25–29, and 33, and James A. Mundy, pp. 23–25.

32. *Chicago Defender,* p. 12. Interview, the Reverend Junius C. Austin, Jr. (Chicago), Jan. 24, 1977, ll. 295–98. Directors James Mundy and J. Wesley Jones, of Bethel and Metropolitan, respectively, had special reason to challenge each other's reputation. Jones had been Mundy's successor at Bethel when Mundy moved to Pilgrim to direct the choir there in 1920. In 1924, Jones "defected" with Dr. Cook, then the pastor of Bethel, to direct the choir at Cook's new church, Metropolitan. In 1930, Mundy returned to Bethel. In the April 26, 1930, *Defender,* however, the contest was characterized as "purely friendly" (p. 10). Interviews: the Reverend Esther Greer, Assistant Pastor, Metropolitan Community Church (Chicago), Dec. 6, 1977, p. 4; James Mundy, pp. 18, 23, 25); Mrs. Bertha Curry (Chicago), Dec. 9, 1977, pp. 7 and 25.

33. Interview, Augustus Evans, Dec. 13, 1976, p. 13.

34. "Great Musical," *Chicago Defender,* Sept. 22, 1923, p. 5. Interview, Augustus Evans, Dec. 13, 1976, p. 22.

35. Interview (Chicago), Dec. 6, 1977, ll. 154–68 and 148–50.

36. Illinois Writers Project, MS 89, passim. William Page, "Young Negro Musicians in Chicago: Outlets for Musical Expression," Microfilm No. 5, Illinois Writers Project, Chicago: n.d.

37. Dena J. Epstein, *Sinful Tunes and Spirituals* (Urbana: Univ. of Illinois Press, 1977), 105, 109–10, 197–99. See also Southern, *Music of Black Americans,* 36–42, and "'I Love the Lord, He Heard My Cry': Black Meter Music" and "'What a Friend We Have in Jesus': Hymns of Improvisation," in Wyatt Tee Walker, *"Somebody's Calling My Name": Black Sacred Music and Social Change* (Valley Forge, Penn.: Judson Press, 1979), 73–96 and 97–126, respectively.

38. Interviews: Edward Boatner, p. 16; James A. Mundy, pp. 14–15, 21, and 29; and Augustus Evans, March 24, 1976, pp. 1–2.

39. Interviews: Edward Boatner, pp. 41–43; Mrs. Sallie Martin (Chicago), March 28, 1976, pp. 12–13.

40. Interviews: Mrs. Bertha Curry, p. 15; and Mrs. Sallie Martin, p. 30.

41. Interviews: James Mundy, p. 15; Augustus Evans, pp. 1–2; Edward Boatner, p. 15.

42. Interview, James Mundy, p. 16.

43. Ibid. Levine, *Black Culture and Black Consciousness,* 158–70.

44. Work, *Folk Song of the American Negro,* 90–99 passim. Antonín Dvořák, "Music in America," *Harper's Magazine* XC (1885): 432.

45. "Introduction," in J. Rosamond Johnson, trans., *Utica Jubilee Singers*['] *Spir-*

ituals: As Sung at the Utica Normal and Industrial Institute of Mississippi (Boston: Oliver Ditson, 1930), v–vi.

46. See Albert B. Lord, *The Singer of Tales* (1960, rpt. New York: Atheneum, 1973), 136–38. Lord's description of the substitution of written and printed texts for the oral epic song in Yugoslavia and the detrimental effect of "this disease" (p. 137) of literacy is strikingly similar to the near-loss of the spirituals of black Americans. Also see "Folk Music," in George Herzog, *Research in Primitive and Folk Music in the United States,* Bulletin No. 24 (Washington, D.C.: American Council of Learned Societies, 1936), 45–97. Herzog notes that students of folk song, usually of literary backgrounds, relied more on the textual transcription than on the live record of folk performances. The result was a science of which the source was a "by-product" (p. 46) of practice rather than the practice itself.

47. Interview, James Mundy, pp. 6–8.

48. *Jubilee Songs: Complete. As Sung by the Jubilee Singers of Fisk University* (New York: Bigelow and Maine, [1872]), 3. On the collection of black music by students of folksong, see "Introduction," in Bernard Katz, ed., *The Social Implications of Early Negro Music in the United States* (New York: Arno Press, 1969), vii–xii; Henry E. Krehbiel, *Afro-American Folksongs: A Study in Racial and National Music* (New York: G. Schirmer, 1914), vii–ix; and [William F. Allen, Charles P. Ware, Lucy M. Garrison], *Slave Songs of the United States* (New York: A. Simpson, 1867). For the most detailed account of the role of whites in encouraging blacks to sing their own songs, see R. Nathaniel Dett, ed., *Religious Folk-Songs of the Negro: As Sung at Hampton Institute* (Hampton, Va.: Hampton Institute Press, 1927). This is the original collection of "jubilee songs" for which Hampton's singers were noted. Dett's new arrangements of this music comprise the fourth edition of *Religious Folk-Songs.* In the prefaces of the three previous editions (1874, 1891, 1909), all of which Dett included with his, there is almost a running account by the white writers of those prefaces of their students' attitudes toward the spiritual as sung at Hampton. See also Work, *Folk Song of the American Negro,* 114.

49. On the musical training of slave song collectors, see, for example, Epstein, *Sinful Tunes,* Chapter 16, "Slave Songs of the United States: Its Editors," 303–20. Quote from interview, Edward Boatner, p. 15. On attitudes toward the spiritual, see James Weldon Johnson, ed., *The Second Book of Negro Spirituals* (New York: Viking, 1926), 18.

50. For a discussion of this manifestation of American musical nationalism within the broader historical context of the idea, see Barbara A. Zuck, *A History of Musical Americanism* (Ann Arbor: UMI Research Press, 1980), passim. She discusses Dvořák on pp. 56–59. See also Dvořák, "Music in America," passim.

51. Arthur Farwell through the Wa-Wan Press he founded was one of the most noted composers of American classical music based on folk music. See Zuck, *A History of Musical Americanism,* 64–66. On Burleigh's songs, see U.S. Copyright Office Records: "Two negro spirituals; words from Jubilee songs, music arr. by H[arry] T[hacker] Burleigh; 4 pt. mixed chorus, 8vo. Contents: 1) Dig my grave. 2) Deep River." Registration Number: E 330130.

52. Neither Mundy nor any of the other directors I interviewed could remember the specific pieces Mrs. Hackley introduced at the Exposition, although each knew of her role. According to records at the U.S. Copyright Office, only three of Burleigh's and one of Dett's songs were published by 1915: Burleigh's *Deep River* (see note

above); *I'll Be Dar to Meet Yo'* from *Two Plantation Songs* (registered April 15, 1907, published by Schirmer); *Child, Jesus Comes from Heav'nly Heights* (registered Dec. 16, 1912 [E 299656], published by Ricordi); and Dett's *Listen to the Lambs* (registered July 30, 1914 [E 346817], published by Schirmer). Quote from interview, James Mundy, pp. 6–7, 15–18. See more about Hackley in Southern, *Music of Black Americans*, 435. Also see the E. Azalia Hackley Collection at the Detroit Public Library. When I surveyed this collection, I was unaware of Hackley's role in Chicago. Judging from the reams of memorabilia, much of which is uncatalogued, I would not consider the effort in vain when in Detroit again to look for documentation of her role in worship music in Chicago within the collection.

53. Nashville, Tenn.: Sunday School Publishing Board, National Baptist Convention, 1927.

54. Illinois Writers Project, MS 99, "Dr. William Henry Smith," 1–2.

55. Zora Neale Hurston, "Spirituals and Neo-Spirituals," in *Negro: An Anthology. Collected and Edited by Nancy Cunard* (1933, rpt. New York: Frederick Ungar, 1970), 224.

56. Interview, James Mundy, p. 21.

Chapter 6

Old-Line Religion and Urban Migrants

1. TADS, 27; interview, Jan. 18, 1977, l. 255.

2. Interview, Jan. 18, 1977, ll. 244–45.

3. Studies of black churches in Chicago have tended to place migrants in churches in which the worship demeanor was highly demonstrative. See Sutherland, "An Analysis of Negro Churches," 4–7; St. Clair Drake, "Churches and Voluntary Associations in the Chicago Negro Community," typescript (Works Progress Administration, 1940), especially "Urbanizing the New-comers['] Church," 146–51; Drake and Cayton, *Black Metropolis,* 412–29, 611–53, and 670–88; Vattel E. Daniel, "Ritual and Stratification in Chicago Negro Churches," *American Sociological Review* 7, no. 3 (June 1942): 352–61, passim. For studies on migrant preferences in black churches outside of Chicago, see, for example, Gunnar Myrdal, *An American Dilemma: The Negro Problem and Modern Democracy,* 2 vols. (New York: Harper and Brothers, 1944), 935–42; and Mays and Nicholson, *The Negro's Church,* 35–37; and Frazier, *The Negro Church,* Chapter 4, "Negro Religion in the City," 52–71.

4. Mays and Nicholson, *The Negro's Church,* 179 and 106; Sutherland, "An Analysis of Negro Churches," 136; Spear, *Black Chicago,* pp. 142 and 178; Chicago Commission on Race Relations, *The Negro in Chicago,* 79; Hall, *Negroes in the United States: 1920–32,* 551.

5. See Spear, *Black Chicago,* 93, and Drake and Cayton, *Black Metropolis,* 612, for two studies of "lower class" and religious preferences. On black ministers' transmittal of white values, see Daniel, *The Education of Negro Ministers,* 27 and 32: "The purpose of this movement [to train former slaves as ministers] seems to have been to enable the freedmen to assimilate the white man's culture more rapidly; . . . [in founding] Negro schools . . . there seems to be no evidence of . . . a desire to change from the type of education offered in the schools controlled by whites. The curricula of the former and the latter are convincingly alike."

6. For a full discussion of this problem, see "Migrant and Northern Negroes," in Louise V. Kennedy, *The Negro Peasant Turns Cityward: Effects of Recent Migrations to Northern Centers* (1930, rpt. New York: AMS Press, 1968), 221–26. In addition to Kennedy, see Spear, *Black Chicago,* 168; Drake and Cayton, *Black Metropolis,* 73.

7. Feb. 10, 1917, [editorial page].

8. Spear, *Black Chicago,* 178; untranscribed interview, Mrs. Lena McLin Franklin, Secretary of Pilgrim Baptist Church (1926 to [1982?]), (Chicago), Jan. 24, 1977; interview, Junius C. Austin, Jr., ll. 149–53.

9. Frazier, *The Negro Church,* 58–60; and Drake and Cayton, *Black Metropolis,* 645–53 passim .

10. See Table 17 in Drake and Cayton, *Black Metropolis,* 414; also Spear, *Black Chicago,* 75–77 and 179.

11. Drake and Cayton, *Black Metropolis,* 612–13 and 614.

12. Ibid., 673–79; Spear, *Black Chicago,* 175; Sutherland, "Analysis of Negro Churches," 6–7. These studies have in common their efforts to investigate—to differing degrees—the social context of religion in black Chicago. But their more significant bond can be found in the data they share. Sutherland's is the oldest, having been completed in 1930 and based on data collected by the author beginning in 1928. Drake and Cayton published theirs in 1938. But since they wrote of the 1920s as well, they used much of Sutherland's data, especially his models. Working with these classifications, they collected data throughout the early and middle thirties that appeared in 1940 as Drake's "Churches and Voluntary Associations. . . ." This work formed the database for the critique of black religion in *Black Metropolis.* Each of these works informed Spear's 1967 *Black Chicago.* He wrote that Sutherland's research results had been "useful" and that the "classic" Drake and Cayton investigation had been helpful in "suggesting a framework for study" (pp. 237 and 234).

13. Statistics calculated from figures available for 1910 and 1920 in Chicago Commission on Race Relations, *The Negro in Chicago,* 106 and 602. For 1916 to 1920, see Drake and Cayton, *Black Metropolis,* 8.

14. Mays and Nicholson, *The Negro's Church,* 38, and Spear, *Black Chicago,* 175. On improvisation and the black preacher, see Charles V. Hamilton, *The Black Preacher in America* (New York: William Morrow, 1972), 28–32, 69, and passim. This idea is well developed in historical and literary sources on black Americans. Hamilton is mentioned here because of his subthesis that the black preacher's ability to improvise made him a "linkage figure" to help ease the emotional stress on black Americans at three "crucial" points in their history—enslavement, emancipation, and migration. On 'bearing up' a black preacher, see Zora Neale Hurston's "Spirituals and Neo-Spirituals," in Cunard's *Negro,* 225. Accounts of this type of worship response are usually only descriptive, with the result being an emphasis on the pervasiveness of emotionalism. Hurston's article (pp. 223–25) and two others she prepared for *Negro* ("Shouting," 34–35, and "The Sermon," 35–39) are useful because she analyzes the structure of this type of worship and the patterns of responses.

15. Miles M. Fisher, *The Master's Slave: Elijah John Fisher, A Biography* (Philadelphia: Judson Press, 1922), 88; interview, Junius C. Austin, Jr., ll. 408–13; Drake and Cayton, *Black Metropolis,* 673–74.

16. Mays and Nicholson, *The Negro's Church,* 51 and Chapter 3, "The Negro Ministry," passim. Frazier, *The Negro Church,* 57.

17. Interview, Jan. 22, 1977, p. 13.

18. "Mother," in *Inspirational Thoughts,* 59.

19. TADS, 41; interview, Jan. 19, 1977, pp. 12–16.

20. TADS, 61.

21. Lomax, *Mister Jelly Roll,* 184–88. Also O'Neal and O'Neal, "Georgia Tom Dorsey," 23–24.

22. Thomas A. Dorsey, "President's Annual Address to the National Convention of Gospel Choirs and Choruses, Inc., at Washington, D.C. [1947]" (unpublished), [p. 1]. Dorsey's recollection may contain inaccuracies. The Godrich and Dixon discography lists no recording for the Pace Jubilee Singers before 1927; in fact, no recording of *I'm Going Through Jesus* appears for this group. But the discography is not conclusive evidence that the Pace singers failed to record the piece, since their songs "of little interest" (p. 575) were not listed. Dorsey's recollection may be correct; the recording quite possibly could have failed to meet the criteria for Godrich's and Dixon's listing of "genuinely 'black' records" (p. 7). Even more questionable, then, is why it would have "sold into the millions." In an address to the Convention, Dorsey was not obligated to fix dates and otherwise relate information factually; he emphasized broad ideas. This address in particular may have been constructed with a broader theme in mind, in that it was presented at the fifteenth anniversary of the Convention.

23. Interview, Jan. 19, 1977, p. 10.

24. Theodore Winton Thorson, "A History of Music Publishing in Chicago: 1850–1960" (Ph.D. diss., Northwestern University, 1961), 202.

25. TADS, 65.

26. Interviews: Augustus A. Evans, Mar. 24, 1976, pp. 6–8, 15–16, and Sallie Martin, p. 22.

27. TADS, 63 and 65.

28. TADS, 64; interview, Jan. 21, 1977, p. 35.

29. Theodore Thorson, "A History of Music Publishing in Chicago," 205.

30. TADS, 65. Dixon and Godrich, *Recording the Blues,* 42. See also Godrich and Dixon, *Blues and Gospel Records,* 20–21, for a general description of Brunswick's "race" series between 1923 and 1932.

31. TADS, 66. Godrich and Dixon, *Blues and Gospel Records,* 721–22. Godrich and Dixon mention that Whitaker is an "assumed" name and that Tampa Red's real name is "Hudson Woodbridge" (p. 721). In an interview with the author, Whitaker makes no mention of another name other than Tampa Red. He lived in a public nursing home under the name Hudson Whitaker (non-recorded interview, Chicago, April 3, 1976).

32. TADS, 67.

33. Dixon and Godrich, *Recording the Blues,* 60–61.

34. Howard W. Odum and Guy B. Johnson, *The Negro and His Songs: A Study of Typical Negro Songs in the South* (Chapel Hill: Univ. of North Carolina Press, 1925), 166.

35. For information on the recording industry's setting trends as opposed to blacks' doing so, see Mike Rowe, *Chicago Breakdown* (New York: Da Capo Press,

1979), 15: The blues sound was not always a "barometer of black taste but more . . . the commercial interpretation of that feeling." Hudson Whitaker defined "hokum" as a dance "a little different from a slow drag" (unrecorded interview). On Dorsey's and Whitaker's recordings, see TADS, 36–37, and Dixon and Godrich, *Recording the Blues,* 62–63. Also see Godrich and Dixon, *Blues and Gospel Records,* 206–8, 233, 360, 368–69, 608, and 721–25.

36. TADS, 67.

37. Interview, Jan. 21, 1977, p. 27.

Chapter 7

Preachers and Bluesmen

1. Interview, Jan. 22, 1977, p. 16; Ira D. Sankey, *My Life and the Story of the Gospel Hymns and of Sacred Songs and Solos* (Philadelphia: Sunday School Times, 1907), 50.

2. Of the 278 churches in Sutherland's "An Analysis of Negro Churches in Chicago," 47.8% were Baptist (p. 55). *Gospel Pearls,* p. [4]. On "gospel" singers at the 1925 National Baptist Convention meetings, see *Journal of the Forty-fifth Annual Session of the National Baptist Convention: Held with the Baptist Churches: Baltimore, Maryland, September 9–14, 1925,* 31 and 108.

3. Dixon and Godrich, *Recording the Blues,* 37–38. For a thorough history of African American quartet singing and recording in the early decades of the twentieth century, see "'One Hundred Years of Harmony Singing,'" in Kip Lornell's *"Happy in the Service of the Lord": Afro-American Gospel Quartets in Memphis* (Urbana: Univ. of Illinois Press, 1988), 11–35.

4. *His Eye Is on the Sparrow,* recorded September 1927; released by Paramount (Pm 12630). *Monday Morning Blues,* released by OKeh (4345); *Big Fat Mamma, Strut Miss Lizzie* (Okeh 4380 and 8007, respectively), *Who Built the Ark?* and *I Hope I May Join the Band* (both OKeh 4400). All listings of these recordings are referenced in Godrich and Dixon, *Blues and Gospel Records,* 564–65 and 567, respectively.

5. Interview, Jan. 21, 1977, pp. 33–36.

6. Interview, Jan. 21, 1977, ll. 2021–33.

7. See Levine, *Black Culture and Black Consciousness,* 217, for the "communal" context for slave music; see pp. 217–21 for a discussion of the rise of the solo voice in secular song after slavery. See also Epstein, *Sinful Tunes,* passim, for discussions of various aspects of slave music.

8. The idea of the solo and choral orientation of Afro-American song has been applied to secular and sacred music, respectively, and has been alluded to in several studies, but needs more extensive analysis. Gilbert Chase put it most eloquently in an earlier edition of *America's Music:* "The spirituals are the manifestation of Afro-American folk music in choral singing. The blues are the manifestation of Afro-American folk music in solo singing" (448).

9. For a representative critique of the declaratory role of the blues, see Janheinz Jahn, *Muntu: An Outline of the New African Culture,* Marjorie Grene, trans. (1958; 2nd ed., New York: Grove Press, 1961), 221: "One song *in* the community becomes one song *before* the community, for the community is now only a listener."

10. For an extensive discussion of the similarities between the bluesman and the preacher, see Charles Keil, *Urban Blues* (Chicago: Univ. of Chicago Press, 1966): "Participation in the musical life of the church and intimate knowledge of and passionate living within the Negro reality provide both the mold and the raw materials for blues lyrics and sermons" (pp. 143–44). On sermon structure, particularly chanting and its similarity to blues, see Bruce A. Rosenberg, *The Art of the American Folk Preacher*, Chapter 4, "Chanting," 35–45.

11. See Epstein, *Sinful Tunes*, 217.

12. Frazier, *Negro Church*, 35–40.

13. Daniel, *The Education of Negro Ministers*, 27 and 32.

14. See Keil, *Urban Blues:* "The transition . . . from blues role to preacher role is unidirectional but peculiarly appropriate and smooth for anyone who cares to make the shift" (p. 148). See also Rosenberg, *The Art of the American Folk Preacher*, 41.

15. Oliver, *Songsters and Saints*, 140–41 and 145.

16. Dixon and Godrich, *Recording the Blues*, 38 and 56–57.

17. See Paul Oliver's description of the formulaic qualities of the recorded sermon on p. 153 of *Songsters and Saints*. He finds the introductory part represented so consistently "as to suggest that it was a formula required by the recording companies which accorded with common practice" (p. 153). Also see pp. 274–75 for annual income figures for blacks and pp. 145–46 on length of time for recordings.

18. For a list of Nix's 1927 recordings, see Godrich and Dixon, *Blues and Gospel Records*, 562–63. On his *Black Diamond Express to Hell* sermon and sales figures, see Dixon and Godrich, *Recording the Blues*, 56–57.

19. Vocalion Records No. 1149, recorded October 1927.

20. For a complete listing of Nix's recorded sermons, see Godrich and Dixon, *Blues and Gospel Records*, 562–64.

21. Interview, Dec. 12, 1977, ll. 330 and 340.

22. On the climax in black sermons, see Henry H. Mitchell, *Black Preaching* (1970, rpt. San Francisco: Harper and Row, 1979): "In order to accomplish [the Black climax], the Black preacher has shifted from objective fact to subjective testimony—from "he said" and "it happened" to "I feel" and "I believe" (pp. 188–89).

23. Interview, Jan. 21, 1977, pp. 33–36; TADS, 64.

24. In a rather probing analysis of the contrast between responses to the bluesman and to the preacher, anthropologist John Szwed has concluded that "[Afro-American] church music is directed *collectively* to God; blues are directed *individually* to the *collective* ("Musical Adaptation among Afro-Americans," *Journal of American Folklore* 82 [1969]: 117 [emphasis added]).

25. Interview, Jan. 29, 1976, ll. 2360–62.

26. Ibid., ll. 2370–73, 2425–27, and 2374–76.

27. "Baptists, Inc., Gather for Golden Jubilee in Chicago," *Chicago Defender*, Aug. 16, 1930, pp. 1 and 3. "Baptist Convention, Inc., Delegates Fail to Register," *Chicago Defender*, Aug. 24, 1930, pp. 1 and 16. On the divisiveness that had plagued the Convention since its founding, see Washington, *Frustrated Fellowship*, especially Chapter 7, "The Seeming End of a Painful Quest, 1889–1895," 159–85.

28. *Proceedings of the 50th Annual Session Jubilee Anniversary of the National Baptist Convention*, 44. *Chicago Defender*, Aug. 24, 1930, p. 16. For background information on Anita Brown and Florence Price, see Southern, *Music of Black Americans*, 277–78 and 416–18.

29. *Proceedings*, 34, 36, 47–48, 51, and 58. According to Clarence Boyer, a specialist in African American gospel music history, Fisher was Willa Mae Ford Smith, the well-known gospel singer who was most recently featured in the film *Say Amen, Somebody*, produced and directed by George T. Nierenberg (1986). There is no evidence other than Smith's verification of this in a telephone conversation with Boyer sometime around June 1988.

30. TADS, 70; interview, Feb. 2, 1976, ll. 3845–82.

31. Interview, Feb. 2, 1976, ll. 3830–38. Godrich and Dixon, *Blues and Gospel Records, 1902–1943,* for Dorsey with Broonzy, p. 75, with Brasswell, p. 108, as Georgia Tom, pp. 207–8, with the Famous Hokum Boys, p. 233, with Kansas City Kitty, pp. 420–21, with Lucas, pp. 458–9, as George Ramsey, p. 608, with Tampa Red, p. 724, and with Peggy Waller, p. 798. *She Can Love So Good* and *You Rascal You* were recorded together "c. mid-August 1930" (p. 724).

32. TADS, 65 and 69–70; interviews: Dec. 3, 1977, ll. 396–409, 111–28, and 210–25, and Feb. 2, 1976, ll. 3883 and 3893. "Baptists, Inc., Gather for Golden Jubilee in Chicago," *Chicago Defender*, Aug. 16, 1930, p. 16. On Lucie Campbell, see Southern, *Music of Black Americans,* 453.

33. Interview, Dec. 3, 1977, ll. 103–6 and 127–28.

34. TADS, 69–70; interviews: Dec. 3, 1977, ll. 152–66, 248–70, and Feb. 2, 1976, ll. 3886–3905.

35. TADS, 69; interview, Dec. 3, 1977, ll. 424–34.

Chapter 8

The emergence of Gospel Blues

1. Interview, April 2, 1976, ll. 1251–79.

2. Interview, Jan. 15, 1977, ll. 416–24.

3. Interviews: Jan. 19, 1977, ll. 763–69, and March 29, 1976, ll. 439–42.

4. Interview, Jan. 19, 1977, ll. 286–314.

5. Charles L. Perdue, Jr., Thomas E. Barden, and Robert K. Phillips, eds., *Weevils in the Wheat: Interviews with Virginia Ex-Slaves* (1976, rpt. Bloomington: Indiana Univ. Press, 1980), 119. Willis Laurence James, "The Romance of the Negro Folk Cry in America," in Alan Dundes, [ed.], *Mother Wit from the Laughing Barrel: Readings in the Interpretation of Afro-American Folklore* (1973, rpt. New York: Garland, 1981), 438–39.

6. *My Southern Home: Or, The South and Its People* (Boston: A. G. Brown, 1880), 193.

7. Interviews: Dec. 3, 1977, ll. 619–22 and 1628–31, and Jan. 22, 1977, pp. 14 and 16; TADS, 63–64.

8. Interview, April 3, 1976, pp. 13–14.

9. Ibid., 14.

10. *Chicago Defender,* Aug. 24, 1930, p. 16.

11. Interview, Junius C. Austin, Jr., ll. 408–10.

12. *Chicago Defender,* Sept. 10, 1921, p. 16. Miles Mark Fischer, "Organized Religion and the Cults," *The Crisis* 44, no. 1 (Jan. 1937): 9. On Elder Lucy Smith, pastor of the All Nations Pentecostal Church, see Spear, *Black Chicago,* 176–77.

13. Interview, James A. Mundy p. 28.

NOTES TO PAGES 187-92

14. Ibid.

15. Interview, Esther Greer, ll. 521–23, 556–57, 857–63, and 601. See also George D. Lewis, "Spirituals of Today," p. 9: This gospel chorus, "the first one in Chicago . . . existed since early in 1928 under the direction of Mrs. Magnolia Lewis (Butts)." Also see Lewis's "Negro Music and Musicians," Microfilm No. 5, n.p.: "In trying to trace the gospel choir to its foundation we found that The Metropolitan Community Center had a choir in 1929 [sic] under the direction of Mrs. Magnolia Lewis (Butts)." Mundy's, Greer's, and Lewis's use of the term "gospel chorus" should not be construed as the designation of those early groups. Lewis was writing in the late thirties or early forties about the gospel movement. By that time almost any large group devoted to indigenous music was labeled a gospel "chorus" or "choir." Mundy and Greer were interviewed in 1977. The term might have slipped into their narratives because "gospel" was the topic of discussion at that point in the interview. Moreover, Metropolitan's choir was named the W. D. Cook Gospel Choir in 1930. Bethel's and Quinn's choirs seem not to have had that designation before then either.

16. Bethel's series of Sunday forums was but one of the pioneering efforts of Reverdy C. Ransom that made Bethel a truly sophisticated church. He later left Bethel in order to found the Institutional Church and Social Settlement where he placed more emphasis on social concerns. See his autobiography, in which he also describes the building and location of Quinn Chapel: *The Pilgrimage of Harriet Ransom's Son* (Nashville: Sunday School Union, 1949), 81–83; also Spear, *Black Chicago,* 178. Lewis, "Spirituals of Today," 6.

17. For descriptions and history of Metropolitan Community Church, see *A Half Century of Christian Service* (Chicago: Metropolitan Community Church, 1970), 5; Sutherland, "An Analysis of Negro Churches," 7 and 133. Also interview, Esther Greer, ll. 931–53.

18. Spear, *Black Chicago,* 93–97 and 175–77. Drake and Cayton, *Black Metropolis,* 673–74.

19. In 1925 Alain Locke argued that the northern migration was not fully explained by labor and racial conditions in the South or natural disasters such as the boll weevil: "The wash and rush of this human tide on the beach line of the northern city centers is to be explained primarily in terms of a new vision of opportunity, of social and economic freedom, of a spirit to seize, even in the face of an extortionate and heavy toll, a chance for the improvement of conditions. With each successive wave of it, the movement of the Negro becomes more and more a mass movement . . . from medieval America to modern" (*The New Negro* [1925, rpt. New York: Atheneum, 1968], 6).

20. TADS, 71. The W. D. Cook Gospel Choir may not have been the name of this group, since Dorsey allows that a "very few groups" had the name "gospel" [TADS, 71]. Quite possibly, however, the "gospel" designation was included after it became the W. D. Cook Singers in 1930 in memory of the first pastor of Metropolitan who had died in 1930 (*A Half Century of Christian Service,* n.p.).

21. Spear, *Black Chicago,* 178.

22. See George D. Lewis, "Mabel Sanford Lewis," in "Musicians," Illinois Writer's Project, MS 101, p. 2 and passim; also Sutherland, "An Analysis of Negro Churches," 89.

23. Xerox copy of printed "History of the Ebenezer Baptist Church," n.d., [pp. 1–2].

24. Interview, June Levell (Chicago), Dec. 8, 1977, p. 5. Mrs. Levell was a charter member of the gospel chorus at Ebenezer and served as its historian.

25. TADS, 72. Biographical information on Smith has not been located. The information used here was obtained from conversations with members of Ebenezer Baptist Church and is therefore undocumented.

26. Spear, *Black Chicago,* 177–78; interview, Junius C. Austin, Jr., ll. 149–51. Ransom, *The Pilgrimage of Harriet Ransom's Son,* 89.

27. In *Proceedings* (1930), 53, there is a record of Professor Frye singing a solo, *I'm Going Through.* TADS, 72; interview, Dec. 3, 1977, ll. 1055–94.

28. Interview, June Levell, ll. 1029–46 and 220–23.

29. Ibid., ll. 1347–77, 1381–97, 1112–13.

30. Ibid., ll. 217, 221–27, 1137–42, 229–31, 508–9, 1107, and 1117. Also see TADS, 72. "Ebenezer Boasts Largest Gospel Chorus," *Chicago Defender,* Feb. 6, 1932, p. 22.

31. Interview, Junius C. Austin Jr., l. 22: "My father began his pastorate at Pilgrim Baptist Church back in 1926." TADS, 73.

32. Interview, June Levell, ll. 723–28. TADS, 73.

33. Interviews: Junius C. Austin, Jr., ll. 341–47, and Thomas A. Dorsey, Dec. 3, 1977, ll. 1384–85.

34. Interview (New York), Sept. 26, 1977, pp. 44 and 46.

35. Ibid., 45–46.

36. Ibid., 45.

37. Interview Junius C. Austin, Jr., ll. 74–79, 162–63, 335–37, and 67.

38. Interviews: Ibid., ll. 84 and 402–12; Dorsey, Jan. 29, 1976, p. 27.

39. Interview, Dec. 10, 1978, ll. 189–91 and 217–25.

40. Interview, Junius C. Austin, Jr., ll. 335–36, 325–26, 352–58, 441–42.

41. Interview, Dec. 10, 1977, ll. 271–88.

42. Interview, Dorothy Austin Brown (Chicago), March 1976 (partially transcribed).

43. Interview, Mabel Mitchell Hamilton Davis (Chicago), Jan. 22, 1977, ll. 252–55, 277–78, and 330–42.

44. Ibid., ll. 315–24 and 355–68. The latter part of this quotation is a partial paraphrase of the following portions of the interview:

HARRIS Would you say other than the words, other than the words of the music, was there much difference?

MITCHELL Huh uh, none at all.

HARRIS Uh huh. So, you could just play from one to another?

MITCHELL Just play, that's right. . . .

HARRIS I, I was thinking that. 'Cause that's exactly where Mr. Dorsey got his.

MITCHELL Uh huh. That's it, yeah.

HARRIS I mean, he took it right from the pop music.

MITCHELL That's it.

45. Ibid., ll. 385–405.

46. Interviews: Lillian Reescer (Chicago), March 31, 1976, ll. 1406–73, and Mabel W. Craft (Chicago), April 2, 1976, ll. 417–44.

47. Payne, *Recollections,* 253–54.

48. Partially transcribed interview, Bertha Curry, p. 3.

49. *The Souls of Black Folk,* 3.

50. Interview, Augustus Evans, Dec. 13, 1976, 25–26.

Chapter 9

Giving the Gospel a Blues Voice

1. Interview, Jan. 22, 1977, p. 16.

2. Interview, Dec. 10, 1978, ll. 39–52.

HARRIS   So Smith and Frye got together and decided they wanted a chorus?

DORSEY   Yeah.

HARRIS   But you feel that perhaps Frye initially had the idea of a chorus?

DORSEY   Oh, yes. It was his idea.

HARRIS   It appeared that Smith wanted some singing in his church different than the anthems and stuff.

DORSEY   Maybe so, but until he heard it, he didn't know what he was going to get.

3. Interviews: Dec. 10, 1978, ll. 85–86, 93–95, and 143–46; Dec. 3, 1978, ll. 305–6.

4. TADS, 72; interview, Dec. 10, 1978, ll. 223–24.

5. Interview, Dec. 3, 1978, l. 1321. "President's Annual Address to the National Convention of Gospel Choruses at St. Louis, Missouri: August 6th 1942," [p. 1], and "President's Annual Address to the National Convention of Gospel Choirs and Choruses, Inc., Detroit, Michigan," Aug. 9, 1945, [pp. 2–3].

6. The lack of a date of composition, or at least of first performance, for almost all of Dorsey's songs makes for little or no correlation between the composing and publishing of a Dorsey song. This ambiguity is even more a problem when copyright dates are factored in. Dorsey would copyright a song years after it was composed and, in some cases, relatively well known. An example is *Take My Hand, Precious Lord,* which will be discussed later in this chapter. Dorsey wrote it at the end of August or beginning of September 1932. It was sung widely, even appearing in the minutes of the National Baptist Convention in 1935. He copyrighted it, however, in 1938. His first gospel, *If You See My Savior,* was probably composed in late 1927 or early 1928. He copyrighted it in 1928. There is one possible reason, among others, for this variance. In 1928, he was still active in the blues world where one—especially Dorsey, it seems—protected one's songs by copyright. That motivation was virtually non-existent in the early years of gospel, much as it was lacking in the early years of urban blues.

7. Interview, Feb. 2, 1976, ll. 1528–30; TADS, 73.

8. TADS, 72.

9. Interview, Feb. 2, 1976, ll. 2448–55.

10. Interviews: Feb. 2, 1976, ll. 1531–36, and Jan. 26, 1977, ll. 43–47.

11. Interview, Feb. 2, 1976, l. 1777.

12. Interview, Augustus A. Evans, Dec. 13, 1979, ll. 714–30.

13. Interviews: ibid.; Dorsey, Jan. 25, 1977, l. 626.

14. Interview, Dorsey, Jan. 25, 1977, ll. 1056–62. In TADS, Dorsey writes that the singer was Eddie Clifford Davis, "another singer and songwriter" (p. 94). Dorsey never mentioned Davis in any other context, but mentions Allen often. In fact, he links Allen clearly to this venture by remarking that "Gus Evans and . . . Allen were going around singing up the convention" (Jan. 25, 1977, ll. 614–15). Which of the two is insignificant, considering that Dorsey would only allow a singer who most likely had the same "it" to which Evans refers to demonstrate his songs.

15. Interviews: Feb. 2, 1976, l. 1576; Elizabeth Marshall, Dec. 3, 1977, l. 1303. Marshall is a first cousin to Dorsey. She lived with Nettie and Dorsey at their Uncle Joshua's home and was Nettie's closest friend.

16. TADS, 94–95; interview, Jan. 25, 1977, l. 791.

17. Interview, Elizabeth Marshall, l. 1380. Myrtle H. Jones, "Informant" (sister of Nettie), Cook County Coroner's Certificate of Death No. 25300.

18. Interviews: Dorsey, Jan. 15, 1977, ll. 299–311; Evans, Dec. 13, 1979, ll. 909, 928–30; Elizabeth Marshall, ll. 1437, 1444–45.

19. TADS, 96. Interview, Elizabeth Marshall, ibid.

20. Interviews: Dorsey, Jan. 15, 1977, ll. 273–74, and Elizabeth Marshall, ll. 1494 and 1512. TADS, 96–97.

21. Interview, Jan. 25, 1977, l. 476. Godrich and Dixon, *Blues and Gospel Records*, 208. Dorsey recorded *Don't Leave Me Here* on Feb. 3, 1932, *If You Want Me to Love You* on Feb. 5, and *M and O Blues* (Parts I and II) on April 21. He recorded two of his printed gospels, *How About You* and *If You See My Savior* on March 17.

22. TADS, 62.

23. Interviews: Augustus Evans, Dec. 13, 1979, ll. 714–30, and Dorsey, Jan. 21, 1977, l. 479. TADS, 65 and 70. Godrich and Dixon, *Blues and Gospel Records*, 208.

24. TADS, 69 and 71.

25. Ibid., 98.

26. *Hymnal*, No. 404, p. 333. On the hymn, tune, author, and composer of *Must Jesus*, see Katharine Smith Diehl, ed., *Hymns & Tunes: An Index* (New York: Scarecrow Press, 1966), 183 and 737–38. Interviews: Jan. 15, 1977, l. 337, and Dec. 12, 1977, ll. 631, 636, and 638–39.

27. For a discussion of Shepherd and Mason and the introduction of hymns into Nonconformist worship, see John Julian, ed., "Shepherd, Thomas" and "English Hymnody, Early [secs. 11–12]," in *A Dictionary of Hymnology: Setting Forth the Origin and History of Christian Hymns of All Ages and Nations*, rev. ed. (London: John Murray, 1915), 1054–55 and 349, respectively.

28. (Oberlin: James M. Fitch, 1844). On background and history of *Must Jesus Bear the Cross Alone?*, see Robert Guy McCutchan, *Our Hymnody: A Manual of the Methodist Hymnal* (New York: Methodist Book Concern, 1937), 313–14. Mc-Cutchan indicates that the first stanza had been altered substantially, before Allen became known for his setting, presumably; by whom, no has been able to document: "Shall Simon bear the Cross alone, / and other Saints be free? / Each Saint of thine

shall find his own, / And there is one for me" (p. 313). On the appearance of Allen's *Must Jesus* in hymnals, see Diehl, *Hymns & Tunes*. Her selection of hymnals to index and her criteria for doing so (pp. v–vi, xx, and xxii) show that this hymn appears widely throughout American hymnals.

29. Mitchell, *Black Preaching*, 188–89.

30. On Allen as a pupil of Mason, see Samuel J. Rogal, comp., *Guide to the Hymns and Tunes of American Methodism*, Music Reference Collection, No. 7 (New York: Greenwood Press, 1986), 219. On Lowell Mason in general, see Chase, *America's Music*, 151–61; quotes from pp. 153–55.

31. Interview, Feb. 2, 1976, pp. 38–39.

32. Interview, Jan. 15, 1977, pp. 10–12 and 77.

Chapter 10

A Place for Gospel Blues in Old-Line Religion

1. Interview, Feb. 2, 1976, p. 40.

2. Mays, *The Negro's God as Reflected in His Literature* (1938, rpt. New York: Negro Universities Press, 1969), 245, and 248–49.

3. Hurston, "The Sanctified Church," in *Zora Neale Hurston: The Sanctified Church,* [Netzahaulcoyotl Historical Society, ed.] (Berkeley: Turtle Island, 1981), 103 and 104. Hurston's article, coming out as it did in the 1920s, antedates the most noted study of spirit possession as an Africanism in African American worship: Melville J. Herskovits, *The Myth of the Negro Past* (1941, rpt. Gloucester, Mass.: Peter Smith, 1970). See particularly sec. 4 of Chapter 7, "The Contemporary Scene: Africanisms in Religious Life," 224–35. For a more recent analysis of the Africanness of African American culture, especially its development in slavery and its evolution thereafter, see Sterling Stuckey, "Introduction: Slavery and the Circle of Culture," Chapter 1 in *Slave Culture: Nationalist Theory and the Foundations of Black America* (New York: Oxford Univ. Press, 1987), 3–97.

4. Fisher, "Organized Religion and the Cults," 9. Payne *Recollections*, 254 and 256.

5. Dorsey had his music typeset and printed by the Chicago music printing firm of Raynor and Dalheim. In my conversations with company officials, they revealed that Raynor merged with Carqueville Printers, another music printing company in Chicago, "in the late '40s." Carqueville has some of the records related to printing Dorsey's songs, but not all since, according to those officials, Raynor did not have complete ones either. When searching through company records, the earliest "Job Ticket" card I found was for a printing (none of the cards indicates how many copies) of *It's My Desire* dated Sept. 17, 1942. Dorsey registered this piece with the Copyright Office, however, on July 1, 1937. Given that the copyright dates correspond little to the composition of a Dorsey song and given as well that the first circulation of Dorsey's pieces do not correlate necessarily with either composition or copyright dates, it should not be surprising that neither Raynor nor Carqueville has any extant record of printing *Take My Hand, Precious Lord* in 1932. If the number of persons from different parts of the United States who performed this piece at the 1937 National Baptist Convention is an indication, however, some printed version

had to be in circulation prior to its 1938 registration. Interviews: March 29, 1976, ll. 932–33; Feb. 2, 1976, pp. 29 and 40; Dec. 10, 1977, p. 78.

6. Mays, *Negro's God*, 19; John Lovell, Jr., *Black Song: The Forge and the Flame: The Story of How the Afro-American Spiritual Was Hammered Out* (New York: Macmillan, 1972), 190–92. James Weldon Johnson, *God's Trombones* (1927, rpt. New York: Viking Press, 1955), 2. Eugene D. Genovese, *Roll, Jordan, Roll: The World the Slaves Made* (1972, rpt. New York: Vintage, 1976), 266. Also see Raboteau, *Slave Religion*, 243–66, for a full discussion of the role of slave religious song, especially an explanation of performance patterns.

7. J. William Harris, *Plain Folk and Gentry in a Slave Society: White Liberty and Black Slavery in Augusta's Hinterlands* (Middletown, Conn.: Wesleyan Univ. Press, 1985), 54. Perdue, *Weevils in the Wheat;* quotations from interviews with "Rev. Ishrael Massie," p. 208, "Mr. Beverly Jones," pp. 182–83, and "Mrs. Marriah Hines," p. 141. For cross-confirmation of accounts, see, for example, interviews with "Arthur Greene," pp. 123–27, "Mrs. Minnie Folkes," pp. 92–96, "Charles Grandy," pp. 114–19, and "Mrs. Alice Marshall," pp. 201–3. See a broad discussion of meetings in Raboteau, *Slave Religion*, "'Steal Away'," in Chapter 5, pp. 213–19.

8. Ex-slave Hannah Lowery quoted in Raboteau, *Slave Religion*, 217.

9. James O. Breeden, ed., *Advice Among Masters: The Ideal in Slave Management in the Old South,* Contributions in Afro-American and African Studies No. 51 (Westport, Conn.: Greenwood Press, 1980), 276. Raboteau, *Slave Religion*, 217.

10. Interview (Chicago), March 31, 1976: ll. 997–1014 and 1037–39. Nicholas C. Cooper-Lewter and Henry H. Mitchell, *Soul Theology: The Heart of American Black Culture* (San Francisco: Harper & Row, 1986), 149.

11. Interview, Feb. 3, 1976, ll. 957–60.

12. TADS, 78. Interview, Sallie Martin, ll. 647–61 and 751.

13. Interviews: Martin, ll. 604–6, 1290–92, and 1304–7; Dorsey, Jan. 21, 1977, ll. 2147–48.

14. TADS, 79.

15. Ibid., 82.

16. Interview, Feb. 3, 1976, ll. 818–24 and 829–40. Jackson material quoted in Laurraine Goreau, *Just Mahalia, Baby: The Mahalia Jackson Story* (Waco, Tex.: Word Books, 1975), 54–55. The Johnson Singers achieved considerable notoriety. The *Defender* regularly reported on their concerts in the early 1930s and referred to them as famous. See, for example, the *Chicago Defender,* Dec. 24, 1932, p. 13.

17. Goreau, *Just Mahalia*, 54–55 and 57.

18. Interviews: Feb. 3, 1976, ll. 890–91; Dec. 10, 1977, ll. 873–74.

19. Interviews: Feb. 3, 1976; ll. 885–86 and 887–88; Dec. 10, 1977, ll. 883 and 875–79. TADS, 87 and 91.

20. TADS, 91. Goreau, *Just Mahalia*, 52.

21. Jackson sang for the political campaigns and ward meetings of Aldermen Louie B. Anderson and William L. Dawson, the latter in his 1932 race for Congress. She was retained and "managed" by undertaker Robert H. Miller. See Goreau, *Just Mahalia,* 58–59 and 61–62. Frazier, *The Negro Church,* 77–79.

22. Miles M. Fisher, "Organized Religion and the Cults," 9 and 10. Drake and Cayton, *Black Metropolis,* 632. Spear, *Black Chicago,* 176. Robert Weisbrot, *Father Divine and the Struggle for Racial Equality* (Urbana: Univ. of Illinois Press, 1983), 60–61.

23. Interview, Feb. 2, 1976, ll. 1793–96. Interview, Sallie Martin, ll. 1710–13. TADS, 79.

24. Interview, Lilian Reescer, ll. 889–90.

25. George D. Lewis, "Spirituals of Today," 10. "Says Modern Church Music Stirs Feet," *Chicago Defender,* Dec. 24, 1932, p. 11.

26. TADS, 73.

27. "Gospel Choruses Plan Gala Songfest Aug 29," *Chicago Defender,* Aug. 19, 1933, p. 13. There is a problem of dates in this article. It claims that "within two months" the 20 churches had responded to the call to organize choruses issued by Dorsey and colleagues in April 1932. None of the other sources suggests that the rapid proliferation of choruses was quite so precipitous. The others concur in dating the foundings of the various choruses over a year, beginning in April 1932.

28. TADS, 73–74. Interview, Jan. 22, 1977, ll. 733–34.

29. Interview, Fannie P. Hunt (Chicago), March 31, 1976, ll. 477–79, 794–97.

30. Interviews: ibid., ll. 575–80; Lilian Reescer, ll. 664–65, 714–16.

31. TADS, 75. Interview, Lilian Reescer, ll. 470–74.

32. "Gospel Singers Close National Meeting," *Chicago Defender,* Sept. 9, 1933, p. 15.

33. Ibid.

34. Ibid.

35. "Jazz Age Ruining Church Music, Says Choir Director," *Chicago Defender,* Sept. 30, 1933, p. 10.

36. Ibid.

37. Goreau, *Just Mahalia,* 91, Interview, Sallie Martin, ll. 1700–1704.

38. *Proceedings, National Baptist Convention, for 1935,* pp. 40, 41, 46, 50, and 52. *Proceedings, National Baptist Convention for 1937,* pp. 53–54, 57, and 245.

Bibliography

Primary Sources

Archives and Collections

Atlanta Historical Society, Atlanta, Georgia.

Center for the Study of Southern Folklore, Memphis, Tennessee. Information on southern black churches.

Chicago Historical Society, Chicago, Illinois.

E. Azalia Hackley Collection, Detroit Public Library, Michigan.

Georgia State Archives, Atlanta. Carroll and Fulton counties and Atlanta city records.

Private record collection of Bob Vinisky, Memphis, Tennessee. Original sermon and quartet recordings on 78 rpm disks.

National Archives, Atlanta Branch, Atlanta, Georgia. Census tracts and World War I draft registration cards.

State of Illinois, Cook County Department of Health.

Union Theological Seminary Library, New York, New York. National Baptist Convention Annual Proceedings.

United States Copyright Office, Washington, D.C.

Vivian G. Harsh Collection, Carter G. Woodson Branch of the Chicago Public Library, Chicago, Illinois. WPA Illinois Writers Project Papers and miscellaneous primary sources on black Chicagoans.

Dorsey Papers

Dorsey, Thomas A. *Inspirational Thoughts*. Chicago: pub. by author, 1935.

_____. Presidential Addresses delivered to the National Convention of Gospel Choirs and Choruses. 1934–1967.

_____. *Songs With a Message: With My Ups and Downs*. Chicago: pub. by author, 1941.

BIBLIOGRAPHY

————. "The Thomas A. Dorsey Story: From Blues-Jazz to Gospel Song." Chicago, c. 1961. [Referenced throughout as TADS.]

Interviews

Unless noted otherwise, all interviews have been tape-recorded and transcribed. Untranscribed interviews exist only as tape recordings. Partially transcribed interviews exist as transcribed sections and as full tape recordings.

Austin, the Reverend Junius C., Jr. Chicago, Jan. 24, 1977.

Boatner, Edward H. S. New York, Sept. 26, 1977.

Brown, Dorothy Austin. Chicago, March 1976. (Partially transcribed.)

Butler, Velma Johnson. Atlanta, June 7, 1976.

Craft, Mabel W. Chicago, April 2, 1976.

Curry, Bertha. Chicago, Dec. 9, 1977.

Davis, Mabel Mitchell Hamilton. Chicago, Jan. 22, 1977.

Dorsey, Thomas A. Chicago: Jan. 29, 30, Feb. 2, 3, March 29, April 5, 1976; Jan. 15, 17, 18, 19 (the tape of this interview was stolen and was approx. half transcribed), 21, 22, 25, Dec. 3, 10, 1977.

Evans, the Reverend Augustus A. Memphis, March 24, Dec. 13, 1976.

Franklin, Lena McLin. Chicago, Jan. 24, 1977. (Untranscribed.)

Greer, the Reverend Esther. Chicago, Dec. 6, 1977.

Hunt, Fannie P. Chicago, March 31, 1976.

Jones, Bessie. Boston, April 1976. St. Simons Island, Georgia: June 1976. (Both untranscribed.)

Levell, June. Chicago, Dec. 8, 1977.

Marshall, Elizabeth. Chicago, Dec. 3, 1977. (Untranscribed.)

Martin, Sallie. Chicago, March 28, 1976.

Mundy, James Ahlyn. Chicago, April 2, 1976.

Phillips, Carrie Lee Hindsman. Atlanta, July 10, 1976.

Plant, Leon. Villa Rica, Georgia, July 18, 1976.

Reescer, Lilian. Chicago, March 31, 1976.

Whitaker, Hudson ("Tampa Red"). Chicago, April 3, 1976. (Unrecorded.)

Serialized Sources

American Missionary Magazine. 1865–75.

The Atlanta Catalogue of Morehouse College. 1916–20.

Atlanta City Directory. 1896–1918.

The Atlanta Independent. 1912–18.

The Chicago Defender. 1923–34.

Proceedings [or Journal] of the Annual Meeting of the National Baptist Convention. 1921–40.

"Tax Digest." Carroll County Georgia. 1901–8.

BIBLIOGRAPHY

Miscellaneous Primary Sources

[Allen, Richard.] *The Life Experience and Gospel Labors of the Rt. Rev. Richard Allen*. N.d. Reprint. Nashville: Abingdon Press, 1960.

"Carroll County, Georgia, Book of Deeds: Book Y."

"Carroll County, Georgia, Superior Court General Index to Deeds and Mortgages: Grantees L–Z—1828–1934."

Drake, St. Clair. "Churches and Voluntary Associations in the Chicago Negro Community." Works Progress Administration, 1940. Typescript.

Fisher, Miles M. *The Master's Slave: Elijah John Fisher, A Biography*. Philadelphia: Judson Press, 1922.

Green, Eddie, *A Good Man Is Hard to Find*. New York: E. H. Morris & Co., 1917.

"A Half Century of Christian Service." Chicago: Metropolitan Community Church, 1970.

Henry, Louise. "History of Negro Music and Musicians: Data on Early Chicago and the Negro." MS 101. In "Musicians." Illinois Writers Project, Chicago.

Hindsman, C[orrie] M. *The History of Mt. Prospect Baptist Church of Villa Rica[,] Georgia*. Villa Rica: n.p., 1949.

———. *Inspirational Songs*. Atlanta: pub. by author, n.d.

"History of the Ebenezer Baptist Church." Chicago, n.d.

Lewis, George D. "The Chicago Choral Study Club." MS 89. Illinois Writers Project, Chicago.

[———]. "Dr. William Henry Smith." MS 99. Illinois Writers Project, Chicago.

———. "Mabel Sanford Lewis." MS 101. In "Musicians." Illinois Writers Project, Chicago.

———. "Negro Music and Musicians." Microfilm 5. Illinois Writers Project, Chicago.

———. "Spirituals of Today." MS 89. Illinois Writers Project, Chicago.

Logan, Gussie Mims. "The Carrie Steele Orphanage." *The Voice* 1(Nov. 11, 1904): 538–40.

Music Committee of the Sunday School Publishing Board. *Gospel Pearls*. Nashville: Sunday School Publishing Board [of the] National Baptist Convention, U.S.A., [1921].

Page, William. "Young Negro Musicians in Chicago: Outlets for Musical Expression." Microfilm 5. Illinois Writers Project, Chicago.

Payne, Bishop Daniel E. *History of the African Methodist Episcopal Church*. Ed. C. S. Smith. 1891. Reprint. New York: Johnson Reprint Corporation, 1968.

———. *Recollections of Seventy Years*. 1888. Reprint. New York: Arno Press and the New York Times, 1968.

Smith, Ruth A. *The Life and Works of Thomas A. Dorsey*. Chicago: Thomas A. Dorsey, 1935.

State of Georgia, County of Carroll. "Colored Marriage Book." N.p, n.d.

Thompson, John. *The Life of John Thompson, a Fugitive Slave: Containing His History of 25 Years in Bondage and His Providential Escape*. 1856. Reprint. New York: Negro Universities Press, 1968.

Townsend, Mrs. A. M., ed. *The Baptist Standard Hymnal: with Responsive*

Readings: A New Book for All Services. Nashville: Sunday School Publishing Board [of the] National Baptist Convention, U.S.A., 1924.

U.S. Bureau of the Census. *State of Georgia, [9th–12th] Decennial United States Census[es].* Washington, D.C.

————. *State of Illinois, 13th Decennial United States Census.* Washington, D.C.

————. *Negro Population in the United States: 1790–1915.* 1918. Reprint. New York: Arno Press and the New York Times, 1968.

Secondary Sources

Books

Albertson, Chris. *Bessie.* New York: Stein and Day, 1972.

[Allen, William F., Charles P. Ware, and Lucy M. Garrison]. *Slave Songs of the United States.* New York: A. Simpson, 1867.

Anderson, Mary Tally. *The History of Villa Rica: [City of Gold].* Villa Rica, Ga.: Georgia Bicentennial Committee, 1976.

Benson, Louis F. *The English Hymn: Its Development and Use in Worship.* New York: Hodder and Stoughton, 1915.

Bonner, James C. *Georgia's Last Frontier: The Development of Carroll County.* Athens: Univ. of Georgia Press, 1971.

Bowers, Q. David. *Nickelodeon Theaters and Their Music.* Vestal, N.Y.: Vestal Press, 1986.

Bradford, Perry. *Born With the Blues: Perry Bradford's Own Story: The True Story of the Pioneering Blues Singers and Musicians in the Early Days of Jazz.* New York: Oak Publications, 1965.

Breeden, James O., ed. *Advice Among Masters: The Ideal in Slave Management in the Old South.* Contributions in Afro-American and African Studies No. 51. (Westport, Conn.: Greenwood Press, 1980).

Broderick, Francis. *W. E. B. Du Bois: Negro Leader in a Time of Crisis.* Stanford, Cal.: Stanford University Press, 1959.

Brown, William Wells. *My Southern Home: Or, The South and Its People.* Boston: A. G. Brown, 1880.

Burlin, Natalie Curtis. *Negro Folk Songs.* Hampton Series, Nos. 6716, 6726, 6756, and 6766. New York: G. Schirmer, 1918.

Chase, Gilbert. *America's Music from the Pilgrims to the Present.* 1955. Revised 2d ed. New York: McGraw-Hill, 1966.

Charters, Samuel B., IV. *Jazz: New Orleans[,] 1885–1963: An Index to the Negro Musicians of New Orleans.* 1958. Revised. New York: Oak Publications, 1963.

Chicago Commission on Race Relations. *The Negro in Chicago: A Study of Race Relations and a Race Riot.* Chicago: Univ. of Chicago Press, 1922.

Cone, James H. *The Spirituals and the Blues: An Interpretation.* San Francisco: Harper and Row, 1972.

Cooper-Lewter, Nicholas C., and Henry H. Mitchell. *Soul Theology: The Heart of American Black Culture.* San Francisco: Harper & Row, 1986.

Daniel, William A. *The Education of Negro Ministers.* 1925. Reprint. New York: Negro Universities Press, 1969.

Dauer, Alfons M. *Der Jazz: Seine Ursprünge und Seine Entwicklung.* Kassel, Germany: Erich Röth-Verlag, 1958.

Dett, R. Nathaniel, ed. *The Dett Collection of Negro Spirituals: Originals, Settings, Anthems, Motets.* Chicago: Hall & McCreary, 1936.

———. *Religious Folksongs of the Negro: As Sung at Hampton Institute.* Hampton, Va.: Hampton Institute Press, 1927.

Diehl, Katharine Smith, ed. *Hymns & Tunes: An Index.* New York: Scarecrow Press, 1966.

Dittmer, John. *Black Georgia in the Progressive Era, 1900–1920.* Urbana: Univ. of Illinois Press, 1977.

Dixon, Robert M. W., and John Godrich. *Recording the Blues.* New York: Stein and Day, 1970.

Drake, St. Clair, and Horace Cayton. *Black Metropolis: A Study of Negro Life in a Northern City.* 2 vols. 1945. Revised and enlarged. New York: Harper and Row, 1962.

Du Bois, William E. B., ed. *The Negro American Family.* [The Atlanta University Publications No. 13.] 1908. Reprint. New York: Negro Universities Press, 1969.

———. *The Souls of Black Folk.* 1903. Reprint. Millwood, N.Y.: Kraus-Thomson Organization, 1973.

Ecke, Melvin W. *From Ivy Street to Kennedy Center: Centennial History of the Atlanta Public School System.* [Atlanta]: Atlanta Board of Education, 1972.

Epstein, Dena J. *Sinful Tunes and Spirituals.* Urbana: Univ. of Illinois Press, 1977.

Frazier, E. Franklin. *The Negro Church in America.* 1963. Reprint. New York: Schocken Books, 1974.

———. *The Negro Family in Chicago.* 1932. Reprint. Chicago: Univ. of Illinois Press, 1966.

———. *The Negro Family in the United States.* 1939. Revised and abridged. 1948. Reprint. Chicago: Univ. of Chicago Press, 1969.

Garrett, Franklin M. *Atlanta and Environs: A Chronicle of Its People and Events.* 2 vols. 1954. Reprint. Athens: Univ. of Georgia Press, 1964.

Genovese, Eugene D. *Roll, Jordan, Roll: The World the Slaves Made.* 1972. Reprint. New York: Vintage, 1976.

George, Carol V. R. *Segregated Sabbaths: Richard Allen and the Emergence of Independent Black Churches 1760–1840.* New York: Oxford Univ. Press, 1973.

Godrich, John, and Robert M. W. Dixon, comps. *Blues and Gospel Records: 1902–1943.* 3d ed., fully revised. Essex, Eng.: Storyville Publications, 1982.

Goreau, Laurraine. *Just Mahalia, Baby: The Mahalia Jackson Story.* Waco, Tex.: Word Books, 1975.

Gutman, Herbert G. *The Black Family in Slavery and Freedom, 1750–1925.* New York: Vintage, 1976.

Hall, Charles E. *Negroes in the United States: 1920–1932.* 1935. Reprint. New York: Arno Press, 1969.

Hamilton, Charles V. *The Black Preacher in America.* New York: William Morrow, 1972.

Handy, William C., ed. *Blues: An Anthology.* New York: Albert and Charles Boni, 1926.

———. *Father of the Blues: An Autobiography by W. C. Handy.* Arna Bontemps, ed. New York: Macmillan, 1941.

Harlan, Louis R. *Booker T. Washington: The Making of a Black Leader.* New York: Oxford Univ. Press, 1972.

———, ed. *The Booker T. Washington Papers.* Vol. II. Urbana: Univ. of Illinois Press, 1972.

Harris, J. William. *Plain Folk and Gentry in a Slave Society: White Liberty and Black Slavery in Augusta's Hinterlands.* Middletown, Conn.: Wesleyan Univ. Press, 1985.

Heilbut, Tony. *The Gospel Sound: Good News and Bad Times.* New York: Simon and Schuster, 1971.

Hemperley, Marion R., comp. *Cities, Towns and Communities of Georgia Between 1847 [and] 1962[:] 8500 Places and the County in Which Located.* Easley, S.C.: Southern Historical Press, 1980.

Herskovits, Melville J. *The Myth of the Negro Past.* 1941. Reprint. Gloucester, Mass.: Peter Smith, 1970.

Holmes, Dwight O. W. *The Evolution of the Negro College.* 1934. Reprint. New York: Arno Press and the New York Times, 1969.

Holmes, William F. "Economic Developments: 1890–1940." In *A History of Georgia.* Kenneth Coleman, gen. ed. Athens: Univ. of Georgia Press, 1977, pp. 257–76.

Horn, Dorothy D. *Sing to Me of Heaven: A Study of Folk and Early American Materials in Three Old Harp Books.* Gainesville: Univ. of Florida Press, 1970.

Jackson, George Pullen, ed. *Spiritual Folk-Songs of Early America: Two Hundred and Fifty Tunes and Texts with an Introduction and Notes.* 1937. Reprint. New York: Dover, 1964.

Jahn, Jahnheinz. *Muntu: An Outline of the New African Culture.* Marjorie Grene, trans. 1958; 2d ed. New York: Grove Press, 1961.

James, Willis Laurence. "The Romance of the Negro Folk Cry in America." In *Mother Wit from the Laughing Barrel: Readings in the Interpretation of Afro-American Folklore.* Ed. Alan Dundes. 1973. Reprint. New York: Garland, 1981, pp. 430–44.

Johnson, J. Rosamond, transcriber. *Utica Jubilee Singers['] Spirituals: As Sung at the Utica Normal and Industrial Institute of Mississippi.* Boston: Oliver Ditson, 1930.

Johnson, James Weldon. *God's Trombones.* 1927. Reprint. New York: Viking, 1955.

———, ed. *The Second Book of Negro Spirituals.* New York: Viking, 1926.

Jones, Bessie. *For the Ancestors: Autobiographical Memories.* Collected and edited by John Stewart. Urbana: Univ. of Illinois Press, 1983.

Jones, Bessie, and Beth Lomax Hawes. *Step It Down: Games, Plays, Songs, and Stories from the Afro-American Heritage.* New York: Harper and Row, 1972.

Jones, Jacqueline. *Soldiers of Light and Love: Northern Teachers and Georgia Blacks, 1865–1873.* Chapel Hill: Univ. of North Carolina Press, 1980.

Jordan, Lewis G. *Negro Baptist History U.S.A.: 1750[–]1930.* Nashville: Sunday School Publishing Board, N.B.C. [National Baptist Convention], [1930].

Jubilee Songs: Complete. As Sung by the Jubilee Singers of Fisk University. New York: Bigelow and Maine, [1872].

Julian, John, ed. *A Dictionary of Hymnology: Setting Forth the Origin and History of Christian Hymns of All Ages and Nations.* Revised. London: John Murray, 1915.

Katz, Bernard, ed. *The Social Implications of Early Negro Music in the United States.* New York: Arno Press, 1969.

Keil, Charles. *Urban Blues.* Chicago: Univ. of Chicago Press, 1966.

Kennedy, Louise V. *The Negro Peasant Turns Cityward: Effects of Recent Migrations to Northern Centers.* 1930. Reprint. New York: AMS Press, 1968.

Krehbiel, Henry E. *Afro-American Folksongs: A Study in Racial and National Music.* New York: G. Schirmer, 1914.

Levine, Lawrence W. *Black Culture and Black Consciousness: Afro-American Folk Thought from Slavery to Freedom.* New York: Oxford Univ. Press, 1977.

Locke, Alain. *The New Negro.* 1925. Reprint. New York: Atheneum, 1968.

Lomax, Alan. *Mister Jelly Roll: The Fortunes of Jelly Roll Morton, New Orleans Creole and "Inventor of Jazz."* 1950. 2d ed. Berkeley: Univ. of California Press, 1973.

Lord, Albert B. *The Singer of Tales.* 1960. Reprint. New York: Atheneum, 1973.

Lornell, Kip. *"Happy in the Service of the Lord": Afro-American Gospel Quartets in Memphis.* Urbana: Univ. of Illinois Press, 1988.

Lovell, John, Jr. *Black Song: The Forge and the Flame: The Story of How the Afro-American Spiritual Was Hammered Out.* New York: Macmillan, 1972.

Mays, Benjamin E. *The Negro's God as Reflected in His Literature.* 1938. Reprint. New York: Negro Universities Press, 1969.

———, and Joseph W. Nicholson. *The Negro's Church.* 1933. Reprint. New York: Arno Press, 1969.

McClain, William B. *Black People in the Methodist Church: Whither Thou Goest?* Cambridge, Mass.: Schenkman, 1984.

McCutchan, Robert Gay. *Our Hymnody: A Manual of the Methodist Hymnal.* New York: Methodist Book Concern, 1937.

McPherson, James M. *The Abolitionist Legacy: From Reconstruction to the NAACP.* Princeton: Princeton Univ. Press, 1975.

Mitchell, Henry H. *Black Preaching.* 1970. Reprint. San Francisco: Harper and Row, 1979.

Myrdal, Gunnar. *An American Dilemma: The Negro Problem and Modern Democracy.* 2 vols. New York: Harper and Brothers, 1944.

[Netzahaulcoyotl Historical Society, ed.]. *Zora Neale Hurston: The Sanctified Church,* Berkeley: Turtle Island, 1981.

Oakley, Giles. *The Devil's Music: A History of the Blues.* New York: Toplinger, 1976.

Odum, Howard W., and Guy B. Johnson. *The Negro and His Songs: A Study of Typical Negro Songs in the South.* Chapel Hill: Univ. of North Carolina Press, 1925.

Oliver, Paul. *Songsters and Saints: Vocal Traditions on Race Records*. Cambridge, Eng.: Cambridge Univ. Press, 1984.

Ottley, Roi. *The Lonely Warrior: The Life and Times of Robert S. Abbott*. Chicago: Henry Regency, 1955.

Parrish, Lydia. *Slave Songs of the Georgia Sea Islands*. 1942. Reprint. Hatboro, Penn.: Folklore Associates, 1965.

Payne, Bishop Daniel E. *History of the African Methodist Episcopal Church*. Ed. C. S. Smith, 1891. Reprint. New York: Johnson Reprint, 1968.

Perdue, Charles L., Thomas E. Barden, and Robert K. Phillips, eds. *Weevils in the Wheat: Interviews with Virginia Ex-slaves*. 1976. Reprint. Bloomington: Indiana Univ. Press. 1980.

Raboteau, Albert J. *Slave Religion: The "Invisible Institution" in the Antebellum South*. New York: Oxford Univ. Press, 1978.

Range, Willard. *The Rise and Progress of Negro Colleges in Georgia: 1865–1949*. Athens: Univ. of Georgia Press, 1951.

Ransom, Reverdy C. *The Pilgrimage of Harriet Ransom's Son*. Nashville, Sunday School Union, [1949].

Rampersad, Arnold. *The Art and Imagination of W. E. B. Du Bois*. Cambridge, Mass.: Harvard Univ. Press, 1976.

Redkey, Edwin S. *Black Exodus: Black Nationalist and Back-to-Africa Movements, 1890–1910*. New Haven: Yale Univ. Press, 1969.

Rogal, Samuel J., comp. *Guide to the Hymns and Tunes of American Methodism*. Music Reference Collection No. 7. New York: Greenwood Press, 1986.

Rosenberg, Bruce A. *The Art of the American Folk Preacher*. New York: Oxford Univ. Press, 1970.

Rossiter, William S. *Increase of Population in the United States: 1910–1920: A Study of Changes in the Population of Divisions, States, Counties, and Rural and Urban Areas, and in Sex, Color, and Nativity, at the Fourteenth Census*. Census Monographs I. Washington, D.C.: Government Printing Office, 1922.

Rowe, Mike. *Chicago Breakdown*. New York: Da Capo Press, 1979.

Rust, Brian, ed. *Jazz Records: 1897–1942*. 4th rev. and enl. ed. 2 vols. New Rochelle, N.Y.: Arlington House, 1978.

Sankey, Ira D. *My Life and the Story of the Gospel Hymns and of Sacred Songs and Solos*. Philadelphia: Sunday School Times, 1907.

Scott, Emmett J. *Negro Migration During the War*. [1920]. Reprint. New York: Arno Press, 1969.

Smith, Willie the Lion. *Music on My Mind: The Memoirs of an American Pianist*. Garden City, N.Y.: Doubleday, 1964.

Southern, Eileen. *The Music of Black Americans: A History*. 2d ed. New York: W. W. Norton, 1983.

Spear, Alan H. *Black Chicago: The Making of a Negro Ghetto: 1890–1920*. Chicago: Univ. of Chicago Press, 1967.

Stackhouse, Perry J. *Chicago and the Baptists: A Century of Progress*. Chicago: Univ. of Chicago Press, 1933.

Stevenson, Robert. *Protestant Church Music in America: A Short Survey of Men and Movements from 1564 to the Present*. New York: W. W. Norton, 1966.

Stewart-Baxter, Derrick. *Ma Rainey and the Classic Blues Singers*. New York: Stein and Day, 1970.

Strickland, Arvarh E. *History of the Chicago Urban League*. Urbana: Univ. of Illinois Press, 1966.

Stuckey, Sterling. *Slave Culture: Nationalist Theory and the Foundations of Black America*. New York: Oxford Univ. Press, 1987.

Titon, Jeff Todd. *Early Downhome Blues: A Musical and Cultural Analysis*. Urbana: Univ. of Illinois Press, 1977.

Walker, Wyatt Tee. *"Somebody's Calling My Name": Black Sacred Music and Social Change*. Valley Forge, Penn.: Judson Press, 1979.

Washington, Booker T. *Up from Slavery*. 1902. Reprint. New York: Avon, 1965.

Washington, James M. *Frustrated Fellowship: The Black Baptist Quest for Social Power*. Macon, Ga.: Mercer Univ. Press, 1986.

Weisbrot, Robert. *Father Divine and the Struggle for Racial Equality*. Urbana: Univ. of Illinois Press, 1983.

Woodson, Carter G. *The History of the Negro Church*. 2d ed. Washington, D.C.: Associated Publishers, 1945.

Wright, R. R., Jr. *The Bishops of the African Methodist Episcopal Church*. N.p.: A. M. E. Sunday School Union, 1963.

Work, John Wesley. *Folk Song of the American Negro*. 1915. Reprint. New York: Negro Universities Press, 1969.

Zuck, Barbara. *A History of Musical Americanism*. Ann Arbor: UMI Research Press, 1980.

Articles

Daniel, Vattel E. "Ritual and Stratification in Chicago Negro Churches." *American Sociological Review* 7, no. 3 (June 1942): 352–61.

Du Bois, W. E. Burghardt. "Caste: That Is the Root of Trouble." *Des Moines Register and Leader*. Oct. 19, 1904: 5.

———. "The Development of a People." *International Journal of Ethics* 14 (1904): 292–311.

———. "Georgia Negroes and Their Fifty Millions of Savings." *World's Work* 18 (May 1908): 11550–54.

———. "The Problem of Amusement." *Southern Workman* 26 (Sept. 1897): 181–84.

———. "The Work of Negro Women in Society." *Spelman Messenger* 18 (no. 5): 1–3.

Dvořák, Antonín. "Music in America." *Harper's Magazine* XC (1885): 428–34.

Fisher, Miles Mark. "Organized Religion and the Cults." *The Crisis* 44, no. 1 (January 1937): 8–10, 29–30.

Herzog, George. "Folk Music." In *Research in Primitive and Folk Music in the United States*. Bulletin No. 24. Washington, D.C.: American Council of Learned Societies, 1936, pp. 45–97.

Hurston, Zora Neale. "Spirituals and Neo-Spirituals." In *Negro: An Anthology. Collected and Edited by Nancy Cunard*. 1933. Reprint. New York: Frederick Ungar, 1970, pp. 223–25.

McRae, Barry. "The Ma Rainey and Bessie Smith Accompaniments: A Survey." *Jazz Journal* 14 (no. 3): 6–8.

O'Neal, Jim and Amy. "Living Blues Interview: Georgia Tom Dorsey." *Living Blues: A Journal of the Black American Blues Tradition* 20 (March–April 1975): 16–34.

Shaw, Arnold. "The Vocabulary of Tin-Pan Alley Explained." *Music Library Association Notes,* Dec. 12, 1949: 33–53.

Southern, Eileen. "Musical Practices in Black Churches of Philadelphia and New York, ca. 1800–1844." *Journal of the American Musicological Society* 30, no. 2 (1977): 296–312.

Szwed, John. "Musical Adaptation among Afro-Americans." *Journal of American Folklore* 82 (1969): 112–21.

Dissertations

Adams, Olin Burton. "The Negro and the Agrarian Movement in Georgia, 1874–1908." Florida State University, 1973.

Harris, Michael W. "The Advent of Gospel Blues in Black Old-Line Churches in Chicago, 1932–33, as Seen Through the Life and Mind of Thomas Andrew Dorsey." Harvard University, 1982.

Piper, David R. "Community Churches: The Community Church Movement." University of Chicago, 1928.

Raichelson, Richard M. "Black Religious Folksong: A Study in Generic and Social Change." University of Pennsylvania, 1975.

Ricks, George R. *Some Aspects of the Religious Music of the United States Negro: An Ethnomusicological Study with Special Emphasis on the Gospel Tradition.* Northwestern University, 1960. Reprint. New York: Arno Press, 1977.

Sutherland, Robert L. "An Analysis of Negro Churches in Chicago." University of Chicago, 1930.

Thorson, Theodore Winton. "A History of Music Publishing in Chicago: 1850–1960." Northwestern University, 1961.

Index

Page references for composers and titles followed by (M) indicate that musical examples are included.